THE GUINNESS BOOK OF
AMAZING NATURE

GUINNESS PUBLISHING

Managing Editor
Elizabeth Wyse

Editors
Roz Hopkins
Frances Williams

Research Editor
Sandip Shah

Researchers
Ben Keith
James Raiher
Simon Stewart

Writers
Nicolas Andrews
Sarah Angliss
Hanna Bolus
Caroline Chapman

Pre-production Manager
Patricia Langton

Publishing Director
Ian Castello-Cortes

Designer
Karen Wilks

Page Production
Keith Bambury

Picture Research
Rebecca Watson

Colour Origination
Essex Colour Services Ltd,
London

Printed and bound
in Italy by
Rotolito, Milan

THE GUINNESS BOOK OF

AMAZING NATURE

GUINNESS PUBLISHING

SPECTACULAR EARTH; UNTAMED

CONTENTS

ENERGY; DIVERSE LIFEFORMS

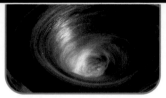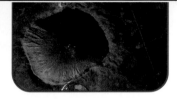

The Guinness Book of Amazing Nature reveals things about the world you never dreamt were possible. To sample a few...

#016 TALLEST TOWERING ASH COLUMN 80 KM #018 **RED HOT LAVA** FLOWS AT RECORD SPEED OF 100 KM/H #022 20,00 PEOPLE KILLED IN **COLOMBIAN MUDSLIDE** #036 ROAR OF VICTORIA FALLS HEARD 40 KM AWAY #040 **FASTEST HURRICANE** SPEED 371 KM/H #050 LARGEST HAILSTONE 19 CM IN DIAMETER #052 **LIGHTNING KILLS** 1,000 PER YEAR #056 700 STRIKES A YEAR IN **TORNADO ALLEY** #076 14 HIMALAYAN PEAKS EXCEED 8,000 M #082 6% OF THE EARTH'S SURFACE IS WETLAND #086 **ANTARCTIC TEMPERATURES** PLUMMET TO -35°C #090 THE DEEPEST **GORGE PLUNGES** 2,400 M #100 AUSTRALIA'S GREAT BARRIER REEF EXTENDS FOR 2,010 KM #102 **ICEBERGS TRAVEL** UP TO 44 KM PER DAY #118 THE SEA HAS RISEN 15 CM OVER THE LAST

PREFACE

100 YEARS **#126** ALASKAN **OIL SPILL** KILLS 300,000 BIRDS **#134** THE OZONE HOLE IS THE SIZE OF NORTH AMERICA **#144** EEL EMITS **ELECTRIC SHOCK** OF 650 VOLTS **#146** BEETLE CAN RELEASE **HOT GAS** UP TO 100°C **#150** MALE **MOTH SMELLS** FEMALE AT 11 KM **#152** CAMELS GO WITHOUT WATER FOR 17 DAYS **#156** **HUMAN TAPEWORM** CAN GROW TO 22.9 M **#162** CHIMPANZEE UNDERSTANDS 300 DIFFERENT SIGNS **#166** GREY WHALE SWIMS 10,000 KM A YEAR **#168** **300 MILLION RABBITS** BRED FROM 24 INDIVIDUALS **#174** **DIVORCE RATE** OF SWAN LESS THAN 1% **#180** AVERAGE ORB WEB IS **SPUN IN 1 HOUR** **#182** 400 MILLION PRAIRIE DOGS IN ONE COLONY **#202** YACHT RACE SPECTATORS **SHOWERED WITH MAGGOTS** **#212** 50 SHIPS LOST IN BERMUDA TRIANGLE

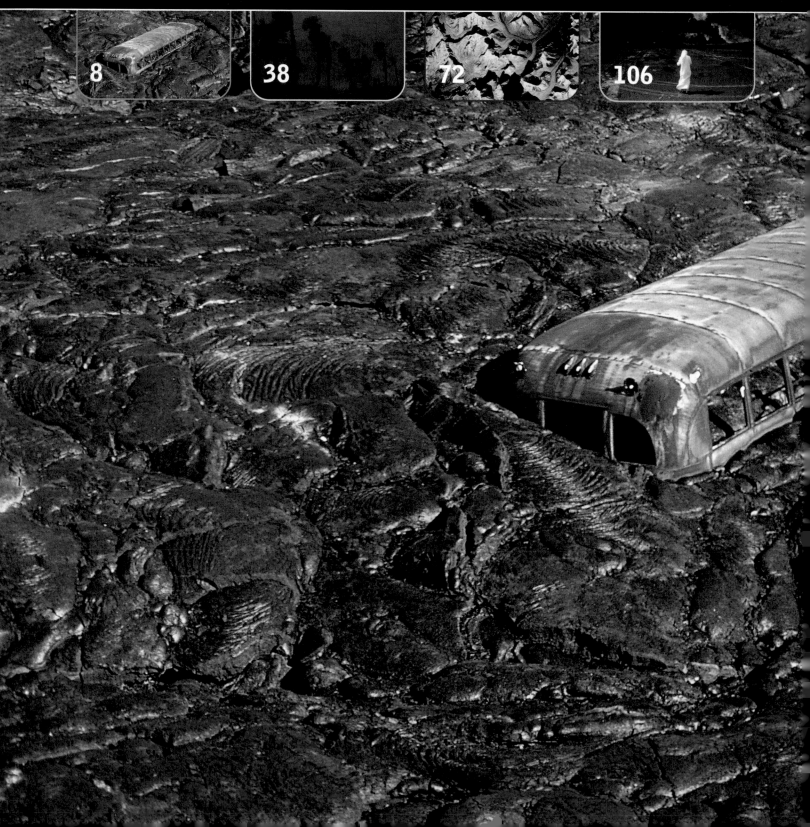

POWERFUL FORCES SHAPE AN

RESTLESS EARTH

TRANSFORM EARTH'S SURFACE

136

170

192

220

EARTHQUAKES 1

18 MASSIVE QUAKES

An earthquake is the trembling of the ground produced by a sudden displacement of rock in the Earth's crust. The energy of the break is transmitted in waves, which have the potential to cause colossal damage—opening fissures in the ground, distorting the contours of the land, destroying buildings, diverting rivers, triggering landslides, avalanches and tidal waves and, in the worst cases, turning the ground into an undulating quicksand-like mass, and hurling objects into the air.

Measuring a quake
The size of an earthquake is defined by the amount of energy it releases. The scale most commonly used to measure earthquakes is 'surface-wave magnitude' (Ms). This scale was invented by US seismologist Dr Charles Richter in 1935. Known as the Richter scale, the system can accurately grade earthquakes on a scale of one to eight. At 1Ms an earthquake can only be detected by scientific instruments; at 8Ms widespread chaos results. New scales and

relative impact of the quake on three factors: damage to humans, objects and nature, and buildings.

Mississippi shakes
In the winter of 1811–12 the USA's Mississippi Valley was struck by three of the most powerful earthquakes in US history, each measuring over 8Ms on the Richter scale. The first hit on 16 Dec 1811, the second on 23 Jan 1812 and the third just over two weeks later on 7 Feb. The violence of the initial shocks

STRIKE EACH YEAR

EVERY YEAR HALF A MILLION EARTHQUAKES SHAKE THE EARTH. MANY ARE RELATIVELY MILD, BUT ONE IN 5,000 (OR ABOUT 100 A YEAR) ARE SO VIOLENT THAT THEY RELEASE MORE ENERGY THAN AN ATOMIC BOMB

Why do quakes happen?
Earthquakes are caused when huge forces are exerted on the rock of the Earth's crust, causing it to fracture. These forces are usually created by movement of the Earth's plates, volcanic activity, landslides or subterranean collapse. When the force created by one of these phenomena becomes greater than the strength of the rock it is exerted upon, the rock cracks along a new or already existing line of weakness. The enormous energy of the break is then transmitted outwards from the focus in spherical waves. It is these waves that constitute the earthquake and that can cause great damage.

means of measuring earthquakes have been developed to cope with the great intensity of quakes, especially in Russia and Japan. In 1966, Kei Aki developed a new concept known as 'seismic moment' (Mo) for measuring quakes greater than 8Ms. This system can also be used to work out an earthquake's 'moment magnitude' (Mw), which measures the size of an earthquake in terms of the whole range of frequencies in the wave spectrum of the tremor, including duration, surface movement and fault rupture. A European Standard Scale was devised in 1993, which measures the intensity of earthquakes on 12 levels, each one assessing the

caused the Mississippi River to temporarily flow upstream. Church bells rang in Boston 1,700 km away. Powerful aftershocks caused the ground to shake intermittently and tremors to be felt all year. A total area of 600,000 km² was damaged, with trees uprooted, fissures carved into the ground and land uplifted by over 3 m. Legend has it that at the same time in Alabama the Shawnee Indian chief, Tecumseh, told the Creek Indians that he had been sent to them by a Great Spirit and to prove it he would stamp his foot at his next destination—Detroit—and that this would make their houses fall down. On the morning of his estimated arrival there, an aftershock of the Mississippi quake was felt in Alabama.

Greatest devastation
Geologists have discovered that about every 500 years the Kanto plain in Japan is hit by an earthquake of enormous magnitude. On 1 Sept 1923, this area experienced the greatest physical destruction ever caused by a single earthquake. The densely populated cities of Tokyo and Yokohama were effectively bull-dozed by the force of a quake that measured 8.3Ms. An estimated 575,000 dwellings were reduced to rubble and as many as 143,000 people died, either trapped in the collapsing buildings or burned to death in the fires that broke out in

the wake of the impact. The effects of the earthquake were particularly bad because the land on which the cities are built is made of soft sediments, accumulated over millions of years. When an earthquake strikes soft ground such as this it is liable to liquefy, turning into an unstable quicksand. The 1923 earthquake permanently distorted even the most solid land. Some areas were uplifted by up to 2 m and the floor of Tokyo Bay moved about 3 m north. The upheaval even fused the island of Nojima, situated just off the Chiba peninsula, to the mainland, forming Cape Nojima.

Catastrophe in Kobe
In the early hours of 17 Jan 1995 a 20-second earthquake measuring 7.2Ms shook the city of Kobe, Japan, killing 4,500 people and injuring 15,000 more. Over 67,000 structures collapsed, sparking a total of about 175 separate fires which burned over an area of nearly 800 km² and razed another 7,000 buildings to the ground. The Hanshin Expressway, an elevated road linking Kobe with the city of Osaka, toppled onto its side. The total damage caused by the quake amounted to 6.9 trillion yen. But the catastrophe brought one ray of hope: up to an hour before the earthquake, people saw flashes of red and blue light. Geologists believe this light effect was caused by fractoluminescence, a phenomenon observed when quartz, a mineral found in many types of rock, is fractured. They believe that fractoluminescence might provide warning signs of an approaching earthquake.

DATA-BURST

HOW OFTEN DO EARTHQUAKES OCCUR?
EARTHQUAKES OCCUR, ON AVERAGE, EVERY MINUTE. THERE ARE OVER 500,000 A YEAR. HOWEVER MOST ARE MINOR TREMORS, WITH ONLY ABOUT 18 MAJOR EARTHQUAKES EACH YEAR. MAJOR QUAKES REGISTER 7.0-7.9 ON THE RICHTER SCALE.

HOW MANY EARHTQUAKES HAVE THERE BEEN THIS CENTURY?
SINCE 1900, THERE HAVE BEEN 78 EARTHQUAKES THAT HAVE CLAIMED MORE THAN 1,000 LIVES. THE WORST WAS IN TANGSHN, CHINA IN 1976, WHEN MORE THAN HALF A MILLION DIED.

CAN EARTHQUAKES TRIGGER OTHER PHENOMENA?
EARTHQUAKES ARE ASSOCIATED WITH OTHER PHENOMENA SUCH AS TSUNAMI, VOLCANIC ERUPTION AND LANDSLIDES.

HOW LONG DO EARTHQUAKES LAST?
THE AVERAGE EARTHQUAKE LASTS FOR LESS THAN ONE MINUTE. SOME HAVE BEEN KNOWN TO LAST OVER FOUR MINUTES.

HOW FAST CAN EARTHQUAKES TRAVEL?
EARTHQUAKE SHOCKWAVES CAN TRAVEL THROUGH ROCK FROM THE HYPOCENTRE AT NEARLY 7 KM PER SECOND, WHICH IS MORE THAN 20 TIMES THE SPEED OF SOUND

WHAT HAPPENS WHEN TECTONIC PLATES COLLIDE?
THERE ARE THREE SORTS OF FAULT RUPTURE: 'NORMAL' FAULTS RESULT IN THE PLATES MOVING APART WHILE 'REVERSE' FAULTS SEE THE PLATES COLLIDING; 'STRIKE SLIPS', RESULT IN PLATES SLIDING PAST EACH OTHER.

LEFT: A LONG SECTION OF KOBE EXPRESSWAY LIES TWISTED FOLLOWING THE MASSIVE EARTHQUAKE WHICH STRUCK THE CENTRAL-WESTERN JAPANESE CITY ON 17 JANUARY 1995

Biggest ever earthquake

The largest earthquake recorded in terms of moment magnitude hit Chile on 22 May 1960, measuring 9.5Mw. Many of the country's cities were badly damaged and the shock created a 10-m-high tsunami which swept along the Chilean coast, obliterating entire villages. Hundreds of landslides were triggered by the earthquake, including several that blocked Lake Rinihue in the south of the country for 63 days as its water level rose to over 25 m. The impact of the earthquake remoulded parts of the coastal landscape, with some areas permanently raised or submerged by more than 3 m. It created a fault rupture 300 km long and

Highest death toll

The greatest estimated number of deaths due to an earthquake is 830,000. This almost unbelievable number of fatalities occurred during a prolonged earthquake which hit the Chinese provinces of Shaanxi, Shanxi and Henan on 2 Feb 1556. The highest death toll in modern times was also reported in China. When an earthquake of magnitude 7.9Ms struck Tangshan in eastern China on 28 July 1976 it reduced almost the entire city to

people were killed, 13,000 injured and 500,000 left homeless. Rescuers battled for days to pull survivors from the rubble—they managed to bring 7,000 people out of the wreckage alive on the third day. The huge number of casualties was blamed on the fact that houses in the region had been constructed quickly and poorly during a period of rapid population growth. Most of the flimsy structures toppled the instant the seismic waves shook the area.

came crashing ashore, worsening the chaos. A total of 60,000 people were killed.

Ancient frescoes damaged

While the human cost of earthquakes can be incalculable, the damage done to historical and cultural sites can also be beyond value. Among the worst artistic victims of quakes in recent years were the two frescoes by Giotto of the life of St Francis of Assissi. A series of tremors in central Italy

EARTHQUAKES 2

90% OF GUATEMALANS LEFT

cracked open an area of land 850 km long and 130 km wide. This mega-quake has even been blamed for the eruption of the volcano Puyehue two days later.

Million homeless in Guatemala

At 3:02 am on 4 Feb 1976, a giant earthquake ripped along the Montagua Fault which forms the boundary between the Caribbean and North American plates of the Earth's crust. The effects of the quake felt in the Central American country of Guatemala were phenomenal: 23,000 people were killed, 76,000 were injured and over a million people—90% of the total population—were left homeless. The quake, which measured 7.5Ms, was felt over an area of 100,000 km² and produced the most extensive surface faulting in the western hemisphere in 70 years.

rubble. The aftershock, which hit the following afternoon and measured 7.1Ms, destroyed almost all the buildings that had been left intact. Only one house in 50 and one factory in 10 remained standing. Seven moving trains were derailed and all four of the city's hospitals were flattened. The exact numbers reported dead has varied over time, but the first total, issued on 4 Jan 1977, stood at 655,237. The figure was later adjusted to 750,000, although two years later the New China News Agency reported the official death toll as 242,000. Whatever the actual total, it was a human tragedy of massive proportions.

Homes flattened in Armenia

When an earthquake of magnitude 6.8Ms hit the mountainous border region of Spitak, Armenia, at 11:41 am on 7 Dec 1988, 25,000

Crime and disorder

The example of the Managua earthquake in Nicaragua in 1972 shows how easily the usual civic calm is disrupted with the onset of such a major disaster. In the series of quakes that hit the city on 23 Dec, 5,000 people were killed, 20,000 injured and 300,000 made homeless. Shops, businesses, homes, hospitals, schools and the local prison were destroyed, causing damage to the tune of a billion dollars. The police, who had also suffered terrible casualties during the quake, were powerless to defend against the looting which began a few hours after the quake and the authorities, operating from emergency headquarters were forced to declare martial law within 38 hours. Firemen tried to extinguish the numerous fires that burned in the aftermath of the quake, despite the fact that fire had damaged their own station, crushing men and destroying radios and other equipment. Traffic congestion and chaos ensued as the many thousands of people made homeless tried to make their way out of the city.

Europe's biggest earthquake

On 1 Nov 1755 an earthquake estimated at a magnitude of 8.7Ms hit the city of Lisbon, Portugal. The violence of the initial jolt destroyed many of the city's buildings but the devastation did not end there. Many structures left standing collapsed in the aftershock that followed two hours later. In the city's harbour giant waves, as much as 10 m high,

---

JARGON

AFTERSHOCK
QUAKE WHICH FOLLOWS AFTER A LARGER EARTHQUAKE

CIRCUM-PACIFIC BELT
THIS ZONE SURROUNDING THE PACIFIC OCEAN ACCOUNTS FOR ABOUT 90% OF THE WORLD'S EARTHQUAKES

EPICENTRE
THE POINT ON THE EARTH'S SURFACE DIRECTLY ABOVE THE FOCUS OF THE EARTHQUAKE

FAULT
A WEAK POINT IN THE EARTH'S SURFACE WHERE ROCK LAYERS HAVE RUPTURED AND SLIPPED

FAULT CREEP
THE SLOW CONSTANT MOVEMENT OF FAULTS IN THE EARTH'S CRUST

FORESHOCK
A SMALL TREMOR WHICH CAN PRECEDE A LARGER EARTHQUAKE BY AS LITTLE AS SECONDS OR AS MUCH AS WEEKS

HYPOCENTRE
THE FOCUS OF AN EARTHQUAKE

MAGNITUDE
A MEASURE OF THE STRENGTH OF THE QUAKE

PLATE
ONE OF THE SEGMENTS THAT MAKES UP THE EARTH'S CRUST. THERE ARE SEVEN MAJOR PLATES, ALL INTERACTING AND MOVING RELATIVE TO ONE ANOTHER

PLATE TECTONICS
THE THEORY OF HOW THE PLATES RELATE TO ONE ANOTHER

SEISMIC BELT
AN EXTENDED EARTHQUAKE ZONE

SEISMOGRAPH
AN INSTRUMENT THAT RECORDS THE MOTIONS OF THE EARTH'S SURFACE

LEFT: COFFINS LIE WAITING FOR THE BODIES OF VICTIMS OF THE ARMENIAN EARTHQUAKE DISASTER, LENINKAN, 1988 · RIGHT: COMPUTER-GENERATED IMPRESSION OF AN EARTHQUAKE

in 1997 followed by a large quake, measuring 5.5Ms, shattered frescoes in the main entrance hall of the Basilica at Assissi. Falling masonry there killed four people including two Franciscan friars. More than 20 aftershocks and another quake a few days later caused further damage. The Basilica, and the Giotto frescoes that adorned it, was one of the most important Christian shrines in Europe. A major pilgrimage site, the monument dedicated to the founder of the Franciscan order dates back to the 13th century. Painstaking restoration is now underway to piece together the remain of the frescoes, in order to reconstruct the artwork.

MAN-MADE EARTHQUAKES?

SCIENTISTS BELIEVE THAT NOT ALL EARTHQUAKES ARE NATURAL PHENOMENA. THE FILLING OF RESERVOIRS IS THOUGHT TO TRIGGER SEISMIC TREMORS BY PLACING A MASSIVE STRAIN ON THE SURROUNDING ROCK. WHEN THE FORCE BECOMES GREAT ENOUGH, THE ENERGY IS TRANSMITTED AS A SEISMIC WAVE THROUGH THE ROCK. ANOTHER POSSIBLE EXPLANATION IS THAT WATER FROM NEW RESERVOIRS SEEPS ALONG 'DEAD' FAULT LINES IN THE EARTH'S CRUST, LUBRICATING THEM AND ALLOWING ROCK MOVEMENT TO OCCUR WHERE BEFORE THE CRUST WAS SOLID. ALTHOUGH SCIENTISTS ARE NOT CERTAIN OF THE CONNECTION BETWEEN THE CREATION OF RESERVOIRS AND THE INCIDENCE OF EARTHQUAKES, THERE IS SIGNIFICANT EVIDENCE POINTING TO A LINK. FOR EXAMPLE, IN THE USA BETWEEN 1935, WHEN THE HOOVER DAM WAS COMPLETED, AND 1940, WHEN THE RESERVOIR BEHIND THE DAM HAD FILLED TO CAPACITY, HUNDREDS OF EARTHQUAKES WERE REPORTED. SIMILARLY, IN SATARA, INDIA, A SERIES OF TREMORS BEGAN TO BE FELT IN 1965 AS SOON AS THE KOYNA RESERVOIR HAD BEEN FILLED. THE TREMORS CONTINUED UNTIL TRAGEDY STRUCK IN 1967 WHEN AN EARTHQUAKE MEASURING 6.4MS CAUSED 177 DEATHS AND LEFT 2,000 PEOPLE INJURED. THE WORST KNOWN CASE OF A MAN-MADE EARTHQUAKE, HOWEVER, CAME IN KILLARI, INDIA, ON 30 SEPT 1993. THE FILLING OF THE LOWER TIMA RESERVOIR IS THOUGHT TO HAVE BEEN THE CAUSE OF AN EARTHQUAKE MEASURING 6.4MS WHICH HIT A DENSELY POPULATED REGION KILLING 10,000 PEOPLE AND FLATTENING THE MUD AND STONE-BUILT HOUSES OF 20 ENTIRE VILLAGES.

HOMELESS BY 1976 QUAKE

WHEN AN EARTHQUAKE STRIKES, THE COST TO HUMAN LIFE CAN BE MASSIVE—AS HUGE STRUCTURES TOPPLE OVER UNDER THE FORCE OF THE QUAKE, VICTIMS ARE OFTEN CRUSHED IMMEDIATELY BY TUMBLING MASONRY

EARTHQUAKES 3

THE SAN ANDREAS

Restless earth

Geologists estimate that over the past 5 million years the Earth's crust has been displaced by over 1,000 km in the San Andreas fault zone. The Pacific and North American plates grind against each other in a 'strike-slip' motion, with movement occurring either as a sudden jolt or a steady creep. The creeping fault causes a constant stream of minor quakes, whereas if the section is locked, pressure builds up until the stress is so great that energy is released in a spasm.

The big one

It is these locked sections of the San Andreas fault that give geologists the greatest cause for

deep—a quarter of the thickness of the continental crust on which California sits—so even the mightiest of fractures is unlikely to split the state from the rest of the USA. Nevertheless, California is a very highly populated area and this gives seismologists justifiable cause for concern. They estimate that depending on variable factors an earthquake of 6Ms or more could easily cause between 2,000 and 100,000 deaths.

San Francisco earthquake

The San Andreas fault's most devastating earthquake struck the San Francisco Bay area of California on 18 April 1906. A locked section of the fault,

FAULT IS 15KM DEEP

RUNNING LIKE A SCAR DOWN THE STATE OF CALIFORNIA, THE SAN ANDREAS FAULT IS THE POINT WHERE THE TWO PLATES OF THE EARTH'S CRUST GRIND AGAINST ONE ANOTHER, TRIGGERING VERY POWERFUL EARTHQUAKES

concern, and convince some that California is sitting on a time bomb. They fear the arrival of the big one—a quake of inestimable proportions which they believe could even break California off from the mainland and cast it adrift into the Pacific. Fortunately, the San Andreas fault is only 15 km

430 km long, ruptured, unleashing an earthquake measuring a phenomenal 8.3Ms on the Richter scale. The first warning of the disaster came in a foreshock which was felt at 5:12 am. Just 20–25 seconds later, the full force of the quake let rip. Violent waves of shaking, lasting 45–60 seconds,

and punctuated by massive jolting shocks, destroyed buildings and caused the deaths of up to 800 people. The earthquake started a fire that raged for three days, destroying 28,000 buildings and bringing the death toll to over 3,000. In the aftermath of the quake 225,000 people, out of a total population of 400,000, were left homeless. The earthquake's epicentre was near San Francisco, but its force was felt from southern Oregon as far south as Los Angeles and inland as far as central Nevada. Its force displaced areas of ground near the town of Olema and parts of the ocean floor by a massive 6 m. After this tragic quake, the San Andreas zone was quiet for over 80 years, but stresses were building up for the next major shock.

The Loma Prieta quake

On 17 Oct 1989, the San Andreas fault shook California again. At 5:04 pm, at the height of the rush hour, an earthquake lasting approximately 16 seconds rocked San Francisco and the surrounding towns. Buildings toppled and bridges and roads were destroyed. A total of 63 people were killed, nearly 4,000 were injured and 1,000 were left homeless. Although

all of San Francisco's major skyscrapers survived, damage to property caused by the earthquake amounted to almost $6 billion— making this quake the most costly natural disaster in the USA at the time. The epicentre of the 1989 earthquake was located near the Loma Prieta peak in the Santa Cruz mountains 120 km south of San Francisco. It ruptured the southernmost 40-km stretch of the break in the San Andreas fault left by the 1906 earthquake.

Los Angeles rocked

At 4:31 am on 17 Jan 1994, California was again struck by an earthquake of devastating proportions. The quake occurred just south of the San Andreas fault zone. Just 14 km below the city of Northridge in the San Fernando Valley, north of Los Angeles, a seismic wave measuring 6.6Ms was caused by movement along the Santa Monica Mountains thrust fault. The earthquake killed 63 people and left 15,000 homeless. It smashed buildings and destroyed roads, including an elevated section of the Santa Monica freeway—the USA's busiest major road. The total cost of the damage was estimated at $30 billion—five times that caused by the region's last serious seismic tragedy in 1989.

Quake-proof

In especially active quake-zones, architects have designed buildings to cope with excessive lateral strain, raising them from the ground on rubber or steel pads and formulating complex structures of metal and concrete which absorb the vibrations but ensure that the buildings do not collapse. In San Francisco, the modern pyramid building is designed to earthquake-resistant standards.

THE USA'S SECOND DANGER ZONE?

SOME GEOLOGISTS FEAR THAT THE SAN ANDREAS FAULT ZONE IS NOT THE USA'S ONLY EARTHQUAKE DANGER ZONE. THEY BELIEVE THAT THE MIDWEST MAY ALSO FALL VICTIM TO THE 'BIG ONE' IN THE FUTURE. THEY ARE CONCERNED THAT THE SERIES OF EARTHQUAKES WHICH STRUCK IN THE MIDWEST IN 1811–12 DEMONSTRATE ENORMOUS SEISMIC ACTIVITY IN THE AREA. SINCE THEN THERE HAVE BEEN OVER 4,000 EARTHQUAKES IN THE AREA, SOME WITH SEISMIC MAGNITUDES OF UP TO 6MS. GEOLOGISTS ALSO POINT TO THE HIGH NUMBER OF FAULT AND FOLD ZONES —A TOTAL OF OVER 100—LOCATED IN CENTRAL AREAS OF THE CONTINENT, WHICH PROVIDE THE POTENTIAL FOR A DISASTROUS UPHEAVAL. GEOLOGISTS HAVE CALCULATED THAT THERE IS A 50% CHANCE OF AN EARTHQUAKE MEASURING 6MS OR MORE HITTING THE MIDWEST BY THE YEAR 2000, AND A 90% CHANCE OF A SIMILAR STRIKE BY 2040. IF THEIR CALCULATIONS PROVE CORRECT, THEN THE LOSS OF LIFE AND DAMAGE TO BUILDINGS, NOT TO MENTION THE FINANCIAL COST, WOULD BE ABSOLUTELY AWESOME.

LEFT: THE SAN ANDREAS FAULT LINE WHICH EXTENDS THROUGH SOUTHERN CALIFORNIA, USA, FOR 1,050 KILOMETRES · RIGHT: THE RUINS OF SAN FRANCISCO IN 1906

VOLCANOES 1

TALLEST TOWERING

Named after Vulcanus, the Roman god of fire, volcanoes are formed when molten rock and gases from the Earth's upper mantle force their way upwards and erupt through cracks in the surface. Volcanoes occur in areas where the Earth's crust or plates are unstable. Eruptions can propel ash and debris high into the air while lava flows may spread across a wide area. Poisonous gases often add to the devastation. Once lava and ash have piled up around the vent, a young volcano is formed.

smoother shape. At 4,170 m high, 120 km long and 103 km wide, Mauna Loa is the largest volcano in the world today. It erupts every three to four years.

Sea creatures

Most volcanoes are situated within 250 km of the sea. Over half of active volcanoes form islands or occupy coastal sites. Raised sea levels can precipitate eruptions. In Iceland, for example, ice-covered volcanoes tend to erupt if the ice melts.

ASH IN THE ATMOSPHERE

WHEN A VOLCANO ERUPTS, IT SENDS TINY PARTICLES OF SULPHUR HIGH INTO THE STRATOSPHERE. THESE PARTICLES PREVENT THE SUN'S ENERGY FROM PENETRATING THE ATMOSPHERE, AND THIS CAN LEAD TO A DROP IN TEMPERATURES ACROSS THE GLOBE. THE ERUPTION OF MT PINATUBO, ON LUZON, NORTHWEST OF MANILA, IN THE PHILIPPINES IN 1991 IS BLAMED FOR CAUSING GLOBAL TEMPERATURES TO FALL BY HALF A DEGREE CENTIGRADE. THE EFFECTS OF THIS ERUPTION COULD BE MEASURED ACROSS THE WORLD FOR TWO YEARS FOLLOWING THE DISASTER.

ASH COLUMN 80 KM

VOLCANOES ARE FORMED AS THE RESULT OF VIOLENT AND DRAMATIC ERUPTIONS IN THE EARTH'S CRUST. RED HOT MOLTEN LAVA CAN TRAVEL AT SPEEDS OF 100 KM/H WHILE CLOUDS OF POISONOUS DUST BLAST INTO THE AIR

Conical perfection

The Mayon volcano, on the island of Luzon in the Philippines, rises above the city of Legaspi and is said to have the world's most perfect cone. The circumference of its base extends for 130 km and the volcano rises up as high as 2,421 m from the shores of the Albay Gulf. Whilst it is popular with climbers and campers, Mayon is still an active volcano and there have been more than 30 recorded eruptions since 1616. The town of Cagsawa was buried by volcanic ash in 1814, while another eruption claimed the lives of 75 people as recently as 1993.

Shaped by temperament

If a volcano ejects a large amount of lava, the red hot flow will spread out across the surrounding terrain. If it ejects only a small amount, then cooling mounds will form near the vent. Volcano shape is also affected by whether ash columns or magma are ejected. Magma is the molten rock containing silicate which erupts as lava flows. 'Cinder Cones' are steep volcanoes which tend to erupt irregularly, but fiercely. Mount Fuji in Japan is a good example of a classic volcano, with steep sides which curve upward to reach a sharp peak. In contrast, a volcano which ejects lava regularly, such as Mauna Loa, in Hawaii, will display a much

The sound of violence

When Krakatau (or Krakatoa) erupted on the uninhabited Pulau Island, in Indonesia, on 26–27 Aug 1883, the explosion is estimated to have been 26 times more powerful than the largest ever H-bomb test. The noise, which could be heard in Australia, 4,800 km away, travelled across 8% of the Earth's surface. A resulting tidal wave, more than 30 km high, killed 36,000 people and wiped out 163 villages on the nearby islands of Java and Sumatra. A total of 18 km³ of magma was expelled, sending debris flying 55 km into the air while an ash cloud rose to 80 km, plunging much of Java and Sumatra into darkness and making

it the highest ash column and highest ash cloud ever recorded. Dust was still falling 5,330 km away 10 days later.

Ice breakers

A series of earthquakes on 30 Sept 1996 alerted scientists to an eruption underneath a 600-m-thick glacier between the volcanoes of Bardarbunga and Grimsvotn in central Iceland. Within a few days, the force of this underground or fissure volcano had broken through the glacier, expelling ash plumes several kilometres into the air and forcing the cancellation of flights in north and east Iceland as the ash cloud headed in that direction.

The Ring of Fire

Almost all volcanoes erupt in coastal areas or beneath the sea, often creating fantastic mountain ranges under water. Certain parts of the Earth's crust are particularly at risk of extreme seismic activity. The Ring of Fire is the name given to a huge belt of volcanic activity that stretches around the Pacific Ocean, including Papua New Guinea and the Philippines. Characterized by a series of explosions and quakes in close proximity, almost every major city in the region has been devastated at least once by an earthquake or volcanic activity. There is more seismic activity in this area than anywhere else in the world.

JARGON

ASH
PARTICLES OF PULVERIZED ROCK WHICH HAVE BEEN BLOWN FROM A VOLCANIC ERUPTION

CENTRAL VOLCANOES
THE MOST COMMON FORM OF VOLCANO, USUALLY CONE-SHAPED WITH ONE VERTICAL PIPE OF LAVA

CINDER CONES
SMALL, STEEP VOLCANOES THAT TEND TO ERUPT FEROCIOUSLY

DORMANT
A VOLCANO WHICH IS CURRENTLY INACTIVE, BUT WHICH MAY ERUPT AT SOME POINT IN THE FUTURE

ERUPTION CLOUD
THE COLUMN OF ASH, ROCKS AND GAS WHICH CAN RISE SEVERAL KM INTO THE SKY FROM A VOLCANO

MAGMA
MOLTEN ROCK CONTAINING SILICATE AND OTHER CHEMICALS

LAHAR
TORRENTIAL MUDFLOW CAUSED WHEN VOLCANIC ASH MEETS SNOW, ICE OR WATER

LAVA
EJECTED MAGMA, WHICH FLOWS LIKE MOLTEN WAX, COOLING, HARDENING AND SLOWING AS IT MOVES FURTHER FROM SOURCE

VOLCANOLOGIST
PERSON WHO STUDIES THE GEOLOGY, PAST BEHAVIOUR AND CURRENT ACTIVITY OF VOLCANOES TO UNDERSTAND HOW THEY WORK

DATA-BURST

HOW FAR CAN ASH SPREAD FROM THE VOLCANO?
ASH FROM VIOLENT ERUPTIONS CAN SPREAD AS FAR AS 200 KM.

HOW HIGH CAN THE TOWERING ASH COLUMNS REACH?
COLUMNS OF DEBRIS CAN REACH AS HIGH AS 80 KM IN SOME CASES— EQUIVALENT TO MORE THAN FIVE TIMES THE SIZE OF MT EVEREST.

ARE THERE ANY OTHER DANGERS APART FROM ASH SUFFOCATION?
THE VOLCANO MAY RELEASE POISONOUS GASES, OR MAY SHOWER ENTIRE CITIES WITH DEBRIS. VIOLENT RAINSTORMS CAN ALSO INTERACT WITH THE DEBRIS, CREATING FAST AND HARD BULLETS THAT HURTLE DOWN TO THE EARTH. PLANES HAVE BEEN FORCED TO MAKE EMERGENCY

LANDINGS DUE TO THE SHEER LOSS OF POWER AS PARTICLES FROM THE ERUPTION GET CLOGGED IN ENGINES.

WHAT VOLUME OF MATERIAL CAN BE DISPERSED?
MATTER IN EXCESS OF 100 KM3 CAN BE EJECTED IN THE HEAT OF A VOLCANIC ERUPTION. THIS AMOUNT OF MATERIAL COULD FILL WEMBLEY STADIUM 85,000 TIMES OVER.

HOW FAR CAN MATTER BE DISPERSED?
MATTER CAN BE THROWN OVER AN AREA AS WIDE AS 500 KM².

HOW LONG DO ERUPTIONS LAST?
ON AVERAGE VOLCANIC ERUPTIONS LAST LESS THAN TWO DAYS. RARELY IN NATURE ARE SUCH VAST CHANGES TO THE LANDSCAPE WROUGHT IN SUCH A SHORT TIME.

LEFT: AUGUSTINE VOLCANO, SATELLITE VIEW OF ASH COLUMN · INSET: HOUSES ENGULFED BY LAVA AND ASH FOLLOWING THE ERUPTION OF HEIMAEY VOLCANO, ICELAND

Volcanic myth and legend

The oldest and most active volcano in Europe is Mount Etna. Situated on the island of Sicily, south of the Italian mainland, its name comes from the Greek and means 'I burn'. The ancient Greeks created many legends about the volcano. It was believed to be the workshop of Hephaestus, the god of fire. A giant named Typhon was thought to lie beneath the mountain making the Earth tremble when he turned. Mt Etna is more than 3,200 m high and covers 1,600 km. It was at its most active between 1500 BC and AD 1669 when 71 eruptions were recorded. However, it is thought to have been active for 2.5 million years.

The power to destroy

One of the most powerful eruptions ever recorded occurred on the Indonesian island of Sumbawa on 10–11 April 1815. Known as

as a sacred symbol in Japan. Thousands of Japanese climb its eight peaks every summer to visit the temples and shrines, some of which are located at the bottom of the crater. The volcano is part of the Fuji Volcanic Zone, which extends from the Mariana islands to northern Honshu.

Deadly lava

The eruption of Laki, in south-east Iceland, which began on 8 June 1783 and continued until February

contributed to the demise of the Minoan empire in the region and helped to create the legend of the lost city of Atlantis. The Greek philosopher, Plato, described Atlantis as a 'rich and proud land' that was apparently 'swallowed by the sea' when it provoked the anger of the gods Poseidon and Zeus. Despite speculation about the location of the underwater city, there is still no firm evidence to prove that Atlantis ever existed.

of ash 11,000 m into the air. By September 1997, successive eruptions had devastated large parts of the island. Nearly all the inhabitants of Montserrat were forced to evacuate their homes and relocate onto neighbouring islands. An emergency relief programme was put into operation by the British Government.

No protection

According to native American Indian legend, Mt St Helens, in

VOLCANOES 2
RED HOT LAVA FLOWS

Tambora, the eruption was one of the most devastating of the past 200 years. Some 180 km³ of volcanic matter was expelled across 500,000 km² of farmland, which was then covered in a layer of ash 1 cm thick. As many as 10,000 people died as a direct result of the eruption and the tidal waves that it produced, while 82,000 deaths were caused by the subsequent famine and disease.

Eternal damnation

At 3,776 m, Mt Fuji is the highest mountain in Japan. Located 95 km west of Tokyo, it has not erupted since 1707 but is still considered active. Its name means 'everlasting life' and the mountain is regarded

1784, was responsible for the longest lava flow ever recorded. The volume of lava expelled by the volcano was 12.3 km³ and covered an area of 565 km², travelling up to 70 km from the source. Sulphurous gases, which could be detected as far away as Siberia and Syria, destroyed crops and grasses and killed most of Iceland's farm animals. The resulting famine caused the deaths of a fifth of Iceland's population.

The lost city of Atlantis

A huge eruption in 1640 BC on Santorini in the Aegean Sea completely blew the volcano apart, leaving a few, scattered remnant islands. This event probably

Glowing flow

When Mt Pelee, on Martinique in the Caribbean, erupted on 8 May 1902, fast flowing lava poured down towards the port of St Pierre at such a rate that 29,000 people living there were unable to flee in time and were killed. Lava with low viscosity can flow faster, travelling at speeds of up to 100 km/h. These are commonly known as 'glowing avalanches' or 'ash flows'. These sudden lava eruptions have been called Pelean volcanoes ever since.

Black volcanic tide

Volcanic eruptions can have devastating knock-on effects. An apparently minor eruption at Nevada del Ruiz, in Colombia, on 13 Nov 1985 occurred under a glacial ice cap. For three hours, the volcano belched forth hot ash, which melted the snow and ice. An enormous mud flow, called a lahar, was sent hurtling towards the town of Armero, mixing with hot ash from the volcano. Some 25,000 people were killed in the wake of the black ooze.

Crisis on Monserrat

On 18 June 1995 the island of Montserrat in the Caribbean experienced its first volcanic eruption. An initial eruption in the Soufriere Hills resulted in minor ashfalls, steam explosions and earthquakes. Then, on 21 Aug, a huge steam explosion plunged Plymouth, the island's capital, in total darkness for over half an hour. Another serious eruption, on Boxing Day 1995, sent a column

Washington State, USA, was a beautiful maiden sent to protect the Columbia River from her two battling brothers, the nearby Mt Adams and Mt Hood. However, Mt St Helens has erupted 20 times over the past 4,500 years, most devastatingly in March 1980. After several days of volcanic activity, which sent a cloud of ash surging 20 km into the sky, the mountain's height was reduced by 1,100 m and its crater formed a basin up to 500 m wide and 200 m deep. These ash clouds, and a resulting avalanche which reached speeds of up to 250 km/h, destroyed 550 km² of land, including 10 million trees. About 60 people were killed and the town of Ritzville was covered in a layer of ash 8 cm thick. Damage caused by volcanic activity in the 1980s amounted to in excess of $1,000 million.

Pinatubo blast

In 1991, one of the largest and most serious eruptions of the 20th century took place on Mt Pinatubo, north-west of Manila on the island of Luzon in the Philippines. It was the first time that the volcano had erupted in 600 years. At least 700 people died and 100,000 were left homeless by the eruption, which sent a column of ash 30 km high into the air and adversely affected global temperatures for the next two years.

Monitoring Vesuvius

Mt Vesuvius is one of the most famous of all volcanoes. Its pyramid shape looms behind the

LEFT: VIEW AT NIGHT OF A LAVA CHANNEL BELOW THE ACTIVE VENTS OF MOUNT ETNA, SICILY · RIGHT: A BUS SITS BURIED IN A COOLING LAVA FLOW FROM KILAUEA, HAWAII

city of Naples in southern Italy. Over 1,900 years ago, it covered the ancient Roman cities of Pompeii and Herculaneum with tonnes of pumice ash and poisonous gases. Scientists today believe that the threat of a further explosion from Vesuvius remains a dangerous possibility. Watchful of its seismic activity, they monitor gases emerging from its simmering caldera. Experts who have probed the surrounding area for electronic currents have discovered an enormous rock plug jammed in the 60 m-wide conduit of the volcano—like a stopper in a champagne bottle. If this cork were to pop, the effect would be cataclysmic for the 2 million people who currently live in the shadow of the volcano. Rather than falling prey to red hot lava, it is the danger of 'pyroclastic flow'—superheated ash combined with poisonous gases—that has been identified as a potential mass killer. In 1995, the Italian government set up a commission which aimed to put together a precautionary emergency plan for people living in the high risk area. However, experts disagree with one another about how long it will be before the next eruption takes place. The current evacuation plan would take a week to implement, but volcanologists warn that Vesuvius has the power to destroy everything within an 8-km radius 'within minutes'.

ANCIENT CITY PRESERVED IN ASH

WHEN VESUVIUS ERUPTED IN THE YEAR AD 79, THE ROMAN TOWNS OF POMPEII AND HERCULANEUM WERE BURIED UNDER POISONOUS ASH AND MUD WITHIN 12 HOURS. THE ANCIENT GREEK WRITER, PLINY, GAVE THE FIRST EYE-WITNESS ACCOUNT OF A VOLCANIC ERUPTION: "A DARK AND HORRIBLE CLOUD WAS COMING UP BEHIND US AS WE WERE FLEEING, SPREADING OVER THE EARTH LIKE A FLOOD". THE CITY WAS PUMMELLED BY VOLCANIC ROCK AND PUMICE, BURIED IN ASH AND THEN SEALED WITH BOILING MUD AND LAVA WHICH LATER ALLOWED ARCHAEOLOGISTS TO UNCOVER THE HISTORICAL CITY WHEN THEY STARTED TO DIG AT THE SITE 250 YEARS AGO. TO THEIR AMAZEMENT, THEY FOUND ROMAN BUILDINGS PRESERVED JUST AS THEY WERE ON THE DAY OF THE EXPLOSION AND EVERY DETAIL OF ROMAN LIFE REMAINED INTACT. EVEN SOME OF THE BODIES OF POMPEII'S 15,000 FORMER INHABITANTS WERE PRESERVED IN THE ASH. MOST OF THE PEOPLE DIED AS A RESULT OF SUFFOCATION BY SULPHURIC ASH. USING A METHOD OF PLASTER CASTING, ARCHAEOLOGISTS HAVE BEEN ABLE TO REVEAL THE ANGUISHED EXPRESSIONS ON THEIR FACES ON THAT FATEFUL DAY.

AT RECORD SPEEDS OF 100 KM/H

THE ERRATIC AND DESTRUCTIVE POWERS OF VOLCANOES HAVE DESTROYED MANY CITIES, FAMOUSLY COVERING ANCIENT POMPEII WITH BURNING ASH IN AD 79, BUT ALSO WREAKING HAVOC IN MODERN DAY MONTSERRAT

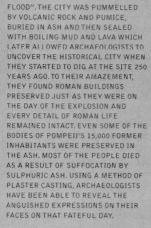

A landslide is the sudden downward movement of a mass of soil or rocks from a cliff or steep slope. This occurs when a slope becomes unstable, usually because the base has been undercut or materials within the mass of earth itself have become lubricated. Heavy rainfall, frost and melted snow can all increase the movement of a slide, adding weight to the debris and lubricating its slide down an incline. Other contributory factors which can affect the magnitude of a landslide include the scarcity of vegetation, differences in rock structures, the steepness of the slope and the amount of undercutting at the base.

reached a depth of 58 m. The landslide occurred just before midnight as campers in the park were sleeping in their tents; 24 people were killed and many others were badly injured.

Earth shaking
Although landslides are usually caused by earthquakes, the reverse process can also take place when landslides produce seismic waves equivalent to a small to moderate earthquake. On 25 April 1974 a

Dam disaster
The Vajont Dam was built between 1957 and 1960 in a tributary of the River Piave in the Southern Alps in Italy. Rising to a height of 276 m, it was one of the highest dams in the world. In 1960, as the reservoir of the dam was being filled, a landslide of 70,000 m³ of rock hit the reservoir. Slow, incremental landslides, known as 'creeps', continued at the site over the next three years, increasing in speed over time. Then, on 9 Oct

Water power
Water plays a key role in the generation of landslides. Heavy rains and snowmelts can play havoc in regions with unstable geological conditions, triggering landslides with alarming frequency. The annual monsoon season in Nepal causes landslides on main roads, and the key road south to India from Pokhara is blocked almost every year. While these perennial slides are destructive, they are not usually catastrophic.

LANDSLIDES

LANDSLIDE TRAVELLED OVER

The Madison slide
The Hebden Lake earthquake on 17 Aug 1959 triggered one of the worst landslides to affect the USA. The earthquake occurred west of the Yellowstone National Park, on the south wall of the canyon cut by the Madison River. Some 31 million m³ of rock debris rushed down the south wall of the canyon, tearing up trees and causing terrific damage as it fell. A block the size of a house rode the landslide's stream as it ravaged the region. At least 1.6 km of the Madison River and highway was buried by a pile of debris up to 67 m deep. This created a dam across the river which resulted in a lake that, after three weeks, extended 9.6 km upstream and

massive landslide along the Mantaro River in Peru triggered an earthquake that killed more than 450 people. This slide fell suddenly, travelling at a speed of around 140 km/h over a distance of about 7 km. Part of its gravitational energy, lost in the rapid downward movement of soil and rock, was converted into seismic waves. A seismograph situated 80 km away from the landslide recorded three minutes of tremors as a result. Earthquakes such as this can shake down seemingly resistant rocks lying above unstable, impermeable rocks. Tremors can also affect the equilibrium of the slope and increase the likelihood of a mass movement of the rock.

1963 disaster struck when a massive rock slide occurred; 275 million m³ of rock debris slid into the reservoir at speeds of up to 250 km/h. This slide caused a massive water wave which spilled 70 m over the top of the dam. The Piave Valley below was flooded in seven minutes, and debris was carried 1,800 m down its length and mounted 260 m up its sides. The villages of Pirago, Villanova, Rivalta and Fae, and the town of Longarone, were instantly wiped off the map. Fatalities were extremely high with some 1,925 deaths recorded. Remarkably, the dam itself somehow withstood the pressure of the water and debris which was calculated at equivalent to 170,000 kw per hour.

However, in 1976, the village of Pahirikhet in Nepal was destroyed by a monsoon-generated landslide which killed 150 villagers. The hills of Hong Kong are also prone to slides. The underlying granite is covered with soil and weathered rock, which often becomes dislodged by the weight of heavy rains. On 18 June 1972 one such slide, over 180 m wide, swept through the Kwun Tong district of Kowloon, burying the shanty town neighbourhood under rock and debris, and killing over 100 people. Later that same year, on 13 Sept, a total of 40 cm of rain fell in a single day causing a landslide on the Japanese island of Kamijima which killed some 112 people.

DATA-BURST

WHAT IS THE BIGGEST NUMBER OF PEOPLE KILLED IN A LANDSLIDE?
ON 16 DEC 1920 A LANDSLIDE WAS TRIGGERED BY A SINGLE EARTHQUAKE IN THE GANSU PROVINCE, CHINA, WHICH KILLED ABOUT 180,000 PEOPLE.

WHAT IS THE MOST MATERIAL DAMAGE CAUSED BY A LANDSLIDE?
FROM 18–26 JAN 1969 A SERIES OF LANDSLIDES BROUGHT ABOUT BY NINE DAYS OF TORRENTIAL RAIN AND A SUBTROPICAL STORM CAUSED ABOUT $138 MILLION WORTH OF DAMAGE IN SOUTHERN CALIFORNIA, USA.

WHAT IS THE LARGEST RECORDED LANDSLIDE?
THE LARGEST IN RECENT HISTORY OCCURRED IN 1911 AT USOY IN THE PAMIR MOUNTAINS IN RUSSIA. 2.5 KM³ OF MATERIAL FLOWED DOWN THE SLOPES. BECAUSE THE AREA WAS SO REMOTE AND SPARSELY POPULATED, IT WAS TWO MONTHS BEFORE THE AUTHORITIES DISCOVERED THE EVENT.

WHAT IS THE SLOWEST TYPE OF LANDSLIDE?
THE MOST GRADUAL FORM OF LANDSLIDE OCCURS IN POLAR OR HIGH-ALTITUDE AREAS OF PERMANENTLY FROZEN GROUND. THIS SLOW DOWNHILL MOVEMENT OF DEBRIS SATURATED BY WATER IS KNOWN AS SOLIFLUCTION. IT OCCURS DURING PERIODS OF THAW, WHEN MELTWATER SATURATES THE THAWED DEBRIS TO A SHALLOW DEPTH, CARRYING IT OVER THE PERMANENTLY FROZEN SURFACE. SOLIFLUCTION CREATES TERRACE-LIKE FEATURES ON THE SLOPES.

HAVE THERE BEEN MAJOR LANDSLIDES IN RECENT YEARS?
YES. SEVERAL HUNDRED PEOPLE DIED ON 29 MARCH 1994 WHEN HEAVY RAIN NEAR CUENCA IN ECUADOR CAUSED A LANDSLIDE THAT BURIED A MINING COMMUNITY. IN JUNE 1997, IN YUNNAN PROVINCE, CHINA, TWO LANDSLIDES IN A GOLD MINE RESULTED IN THE DEATHS OF AT LEAST 227 MINERS.

LEFT: FALLEN ROCKS FROM LANDSLIDE BLOCK ROAD IN NAGAR, PAKISTAN, 1996 · RIGHT: LUXURY HOME IN ORANGE COUNTY, USA, SLIPS DOWN HILL DURING A LANDSLIDE CAUSED BY HEAVY RAINS

Air blast

As landslides cascade down their path of destruction, they create an air blast. This is caused by the pressure of rapidly expelled air trapped by the descending slide mass. This air can make a thunderous noise: survivors of the Madison tragedy spoke of a violent slam of air that boomed when the mountainside slid from its foundations as the landslide struck. Many experts believe that the cushion of air that travels with a landslide gives it extra motion and allows it to travel longer distances. The trapped air acts in the same way as a lubricant, propelling the landslide further along its course.

THE ABERFAN TRAGEDY

IN 1966 AN HORRIFIC LANDSLIDE ENGULFED A WELSH MINING COMMUNITY AT ABERFAN, IN THE SOUTH-EAST PART OF MERTHYR TYDFIL. AMONG THE 144 FATALITIES WERE 116 CHILDREN AND FIVE TEACHERS, WHOSE PRIMARY SCHOOL WAS CRUSHED BENEATH THE DEBRIS. DURING THE MINING PROCESS, WASTE MATTER KNOWN AS TAILINGS (INCLUDING WET CLAY AND SHALE LAYERS) IS BROUGHT OUT OF THE MINE AND DUMPED, FORMING AN ARTIFICIAL HILL CALLED A SLAG HEAP. IN ABERFAN, SEVEN SLAG HEAPS LAY BETWEEN 40 AND 200 M ABOVE THE TOWN ON THE MERTHYR MOUNTAIN SLOPES. IN OCTOBER 1966, WATER FROM NEARBY STREAMS COMBINED WITH HEAVY RAIN, LOOSENING THE SLAGHEAP, AND STARTING A LANDSLIDE WHICH ENVELOPED THE TOWN.

JARGON

CREEP
GRADUAL MOVEMENT OF ROCK, SOIL AND SEDIMENT DOWN A SLOPE; SLOW CREEP IS THE RESULT OF GRAVITY ACTING ON MATERIAL THAT HAS LOST ITS COHESION

MASS-WASTING
THE TRANSFER OF EARTH MATERIAL DOWN HILL SLOPES INCLUDING MOVEMENT SUCH AS FLOW, SLIDE, FALL AND CREEP

OVERSTEEPENING
THE CREATION OF A SLOPE STEEP ENOUGH FOR DEBRIS TO DESCEND

SOLIFLUCTION
THE GRADUAL MOVEMENT DOWN A SLOPE OF SOIL SATURATED BY WATER

7 KM AT A SPEED OF 140 KM/H

LANDSLIDES HAPPEN SUDDENLY AND WITHOUT WARNING. MASSIVE ROCKS AND HUGE AMOUNTS OF DEBRIS RUSH DOWN MOUNTAIN SLOPES, SWEEPING AWAY ANYTHING IN THEIR PATH, FLATTENING ENTIRE VILLAGES AND TOWNS

Mudslides are caused by the potent combination of loose earth and added water. This creates a tide of debris that flows faster and further than a typical, less fluid, landslide. Mudslides either follow in the wake of volcanic activity, where melting snow adds to the molten lava mix, or they occur after a period of heavy rain in a previously dry, hilly area where vegetation is sparse. Rivers become swollen and burst, sending mud and debris streaming through nearby towns and villages. The high density of mudslides enables them to sweep away buildings and boulders weighing several tonnes. Some mudslides have travelled for distances of up to 100 km.

Worst mudslide

One of the worst mudslides on record occurred in west-central Colombia on 13 Nov 1985, when a volcanic eruption on Nevado del Ruiz melted large quantities of snow and ice around the summit. Nevado del Ruiz is 5,400 m high and the northernmost of nearly 300 active volcanoes in the Cordillera Central range of the Andes. A famous earlier eruption in 1845 had caused devastating mudslides that killed 1,000 people.

Geological evidence suggests that there had been another similar occurrence in 1595. In 1985, however, the damage was far greater. The mud caused by the melting snow and ice poured down the slopes at high speed and into the valleys below, destroying everything in its path. The town of Armero, nearly 50 km from the mountain on the Lagunilla River, was particularly badly hit. Around 20,000 inhabitants were killed and the majority of houses destroyed.

There were thousands more deaths in surrounding villages, with 1,000 reported killed at Chinchina, on the western side of the mountain. The consequences were so devastating because of the lethal combination of mud and magma (molten lava), which is known as lahar and has the consistency of wet cement. After a volcano erupts, the slightest addition of water mobilizes the layers of ash below. This greatly increases the slide's weight and reduces its cohesion,

MUDSLIDES

20,000 PEOPLE KILLED IN

TOWN SWALLOWED UP

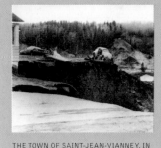

THE TOWN OF SAINT-JEAN-VIANNEY, IN THE CANADIAN PROVINCE OF QUEBEC, HAD TO BE ABANDONED WHEN A MUDSLIDE STRUCK IN MAY 1971. THE TOWN HAD BEEN BUILT IN A SHELTERED HOLLOW AT THE UPPER END OF A SLIDE THAT OCCURRED IN THE 15TH OR 16TH CENTURY.

THE INHABITANTS LIVED WITHOUT INCIDENT FOR SEVERAL HUNDRED YEARS. THEN ON 4 MAY 1971, THE FIRST INDICATIONS OF IMPENDING DISASTER CAME WHEN FARM ANIMALS REFUSED TO ENTER FIELDS ON THE EDGE OF TOWN, PRESUMABLY BECAUSE THEY COULD SENSE SOME EARTH MOVEMENT. THAT NIGHT, A HUGE SLIDE APPROACHED, DESTROYING THESE FIELDS AND OPENING UP A CRATER 800 M WIDE AND 23 M DEEP. ROADS, VEHICLES AND HOUSES WERE ALL SWALLOWED UP AS A MASSIVE WAVE OF MUD 15 M HIGH FLOWED FOR FOUR HOURS FOR NEARLY 3 KM UNTIL IT REACHED THE SAGUENAY RIVER. A TOTAL OF 31 PEOPLE DIED IN THE DISASTER AND THE TOWN HAS SINCE BEEN ABANDONED DUE TO THE EXTREME INSTABILITY OF THE UNDERLYING CLAY.

effort to prevent a repeat occurrence, an artificial landslide was created in 1966 by setting off an explosion. The contents of the slide were then used to dam up the nearby Medeo Gorge, creating a formidable barrier around 100 m long. The experiment proved successful, dramatically reducing the impact of another potentially devastating mudslide which occurred in 1973.

Entombed in mud

Mudslides are a common consequence when flash floods hit an unstable area. The year 1997 was a particularly bad one for flooding in Brazil. In the poorer parts of São Paulo, Rio de Janeiro

Storm damage

In the hurricane season of 1993, a tropical storm named Bret caused severe flooding in Colombia, Venezuela, Nicaragua and Costa Rica. When the storm reached the Mexican state of San Luis Potosi, there was 400 mm of rainfall and the resulting mudslides killed 14 people and left 100,000 homeless.

Black tide

Up to 70 people were killed, many others went missing and 2,000 were made homeless by the mudslide that swept down from the hills and through the town of Sarno, near Naples, in southern Italy in May 1998. What became known as 'the black tide' destroyed buildings and swept away cars and trees after a period of very heavy rain. One local resident described how, when he tried to reach his house, he was faced by a wall of mud 2.5 m high. Again, many of the victims came from poorer areas, where badly built houses offered little protection. The local authorities were criticized for failing to protect potential disaster areas and allowing unregulated construction of local buildings. The Italian government promised £18 million in aid to rejuvenate Sarno.

COLOMBIAN MUDSLIDE

AFTER HEAVY RAIN, OR VOLCANIC ACTIVITY ON SNOW-CAPPED MOUNTAINS, MUDSLIDES CAN SWEEP DOWN THROUGH HILLS AT DEVASTATING SPEEDS, FLUSHING AWAY ENTIRE VILLAGES IN A FOUL AND LETHAL WALL OF SEDIMENT.

enabling it to travel further and faster than an ordinary lava flow. These flows can move at speeds of up to 110 km/h, picking up stones, rocks, boulders, tree trunks and the remains of buildings in their wake.

Pre-empting a mudslide

Almaty, the capital city of Kurdistan, is an area of extensive geological risk. The city stands

about 900 m above sea level in the northern foothills of the Trans-Alay Alatau, near the Bolshaya and Malaya Almaatinka rivers. There have been many earthquakes in the region, most notably in 1887 and 1911, and the area is particularly prone to mudslides. In 1921, a serious mudslide flowed down the Malaya Almaatinka River and caused widespread damage and considerable loss of life. In an

and Recife thousands of people lost their homes, while many were killed in mudslides that swept through the area in February and again in April. Many of the makeshift shanty-style homes lacked solid foundations and as a result offered no protection from the sheer force of the mudslide. Some victims were unable to escape and were entombed within their houses.

Fired up

In Southern California in 1993, major mudslides were triggered in the wake of forest fires. The fires had denuded the vegetation and changed the nature of the soil making it more impervious, so that when the rains came, little more than a shower turned vast areas of land into muddy black slides which damaged homes and blocked transport routes.

DATA-BURST

WHAT IS THE DIFFERENCE BETWEEN A MUDSLIDE AND A LANDSLIDE?
A MUDSLIDE IS ESSENTIALLY A LANDSLIDE WITH ADDED WATER. THIS MAY COME FROM HEAVY RAIN OR THE MELTING OF SNOW AND ICE. IT LIQUIFIES THE DEBRIS, CAUSING IT TO FLOW FASTER, FURTHER AND OFTEN WITH MORE DEVASTATING EFFECT.

WHERE DO MUDSLIDES OCCUR?
USUALLY IN AREAS OF VOLCANIC ACTIVITY OR HILLY, SPARSELY VEGETATED AREAS WHERE RAIN IS RARE BUT OCCASIONALLY VERY INTENSE.

WHAT MEASURES CAN BE TAKEN TO LESSEN THE DAMAGE CAUSED BY MUDSLIDES?
SOME MEASURES CAN BE TAKEN TO LESSEN THE IMPACT OF POTENTIAL MUDSLIDES. WHEN MOUNT UNZEN IN JAPAN ERUPTED IN 1991, IT SWAMPED LOCAL HOMES WITH A LAYER OF MUD 2 M DEEP WHEN RAINS WASHED DOWN

THE VOLCANO'S ASH-COVERED SLOPES. IN RESPONSE, THE MIZUNASHI RIVER, A SEASONALLY DRY RIVERBED, WAS WIDENED AND PAVED WITH CONCRETE WALLS TO FUNNEL FUTURE MUDSLIDES INTO SHIMABARA BAY.

WHAT DIRECTIONS DO MUDSLIDES FOLLOW?
MUDSLIDES FOLLOW STREAM VALLEYS AND CHANNELS AND SPILL OUT INTO LOBES OR FANS WHEN THEY REACH LOW-LYING TERRAIN.

CAN MUDSLIDES MOVE HEAVY OBJECTS?
THE HIGH DENSITY OF MUDSLIDES ENABLES THEM TO CARRY BUILDINGS AND BOULDERS WHICH MAY WEIGH MANY TONNES.

HOW IS IT POSSIBLE TO TELL WHERE A MUDSLIDE HAS TAKEN PLACE?
MUDSLIDES LEAVE SCARS ON THE SLOPES THEY RIDE DOWN AND LEAVE A TRAIL OF BOULDERS, STONES AND DIRT.

LEFT: ITALIAN SOLDIERS DIG FOR SURVIVORS IN THE WAKE OF MUDSLIDES WHICH TURNED INTO RIVERS OF DEATH, SARNO, ITALY, MAY 1998. · RIGHT: MUDSLIDE IN THE PERUVIAN HIGHLANDS

Subsidence can take several forms. Settlement occurs when fluid is squeezed or removed from a land mass. It is a gradual process and leads to changes in the soil and rock structures. Similarly, the continual deposition of sediment, or the weight of heavy artificial structures can cause the land beneath it to contract and sink. The wetting of soil or rock materials, such as clay or sand, can also lead to a change in structure as the land shifts and resettles in a denser, more compact form. A more drastic event occurs when water, oil or minerals are extracted from deep underground, causing the soil and rock above to collapse.

Mining peril

Many of the biggest subsidence problems are the result of human intervention. The extraction of underground minerals through mining, for instance, has resulted in death and tragedy all around the globe. In China alone, government statistics suggest that around 10,000 miners are killed every year. The direct causes are usually either the collapse of a mine shaft or underground explosions. The situation is exacerbated in countries like China, where there are thousands of small mines some of which fail to observe safety instructions. Following a 15% increase in mining-related deaths in China in 1994, investigators found one-third of small coal mines operating without a licence. Around 75% failed to meet basic safety standards.

Tunnel trouble

The building of underground tunnels is always a dangerous engineering feat, and tunnel-building casualties have always been high. In 1908, a tunnel being developed under the Kandar Valley at Lotschberg, Switzerland, collapsed due to sudden subsidence, killing all 25 people who were working on it at the time. The 1,000-m tunnel was entirely filled by a vast inflow of water, gravel and broken rock. The tragedy followed the report of a geological panel which gave the tunnel the go-ahead, believing that it would be drilled through solid bedrock far beneath the floor of the valley. It later transpired that the bedrock was some 300 m underground, at least 100 m below the level of the tunnel.

DATA-BURST

IS SUBSIDENCE STILL CAUSING FATALITIES?
SUBSIDENCE CONTINUES TO CAUSE MINING DISASTERS. IN SEPTEMBER 1996, 80 PEOPLE WERE BURIED WHILE ILLEGALLY MINING FOR TIN IN NIGERIA. IN THE FIRST THREE MONTHS OF 1997, 178 MINERS WERE KILLED AND 2,400 INJURED IN SOUTH AFRICA, WHILE IN JUNE 1997, A FURTHER 227 MINERS WERE KILLED AT A CHINESE GOLD MINE.

WHAT ARE SINKHOLES?
SINKHOLES OCCUR ON ROLLING PLAINS WITH FEW SURFACE STREAMS AND ARE THE RESULT OF A DRAMATIC FORM OF SETTLEMENT. THERE CAN BE TENS OF THOUSANDS OF SUCH HOLES PER SQUARE KILOMETRE, RANGING IN DEPTH FROM THE BARELY DISCERNIBLE TO HUGE DEPRESSIONS MORE THAN 1 KM WIDE AND HUNDREDS OF METRES DEEP. SINKHOLES FORM BECAUSE OF THE DISSOLUTION OF BEDROCK AT INTERSECTION JOINTS

AND AFTER THE COLLAPSE OF CAVE ROOFS. OTHER SINKHOLES OCCUR ENTIRELY UNDERGROUND, WITHIN THE SOIL. THIS KIND OF SUBSIDENCE OCCURS WHERE SOIL IS WASHED DOWNWARDS INTO THE SUBSURFACE, LEAVING AN ARCHED VOID ABOVE. SUCH SOIL-BASED SINKHOLES CAN CAUSE A PARTICULAR PROBLEM IN BUILT-UP AREAS, WHERE THE UNDERGROUND ROOF COLLAPSES BENEATH ROADS OR BUILDINGS.

IS ANYTHING BEING DONE TO SAVE THE TOWER OF PISA FROM FALLING OVER?
YES, A CONSERVATION PLAN IS UNDERWAY WHEREBY THE TOWER WILL BE ANCHORED BY STEEL CABLES TO A PROVISIONAL STRUCTURE. A WEDGE OF SOIL WILL THEN BE SLOWLY REMOVED FROM THE EARTH UNDERLYING THE TOWER'S FOUNDATION. SOIL WILL BE SCOOPED FROM THE DIRECTION OPPOSITE TO THE LEAN, CORRECTING THE ANGLE OF THE TOWER, WHICH WILL THEN BE CONSOLIDATED.

SUBSIDENCE

VENICE SINKS 1 CM

Collapsing walls

The Tanna Tunnel, which was driven through the Takiji Peak in Japan during the 1920s, was the scene of many tunnelling disasters. An initial collapse killed 16 people and was followed by an extremely large influx of water and debris. A further 17 men who were also buried in the rubble survived after being uncovered several days later. However, three years later, another collapse at the tunnel brought more deaths. To prevent further problems, Japanese engineers dug a drainage tunnel parallel to the main tunnel, which was used to syphon off excess groundwater that was making the land unstable.

Submerged subsidence

Darwin Rise is a topographical rise covering an area that stretches 10,000 km by 4,000 km across the western and central Pacific Ocean. With the discovery of shallow water organisms living in deep areas, the area provides plenty of evidence of marine subsidence. Oxidized iron has also appeared in dredged samples. This suggests that considerable erosion and weathering have taken place and that a large number of long-vanished volcanic cones and atolls must have been exposed above sea level at some point in the past. The area was named after Charles Darwin, the evolutionist, who identified the subsidence which has been occurring continuously since the Cretaceous Period. The area confirms that there have been large vertical movements of the Earth's crust beneath the sea.

Faulty towers

Subsidence is often caused by the removal of groundwater and over-extensive mining. However, it also occurs when a building is simply too heavy for the ground beneath it. The Leaning Tower of Pisa, Italy, is perhaps the most famous example of a building constructed on land incapable of bearing its weight. Work began on the tower's construction in 1174, but the underlying sand and clay mix meant that it has never been entirely vertical. The architect in charge gave up on the project after three years, and the tower was eventually completed in 1350 without him. Since then it has continued to lean at a rate of about 1 mm per year, and is now more than 5 m off the vertical. At least the tower has not collapsed, which is more than can be said for several medieval English cathedrals built in similar circumstances. Winchester and Gloucester cathedrals both collapsed in the 12th century, Lincoln in the 13th and Ely and Norwich went the same way in the 14th century. All of these collapses were the result of excessive surface loading based on insufficient knowledge of the geology of the underlying land.

CITY IN PERIL

VENICE IN NORTHERN ITALY IS ONE OF EUROPE'S MOST HISTORICAL AND BEAUTIFUL CITIES. BUILT ON RECLAIMED LAND JUST NORTH OF THE DELTAS OF THE ADIGE, BRENTA AND PO RIVERS, THE CITY HAS BECOME INCREASINGLY PRONE TO SUBSIDENCE. THIS IS PARTLY BECAUSE OF THE WATERLOGGED LAND ON WHICH IT IS BUILT BUT ALSO DUE TO THE INADEQUATE FOUNDATIONS OF MANY OF ITS GREAT BUILDINGS. THE CITY WAS ESTIMATED TO SINK AT A RATE OF ABOUT 1 CM EVERY 10 YEARS, BUT THE LEVEL OF DECLINE IS NOW THOUGHT TO BE INCREASING. THIS IS POTENTIALLY

DISASTROUS SINCE MOST OF THE CITY LIES LESS THAN 1.25 M ABOVE SEA LEVEL. SEASONAL FLOODS ARE ALSO ON THE INCREASE AND THE OCCASIONAL SEVERE STORM CAN CAUSE GREAT DAMAGE. ON 3–5 NOV 1966 EXTREMELY HIGH WINDS IN THE ADRIATIC BASIN CREATED A STORM SURGE OF 1.9 M, FLOODING FOUR-FIFTHS OF THE CITY AND CAUSING $70 MILLION WORTH OF DAMAGE. DESPERATE PRESERVATION ATTEMPTS ARE NOW UNDERWAY BUT IT APPEARS THAT VENICE IS SUFFERING A SLOW, LINGERING DEATH, WITH SUBSIDENCE CONDEMNING IT TO A WATERY GRAVE.

RIGHT: CLOSE-UP VIEW OF THE ARCADES ON THE LEANING TOWER OF PISA, ITALY · INSET: THE LEANING TOWER OF PISA, NOW 5 M OFF THE VERTICAL

EVERY TEN YEARS

SUBSIDENCE IS THE SINKING OF THE EARTH'S SURFACE IN RESPONSE TO A MAN-MADE OR NATURAL STIMULUS. IT MAY HAPPEN GRADUALLY OR THE EARTH MAY FALL AWAY SUDDENLY, CAUSING INJURY, DEATH AND DESTRUCTION

An avalanche Is a build-up of snow in a hilly or mountainous region that loses its cohesion and so tumbles down the mountain, gathering in size and momentum as it does so. The conditions that determine the likelihood of an avalanche are similar to those that dictate whether a layer of soil will produce a landslide. However, avalanches are less predictable than landslides because snow is acutely affected by pressure and temperature. A small change in either may be enough to dislodge a large quantity of snow.

Worst avalanches

Some regions are particularly prone to avalanches because of their particular geological or geographical conditions. Mt Huascaran is a 6,700-m mountain at the northern end of the Andes in Peru. Around the peak, a summit glacier and snow field is hundreds of metres thick. Large quantities of snow and ice break off the glacier every year. On 10 Jan 1962, a particularly large mass of ice broke away from the glacier and fell vertically downwards for almost a kilometre. Its impact below broke up the ice and snow, forming a dense cloud of suspended particles which careered down the mountain at incredible speed, gathering up soil and boulders in the process. The combined avalanche and mudslide hit the small town of Ranrahirca and six other villages at an elevation of 2,700 m. By this time it had already fallen 3,500 m

and expanded to a volume of approximately 13 million m³. Some 4,000 people were killed and Ranrahirca and the neighbouring villages were largely destroyed. The avalanche finally travelled about 20 km in around seven minutes and blocked the river at the end of its path. This caused severe flooding, adding to the disaster in the region.

Alpine avalanches

Avalanches in the Alps between France, Austria, Switzerland and Italy have been written about for thousands of years. It is thought that part of Hannibal's army, who crossed the Alps in 218 BC, fell victim to avalanches since about half of the 38,000 men who set out died on the journey. The writer Strabo also mentions Alpine avalanches around 2,000 years ago. Many villages in the Dauphiné region of France were completely destroyed by avalanches in the 15th century, while an avalanche above the Swiss village of Randa, near the Weisshorn, killed 36 people in 1639. Switzerland has the greatest number of avalanche

AVALANCHES
AUSTRIAN POSTMAN

fatalities of anywhere in the world because of the density of mountain settlements at high altitudes. Between 1975 and 1986, 210 people died as a result of avalanches in the Alps. A quarter of these victims were Swiss.

Canadian catastrophe

Camp Leduc is a small copper mining community situated on a ridge in the Rocky Mountains of British Columbia, Canada. In February 1965, 154 men were working there, driving tunnels into the mountain to excavate a large seam of copper ore which had been discovered at high altitude, where the annual snowfall frequently exceeds 15 m. However, on 18 Feb 1965, a huge avalanche careered down the mountain slope, covering the southern half of the camp area and destroying the building at the head of the mine tunnel. Some 70 miners were buried; 43 were rescued while the other 27 died.

War-time weapon

Most avalanches are natural disasters, but some have been set off deliberately to devastating effect. The highest avalanche death toll in history occurred during World War I when Italian and Austrian troops fighting in the Tyrolean Alps realized that avalanches triggered by gunfire were an efficient and ruthless means of destroying the enemy. Over the course of the three World War I winters, the loud booms of

guns set off many avalanches and as many as 80,000 soldiers may have perished. The bodies of soldiers were still being recovered 30 years after the war ended.

Deadly avalanches

On 11 Jan 1954 two avalanches in 12 hours roared into the village of Blans near the Arlberg Pass, Austria. Of the 376 residents of the village, 111 were killed and 29 out of 90 homes were destroyed. In the biggest recorded mass burial in an avalanche, some 300 miners were buried alive in the nearby Leduc mine. On 20 Jan 1951, 240 people died and more than 45,000 were trapped when avalanches thundered through the Swiss, Austrian and Italian Alps.

AVALANCHE RESCUE

THE CHANCES OF BEING RESCUED FROM AN AVALANCHE FALL ARE OFTEN VERY SLIM INDEED. MANY VICTIMS ARE KILLED INSTANTLY BY THE IMPACT OF THE AVALANCHE AND THOSE WHO BECOME BURIED ARE DIFFICULT TO LOCATE AND WILL NOT SURVIVE VERY LONG IN THE FREEZING CONDITIONS. IT HAS BEEN ESTIMATED THAT, OVERALL, ONLY ABOUT 5% OF AVALANCHE VICTIMS ARE FOUND ALIVE AND THOSE THAT ARE FOUND MORE THAN 30 MINUTES AFTER BEING BURIED HAVE ONLY A 50% CHANCE OF SURVIVAL. DEATHS IN SUCH CIRCUMSTANCES ARE PARTICULARLY TRAUMATIC BECAUSE

VICTIMS ARE OFTEN TRAPPED BENEATH JUST A METRE OR TWO OF SNOW BUT THE WEIGHT OF SNOW AROUND THEIR FEET MAKES ESCAPE VERY DIFFICULT. DESPITE THE MANY ADVANCES IN MOUNTAIN RESCUE TECHNIQUES, THE USE OF TRACKER DOGS REMAINS ONE OF THE MOST EFFECTIVE METHODS OF LOCATING AVALANCHE VICTIMS. A WELL-TRAINED DOG CAN SEARCH AN AREA OF 100 M² IN LESS THAN 30 MINUTES WHEREAS IT WOULD TAKE A TEAM OF 20 MEN APPROXIMATELY FOUR HOURS TO COVER THE SAME GROUND EQUALLY THOROUGHLY.

RIGHT: SNOW CASCADES DOWN A STEEP VALLEY DURING AN AVALANCHE IN THE HIMALAYAS

BURIED FOR 3 DAYS

AVALANCHES OCCUR WHEN HUGE VOLUMES OF SNOW BECOME DISLODGED FROM THE SIDES OF MOUNTAINS AND CRASH SUDDENLY AND VIOLENTLY TO THE FLOORS OF VALLEYS. THEY CAUSE HUNDREDS OF DEATHS EVERY YEAR

Erosion is the wearing down of land over a period of time by water, wind and other forms of weather. A variety of landscapes, such as steep cliffs and mountains or smooth shorelines, have been shaped over time by erosion. Humans have long tried to halt its effects, particularly on coastlines. However, the sheer power of the elements is overwhelming, and many defences have crumbled as a result of their ceaseless battering.

Coasts at risk

In many parts of the world, homes built along the coasts are at continual risk from the sea. This is apparent on both the USA's eastern and western seaboards.

Many homes along Bodega Bay, California, USA, have been claimed by the sea because of erosion. Tarpaulin, which covers many areas of the coastline at risk from erosion, is a common sight. Fragments of broken homes, which have fallen down crumbling cliffs eroded by the sea, litter the beach. Part of the problem at Bodega Bay is that the soil is crumbly and is therefore vulnerable to collapse when pounded by the sea. Storms, which can be very heavy in the

area, can exacerbate the problem. Another area at risk from coastal erosion is Maine, USA. Here, too, houses have fallen onto the beach as the cliff beneath them is eroded by the sea. In one incident in April 1996, a garage in Rockland, Maine, with a car parked inside, was torn away from a building as the cliff gave way beneath it following serious erosion. Fortunately, the owner of the vehicle, who was in her 90s, escaped injury.

Vanishing beaches

Anguilla, an island in the Lesser Antilles, has beaches that are essential to its social, economic and environmental well-being. They provide habitats for plants and animals as well as being important tourist sites. However, they are under threat from beach erosion. At Cove Bay, erosion is so intense that the road is regularly relocated inland, and Shoal Bay is moving steadily westward because of erosion on the east side. Sea

EROSION

30 M OF COAST DISAPPEARED

walls have been erected to stop the sea's encroachment, but many of these are being eroded as well. In 1995, Hurricane Luis added to the problems; at Maunday's Bay, the erosion of beach and sand dunes left villas perched dangerously near the edge of 3-m sand cliffs. On the other side of the island, Bames Bay was completely stripped of its sand, leaving only a bare rock platform. As a result of this continual coastal erosion, the island is constantly shrinking —30 m was lost in just one day.

Cutting wind

Wind erodes the land because it carries dust and sand, which are blown onto landforms. One of the

LIVING ON THE EDGE

THE NORTH-EAST COAST OF ENGLAND IS PARTICULARLY SUSCEPTIBLE TO COASTAL EROSION BECAUSE OF THE VIOLENT SEAS THAT CRASH AGAINST ITS SHORES THROUGHOUT THE YEAR. THE 60-KM STRETCH OF ENGLISH COASTLINE AROUND SCARBOROUGH LOSES UP TO 25 CM PER YEAR TO THE SEA. EROSION BY THE SEA IS CAUSED PRIMARILY BY THE IMPACT OF THE WAVES CRASHING AGAINST THE SHORE AS WELL AS THE ABRASION OF SAND AND PEBBLES THAT ARE AGITATED INCESSANTLY BY THE ACTION OF WAVES WHICH DRAG THE PARTICLES BACK AND FORTH. ONE VICTIM OF THIS BATTERING WAS THE HOLBECK HALL HOTEL IN SCARBOROUGH. ONCE PERCHED ON TOP OF GENTLE CLIFFS, IT USED TO PROVIDE A PICTURESQUE VIEW OF THE SEA AND THE COAST. HOWEVER, IT WAS THIS PROXIMITY TO THE SEA THAT LED TO ITS LITERAL DOWNFALL. IT COLLAPSED INTO THE SEA ON JUNE 4-5, 1993. THE INCIDENT WAS A RESULT OF ONGOING COASTAL EROSION, WHICH PRECIPITATED A SMALL LANDSLIDE. THE DAMAGE CAUSED TO A LARGE PART OF THE HOTEL WAS SO EXTENSIVE THAT THE SITE WAS DEMOLISHED.

JARGON

ABRASION PLATFORMS
AN ALTERNATIVE NAME FOR WAVE CUT PLATFORMS

DEPOSITION
THE DEPOSITING OF ERODED MATTER

GROYNES
SEA WALLS, BUILT TO PROTECT THE COAST FROM THE SEA'S ENCROACHMENT

KARST LANDSCAPE
LIMESTONE-BASED HEAVILY ERODED LANDSCAPES

WAVE-CUT PLATFORM
GEOLOGICAL PHENOMENA FORMED WHEN SEA ERODES LAND BELOW A CERTAIN LEVEL, LEAVING A WATER-RESISTANT PLATFORM JUTTING OUT FROM THE CLIFF

IN JUST ONE DAY

THE FORCE AND ENERGY OF THE ELEMENTS CONSTANTLY WORK TO TRANSFORM THE EARTH'S SURFACE. THE IMPACT OF WIND AND WATER IS RELENTLESS, SHAPING STUNNING NATURAL SCULPTURES AND CREATING DEADLY HAZARDS

areas in which wind erosion can most clearly be seen is the dry Seistan depression between Iran and Afghanistan. Here, there is so much dust in the wind that the houses have no windows in their north walls because the wind blows from the north with great ferocity on 80 days in a typical summer. These winds are known as Shamal winds, and blow dust in from the floodplains of the Tigris and

Euphrates rivers. Because the area is dry, particles lying on the land are picked up by the wind and carried many kilometres.

Grinding sands

Clay, silt and sand eroded from landforms are all carried by the wind and taken on a journey in which they will erode other landforms. Particles carried by the wind sandblast the rock, slowly

grinding away at the land over many centuries. In arid areas the lack of vegetation means that rock formations have no protection from particles in the wind. A classic example of wind erosion is Petra, Jordan, where rocky outcrops stand above the desert floor. The rock is resistant to erosion and is weathered slowly. The rocky outcrops are larger at the top than at the bottom because

large particles blown by the wind stay closer to the ground, and erode the rock faster than the small, high-flying particles. The wind produces many beautiful designs on the rock as it slowly grinds and polishes it. This process can lead to desolate landscapes. In the desert of Dasht-e-Lut in Iran, the wind has eroded almost all of the rock to form a virtually flat rock desert. Although some rock pillars are still left standing, in time even these will be eroded and taken elsewhere by the wind.

Dust build up

The Great Plains of the USA have a long history of dust erosion, including the famous Dust Bowl of the 1930s. In modern America, 30 million hectares are affected by dust erosion. Sediment can pile up in unexpected areas—a Kansas state highway department removed 965 tonnes of sand from a mere 460-m stretch of road.

DATA-BURST

CAN EROSION AFFECT WATER QUALITY?
YES. THE WATER QUALITY CAN DECLINE DUE TO THE BUILD-UP OF ERODED SEDIMENTS. THIS HAPPENED WHEN EROSION IN THE GREAT LAKES CAUSED SEDIMENT TO ACCUMULATE.

CAN STORMS ASSIST EROSION?
DEFINITELY. SEA LEVELS CAN RISE DRAMATICALLY DURING A STORM, WHICH SENDS LARGE WAVES LASHING AGAINST THE COAST. STORMS INLAND CAN RAISE RIVER LEVELS, WHICH ALSO SERVE TO ERODE BANKS.

WHAT ARE SEA WALLS?
THESE ARE SEA DEFENCES WHICH EXTEND ALONG THE BEACH AND PREVENT THE MOVEMENT OF LARGE AMOUNTS OF SAND. THEY ARE SOMETIMES CALLED GROYNES.

WHAT ARE BEACH REPLENISHMENT PROJECTS?
THESE ARE ATTEMPTS TO COMBAT

EROSION BY BRINGING IN SAND FROM ELSEWHERE. A TREATMENT RATHER THAN A CURE, THEY CAN BE VERY EXPENSIVE. A TOTAL OF $64 MILLION WAS SPENT IN THE LATE 1970S IN ORDER TO REPLENISH MIAMI BEACH. THE RESTORATION LASTED FOR JUST A DECADE, WHEN IT REQUIRED RENEWING.

HOW FAR CAN WIND CARRY PARTICLES?
THE WIND CAN CARRY POTENTIALLY EROSIVE PARTICLES ACROSS MASSIVE DISTANCES. FINE CLAY PARTICLES, SWEPT UP FROM MONGOLIA'S GOBI DESERT, HAVE BEEN FOUND IN ALASKA, 10,000 KM AWAY.

WHY ARE SOME CASES OF EROSION OFTEN DEPICTED AS SUBSIDENCE?
LEGAL WRANGLES OVER INSURANCE MEAN THAT OCCURRENCES OF EROSION ARE OFTEN FILED AS SUBSIDENCE AS IT IS NOT ALWAYS POSSIBLE TO INSURE AGAINST THE FORMER.

LEFT: WAVE-LIKE PATTERNS ERODED INTO THE SANDSTONE IN ARIZONA'S ANTELOPE CANYON · RIGHT: ROYAL TOMB CARVED IN ERODED ROCK FACE, PETRA

GEYSERS
HIGHEST JET ERUPTS

Geysers are large and violent hot water springs. The term derives from the Icelandic word 'geysir', meaning 'to rush forth'. Geysers result when underground waters come into contact with magma following a volcanic eruption. The water becomes very hot very quickly and, as the pressure builds, it is ejected through fissures, or cracks, in the rock. The effects of geysers can be spectacular. Roaring jets of steam and boiling water can shoot several hundred metres high into the air.

Sleeping giants

The frequency with which geysers erupt varies greatly. Some can be active for hundreds of years, while the lifecycle of others is often much shorter. Some discharge almost continuously, while others erupt briefly and violently every few minutes before lying dormant for hours, days or even years. In some instances, it is possible to predict a pattern of behaviour. The former geyser at Atami, Japan, threw water 0.5 m into the air at five-hourly intervals.

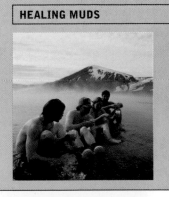

HEALING MUDS

IN THE WESTERN PART OF THE CZECH REPUBLIC THERE ARE MORE THAN A DOZEN THERMAL SPRINGS. THE BEST KNOWN IS THE VRDLO, WHICH SPOUTS WATER OF 72°C AROUND 11 M INTO THE AIR. ALTHOUGH THE GEYSERS WERE IDENTIFIED BY THE ROMANS, IT WAS CHARLES IV, THE HOLY ROMAN EMPEROR, WHO DISCOVERED AND DEVELOPED THE SPRINGS FOR THEIR APPARENT HEALING PROPERTIES IN 1358. WATER FROM THE ALKALINE SULPHUR SPRINGS IS HIGHLY VALUED FOR THE TREATMENT OF DIGESTIVE DISORDERS AND LIVER DISEASES.

TO MORE THAN 460 M

GEYSERS ARE AMONGST THE MOST UNPREDICTABLE AND VIOLENT OF ALL NATURAL PHENOMENA. THESE HOT SPRINGS CAN PROJECT THOUSANDS OF LITRES OF SUPER-HEATED WATER AND STEAMING GASES HIGH INTO THE AIR

Underground cocktail

Although water is the dominant component of the vapour emitted by geysers, gases such as carbon dioxide and hydrogen sulphide are also present. After volcanic activity, the underground water is heated by magma and magmatic gases. As the magma cools and solidifies, so its gases become concentrated under increasing pressure in the residual liquid. When the pressure is high enough, liquid is forced through the cracks in the surrounding solid rock. The pressure then extends the crack upwards until it reaches the surface, where it creates a fumarole, the vent through which the jet erupts.

Tall stories

On average, geysers propel water and steam approximately 50 m into the air. In some cases, however, the jet can be much higher. The tallest geyser ever recorded was the Waimangu Geyser in New Zealand. In 1903, it erupted about every 36 hours reaching a height of more than 460 m. Four people, who were standing 27 m away from the geyser, were killed when it erupted; their bodies were found up to 800 m away. Since 1904, however, the Waimangu Geyser has been dormant. Of the geysers active around the world today, the Steamboat Geyser in Yellowstone Park is probably the tallest,

reaching up to 115 m. During the 1960s, there were times when it erupted every few days. Over the past 20 years, however, the intervals between eruptions have varied from 19 days to four years.

Towers of energy

The power of the jet and the heat from the water have made geysers a valuable potential source of energy. The steam can be tapped and used in turbines to generate electricity. The first commercial geothermal power plant was created at Larderello, Italy, in 1904 and there are others in El Salvador, Japan, Mexico, New Zealand and the USA. A plant in California, north of San Francisco, generates energy levels of up to 1,900 megawatts. However, because geysers occur in areas of volcanic activity, they are often not the most appropriate places on which to build a power station. Also, some of the steam ejected is so full of corrosive minerals that it can threaten industrial processes. Nevertheless, in the right circumstances, geyser power can prove to be a more economically competitive source of energy than fossil fuels.

The geysers of Yellowstone Park

Yellowstone Park is the largest and oldest national park in the USA. It extends across 8,983 km² from north-western Wyoming into southern Montana and eastern

Idaho, and was established as the first park of the nation by the US Congress in March 1872. Yellowstone Park consists largely of volcanic plateaus and its main attractions are the 10,000 hot springs within its boundaries. These include around 200 geysers as well as steam vents, fumaroles, colourful hot pools, rivers and mud cauldrons. The greatest eruption to occur within Yellowstone happened about 600,000 years ago when about 1,000 km³ of magma was ejected in gigantic flows. This created a volcanic basin roughly 45 km wide by 75 km long which now contains the Yellowstone Lake. Today, the total heat flux generated by Yellowstone's thermal features is around 300 megawatts. Old Faithful is probably the world's best-known geyser. Situated in the Upper Geyser basin within the park, it is up to 300 years old but was given its name in 1870 because of the reliable way in which it appeared to erupt every 65 or 70 minutes. However, in reality it discharges steam and water at intervals anywhere between 33 and 148 minutes. Each discharge consists of about 45,000 litres of hot water and billowing steam.

DATA-BURST

HOW DEEP ARE GEYSERS?
THE NECK OF A GEYSER IS A VERTICAL PIPE THAT CAN EXTEND UP TO TENS OF THOUSANDS OF METRES DEEP INTO THE GROUND.

WHY ARE GEYSERS MINERAL-RICH?
THE WATER THAT EMERGES FROM GEYSERS HAS BEEN PERCOLATED THROUGH CRACKS IN THE ROCK. BECAUSE OF THE HIGH TEMPERATURE, IT HAS DISSOLVED A LARGE NUMBER OF THE CHEMICAL AND MINERAL CONSTITUENTS ON ITS JOURNEY.

WHERE IS THE WORLD'S TALLEST GEYSER?
IN 1903 THE WAIMANGU GEYSER IN NEW ZEALAND ERUPTED TO A HEIGHT OF OVER 460 M. THIS GEYSER IS NO LONGER ACTIVE. THE HIGHEST JET FROM A GEYSER TODAY IS EMITTED BY

THE STEAMBOAT GEYSER IN THE USA WHICH CAN REACH UP TO 115 M.

ARE GEYSER ERUPTIONS REGULAR AND FREQUENT?
SOME GEYSERS ERUPT ALMOST CONTINUOUSLY, OTHERS EVERY FEW MINUTES, OTHERS AT INTERVALS VARYING FROM MINUTES TO YEARS.

HOW DO HOT SPRINGS FORM?
A STEAMING HOT SPRING FORMS WHEN UNDERGROUND WATER IS HEATED BY WARM ROCKS. AS IT GETS HOTTER, THE WATER RISES TO THE SURFACE.

HOW DO MUD POOLS FORM?
A POOL OF HOT BUBBLING MUD MAY FORM WHERE HOT WATER MIXES WITH MINERAL PARTICLES. ACIDIC VOLCANIC GASES CORRODE THESE PARTICLES FROM THE SURROUNDING ROCKS.

JARGON

CALDERA
A LARGE, VOLCANIC CRATER

DORMANT
NOT CURRENTLY ERUPTING BUT MAY DO SO IN THE FUTURE

FUMAROLE
THE VENT THROUGH WHICH VOLCANIC VAPOURS ARE EJECTED

LAVA
STREAM OF MOLTEN ROCK THAT RUNS ON TOP OF THE GROUND

MAGMA
MOLTEN, UNDERGROUND ROCK

TURBINE
A ROTARY MOTOR OR ENGINE DRIVEN BY A FLOW OF WATER, STEAM, GAS OR WIND

LEFT: OLD FAITHFUL GEYSER, YELLOWSTONE NATIONAL PARK, WYOMING, USA · INSET: AERIAL VIEW OF MAMMOTH SPRINGS IN YELLOWSTONE NATIONAL PARK

Although they contain only a fraction of the world's water—1% as compared to the 97.2% contained in the oceans—rivers are the main force behind changing landscapes. From its source near a watershed, or from a spring, a stream seeks the steepest and shortest course downwards. Swollen by tributaries, rainfall and ground water, it becomes a river and its power increases, enabling it to erode the landscape as it works its way to the sea. When a river reaches low-lying ground, its pace slackens; meandering along valley floors, it deposits large amounts of sediment which create flood plains, levees and even islands.

The Amazon

The greatest river complex in the world, the Amazon is also the world's longest river. From its source among the snow-covered Andes of southern Peru, the river forms the Apurimac, which joins other streams to become the Ene, the Tambo and the Ucayali. From the confluence of the Ucayali and the Marañón, the river is called the Amazon for its final 3,700-km journey to the Atlantic Ocean. In total, the river is 6,750 km long.

The Nile, which stretches from Burundi to the Mediterranean, was 6,670 km long before the loss of some meanders when Lake Nasser formed behind the Aswan Dam. The Amazon's flow is 60 times greater than that of the Nile, and it drains 7,045,000 km^2 of land—nearly twice that of any other river. It has 15,000 tributaries, 10 of which are over 1,600 km in length. The Amazon also supports the largest tropical rainforest in the world.

The 'father of waters'

As the central river artery of the USA, the Mississippi has become one of the busiest commercial waterways in the world. From its source in northern Minnesota, the river flows south, receiving the waters of the Missouri and the Ohio in its middle reaches, until it empties into the Gulf of Mexico —a distance of 6,020 km, which makes it the third longest river in the world. The Mississippi basin contains 31 US states and two

RIVERS

AMAZON RIVER CARRIES 25%

HOLY WATER

FROM ITS SOURCE IN AN ICE CAVE IN THE HIMALAYAS, THE GANGES FLOWS 2,506 KM THROUGH INDIA AND BANGLADESH TO ITS ENORMOUS DELTA IN THE BAY OF BENGAL. FOR MUCH OF ITS COURSE IT IS A WIDE, SLUGGISH STREAM, FLOWING THROUGH DENSELY POPULATED AND HIGHLY FERTILE LAND. THE RIVER IS SACRED TO THE HINDUS, WHO BELIEVE IT TO BE THE PERSONIFICATION OF THE GODDESS GANGA. LORD SHIVA, THE MALE GOD OF FERTILITY, SUPPOSEDLY CAUGHT THE RIVER IN HIS HAIR TO PREVENT DISASTER AS IT CRASHED TO EARTH. HINDUS BATHE IN THE RIVER AND CAST THE ASHES OF THEIR DEAD ON ITS SACRED WATERS IN THE BELIEF THAT THE SOUL OF THE DEPARTED WILL GO STRAIGHT TO HEAVEN. THE CITY OF VARANASI, OR BENARES, ON THE GANGES IS A CENTRE OF HINDU FAITH.

some 4,960 m³/sec and their waters can carry as much as 3 million tonnes of eroded material downhill from the highlands in a single day. The majority of this sediment is deposited on the plains of Mesopotamia where it forms rich, fertile soil.

Mother Volga
Lying entirely within the Russian Federation, the Volga's catchment area is the largest in Europe. From its source in the Valday Hills, the main river flows south-east through steppe and forest, gathering up the waters of its main tributaries, the Oka, Belaya, Vyatka and Kama on its way.

OF EARTH'S WATER

RIVERS ARE NOT ONLY THE MAIN FORCE IN SHAPING AND TRANSFORMING THE LANDSCAPE, BUT THEY ALSO PROVIDE ESSENTIAL ROUTES FOR EXPLORATION, NAVIGATION AND TRADE AND PLAY A PIVOTAL ROLE IN SETTLEMENT LOCATION

Canadian provinces. When the great river enters its alluvial plain, it winds in enormous curves, forming ox-bow lakes, levees and huge banks of sediment.

Land between the two rivers
The Euphrates is the greatest river of south-western Asia. Together with the Tigris, it originally encompassed the ancient 'Land Between the Two Rivers', the

location of humans' earliest recorded urban civilizations. From its source in the mountains of Erzurum in Anatolia, the Euphrates flows south-east until it joins the Tigris and becomes a muddy waterway known as the Shatt al Arab, which extends through a vast delta into the Persian Gulf. During the heavy rains in spring, the combined discharge of the two rivers is

As it approaches the Caspian Sea, it divides into a delta comprised of about 275 channels. Navigable for nearly its entire length, the Volga has played an important role in Russia's history: in the 9th century Viking invaders sailed down the Volga into the heart of Russia, establishing trade routes which still exist to this day. The river, known in Russian folklore as 'Mother Volga', remains Russia's

most important waterway, and is connected to Moscow and St Petersburg by canals.

Frozen giant
The Ob'-Irtysh (Ob') is the world's seventh longest river. Running along the Siberian slopes of the Altai Mountains, it stretches for some 5,409 km and drains a basin of around 2,990,000 km². The Ob' absorbs massive amounts of seasonal snow and rain. Its entire length is frozen by November, the upper reaches remaining so for 150 days. Up to 80 km wide in places, it is the widest river in the world which regularly freezes over.

DATA-BURST

WHICH RIVER CARRIES THE GREATEST VOLUME OF WATER?
THE AMAZON RIVER IS ESTIMATED TO CARRY 20—25% OF ALL THE WATER THAT RUNS OFF THE EARTH'S SURFACE.

WHICH RIVER HAS CUT THE DEEPEST TRENCHES?
MORE THAN 1,610 KM OF THE COLORADO RIVER, ARIZONA, USA, RUNS THROUGH A DEEP TRENCH. AT A MAXIMUM OF 1,829 M, THE GRAND CANYON IS ITS DEEPEST GORGE.

WHAT ARE A RIVER'S MAIN SOURCES OF WATER?
RAINFALL, MELTWATER AND SPRING WATER. MELTWATER FROM MAJOR MOUNTAIN SYSTEMS IS THE ORIGIN OF SOME OF THE WORLD'S GREAT RIVERS; 19 ORIGINATE IN THE HIMALAYAS.

ARE THERE DIFFERENT TYPES OF RIVER?
THERE ARE THREE TYPES OF RIVER: PERENNIAL, WHEN THE FLOW OF

WATER IS CONSTANT ALL YEAR ROUND; SEASONAL, WHEN THE FLOW OF WATER IS AFFECTED BY SEASONAL CHANGE; AND EPHEMERAL, WHEN A RIVER IS CREATED BY A RARE RAINSTORM.

CAN A RIVER SURVIVE IN A DESERT?
SOME RIVERS, SUCH AS THE COLORADO IN THE USA, MANAGE TO PASS THROUGH DESERT AREAS WITHOUT DRYING UP. THEY CONTINUE TO FLOW BECAUSE FOR MUCH OF THEIR COURSE THEY PASS THROUGH WETTER AREAS.

WHICH IS THE WORLD'S LARGEST RIVER SYSTEM?
IN TERMS OF VOLUME OF WATER AND THE AREA OF THE DRAINAGE BASIN, THE AMAZON IS THE LARGEST RIVER SYSTEM IN THE WORLD.

WHERE IS THE SHORTEST RIVER?
THE ROE RIVER, NEAR GREAT FALLS, MONTANA, USA, FLOWS INTO THE LARGER MISSOURI RIVER, AND THE NORTH FORK IS JUST 17.7 M LONG.

LEFT: RIVER WINDING AROUND THE HORSESHOE BEND IN THE CANYON AT LAKE POWELL, UTAH, USA , RIGHT: AERIAL VIEW OF TRIBUTARIES STEMMING FROM THE AMAZON RIVER, BRAZIL

Deltas are formed by deposits of alluvium laid down by rivers as they enter bodies of relatively still water, such as a lake or the sea. They can range in size from tiny features in a mountain lake to vast areas such as the Nile Delta in Egypt. Although occupying less than 2% of the world's land surface, the deltas of the world's great rivers have historically been sites of important civilizations, and remain major centres of population. The rich deposits carried downriver are distributed by the network of channels and form fertile areas for cultivation. Crops grown in these areas benefit from this natural process despite the annual hazard of flooding.

The world's largest delta
The Ganges-Brahmaputra delta—formed where two great rivers, the Ganges and the Brahmaputra, join and flow through Bangladesh and West Bengal—covers an area of 75,000 km². Bangladesh is a land of rivers which flood regularly, leaving rich deposits of alluvium. The area is home to over 100 million people whose lives are enhanced by the region's fertility, but this fertility also brings risk. In October 1988 the country experienced one of the worst floods in its history; two-thirds of the land was submerged for three weeks and a quarter of its inhabitants were left homeless. The delta is also prone to frequent cyclones which funnel up the Bay of Bengal, causing terrible loss of life and crop damage.

Delta in danger
Surrounded by arid rocky desert, the River Nile and its vast delta have supported most of Egypt's agriculture and 99% of its population since the Ancient Egyptians first planted their crops in soils enriched by deposits carried downriver in the annual flood from the African interior. But the site of such a magnificent early civilization is now in decline: some 150 years ago, 2 million hectares of farmland supported 5 million people; today 2.8 million hectares of farmland must support a population of 60 million. The construction of the Aswan High

RIVER DELTAS

YANGTZE DELTA SUPPORTS

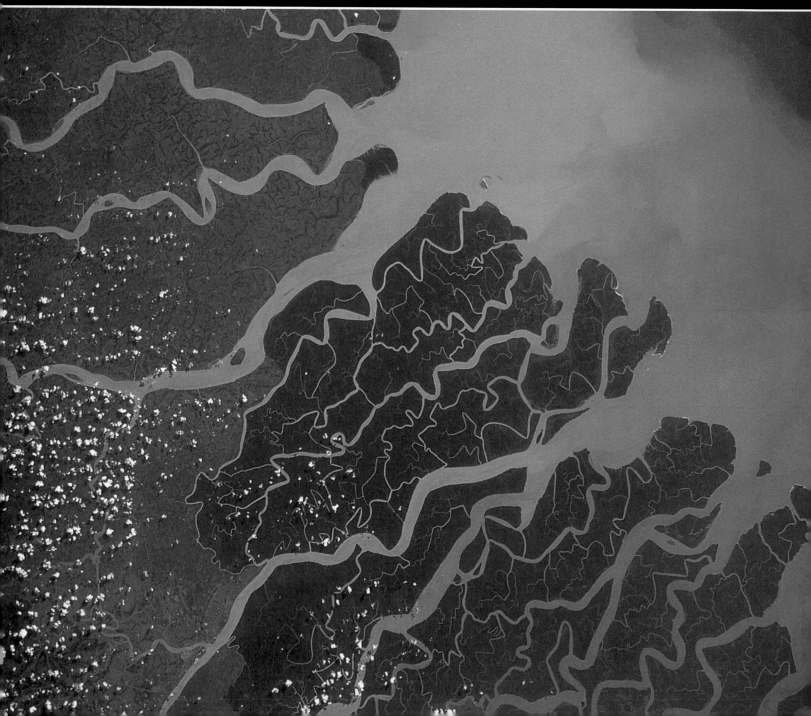

Dam nearly 30 years ago prevented the Nile's annual flooding, and any silt that now reaches the delta is washed away by the Mediterranean's currents faster than it can be replenished. The delta is further imperilled by an increased salinity of the soil, brought about by intensified farming and the use of fertilizers.

Mud pie

The Mississippi delta has been formed by millions of years of sedimentation which spills out in a huge cone over the floor of the Gulf of Mexico. Each year the river adds some 495 million tonnes of sediment to the delta which is advancing its shoreline seawards

China's river deltas

Three of China's greatest rivers, the Yangtze, Zhujiang and Huang Ho (or Yellow River), have all formed vast deltas, each one rich in arable land, natural resources and heavily populated. The Yangtze's delta supports a population of 73 million, 14 cities and produces abundant crops of grain, cotton, hemp and tea. Flowing for some 4,700 km from the Kunlun Mountains to the sea, the Huang Ho carries with it vast quantities of yellow silt which forms the delta that has become one of China's most fertile regions. Beneath its mud flats lie enormous reserves of petroleum and natural gas. Situated in the sub-tropical zone,

widen at the town of Barrancas, about 80 km north-east of Ciudad Guayana, and the delta receives all the silt from the river. The delta itself is really a mangrove jungle that stretches hundreds of kilometres across. It is 60% water and those who live there construct log houses which stand on stilts 5 m above the river. Many of these communities are inaccessible except by small boat. The indigenous Warao Indians call the Orinoco 'a place to paddle' and managed to escape subordination by 18th century European slave traders by disappearing into the difficult waters of the delta. Natural oil has been discovered under this watery landscape.

73 MILLION PEOPLE

SINCE THE BEGINNING OF CIVILIZATION, RIVER DELTAS HAVE ATTRACTED HUMAN SETTLEMENT BY VIRTUE OF THEIR RICH AND FERTILE SOILS, ABUNDANT WATER AND ACCESS, ALONG NAVIGABLE WATERWAYS, TO THE SEA

time the river finally empties into the China Sea, it has seven main branches which weave through the delta. Although two of them have silted up completely, the Vietnamese believe that the number 9 is auspicious and so call the delta Nine Dragons. The area is very fertile: Vietnam is the third biggest exporter of rice in the world and the region provides half of the total national crop. When the delta floods annually, the roads even become covered with rice.

by nearly 10 km every 100 years. The low flat alluvial plain between Memphis and New Orleans used to be extremely vulnerable to flooding and as a result a network of levees now regulates the flow of water. The man-made river control structures are modifying the natural landscape. The original delta area of south-central Louisiana is no longer receiving sediment from the Mississippi, and as a result subsidence is causing loss of land.

the Zhujiang delta's mild climate and plentiful rainfall enable crops like rice and sugar cane to flourish. Utilizing the delta's extensive network of rivers, ships carry on a thriving trade with Hong Kong, Macao and islands in the South China Sea.

Swampy Orinoco

Over the entire 2,000-km course of the Orinoco River there is not a single dam, so it floods annually and prodigiously. The river begins to

Nine Dragons

The Mekong travels from Western China to its delta in Vietnam, a journey of 4,100 km, and is the least developed of Asia's great rivers. The flat hot delta of the Mekong is home to more than a fifth of Vietnam's 69 million people, many of them still living in houses on stilts connected to each other by bamboo bridges. Around 3,200 km of rivers and channels make up the delta, rivalling the total length of the Mekong. By the

The expanding Danube

The River Danube, the second longest river in Europe, rises in the Black Forest of Germany and empties into the Black Sea in Russia. The delta begins near Tulcea, 80 km from the sea, where it splits into three channels that cover a 4,300-km² area. Around 6,500 years ago, this region was once a cove on the Black Sea but the river has deposited 80 million tonnes of silt a year to form the delta. It grows 5–30 m every year.

LEFT: THE NILE DELTA, EGYPT, TAKEN BY LANDSAT SATELLITE · RIGHT: AERIAL VIEW OF THE GANGES DELTA, BANGLADESH

Waterfalls occur when the relatively gradual descent of a river to the sea encounters an abrupt change of level. The fall can be sudden, as water hurtles over a sheer cliff face, or it may descend more slowly in graduated steps or a series of small cascades. Waterfalls often occur where a river flows from hard to soft rock—soft rock is eroded by the water at a much higher rate than the hard rock. Over a period of millions of years the erosion can smooth away the rock and the waterfall gradually disappears. At the foot of a waterfall is the plunge pool, which has been caused by the constant erosion of the river bed by descending water.

The highest fall

On 16 Nov 1933 a US pilot named Jimmie Angel was flying over the rainforests of Venezuela's Caniama National Park when he caught sight of a spectacular chute of water plummeting down from the flat-topped Devil's Mountain; while looking for gold, the pilot had discovered the world's highest waterfall. Almost perpetually obscured by clouds, Angel Falls plunges a total of 979 m into the dense jungle of Devil's Canyon. The falls' longest single drop is 807 m. Although known locally as Churun-Meru, the falls were later named after Jimmie Angel.

The smoke that thunders

With a roar which can be heard 40 km away, the mighty Zambezi River plunges over a precipice 1,700 m wide and 108 m high into a great mist-filled chasm below. With an average yearly flow of 935 m³/sec, the Victoria Falls are twice as wide and twice as deep as Niagara Falls. They are located on the border between Zambia and Zimbabwe, and are known to the local people as Mosi-oa-tunya, or 'the smoke that thunders'. The first European to discover the falls was David Livingstone in 1855; he named them after Queen Victoria. From the chasm, the water flows with increasing speed into a narrow gorge, and from there into a deep pool called the Boiling Pot. The river below the falls is a great attraction for whitewater

WATERFALLS

ROAR OF VICTORIA FALLS

DARE-DEVILS AT NIAGARA

NIAGARA FALLS HAS EXERCISED AN OFTEN FATAL ATTRACTION FOR DARE-DEVILS. POSSIBLY THE MOST FAMOUS DARE-DEVIL WAS THE 19TH-CENTURY FRENCHMAN, JEAN-FRANÇOIS GRAVELET, OR 'BLONDIN', WHO CROSSED THE FALLS BY TIGHTROPE IN 1859. LATER HE CROSSED THEM IN A VARIETY OF WAYS: BLINDFOLDED, ON STILTS AND IN A WHEELBARROW. ON ONE OCCASION HE CROSSED THEM CARRYING HIS MANAGER ON HIS BACK, STOPPING HALF WAY ACROSS TO MAKE AND EAT AN OMELETTE. THE FIRST PERSON TO GO OVER THE FALLS IN A BARREL WAS ANNIE TAYLOR. THOUGH SHE SURVIVED, RED HILL JUNIOR'S ATTEMPT TO DO THE SAME IN A VESSEL MADE FROM INNER TUBES PROVED FATAL. TO PREVENT FURTHER CASUALTIES, SUCH STUNTS HAVE BEEN PROHIBITED BY LAW SINCE 1911.

JARGON

CASCADE
A WATERFALL WITH A SMALL VOLUME OF WATER. SOMETIMES THERE CAN BE A SERIES OF CASCADES ALONG A RIVER

CATARACT
A LARGE WATERFALL WITH A LARGE VOLUME OF WATER

CURTAIN
A CURTAIN OF WATER FORMS WHEN A RIVER HURTLES OVER A CATARACT. IT GRADUALLY ERODES THE LIP OF THE PRECIPICE, CAUSING IT TO RECEDE

PLUNGE POOL
A DEPRESSION IN THE RIVER BED BELOW THE WATERFALL CAUSED BY THE CONTINUAL EROSION OF THE FALLING WATER

River Niagara which forms part of the boundary between Canada and the USA. The Canadian, or Horseshoe, Falls are more than twice as broad but slightly lower than the American Falls.

The falls are a major source of hydroelectricity, which has reduced their power, but they are still powerful enough to produce a spectacular 'curtain' of water. Secreted behind the curtain is a cavern called the Cave of the Winds, which is accessible by boat.

The falls have witnessed some remarkable events: in July 1960 a boat containing a man and two children capsized near the edge of the falls. One child was rescued, but the man and second child went over the edge. The man died, but the child, wearing only a life-jacket and swimming trunks, survived.

The world's widest waterfall
The Khone Falls are a series of cataracts on the Mekong River in Southern Laos on the border with Cambodia. They measure 10.8 km wide and drop from a height of 21 m. They have an average annual flow of 11,500 m^3/sec. The volume of water in the Khone Falls is double that of Niagara.

Biggest flow
The Boyoma Falls in north-west Zaire, central Africa, have a massive average annual flow of 17,000 m^3/sec. Formerly known as Stanley Falls after the English explorer Sir Henry Morton Stanley, they reverted to their African name in 1971. The falls are comprised of seven cataracts that each fall 60 m and extend for 100 km along the river between Kisangani and Ubundu.

HEARD 40 KM AWAY

WHEN A RIVER IS FORCED TO FLOW OVER A SUDDEN BREAK IN THE GROUND LEVEL, SPECTACULAR WATERFALLS RESULT, SENDING THOUSANDS OF LITRES OF WHITE SPRAY AND CHURNING WATER INTO DEEP PLUNGE POOLS BELOW

rafters, while bunjee jumpers hurl themselves 111 m off the Victoria Falls bridge.

Fiercest flow
Flowing through the Sierra Nevada in central California, USA, the Yosemite River races through the Yosemite valley to create one of the world's highest cataracts. The U-shaped canyon with its precipitous sides was formed as a result of glaciation—the erosive power of the glacier gouged out the tall cliffs, leaving high, hanging valleys over which tributary rivers are forced to dive. Yosemite Falls consists of two major waterfalls separated by a series of smaller cascades: the Upper Yosemite Fall drops 436 m, while the Lower drops just over 100 m. The two falls, including the cascades, drop a total of 800 m, equivalent to the height of the Eiffel Tower in Paris. The waterfalls are seen at their best in late spring when the volume of water is greatly increased by snow melting in the mountains. At other times of the year the falls can be almost dry.

Niagara's water curtain
The famous Niagara Falls are in fact two waterfalls, separated from each other by Goat Island in the

DATA-BURST

DO WATERFALLS ERODE DIFFERENT ROCK TYPES?
YES. WATERFALLS ERODE ROCKS OF VARYING RESISTANCE AT DIFFERENT SPEEDS. FALLS CAN ALSO DEVELOP AT JUNCTIONS BETWEEN DIFFERENT ROCK TYPES: NIAGARA FALLS HAS A BLOCKY DOLOMITE CAP OVERLAYING WEAKER SHALE AND SANDSTONE.

DO WATERFALLS RETREAT?
YES. AT NIAGARA, FOR EXAMPLE, THE FALLS HAVE RETREATED 11 KM FROM THE FACE OF THE ESCARPMENT WHERE THEY BEGAN.

WHICH WATERFALL SPILLS THE MOST WATER PER SECOND?
THE YOSEMITE FALLS IN THE USA SPILLS ITS AVERAGE SPRING FLOW AT A RATE OF 9,000 LITRES PER SECOND.

HAVE WATERFALLS EVER BEEN DESTROYED BY HUMAN ACTIVITY?
YES. TWO OF THE WORLD'S GREATEST WATERFALLS, THE GUAIRA AND THE URUBA-PUNGA, BOTH IN ALTO PARANA IN PARAGUAY/BRAZIL, HAVE BEEN INUNDATED BY THE BUILDING OF THE ITAIPU DAM.

CAN WATERFALLS BE USED FOR HYDROELECTRICITY?
YES. NIAGARA FALLS IS USED FOR THE PRODUCTION OF HYDROELECTRIC POWER, WHICH HAS THE EFFECT OF REDUCING THE POWER OF THE FALLS. ABOUT 4.4 MILLION KILOWATTS ARE PRODUCED EVERY YEAR.

HOW DEEP ARE PLUNGE POOLS?
VERY DEEP. IN SOME INSTANCES, THE DEPTH OF THE PLUNGE POOL MAY EQUAL THE HEIGHT OF THE CLIFF CAUSING THE FALLS.

HOW DO WATERFALLS PRODUCE RAINBOWS?
WATERFALLS PRODUCE RAINBOWS AS LIGHT FROM THE SUN IS REFRACTED THROUGH THE WATER DROPLETS IN THEIR SPRAY.

LEFT: A TOURIST BOAT UNDERTAKES A PERILOUS TRIP AT THE HORSESHOE FALLS, NIAGARA, CANADA · RIGHT: ANGEL FALLS, CANIAMA NATIONAL PARK , VENEZUELA

STORMS AND FREAK WEATHER

GLOBAL FORCES

CAUSE MASSIVE DEVASTATION

136 170 192 220

HURRICANES 1

FASTEST HURRICANE

Hurricanes, typhoons and cyclones are all aspects of the same phenomenon. They are different regional names given to strong tropical storms. These storms form over the western Atlantic Ocean, the north-eastern Pacific Ocean and the Caribbean. Hurricanes derive their name from the West Indian god called 'Hurakan' to whom local tribes would pray for mercy from deadly storms. Hurricanes travel over sea and once they reach land they usually degenerate into depressions.

ON FIRST NAME TERMS

HURRICANES ARE ALWAYS LABELLED WITH PEOPLE'S NAMES. THIS CUSTOM FIRST ORIGINATED IN AUSTRALIA DURING THE LATE 19TH CENTURY. A METEOROLOGIST, NAMED CLEMENT WRAGGE NAMED EVERY IDENTIFIABLE SYSTEM HIGH AND LOW, ON HIS WEATHER CHARTS. HE BEGAN BY CALLING THEM AFTER LETTERS IN THE GREEK ALPHABET, AS WELL AS MYTHOLOGICAL CHARACTERS. HE ENJOYED CREATING CONTROVERSY AND SO BEGAN TO LABEL HURRICANES WITH THE NAMES OF PROMINENT LOCAL POLITICIANS. WHEN THEY THREATENED LEGAL ACTION, HE BEGAN TO USE THEIR WIVES' NAMES. HIS HABIT OF NAMING HURRICANES FELL OUT OF FAVOUR WHEN HE LEFT OFFICE, BUT IT WAS REVIVED DURING WORLD WAR II. A RADIO OPERATOR WHO ISSUED HURRICANE WARNINGS IS ALLEGED TO HAVE STARTED WHISTLING A SONG CALLED 'EVERY LITTLE BREEZE SEEMS TO WHISPER LOUISE'. THEREAFTER THE HURRICANE WAS REFERRED TO AS LOUISE. THE OFFICIAL SEAL OF APPROVAL FOR THE NAMING OF HURRICANES CAME FROM THE WORLD METEOROLOGICAL SOCIETY IN 1952.

SPEED 350 KM/H

HURRICANES ARE WHIRLING TROPICAL STORMS THAT CAN BLOW UP TO A SPEED OF 350 KM/H. OVER THE COURSE OF A DAY, THEY PICK UP APPROXIMATELY 2 BILLION TONNES OF WATER VAPOUR, CAUSING GIANT WAVES AND FLOODING

Measuring wind speed

The force of a hurricane can be calculated on two scales. The Beaufort Scale measures wind speeds up to 118 km/h which rate at the top of the scale as force 12. The Saffir-Simpson scale is commonly used to track more powerful hurricanes. The intensity of a hurricane is measured in five levels. Level 1 measures 'weak' winds of 120 km/h whereas level 5 winds can reach 'devastating' speeds of over 250 km/h.

Brewing a storm

Hurricanes develop when rising air currents form over warm oceanic waters creating areas of intense low pressure. These form a well at the centre of the warm, rising air. As the air spirals upwards it cools, causing the water vapour it carries to condense rapidly, forming banks of dense cloud and torrential downpours of rain. The condensed water vapour releases massive quantities of latent heat which further fuels the development of the hurricane. In releasing this latent heat, hurricanes prevent the tropics from overheating.

Spinning an odd line

Hurricanes usually originate between latitudes of 7 and 15 degrees either north or south of the equator. In the northern hemisphere they generally start moving towards the west before curving north-west and later north-east. In the southern hemisphere, the tracks are generally westward, then south-west and eventually south-east. Initial speeds of hurricanes are about 16 km/h but this can double or more, after recurving. There are considerable variations from the basic pattern of behaviour.

The calm before the storm

At the centre—or the 'eye'—of the storm there is relative calm, with cloudless skies and wind speeds of about 24 km/h. The strongest winds rotate around the eye itself, where they can reach speeds of up to 350 km/h. The passing of the eye of the storm suggests that the storm is over, but the brutal winds that follow from the opposite direction can be just as fierce as those in the first wave. The eye itself measures about 25–40 km across, becoming smaller and more circular as the inflowing winds spiral faster, causing some of the most destructive winds of the hurricane to rage within a 100 km radius of it. Cloud banks swirling around the eye can reach heights of 13 to 16 km above the surface of the ocean.

Storm surges

The most destructive aspect of a hurricane is the storm surges that go with it. Triggered by the combination of low air pressure and spiralling winds, vast amounts of water are sucked up from the sea. This water eventually takes the form of huge waves that can reach up to 8 m in height. When a hurricane blows in from the ocean and hits land, the storm surge manifests itself as a great wall of water. This can cause severe flooding. The storm surge is responsible for 90% of deaths, usually through drowning.

DATA-BURST

WHY ARE HURRICANES NAMED?
SO THAT FORECASTERS AND THE PUBLIC CAN EASILY REFER TO THEM.

WHAT IS THE DIFFERENCE BETWEEN HURRICANES AND TWISTERS?
TWISTERS ARE MUCH SMALLER, LAND-BASED VORTICES, WHILST HURRICANES ARE SEA-BASED. TWISTERS LAST FOR HOURS, HURRICANES FOR DAYS.

CAN HURRICANES BE PREVENTED?
EXPERIMENTS TO DATE, SUCH AS SEEDING HURRICANES, HAVE BEEN UNSUCCESSFUL, ALTHOUGH IT IS POSSIBLE TO MONITOR AND THEREFORE PREPARE FOR THEM.

WHY DO HURRICANES OCCUR MOST OFTEN IN THE SUMMER AND AUTUMN?
THIS IS DUE TO FAVOURABLE CLIMACTIC CONDITIONS—WARM OCEANS, PRONOUNCED ATMOSPHERIC CIRCULATION AND CONDUCIVE TROPICAL ATMOSPHERIC CONDITIONS.

IN WHICH DIRECTION DO HURRICANES ROTATE?
ANTI-CLOCKWISE IN THE NORTHERN HEMISPHERE, AND CLOCKWISE IN THE SOUTHERN HEMISPHERE. THE DIFFERENCE CONCERNS THE CORIOLIS EFFECT, A PRINCIPAL BASED ON THE EARTH'S ROTATION.

ARE HURRICANES GETTING MORE INTENSE AND FREQUENT?
NO, THERE HAS BEEN A MARKED DECREASE IN THE INTENSITY OF ATLANTIC TROPICAL HURRICANES.

WHAT IS THE MOST RAINFALL PRODUCED IN A HURRICANE?
THE MOST RAINFALL PRODUCED OVER 10 DAYS IN A HURRICANE IS 3.7 M.

WHICH YEAR HAS HAD THE MOST HURRICANES AND TYPHOONS?
THE MOST TYPHOONS IN ONE YEAR WAS 26 IN 1964, AND THE MOST HURRICANES, 19 IN 1995.

JARGON

CENTRAL DENSE OVERCAST
A SHIELD OF CLOUD THAT FORMS FROM THE THUNDERSTORM IN THE EYEWALL OF A HURRICANE

CORIOLIS EFFECT
NAME GIVEN TO THE INFLUENCE OF THE EARTH'S ROTATION ON THE DIRECTION IN WHICH HURRICANE WINDS SPIRAL. WINDS CURVE TO THE RIGHT IN THE NORTHERN HEMISPHERE AND LEFT IN THE SOUTHERN HEMISPHERE.

DVORÁK TECHNIQUE
A MEANS OF GATHERING DATA ON HURRICANE INTENSITY BASED ON SATELLITE IMAGES

EYE
THE RELATIVELY CALM CENTRE OF A TROPICAL CYCLONE

FUJIWHARA EFFECT
THE ROTATION OF TWO STORMS AROUND EACH OTHER

HURRICANE SEASON
HURRICANES OCCUR MOST FREQUENTLY IN SUMMER AND AUTUMN WHEN THE SEA IS AT ITS WARMEST. IN THE NORTH-EASTERN PACIFIC/WESTERN ATLANTIC REGION, THE HURRICANE SEASON RUNS FROM 15 MAY TO 30 NOVEMBER

LANDFALL
WHEN A HURRICANE HITS LAND

STORM SURGE
DOME OF WATER CREATED BY THE HURRICANE'S LOW PRESSURE CENTRE AND SPIRALLING WINDS, LEADING TO FLOODING ON LAND

TRACK
THE PATH A CYCLONE MAKES ACROSS THE SEA

LEFT: MAROONED BOAT, DRAGGED INTO A FIELD BY THE FORCE OF VIOLENT HURRICANE WINDS

Whirling dervish

The hurricane that hit Galveston, Texas, on 8 Sept 1900, was the most deadly natural disaster ever to befall the USA. Reaching wind speeds of around 170 km/h, an estimated 10,000 to 12,000 people were killed, causing an estimated $20 million worth of damage. Following the disaster, measures were taken to protect the city, specifically by building a seawall. When its effectiveness was tested by another hurricane in 1915, the death toll amounted to a comparatively modest 275, although the cost in damages rose to a staggering $50 million.

Low down in Florida

On the night of the 2 Sept 1935 large parts of North America, stretching from Florida to North Carolina, were hit by the most vicious hurricane ever. The 'Labour Day' hurricane devastated large areas of the country, with islands in the Florida Keys disappearing and hundreds of people going missing from many coastal regions. Air pressure on the mainland reached a record low with barometer readings dropping to 892 mb. This is the lowest ever central pressure recorded of any Atlantic hurricane. Winds travelling at devastating top speeds wrought havoc, snapping tough metal and wooden structures, from trees to steel railings. Local people who were able to respond to the hurricane warnings found travel out of the city impossible: fallen trees littered the railway tracks and many carriages had been derailed.

Belize blown away

Belize was almost wiped out by Hurricane Hattie and its ensuing storm surge on 31 Oct 1961. Hattie's winds were blowing at a sustained speed of approximately 320 km/h, with waves of 3 m, when it reached the city. Two thousand people died and three-quarters of the city's buildings were badly damaged or completely destroyed. As a result, the capital was moved 80 km inland to a safer site.

Betsy changes her mind

Hurricane Betsy began its erratic path of destruction on 27 Aug 1965. On course for the south-eastern Bahamas, it hovered just north of the capital Nassau for 12 hours before heading towards Florida. Locals there were warned of an imminent assault by the hurricane, but Betsy took an

HURRICANES 2

WIDEST RECORDED

unexpected turn towards the Gulf of Mexico, ending its violent outburst with tidal waves and ferocious 200 km/h winds in New Orleans. The town was severely damaged, and those who had refused to evacuate were killed by the floodwaters that swept through the city, devastating the historic French Quarter and leaving over 50,000 people homeless.

Five out of five

Statistically, Force 5 hurricanes are only expected to occur once every 100 years, and yet two have struck within the last decade: hurricanes Gilbert and Andrew. The gigantic Hurricane Gilbert, which began its assault on the Caribbean, Mexico and Texas between 12 and 19 Sept 1988 with winds gusting up to 320-330 km/h, killed over 350 people, left 750,000 homeless and caused at least $10 billion worth of damage. Gilbert blew through Jamaica with sustained wind speeds of 280 km/h and a storm surge whose waves were 6 m high, depositing up to 0.5 metres of rain in only 8 hours. Such was the intensity of Gilbert that its zone of rain stretched for 1,000 km from its centre. Hurricane Andrew holds the record for the most costly hurricane in American history: damages ran to $25 billion. It cut a ruinous course across southern Florida on 15 August 1992, smashing apart houses and offices in the city of Homestead, a suburb just south of Miami, and destroying an Air Force base located there.

The Great Storm

On 16-17 Oct 1987, winds of hurricane force devastated areas of southern Britain. At its peak, the winds gusted at speeds of up to 140 km/h (86 mph), killing 19 people and causing nearly £1 billion worth of damage. Tearing through the counties of Sussex and Kent, the violent winds brought down more than 15 million trees in south-east England, including six of the seven oaks which gave Sevenoaks, in Kent, its name. Roofs were removed, fences flattened, and chimneys sent crashing. The aircraft hangar at Southend collapsed, reducing the planes it housed to scrap. High on the cliffs of East Sussex, over 200 mobile homes were blown over and wrecked at a caravan site in Peacehaven.

Holy smoke

The storm of 1703 was the worst recorded in British history. At least 123 people were killed on land, and the total losses at sea were estimated at 8, 000, including a Channel Squadron of the Royal Navy. In a tragic freak accident, the Bishop of Bath and Wells was crushed to death when a chimney stack came crashing through the ceiling of his bedroom.

TRACKING AND TAMING

BECAUSE OF THE IMMENSE COST, BOTH FINANCIAL AND HUMAN, THAT HURRICANES CAN INCUR, TRACKING AND PREDICTING THEIR PATHS IS BECOMING INCREASINGLY CRUCIAL. SAFE PROCEDURES FOR EVACUATION CAN ONLY BE SET UP IF KNOWLEDGE OF AN IMMINENT HURRICANE IS AVAILABLE AT THE EARLIEST OPPORTUNITY. SPECIALLY EQUIPPED AIRCRAFT MAKE REGULAR RECONNAISSANCE TRIPS WHILE SCIENTISTS MONITOR AND PREDICT LIKELY TROUBLE SPOTS. TO DATE HOWEVER, HURRICANES HAVE PROVED

IMPOSSIBLE TO PREVENT. IN THE MID-1960s, AMERICAN SCIENTISTS UNDERTOOK A PROJECT CALLED 'STORMFURY' WHICH SOUGHT TO REDUCE THE INTENSITY OF HURRICANES. IN 'SEEDING' THE CLOUDS WITH CRYSTALS THEY BELIEVED THAT THE HURRICANE WOULD RELEASE ITSELF AS RAIN, THUS ENLARGING THE EYE AND REDUCING ITS INTENSITY. HOWEVER, CURRENT RESEARCH SHOWS THAT UNMODIFIED HURRICANES ALSO HAVE LARGE EYES, BUT ARE JUST AS DEADLY. PROJECT 'STORMFURY' WAS TERMINATED IN 1971.

LEFT: BOAT TOSSED INTO A PARKING LOT BY HURRICANE MARILYN, VIRGIN ISLANDS, 1995 · RIGHT: PALM TREES BLOW IN THE HIGH WINDS OF HURRICANE ALLEN, GULF OF MEXICO, 1980

HURRICANE 1,100 KM

NORMALLY EXPECTED TO OCCUR EVERY HUNDRED YEARS,
THE FORCE 5 HURRICANES, GILBERT AND ANDREW, HIT THE
USA WITHIN FOUR YEARS OF ONE ANOTHER. TOGETHER
THEY RAN UP A COMBINED DAMAGES BILL OF $35 BILLION

Drought is an insidious hazard of nature, but one that can present a very serious threat to those who live off the land. Lack of rainfall results in severe water shortages which can destroy crops. In the world's poorer countries drought brings famine, disease and death on a massive scale.

Types of drought
There are four different ways of categorizing droughts; while some are a recurrent climatic feature, others are more erratic and less predictable. Permanent drought takes place in some of the world's driest regions where agriculture is only ever possible with the aid of continuous irrigation. Seasonal drought occurs in areas with well defined rainy and dry seasons. Unpredictable drought involves abnormal rainfall and is common in humid climates. Invisible drought is the result of a borderline water deficiency that diminishes crop yields but is not severe enough to destroy them.

Causes of drought
A number of factors influence the occurrence of drought including soil moisture, topography, interactions between the air and sea patterns, global weather and internal climate dynamics. Prolonged droughts occur when there are large scale anomalies in atmospheric circulation patterns. These can persist for months, seasons, even decades. The onset of naturally occurring drought is often aggravated by human-made factors such as over-farming of the land and over-use of the water supply.

High death toll in China
The severe drought in northern China between 1876 and 1879 is considered to be the worst in

history. Between 9 and 13 million people died of starvation. Alleged reports told of children being sold, and record that some people resorted to cannibalism.

African tragedy
The Sahelian drought affects the Sahel region on the southern fringe of the Sahara in Africa. This area suffered from severe drought in the 1980s which lead to devastating famine. Half a million people died in Africa as a result of drought

DROUGHTS
NO RAIN FOR 5 YEARS

in 1985. Ethiopia, in particular, was very badly hit. Over half of the country's cattle died in 1980 alone, a year when the region received absolutely no rainfall at all. One theory suggests that a fluctuation in the oceanic temperature might have played a part in creating the unusually arid conditions during this period.

No water on Java
The island of Java in Indonesia, was particularly badly hit by the drought of 1997. Thousands of farmers in central Java found their livelihoods destroyed by an eight-month period without rain, and crop prices rose sharply. In Gunungkidul, water was available only from one small spring, while in other parts of the island people were forced to walk long distances to reach a limited water supply. The

situation was compounded by smog from forest fires that raged on the neighbouring island of Sumatra and on Kalimantan in Borneo.

Drought in India
India experienced a severe drought in 1998 and the state of Orissa was particularly badly hit. There had been little rainfall there for several years, but this situation worsened when the monsoon failed to arrive that year. Many villages lost their crops, causing a million agricultural labourers to lose their jobs. Half a million people were forced to migrate from drought-affected areas and there were a number of deaths from starvation.

Dust bowl
The most severe drought to hit North America occurred predominantly on the Great Plains

during the 1930s. For five years there was absolutely no rain. The situation was made worse by hot, dry winds that blew away the top layer of soil, piling it 6 m high in places. In May 1934, a cloud of dust stretched from Alberta in Canada, to Texas, in southern USA. Birds suffocated in mid-flight and dust fell on ships 480 km off the east coast of the USA. The following year, a single dust storm deposited 12 million tonnes of dust on Chicago. In 1936, a total of 4,768 people were reported to have died from heatstroke and related breathing problems. While the prolonged lack of rain was in part a result of freak weather conditions, the 'dust bowl' had also been created by a century of bad farming practice. Early pioneers ploughed the prairie plains and slaughtered the herds of bison.

DATA-BURST

WHAT ARE THE NATURAL FACTORS THAT CAN LEAD TO DROUGHT?
SOME DESERT REGIONS, SUCH AS THE KALAHARI AND THE SAHARA, ARE INLAND AREAS OF HIGH PRESSURE. THEY ARE DRY AS A RESULT OF BEING SO FAR AWAY FROM THE SEA, AND MOISTURE CARRYING AIR IS UNABLE TO REACH THEM.

WHAT HUMAN FACTORS LEAD TO DROUGHT?
THE ARID NATURE OF DRY REGIONS IS ALSO RELATED TO THEIR CULTIVATION BY MAN. TWO THOUSAND YEARS AGO, WHAT IS NOW THE SAHARA DESERT WAS FERTILE SOIL. IT WAS AN AREA FARMED BY THE ROMANS AND EGYPTIANS. AS A RESULT OF BEING OVER-CULTIVATED BY THESE ARABLE CIVILIZATIONS, IT LATER TURNED INTO A DRY DESERT REGION.

WHICH PLACES HAVE PERMANENT DROUGHTS?
THE ATACAMA DESERT IN CHILE EXPERIENCES ALMOST NO RAIN. ON SOME OCCASIONS DURING THE CENTURY, A SQUALL BRINGS SOME RAIN TO A LIMITED AREA.

DOES DROUGHT CAUSE FIRE?
YES. IN 1998, FOREST FIRES FUELLED BY DROUGHT HELPED TO DESTROY PART OF THE BRAZILIAN RAINFOREST. SAVANNA HIGHLANDS BURNED OVER TWO MONTHS. THE DROUGHT WAS LINKED TO THE EL NIÑO WEATHER PHENOMENON.

WHEN WAS THE WORST DROUGHT IN RECENT MEMORY?
IN THE 1984—85 DROUGHT IN THE SAHEL, HALF A MILLION PEOPLE DIED FROM THE RESULTING FAMINE.

RELIEF FOR THOSE STARVING FROM DROUGHT

DROUGHT AND FAMINE CAN PROMPT MASS MOBILIZATION TO ALLEVIATE THE CRISIS. ONE OF THE MOST HIGHLY-PROFILED CASES IN RECENT YEARS FOLLOWED THE DROUGHT IN ETHIOPIA IN 1984. EXACERBATED BY CIVIL WAR AND SOIL EROSION, THIS DROUGHT RESULTED IN LARGE SCALE CROP FAILURE. UPWARDS OF 800,000 PEOPLE DIED AND MILLIONS OF LIVES WERE THREATENED. IMAGES OF THE STARVING PEOPLE BROADCAST ON TELEVISION LED TO A CO-ORDINATED EFFORT TO HELP BRING IN FOOD. POP SINGER BOB GELDOF SPEARHEADED 'LIVE AID', A MASSIVE FUND-RAISING CONCERT HELD IN WEMBLEY, LONDON, IN 1985. GLOBAL SATELLITE IMAGES BEAMED THE CONCERT WORLDWIDE RAISING MILLIONS OF POUNDS. LIVE AID SPAWNED SEVERAL OTHER FUND-RAISING EFFORTS IN LATER YEARS.

LEFT: SALT DEPOSITS IN THE ATACAMA DESERT, CHILE · RIGHT: CRACKED MUD IN THE SARIGUA NATIONAL PARK, ONE OF PANAMA'S MOST ARID REGIONS

ON US GREAT PLAINS

WITHOUT WATER THERE CAN BE NO LIFE. WHEN DROUGHT DAMAGES THE SOIL STRUCTURE, CROP FAILURE IS THE INEVITABLE RESULT. IN 1985, HALF A MILLION PEOPLE PERISHED IN ETHIOPIA DURING THE SAHEL DROUGHT

A heatwave is a period of extremely hot weather that lasts much longer than usual. Most of us enjoy hot weather, but it can prove deadly. Long periods of high temperature with no respite tax the human body beyond its cooling capacity. From 1936–1975 nearly 20,000 people were killed by heat in the USA. In 1980 alone, over 1,250 people died in the USA in one of the fiercest heatwaves in living memory. Air-conditioning, often regarded as a luxury, can actually be a life-saver during a heatwave. But it is not just the heat itself that kills; in cities, when winds drop and airborne pollutants hang in the air, smog forms a choking cloud that has deadly potential.

A scorching year

Temperatures all around the world soared to unprecedented levels during unusually fierce heatwaves in 1996. In July in the eastern and mid-western states of the USA, temperatures sizzled at around 38°C, causing the death of around 1,000 people across the country. The city of Chicago was particularly badly hit: over 733 people died of heat-related causes. During the same month in Spain, 10 people died during a heatwave in which the temperature rose to a burning 44°C. Both of these heatwaves were outdone, however, during the previous month in southern Asia. Residents of the states of Uttar Pradesh, Rajasthan, Bihar and Madhya Pradesh in northern and central India sweltered in burning temperatures of over 46°C. This roasting heat killed 550 people.

Month-long heatwave

In the summer of 1980 a huge area of the USA—from the state of Texas in the south, northwards to Dakota and east as far as New England—was gripped by a heatwave that lasted for more than a month. The scorching heat and fiery temperatures shrivelled crops, dried up reservoirs, killed livestock, started fires and caused hundreds of kilometres of roads to buckle. A total of $20 billion worth of damage was caused—with over 80% of crops, including corn, cotton, soybean and wheat, lost in some areas. In one week in the state of Arkansas, 8 million chickens suffocated in the heat.

HEATWAVES

1980 HEATWAVES KILLED

DATA-BURST

HOW DOES THE HUMAN BODY COPE WITH HEAT?
AT AIR TEMPERATURES OF ABOVE 32°C, EVEN BARE SKIN CANNOT RADIATE ENOUGH HEAT TO MAINTAIN NORMAL BODY TEMPERATURE AND SWEAT GLANDS TAKE OVER THE TASK. WHEN AIR IS VERY MOIST, EVAPORATION MAY NOT TAKE PLACE FAST ENOUGH AND SWEAT POURS.

WHAT IS HEATSTROKE?
HEATSTROKE IS THE BREAKDOWN IN THERMAL CONTROL OF EXCESSIVE BODY TEMPERATURE. BODY TEMPERATURE IS MODIFIED BY THE SKIN. IN HOT CONDITIONS, BLOOD VESSELS DILATE AND HEAT IS RADIATED FROM THE SKIN'S SURFACE. PHYSICAL ACTIVITY WILL TRIGGER SWEAT TO ACT AS A COOLING SYSTEM. IF THESE SYSTEMS DO NOT COOL THE BODY, THEN DEHYDRATION RESULTS.

WHAT IS DEHYDRATION?
WATER IS ESSENTIAL FOR EVERY PROCESS IN THE BODY AND SO A LACK OF WATER LEADS TO MENTAL AS WELL AS PHYSICAL CHANGES. THE PHYSICAL SYMPTOMS OF DEHYDRATION INCLUDE DRYNESS OF THE THROAT, THIRST AND MUSCULAR WEAKNESS. MENTAL ASPECTS INCLUDE DISORIENTATION AND THE OCCURRENCE OF HALLUCINATIONS.

CAN WE ADAPT TO HUMIDITY?
HARD PHYSICAL WORK IN HUMID AIR IS EXHAUSTING IF YOU ARE NOT USED TO IT BECAUSE YOUR BODY FINDS IT HARD TO KEEP COOL. WITH PRACTICE IT CAN BECOME MORE EFFICIENT. THE BRITISH ATHLETE, YVONNE MURRAY, DECIDED TO TRAIN IN A GREENHOUSE BEFORE COMPETING IN THE WORLD CHAMPIONSHIPS IN JAPAN, A COUNTRY THAT IS MORE HUMID THAN BRITAIN.

THE HEAT INDEX

THE USA TAKES THE THREAT OF HEATWAVES VERY SERIOUSLY. A SYSTEM CALLED THE HEAT INDEX, MEASURED IN DEGREES FAHRENHEIT, HAS BEEN DEVISED TO WARN PEOPLE WHEN THEY ARE IN DANGER FROM EXTREME HEAT. AS WELL AS AIR TEMPERATURES, THE HEAT INDEX (HI) ALSO RECORDS HUMIDITY. THIS IS BECAUSE IF HUMIDITY IS HIGH, THE EFFECTS OF HEAT ARE INTENSIFIED. GUIDELINES HAVE BEEN DRAWN UP OUTLINING THE DANGER TO LIFE. ACCORDING TO THE HEAT INDEX, AT AN HI OF 43°C, ANYONE REMAINING OUTSIDE IS LIABLE TO EXPERIENCE SUNSTROKE OR HEAT EXHAUSTION IF THEY STAY IN THE HEAT FOR A LONG PERIOD OR ENGAGE IN PHYSICAL ACTIVITY. PROLONGED EXPOSURE TO THE HEAT AT AN HI OF 71°C IS VERY DANGEROUS: HEATSTROKE IS LIKELY, AND IN THE WORST CASES, CAN KILL.

1,250 PEOPLE IN USA

IN INTENSE HEAT, PEOPLE COLLAPSE FROM EXHAUSTION, HEATSTROKE, SUNBURN AND DEHYDRATION. TARMAC ON ROADS CAN MELT INTO GLUEY GUM WHILE POWER LINES CAN STRETCH AND SAG CAUSING ELECTRICAL BLACKOUT

In Dallas, Texas, temperatures stayed at 37°C for 42 days, once soaring to 45°C. In all, 1,265 people lost their lives.

Burning down under
In the last 100 years, heatwaves in Australia have claimed more lives than any other natural hazard excluding disease. As many as 4,000 heat-related deaths have occurred there since 1803. On 19 Dec 1994 Australia was hit by the hottest December day for 37 years—thermometers recorded temperatures of up to 44°C. Many people were treated for heat exhaustion and dehydration and 34 people were hospitalized in New South Wales. Other problems resulted from road surfaces melting and overhead wires being affected by the heat. The weather also contributed to the bloom of a toxic green algae in the Barwon and Darling river systems. High levels of ozone pollution were also recorded during the heatwave.

Heat horror strikes Chicago
In July and August 1995 the city of Chicago, Illinois, USA, was afflicted by one of the deadliest heatwaves in its history. A total of 592 people died. The city's mayor was criticized for underestimating the effects of the heat. But his was not the only city affected: from Los Angeles, California, in the west, to Philadelphia, Pennsylvania, in the east, record temperatures were reached. In Phoenix, Arizona, the intense heat reached a peak temperature of 49°C. In May of the same year the city of New Delhi and the state of Rajasthan, India, were also badly affected. The deaths of 161 people were attributed to the intense heat.

Heatwave plagues
In 1998 in South America, a heatwave, thought to be caused by El Niño, resulted in disastrous health problems. In Chile, as temperature records were far exceeded by the soaring heat, a plague of giant killer rats spread beyond the ability of the authorities to control it. In Argentina, the heat caused a plague of mosquitoes which brought outbreaks of the killer diseases malaria and dengue fever. In Colombia, 2 million chickens perished and the effects of the heatwave, combined with poor hygiene, saw similar problems grip Peru and Ecuador. Only the last visit of El Niño in 1982 saw disaster on the same scale: that time, over $8 billion worth of damage was caused.

Hot tempers
The human body cannot cope with prolonged exposure to intense heat and a wide variety of problems can ensue. At temperatures between 40–54°C, heat stress is likely to cause irrational behaviour, dehydration, sunburn, sunstroke and heat cramps. The young and the old are especially vulnerable to illness during very hot weather. Deaths resulting from cardiovascular failure are likely to increase during a heatwave. One US study showed that even with a degree of acclimatization, heat-related illnesses rose fourfold in the USA after a temperature increase of between 2–4°C.

LEFT: CHILDREN PLAYING IN A COOLING WATER SPRAY DURING A HEATWAVE· RIGHT: DIVING INTO THE RIVER THAMES IS ONE WAY TO COOL DOWN IN THE SUMMER OF 1933

Floods occur when huge amounts of rain fall in just a short space of time. These massive downfalls can cause rivers to burst their banks, inundating the surrounding land with water. Ice melting upstream can also cause a sudden surge in a river's flow that can swell its volume beyond its usual bounds. The sea too can cause devastating floods when storm tides or tsunamis (tidal waves) sweep inland. Floods are rated by the frequency with which they are predicted to occur: a 100-year flood is one so severe that it is expected to occur only once every 100 years. Controlling floods like this requires careful planning. Reinforcing river banks and constructing dams and reservoirs can help to save lives. Planting forests also helps to minimize the catastrophic effects of flooding by absorbing the extra water caused by heavy storms.

River swelled to 28.6 m—a level almost as great as its all-time high which it reached in 1954.

Storm-tide tragedy

In 1953 a storm tide destroyed 500 km of sea defences along the Dutch coast between Rotterdam and the estuary of the Sheldt river, bursting through protective dykes in 67 places. The surge of water flooded 133 houses almost immediately and continued inland where it inundated an area of

short-circuited underground transformers, cutting off electricity to the region. Its force ripped oil tanks off their supports, adding oil to the swirling water that swept through the city. People were sucked under by irresistible currents and debris was tossed around on the waves. The city's sewers could not cope with the sudden influx of water and human waste burst out of man-holes to join the chaos. In Florence's historic Piazza del Duomo, a pair

along the banks of the Dasht and the Rivers Kech and Nihing were destroyed.

Stemming the flow

The Aswan High Dam, completed in 1970, was constructed on the River Nile in Egypt, 960 km upstream from Cairo, to prevent flooding in Egypt and Sudan. The dam is 3,768 m long at the crest and 984 m wide at the base and towers 109 m above the river bed. Behind the dam, the river has formed a

FLOODS
23 MILLION ACRES

The deadly Yellow River

China's Huang Ho, or Yellow River, has killed more people than any other river in the world. In 1931, four million people were drowned and millions more lost their homes. Eight years later, a further million died when the river once again breached its banks. The reason for the frequent flooding of the Huang Ho is its high silt content. In the 4,830-km stretch of the Yellow River's course, silt makes up 60% of the river's volume. This yellow mud can block the smooth passage of water and force it to change course over fields and villages. China was once again afflicted by massive flooding in July and August of 1996. Nearly 2,300 people died leaving a further 2.36 million stranded or homeless. The Yangtze

1,600 km²—6% of the Netherlands' total farmland. In total around 1,800 people died, 43,000 homes were destroyed and 50,000 cattle drowned.

Italy's deluge

In one of the worst storms ever known in northern Italy, one-third of the expected rain for the year of 1966 fell within the space of just 40 hours. The unbelievable two-day downpour hit the region around the historic city of Florence in November of that year and caused a major flood that killed a total of 144 people. As the torrential rain ran off hillsides, water joined the River Arno flowing towards Florence in an uncontrollable torrent that rushed downstream at 130 km/h. The raging floodwater

of bronze doors was ripped off the cathedral and swept away. Outside the city, along the River Arno, 112 people died, 50,000 farm animals were drowned and 10,000 homes were completely wrecked.

Mississippi drench

Record-breaking rainfall drenched the upper Mississippi basin in the USA in the summer of 1986 causing widespread devastation. By late June the Mississippi River had breached its banks in Minnesota where the National Guard helped to battle against the worst flooding in over 30 years. More than 1.5 million sandbags were used in the west Des Moines region alone. Floods are a fact of life in the Midwest, but they usually arrive in spring when snowmelt fills the streams. That summer, the usual eastward passage of thunderstorms was blocked by a high pressure system, and the rains kept falling. Despite valiant attempts to contruct levees and stem the flow, the floodwater washed across 23 million acres. Fifty people died and damages were estimated at more than 10 billion dollars.

Horror in Pakistan

In March 1998, in south-western Pakistan—an area that is usually arid—abnormally heavy spring rains burst the banks of the River Dasht causing widespread upheaval. About 1,000 people died, many swept into the Arabian Sea or buried in the 1.8 m of mud left by the floodwater. The mud stretched 500 km down the river's course and all the settlements

massive reservoir—Lake Nasser—which stretches about 500 km upstream. A quarter of the total capacity of the lake, known as 'century storage', is reserved for the unusually high flood levels which may occur every 100 years.

Fertile floods

Floods do not only bring destruction. As long as the silt desposits are not too large, then the organic matter and minerals that a flood spreads over soil can leave it more fertile than before. The Ancient Egyptians made use of this benefit and planned their whole agricultural cycle around the River Nile's yearly floods. They realized that the rich nutrients deposited by floodwaters improved the harvests.

JARGON

DISCHARGE
THE AMOUNT OF WATER THAT A RIVER NORMALLY EXPELS

DRAINAGE BASIN
ALSO CALLED THE 'CATCHMENT AREA', THIS IS THE AREA OF LAND INTO WHICH WATERSHEDS FROM A SPECIFIC RIVER DRAIN

ICE JAM
A BLOCKAGE CAUSED BY ICE WHICH HAS BEEN BROKEN UP AT A HIGHER PART OF THE RIVER

LEVEE
RAISED EMBANKMENT OF A RIVER, WHICH RESULTS FROM PERIODIC OVERBANK FLOODING

100-YEAR-FLOOD
A FLOOD EXPECTED TO OCCUR EVERY 100 YEARS (THERE ARE ALSO 500 YEAR FLOODS AND 1,000 YEAR FLOODS)

LEFT: AERIAL SHOT OF FLOODED HOMES · RIGHT: PEOPLE MAKING THEIR WAY DOWN A HIGHWAY AFTER FLOODS IN THE STATE OF MISSOURI, USA

DATA-BURST

WHAT IS THE FLOODPLAIN?

THIS IS PART OF THE RIVER VALLEY THAT IS MADE UP OF UNCONSOLIDATED RIVER-BORNE SEDIMENT. THE RESULT OF PERIODIC FLOODING, IT IS BUILT UP OF RELATIVELY COARSE DEBRIS LEFT BEHIND AS A STREAM CHANNEL MIGRATES LATERALLY, AND OF FINE SEDIMENT DEPOSITED WHEN RIVER BANKS ARE BREACHED.

HOW DOES SOIL CONDITION AFFECT FLOODING?

SOIL IS AN IMPORTANT REGULATOR OF RAIN DISPOSAL. WATER CLINGS BY SURFACE TENSION TO THE TOP LAYER OF SOIL AND THEN IS GRADUALLY FORCED DOWNWARDS. PERCOLATION IS SLOW AND SO SOIL ACTS MOST EFFICIENTLY WHEN RAIN FALLS LIGHTLY BUT PERSISTENTLY, AND IS LEAST EFFICIENT IN HEAVY FALLS.

HOW MUCH SEDIMENT DO RIVERS CARRY?

EACH YEAR, RIVERS DUMP IN THE REGION OF 20 BILLION TONNES OF SEDIMENT INTO THE SEA.

WHAT IS A FLASH FLOOD?

A FLASH FLOOD IS ONE THAT OCCURS VERY SUDDENLY AND UNEXPECTEDLY.

WHY DO PEOPLE OFTEN DIE IN THEIR CARS DURING A FLOOD?

FLOOD WATER OFTEN FLOWS FAST ENOUGH TO CARRY AWAY VEHICLES BUT TOO FAST TO BE NAVIGABLE BY BOAT. CARS CAN BE DEATH TRAPS. BY THE TIME WATER REACHES THE WINDOW, THE WATER PRESSURE IS TOO GREAT FOR THE OCCUPANT TO OPEN THE DOOR. WINDOWS MUST BE OPENED TO EQUALIZE WATER PRESSURE BOTH INSIDE AND OUT.

GREAT FLOODS OF MYTH AND LEGEND

A GREAT DELUGE APPEARS IN THE LEDGENDS OF MANY PEOPLES IN DIFFERENT PARTS OF THE WORLD— ASIA, AUSTRALIA AND THE PACIFIC, AS WELL AS THE AMERICAS. THE BEST KNOWN IS 'NOAH'S FLOOD' FROM THE BOOK OF GENESIS IN THE OLD TESTAMENT OF THE BIBLE, A TALE DERIVED FROM MESOPOTAMIA. THE STORY HAS CLOSE AFFINITIES WITH BABYLONIAN TRADITIONS WHICH TALK OF APOCALYPTIC FLOODS. ONE GILGAMESH EPIC TELLS OF UTNAPISHTIM, A MYTHIC FIGURE WHO—LIKE NOAH—SURVIVED COSMIC DESTRUCTION AND A WORLD FLOOD BY HEEDING DIVINE INSTRUCTIONS TO BUILD AN ARC. IN THE GENESIS MYTH, GOD IS SUPPOSED TO HAVE CREATED A RAINBOW IN THE SKY AS A PROMISE NEVER AGAIN TO VENT HIS WRATH AT MAN BY FLOODING THE EARTH. CURIOUSLY, AFRICA HAS NO UNIVERSAL DELUGE LEGEND AND NEITHER, FOLKLORISTS BELIEVE, DID WESTERN EUROPE UNTIL THE MESOPOTAMIAN MYTH REACHED IT AS THE GREEK LEGEND OF DEUCALION AND PYRRA, AND AS THE BIBLICAL STORY OF NOAH. INSTEAD, EUROPE MAY HAVE HAD A LEGEND OF A MORE LOCAL FLOOD, CAUSED NOT BY RAIN BUT BY THE ENCROACHMENT OF THE SEA.

DEVASTATED BY MISSISSIPPI

WATER IS ESSENTIAL FOR LIFE, BUT WHEN HUGE VOLUMES AMASS, THE UNSTOPPABLE POWER OF A FLOOD CAN BE CATASTROPHIC. WHEN A RIVER BREAKS ITS BANKS, EVERYTHING IN ITS PATH IS SWEPT AWAY IN THE FLOW

HAILSTORMS
LARGEST HAILSTONE

Hail is a form of precipitation comprised of ball-shaped ice particles, or hailstones. Hail forms when turbulent cumulonimbus clouds create strong updrafts of wind. These clouds can rise to vast heights of 16 km where temperatures are as low as -62°C. At such heights, water vapour is sucked up into the cloud. Newly formed ice pellets become heavy as they collect freezing water droplets. Ice crystals acquire one coat of ice after another as the updraft tosses them around the cloud. Eventually, hailstones become too heavy for the updraft to support them in the air and they plummet to the ground. Strong updrafts cause monster hailstones.

STRANGE AND DEADLY HAIL

GEORGE KELLY OF ALABAMA, USA, DISPLAYS THE GOLF BALL-SIZED HAIL WHICH SHATTERED HIS CAR WINDSCREEN ON 26 APRIL 1988. HAILSTONES ARE USUALLY ROUND IN SHAPE BUT CAN FALL IN OTHER LESS REGULAR FORMATIONS. IN AUSTRALIA, KNOBBLY HAIL, WITH SPIKED ICICLE EXTENSIONS, FELL IN THE NORTHERN SUBURBS OF SYDNEY ON 3 JAN 1971. DISTORTION IS THE RESULT OF THE MANNER IN WHICH STONES SPIN IN THE AIR CURRENTS. IN GERMANY, A BIZARRE AND TRAGIC ACCIDENT OCCURRED OVER THE RHON MOUNTAINS IN 1930. FIVE GLIDER PILOTS WHO BAILED OUT OF THEIR AIRCRAFT WERE CAUGHT IN A PASSING THUNDERCLOUD. THEY WERE CARRIED UP AND DOWN WITHIN THE SUPER-COOLED CLOUD UNTIL THEY FELL TO EARTH, FROZEN WITHIN ICE PRISONS.

Outside the city, farm animals were killed and crops were completely flattened. At the airport, 150 small aircraft were wrecked by the hail. One Boeing 757 which had just landed suffered $7 million worth of damage. Total insurance claims amounted to $500 million.

Birds bombarded
A hailstorm that hit the province of Alberta, Canada, on 14 July 1953 flattened crops and killed an estimated 36,000 wild birds with its downpour of golf ball-sized hailstones. It left a trail of destruction 225 km long and 8 km wide. Four days later another hailstorm hit the same area and killed a further 27,000 wildfowl.

Menace in the air
Hail has also been known to cause air disasters. On 4 April 1977 a DC9 aircraft, descending to land through a violent hailstorm, lost engine function and crash-landed on a highway near New Hope, Georgia, USA. The hail smashed a cockpit window and caused the plane's second engine to catch fire. A total of 68 people died.

Protection from hail
Farmers have long sought to protect their crops against the damaging effects of hail, which can cause irreparable damage to young citrus fruits. On the Amalfi coast in Italy, where lemons are grown in abundance, reed matting and netting covers the crop in the winter months when hail may strike. These semi-permeable barriers act as wind breaks while also allowing hail to melt and seep through the cover instead of becoming destructive ammunition.

19 CM IN DIAMETER

DURING SEVERE HAILSTORMS, LUMPS OF ICE RAIN DOWN ON EARTH WITH GREAT FORCE. SUCH ICY BOMBARDMENTS CAN FLATTEN AND DESTROY CROPS, WRECK BUILDINGS AND, IN THE WORST CASES, KILL ANIMALS AND HUMANS

JARGON

CUMULONIMBUS CLOUD
A CLOUD OF BULGING, DENSE FORM, OFTEN TOWERING TO A GREAT HEIGHT IN UNSTABLE AIR. SUCH CLOUDS CREATE STRONG UP-CURRENTS THAT HELP THE FORMATION OF HAILSTORMS

HAIL SUPPRESSION
AN ATTEMPT TO REDUCE THE SIZE OF HAILSTONES TO MINIMIZE DAMAGE TO AGRICULTURE

ICE METEOR
ICE THAT FALLS FROM THE SKY WHOSE ORIGIN IS UNCERTAIN

SEEDING
PART OF THE HAIL SUPPRESSION PROCESS IN WHICH IODINE IS INSERTED INTO CLOUDS

SMALL HAIL
TRANSPARENT HAIL, LESS THAN 0.5 CM IN DIAMETER, THAT IS IRREGULAR, SPHERICAL OR CONICAL IN SHAPE. SMALL HAIL IS FORMED WHEN RAINDROPS FREEZE, WHEN SNOW FLAKES MELT AND REFREEZE, OR WHEN SNOW PELLETS BECOME ENCASED IN A THIN LAYER OF SOLID ICE

SOFT HAIL
HAILSTONES FORMED FROM SMALL CLOUD DROPLETS THAT HAVE FROZEN TOGETHER

WHITE ICE
OPAQUE ICE THAT FORMS QUICKLY WHEN TEMPERATURES ARE SO LOW THAT AIR CANNOT ESCAPE FROM WATER AS IT FREEZES

Bullets of ice
The heaviest known hailstone weighed 1 kg and fell in the Gopalganj district of Bangladesh in 1986. The USA's largest reported hailstone fell in Coffeyville, Kansas, on 3 Sept 1970. This giant lump of ice had a diameter of 19 cm, weighed 757 g with a circumference of 44 cm. In the USA, large hailstones cause up to $25 million worth of property damage every year. In Hunan province, China, on 19 June 1932, a record-breaking hailstorm killed 200 people and injured many thousands more. The highest death toll caused by a hail storm took place in Moradabad, India, on 20 April 1888. During this storm, hailstones the size of cricket balls killed 250 people and more than 1,600 sheep and goats perished.

Germany pelted
On 12 July 1984, the city of Munich in Germany was pelted by a severe hailstorm which caused an almost unprecedented $1 billion worth of damage and injured over 400 people. The storm started at around 8 pm when 5–6-cm hailstones struck the earth, falling at an estimated terminal velocity of 150 km/h. The largest hailstone measured 9.5 cm and weighed 300 g. The storm lasted for only 20 minutes but the damage was immense. Homes and factories were flooded, 70,000 roofs were torn off or badly damaged, 250,000 cars had their windows smashed, greenhouses were demolished and plants stripped away. The following day, hailstones in 20-cm-high piles littered the worst hit eastern part of the city.

DATA-BURST

WHY DO LARGE HAILSTONES FORM CLEAR AND OPAQUE COATS OF ICE?
AT EXTREMELY LOW TEMPERATURES, WATER FREEZES QUICKLY, AIR BECOMES TRAPPED AND WHITE ICE FORMS. IN WARMER TEMPERATURES, WATER FREEZES MORE SLOWLY, THE AIR ESCAPES AND CLEAR ICE FORMS. DUE TO THE FLUCTUATION OF TEMPERATURES, HAILSTONES FORM ALTERNATE LAYERS OF CLEAR AND WHITE ICE RESEMBLING THE SKIN OF AN ONION.

HOW FAST DO HAILSTONES FALL?
SMALL HAILSTONES FALL AT A TERMINAL VELOCITY OF ABOUT 5 M PER SECOND, BUT THE LARGER HAILSTONES, MEASURING 5 CM AND OVER IN DIAMETER, CAN FALL AT A SPEED OF 40 M PER SECOND.

HOW LONG DOES HAIL LAST?
MOST HAIL DOES NOT REMAIN LONG ON THE GROUND AS AIR TEMPERATURES TEND TO BE ABOVE MELTING LEVEL.

WHEN AND WHERE DOES HAIL FALL?
HAIL USUALLY FALLS IN REGIONS OF MIDDLE LATITUDES DURING THE WARMER MONTHS OF THE YEAR. IT FORMS MAINLY OVER LARGE LAND MASSES. THERMAL UP-CURRENTS ARE THEN AT THEIR STRONGEST AND CLOUDS CONTAIN AN ABUNDANCE OF SUPER-COOLED WATER DROPLETS. IN EQUATORIAL REGIONS, HAIL FALLS MAINLY OVER MOUNTAINOUS COUNTRY WHERE ALTITUDES ENSURE LOW TEMPERATURES

HOW DO LARGE HAILSTONES FORM?
THE DIAMETER OF A HAILSTONE IS USUALLY BETWEEN 0.5–5 CM, ANYTHING OVER 1 CM BEING TERMED 'LARGE'. ANY STONES GREATER THAN 5 CM ARE USUALLY CONGLOMERATES OF SMALLER HAILSTONES THAT HAVE BONDED TOGETHER. THE SIZE OF HAILSTONES IS OFTEN DESCRIBED BY COMPARING THEM TO KNOWN OBJECTS SUCH AS PEAS, GOLF BALLS, CRICKET BALLS OR GRAPEFRUIT.

LEFT: A RESIDENT COVERS HIS ROOF AFTER A VIOLENT STORM OF HAIL THE SIZE OF TENNIS BALLS HIT THE TOWN OF REBENACQ IN THE PYRENEES, FRANCE. INSET: LARGE HAILSTONE

LIGHTNING

LIGHTNING KILLS

What we see as a bolt of lightning in the sky is in fact a colossal negative charge, generated by energy from powerful winds during a thunderstorm, surging at phenomenally high speeds down a conductive channel just the width of a pencil and up to 8 km long.

Fatal attraction

Inside a thundercloud powerful swirling winds act like a giant dynamo, churning up water particles and freeing their electrons to create a massive electrical field. Positive charges from the ground and negative charges from the base of the cloud, where electrons have massed, are irresistibly attracted

lightning is an electrical current. In a 1752 experiment he flew a kite in a thunderstorm from which was attached a metal key. When he touched the key with his knuckle, the electric charge that had built up in the metal gave off a spark. His discovery inspired him to invent lightning rods. When Franklin's contemporary, King Louis XVI of France, learned of the American's experiment, he staged a variation for the entertainment of his courtiers. He got 200 monks to re-enact the experiment, holding hands during a storm so that when the electricity was discharged through the kite, the current passed to Earth through all of the monks.

FOOTBALL MATCH ON FIRE

A 16-YEAR OLD SWEDISH GIRL, VERONICA RONN, WAS LITERALLY BLOWN OUT OF HER BOOTS WHEN SHE WAS HIT BY A LIGHTNING BOLT WHILE GUARDING HER GOAL DURING A SOCCER GAME IN GALVE, NORTHERN SWEDEN ON 29 JULY 1994. THE BOLT THREW HER FLYING INTO THE AIR, STOPPING HER HEART FOR FOUR MINUTES, AND CAUSING BURNS ALL OVER HER BODY. THE BLAST TORE HER SOCCER BOOTS TO SHREDS BEFORE THEY ACTUALLY BURST INTO FLAMES. THE BRAVE GOALIE'S FIRST WORDS ON WAKING UP IN HOSPITAL WERE: "HOW DID THE MATCH GO?".

1,000 PER YEAR

EVERY SECOND OF THE DAY AND NIGHT, LIGHTNING STRIKES THE EARTH ABOUT 100 TIMES, EACH TIME SENDING A MILLION VOLTS OF RAW POWER AT SPEEDS OF UP TO 300,000 KM/SEC CRASHING TO THE GROUND

Castle explodes

A terrible fate was visited upon the town of Athlone, Ireland, by a single lightning strike on 27 Oct 1697. By chance, the bolt of lightning struck the arsenal of the castle detonating its contents, which included 260 barrels of gunpowder and 1,000 hand grenades. The force of the huge explosion obliterated the castle and sent fire raging through the thatched roofs of the town.

and as they build up, so does the attraction. At 100 million volts, the attraction is so immense that the air is electrically broken down, or ionized, and negatively charged electrons are pulled downwards. When this column touches the ground, negative and positive meet and complete an electrical circuit.

Kite strike

The 18th-century American scientist Benjamin Franklin was the first person to prove that

Tragedy on high

In Dec 1963, 81 people were killed when lightning struck the wing of a PanAm Boeing 707 flying over Maryland, USA. The strike ignited the fuel tank in the wing's tip and the plane exploded in mid-air.

Three times unlucky

The village of Steeple Ashton in Wiltshire, UK, has gained something of a reputation for lightning encounters. Badly damaged by a strike during a

violent storm on 25 July 1670, the 28 m steeple of the church of St Mary the Virgin had almost been repaired when lightning struck it again less than three months later. Two workmen were killed and the steeple collapsed onto the church. About 300 years later, on 26 June 1973, an 84-year-old pensioner from Steeple Ashton, aptly named Henry Bolt, was thrown across his kitchen when lightning hit a hay barn a few metres from his house.

Fatal fireball

The worst lightning disaster in recent history happened on 2 Nov 1994 in Durunka, Egypt, when lightning struck a train carrying fuel oil. The train was derailed by the strike and exploded near an army depot, creating a gigantic fireball of ignited fuel which surged through the town, ripping apart houses that lay in its path.

Human conductor

Roy C. Sullivan of Virginia, USA, is the only man in the world to have been struck by lightning seven times. An ex-park ranger, his history of strikes spanned 35 years, causing injuries from scorched hair to stomach burns. He commited suicide in 1983, reportedly rejected in love.

JARGON

ANVIL LIGHTNING
A 'BOLT FROM THE BLUE' IN SEEMINGLY CLOUDLESS SKIES

BALL LIGHTNING
UNEXPLAINED RARE FLOATING BALL OF LIGHT THAT OCCURS DURING THUNDERSTORMS

BEAD LIGHTNING
OCCURS WHEN SOME SECTIONS OF A DISCHARGED LIGHTNING CHANNEL REMAIN ILLUMINATED, LEAVING A BEAD-LIKE PATTERN IN THE SKY

BRANCHES
THE ILLUMINATED PARTS OF THE STEPPED LEADER THAT ARE NOT PART OF THE MAIN CHANNEL AND ARE DIMMER IN APPEARANCE

CHANNEL
PATH OF IONIZED AIR THROUGH WHICH CURRENT FLOWS

IONIZATION
THE PROCESS BY WHICH AIR BECOMES CONDUCTIVE, CAUSED BY A TREMENDOUS DIFFERENCE BETWEEN TWO REGIONS OF OPPOSITE CHARGE

SHEET LIGHTNING
OCCURS WHEN THE CHANNEL IS OBSCURED FROM VIEW, GIVING THE APPEARANCE OF A SHEET OF LIGHT IN THE SKY

STEPPED LEADER
NAME GIVEN TO THE DOWNWARD MOVEMENT OF THE CURRENT IN SHORT BURSTS FROM THE BASE OF THE CLOUD TO THE GROUND

DATA-BURST

HOW FAST CAN LIGHTNING TRAVEL?
LIGHTNING CAN STRIKE AT SPEEDS APPROACHING 50,000 KM/SEC.

HOW HOT CAN THE AIR GET?
A LIGHTNING STRIKE CAN HEAT THE AIR TO 30,000°C.

WHAT IS THUNDER?
LIGHTNING HEATS UP THE AIR TO SEVERAL TIMES THE SURFACE TEMPERATURE OF THE SUN. THIS CAUSES THE AIR TO EXPAND, CREATING A SHOCKWAVE, WHICH IS CONVERTED INTO SOUND ENERGY. IT IS THIS SOUNDWAVE THAT CREATES THE NOISE WE RECOGNIZE AS THUNDER.

HOW CAN YOU WORK OUT HOW FAR AWAY A LIGHTNING STRIKE IS?
COUNT HOW MANY SECONDS ELAPSE BETWEEN SEEING A STRIKE AND HEARING ITS THUNDER. SOUND

TRAVELS AT ABOUT 330 M/SEC, SO FOR EVERY THREE SECONDS THAT ELAPSE, THE LIGHTNING IS 1 KM AWAY.

DOES LIGHTNING STRIKE TWICE?
SINCE LIGHTNING STRIKES SO QUICKLY, WHAT MAY APPEAR TO BE A SINGLE FLASH COULD, IN FACT, BE AS MANY AS 40 INDIVIDUAL STROKES.

WHAT IS A FULGURITE?
A TUBE OF GLASSY MINERAL MATTER FOUND IN ROCK, FORMED BY THE FUSION OF LIGHTNING ON LAND.

CAN LIGHTNING CAUSE FIRES?
LIGHTNING CAUSES, ON AVERAGE, 200 FOREST FIRES EVERY DAY.

HOW MUCH ELECTRICAL CURRENT CAN FLOW FROM A LIGHTNING STRIKE?
A CURRENT OF 10 MILLION AMPS CAN BE GENERATED DURING A STRIKE.

A tornado is a spinning funnel of cloud formed within a stormcloud, which builds up so much energy that it finally bursts out of the main cloud mass. It swoops down to the ground then moves away at speeds of up to 112 km/h, sometimes hovering, sometimes striking down again and again. Some tornadoes have been known to travel for distances of up to 350 km before running out of energy. Their awesome pent-up force is caused by humid air surging upwards at the 'squall line'—a zone within the storm cloud where warm, moist air and cool, dry air meet. As this humid air spirals upwards it is replaced by more and more air which is sucked in faster and faster until the whole mass is rotating furiously at speeds of between 480 km/h and 800 km/h.

LEFT, CENTRE AND RIGHT:
TORNADO SEQUENCE FROM NORTH-WEST
TEXAS ON 28 MAY 1994

Mega-spout

If the tornado forms over water, the funnel creates a water spout, spraying water as it spins and moves forwards at up to 80 km/h. The regions where waterspouts are known to occur most frequently are the Gulf of Mexico, Florida, the Bahamas, the west coast of Africa and over the Gulf Stream. Although they are not uncommon, they are rarely observed. The largest one recorded struck the state of Massachusetts, USA, on 19 Aug 1896. Estimated at 1,095 m high and 256 m wide, tapering to 73 m at the base it lasted for 35 minutes, disappearing and reappearing three times. The spray flying around at the base was reported to be approximately 200 m wide and 120 m high.

THE TWISTER PAPARAZZI

MUCH OF WHAT SCIENTISTS KNOW ABOUT TORNADOES HAS BEEN DISCOVERED BY ANALYZING THE DATA PROVIDED BY 'STORM CHASERS'. THESE ARE PEOPLE WHO FOLLOW AND PHOTOGRAPH TORNADOES, OFTEN RISKING THEIR LIVES. IN 1996, IN DEMMITT, TEXAS, USA, THE FIRST EVER PICTURE OF THE INSIDE OF A TORNADO WAS TAKEN BY A TEAM OF STORM CHASERS WHO DROVE A TRUCK CARRYING RADAR IMAGING EQUIPMENT THROUGH A VIOLENT STORM. THE STORM CHASERS MANAGED TO STAY WITHIN 4 KM OF THE RAGING TORNADO FOR NINE OF ITS 14-MINUTE DURATION. THE RADAR MEASURED THE 'EYE' OF THE VORTEX AT 200 M WIDE. IT WAS SURROUNDED BY A WHIRLING RING OF DEBRIS INCLUDING CARS, A HOUSE AND PIECES OF TORN-UP ROAD SURFACE.

TORNADOES 1

SPINNING TORNADOES

Dust devils

If a tornado forms over a hot, dry region, it creates a 'dust devil' or whirlwind. These spinning funnels of flying dust and sand gather their energy and momentum from the heat of the ground. Their exact scale and size is hard to quantify because they usually occur in sparsely populated areas, such as in the arid regions and deserts of the USA, Australia, India and the Middle East. In the Sahara Desert, dust devils lasting from five minutes to several hours are sighted daily. In urban Tucson, Arizona, USA, inhabitants see an average of 80 per day. One of the largest whirlwinds ever seen hit the salt flats of Utah, USA: it was 750 m high and lasted for seven hours, travelling a distance of 64 km.

Home guard

American scientists are currently researching a tornado-detecting tool to give people early warning about tornadoes approaching their

Eye balled

On 25 May 1955, residents of Blackwell, Oklahoma, USA, witnessed a tornado that shone bright blue with an orange light at its centre. Scientists believe that this light was caused by glowing spheres of ball lightning active within the funnel of the cloud.

Man-made tornado

Fast-flying aircraft can actually create tornadoes. In Dec 1992 in Montana, Canada, a Cessna Citation 550 aircraft crashed when it was caught in a violently spinning mass of air left by the previous plane on its flight path.

High energy, low pressure

It is not only the explosive energy unleashed by tornadoes that makes them so destructive. It is the fact that they inflict their violence by means of a very precise strike point. They vacuum everything in their path. Even when their funnels do not come into contact with the

---

DATA BURST

ARE THERE ANY OTHER NAMES FOR TORNADOES?
A WHOLE HOST OF SLANG NAMES FOR TORNADOES HAVE DEVELOPED—IN ADDITION TO 'TWISTER', OTHER TYPES OF TORNADOES ARE ALSO KNOWN AS DUST-DEVILS, WHIRLWINDS AND LANDSPOUTS.

HOW ARE TORNADOES MEASURED?
TORNADOES ARE RATED ON THE FUJITA SCALE. THE SCALE IS BASED ON WIND SPEED INFERRED FROM STORM DAMAGE. THE WORST TORNADOES ARE F5, WHICH HAVE SPEEDS OF MORE THAN 480 KM/H. F6 TORNADOES ARE THEORETICAL, INCONCEIVABLE TORNADOES WITH SPEEDS OF MORE THAN 510 KM/H. THIS IS MORE THAN TWICE THE SPEED OF HIGH-PERFORMANCE SPORTS CARS.

WHAT IS THE WORST SORT OF DAMAGE THAT A TORNADO CAN INFLICT?
AN F5 TORNADO CAN HURL CARS MORE THAN 100 M, LIFT HOUSES OFF THE GROUND AND STRIP BARK OFF TREES.

HOW FAR CAN TORNADOES TRAVEL?
TORNADOES ARE CAPABLE OF TRAVELLING MORE THAN 150 KM ACROSS SEA AND LAND.

ARE TORNADOES MORE POWERFUL THAN HURRICANES?
A TYPICAL TORNADO WILL HAVE 10,000 KILOWATT-HOURS OF ENERGY, WHICH IS ONLY ONE-MILLIONTH THE ENERGY OF A HURRICANE. HOWEVER, THE EFFECT OF TORNADOES IS VERY LOCALIZED. THEY ARE MUCH MORE PRECISE, AND TOUCH WITH A SMALL STRIKE POINT. THE ENERGY DENSITY IS SIX TIMES HIGHER THAN A HURRICANE, MAKING IT THE STRONGEST STORM EFFECT IN NATURE.

WHERE DO TORNADOES GET THEIR ENERGY FROM?
THE MAIN SOURCE OF A TORNADO'S VIOLENT ENERGY DERIVES FROM THE LATENT HEAT CONTAINED IN THE WARM, MOIST AIR OF POWERFUL THUNDERSTORMS.

WHY ARE TORNADOES ROUND?
THE FORCE OF THE PARTIAL VACUUM AT THE CENTRE PULLS AIR IN. AT THE SAME TIME, THE CENTRIFUGAL FORCE OF THE TORNADO PUSHES AIR OUT.

WHY ARE THE TIPS OF TORNADOES DARK?
THEY CONTAIN THE DEBRIS THAT THE ROTATING VORTEX PICKS UP AS IT TRAVELS.

REACH SPEEDS OF 800 KM/H

RELEASING VAST ENERGY FROM A SMALL STRIKE POINT, TORNADOES UNLEASH A CONCENTRATED POWER SO FAST AND FURIOUS THAT THEY ARE SOME OF THE PLANET'S MOST EXTREME AND FEARED WEATHER PHENOMENA

homes. When a twister struck Huntsville, Alabama, USA, in 1989, killing 29 people, many of the survivors reported that they had felt earth tremors some time before the tornado's impact. The prototype tornado-detecting device works like a seismometer—the gadget devised for detecting the tremors of earthquakes.

ground, the twister's impact can still be frighteningly violent. Its whirling sucks the surrounding air into the tube, leaving a zone of very low air pressure outside. If this happens near a building, the massive and sudden drop in air pressure outside the walls caused by the twister's sucking effect leaves a pressure imbalance which

may cause the building to explode. In the USA, approximately 900 twisters strike every year, an average of almost three a day.

Old Testament twister

Tornadoes have been known and feared by people since ancient times. A story in the Old Testament book Ezekiel, Chapter 1, tells how

the prophet Elijah was snatched up to heaven in a lightning-filled tornado. "Behold, a whirlwind came out of the north, a great cloud, a fire infolding itself, and a brightness was about it. And out of the midst thereof was the colour of amber, out of the midst of fire."

Lift off

There have been curious reports of tornadoes snatching up objects off the ground as they travel across land. Strange showers of fish, frogs, lizards, even cats, have been reported. In 1978, in Norfolk, England, a flock of geese were picked up and dropped out of the cloud over a 45-km area.

Worst disaster
On 18 March 1925, 689 people, the most ever killed by a single tornado, perished in the states of Missouri and Illinois, USA, when a mighty tornado travelling at a top speed of 100 km/h forged a path of destruction 350 km long and 1.5 km wide.

Nashville
On 20 April 1998, two tornadoes tore through the heart of Nashville, Tennessee, USA. Such was the scale of the devastation that six counties were declared disaster areas by the vice president, Al Gore. In Nashville itself, the tops of buildings were blown clean off. Debris was thrown over a 10-km swathe, power lines lay in the street and glass shards dangled from high rise buildings. Fortunately, there were no fatal casualties. "I am absolutely astounded that there were not more deaths," the Nashville mayor, Phil Bredesen told reporters. "If this storm had hit five years ago, we'd probably have had three or four deaths," said Cecil Whaley, Director of the Natural Disaster Emergency Management team. "Ten years ago probably 20 to 25. Technology gives us the jump on approaching storms so we can alert people to take cover."

Lucky escapes
On 10 June 1958 in El Dorado, Kansas, USA, a woman was sucked through the window of her home by the force of a tornado and carried 18 m away, where she landed unscathed. In Oklahoma, USA, a house was reported to have been picked up by a tornado and set down again, twisted through 90°. One school building containing 85 pupils was totally demolished and the pupils hoisted up and carried 137 m over land.

Power pick up
Tornadoes are capable of sucking up into the air extremely heavy objects. One tornado was reported to have lifted five 70-tonne railway carriages off their tracks, one of which was deposited 24 m away.

Three times unlucky
The small western US town of Codell in Kansas must be the unluckiest community in the world when it comes to tornadoes. For three successive years, in 1916, 1917 and 1918, it was struck by a tornado on exactly the same day: 20 May. This phenomenon has never been known to happen elsewhere and has so far defied explanation by scientists.

Serial killers
In the space of just one afternoon and evening, on 11 April 1965, an incredible 37 tornadoes tore through the US states of Illinois, Iowa, Indiana, Michigan and Ohio. Their combined power killed 271 people and injured over 3,000 more. The total damage bill was thought to amount to $300 million.

Strung out
Sometimes whole strings of tornadoes can gather together. On 3 April 1974, a succession of tornadoes, 148 in total, whirled for a period of 21 hours, travelling through 13 American states. Moving from Alabama in the deep South, to Ontario in Canada, they left over 28,000 people homeless in their wake. This tornado epidemic became known subsequently as the '1974 Super Outbreak'.

Pigs can fly
Pigs were thrown almost a kilometre by a wild tornado that struck a farm in Nottinghamshire, UK, on 31 Aug 1997. The ferocious freak winds picked up huts containing about 40 animals at Michael Hewson's farm at Sutton-on-Trent, near Newark. "There were dead pigs everywhere," said Mr Hewson. "We saw these pig huts swirling round 100 ft [30 m] up in the air," a neighbour confirmed. "My son shouted that there were pigs being hurled around among chimney pots and tiles. The low air pressure was quite unbelievable."

Tornado mainstreet
'Tornado alley' is the popular name given to the stretch of land which runs from the Gulf of Mexico, through the states of Texas, Oklahoma, Kansas, Nebraska and the Dakotas. Cold dry air masses from Canada meet warm, wet air from the Gulf of Mexico. Each year, approximately 700 tornadoes occur in this region.

Noise and smell
People who have survived tornadoes have described the noise they make at close quarters as a high pitched scream, a hissing noise similar to that of a jet propelled plane. There is also a strong smell of ozone which one survivor described as being similar to that of rotting seaweed.

Warning signals
The imminent danger of a tornado can be detected by observing the shape and formation of a thundercloud. Those which have a bumpy underbelly warn of the churning conditions within. Each lump is a cell of circulating air that may give rise to a whirlwind. These dark bulges of cloud hang down from thunderclouds, giving an impression of clusters of cows' udders: hence their name, 'mammata' or 'festooned' cloud.

Radar detection
Tornadoes are notoriously erratic both in their origin and movement. But ever since it was introduced in 1977, the Doppler radar system has greatly improved the potential ability for meteorologists to track tornadoes. The radar works by picking up the swirling circular movements within supercell thunderstorms. In this way, the likelihood of a tornado forming can be predicted up to 25 minutes before it emerges from the base of a thunderstorm. The vigilant detective work of the National Severe Storms Laboratory is further aided by recording instruments situated on the ground and information supplied by high altitude air balloons.

TORNADOES 2
700 STRIKES A YEAR

HORROR IN FLORIDA

IN THE MIDDLE OF THE NIGHT, ON 24 FEB 1998, THE PEOPLE OF FLORIDA EXPERIENCED A HORROR OF EPIC PROPORTIONS. AT LEAST 12 TORNADOES RIPPED THROUGH THE STATE, FROM DAYTONA BEACH ON THE ATLANTIC COAST TO TAMPA BAY IN THE WEST, CAUSING DEVASTATION, CHAOS AND LOSS OF LIFE. DURING THE NIGHT OF WEATHER-GONE-MAD, HUNDREDS OF BUILDINGS WERE SMASHED TO PIECES, LEAVING THOUSANDS HOMELESS, AND AT LEAST 39 PEOPLE WERE KILLED, WITH MANY HUNDREDS MORE INJURED. THE TORNADOES TORE ROOFS OFF HOUSES AND DUMPED THEM IN FIELDS HUNDREDS OF METRES AWAY, AND PICKED UP CARS AS IF THEY WERE TOYS HURLING THEM INTO THE RUINS OF THEIR OWNERS' HOMES. A PICK-UP TRUCK WEIGHING OVER A TONNE WAS LEFT LODGED UP A TREE; DOCKS AND PIERS WERE HOISTED OUT OF LAKES AND RIVERS TO COME CRASHING DOWN ON TOP OF HOUSES; OAK AND PINE TREES WERE UPROOTED; FALLEN POWER LINES AND ABANDONED TRUCKS LITTERED THE MAIN HIGHWAY. IN THE MOST TRAGIC INCIDENT OF ALL, AN 18-MONTH-OLD TODDLER WAS RIPPED FROM HIS FATHER'S ARMS BY THE TORNADO'S FORCE AND SIMPLY DISAPPEARED.

JARGON

DUST DEVIL
AN ATMOSPHERIC SYSTEM SIMILAR TO, BUT SMALLER THAN, THE TORNADO. IT DEVELOPS ENERGY FROM THE GROUND UPWARDS AND OCCURS IN HOT ARID REGIONS

FUNNEL CLOUD
A TORNADO WHOSE FUNNEL'S TIP DOES NOT TOUCH THE GROUND

GUSTNADOES
A SORT OF STEALTHY TORNADO, WHICH IS WEAKER THAN NORMAL, AND WHICH IS UNDETECTABLE BY RADAR

HOOK ECHO
A PRESSURE AREA WITHIN THE CLOUDS THAT CAN BE PICKED UP BY RADAR AND USED TO WARN OF AN IMPENDING TORNADO

STORM-CHASER
GROUPS OF AMATEUR METEOROLOGISTS WHO RISK CHASING TORNADOES, COLLECTING SCIENTIFIC MATERIAL AND TAKING DRAMATIC PHOTO-SHOTS

TORNADO ALLEY
AN AREA OF CENTRAL USA, ENCOMPASSING NEBRASKA, KANSAS, OKLAHOMA, NORTH TEXAS AND SOUTH DAKOTA

WATERSPOUT
A WEAK FORM OF TORNADO WHICH OCCURS OVER WATER

RIGHT: DEVASTATION IN FLORIDA AS A TORNADO RIPS THROUGH A CAMP GROUND SWEEPING HOLIDAY HOMES OFF THE GROUND, 23 FEBRUARY 1998

IN TORNADO ALLEY

THE CONCENTRATED FORCE OF A TORNADO CAN CAUSE
UTTER CHAOS, RIPPING ROOFS OFF HOUSES, DERAILING
CARRIAGES FROM TRACKS AND CATAPULTING TRUCKS,
CARS, EVEN ANIMALS AND HUMAN BEINGS INTO THE AIR

Often confused with tidal waves, tsunamis are not caused by sea tide movement. These walls of water are created by the force of earthquakes or violent volcanic eruptions beneath the ocean floor that measure at least 6.5 on the Richter Scale. These seismic sea waves travel at great speed, from 160 to 1,100 km/h, and they can be as long as 200 km. They are about a metre high over deep water, but greatly increase in height over shallow water, and can raise the sea level in bays or estuaries by as much as 30 m. The term tsunami, which means 'harbour wave', derives from earthquake-prone Japan, where these occurences are facts of life.

Global effects

When the volcano Krakatau erupted on a small, uninhabited Indonesian island in 1883, the tsunami it created killed 36,000 people. Initially, the sea bed collapsed, creating a hole 8 km wide 200 m below sea level. A huge volume of water flowed into the hole and this formed a wave 30 m high that swept ashore on the neighbouring islands of Java and Sumatra, destroying 165 villages in the process. The effects of this eruption were so profound that a surge in the sea level could be recorded in the English Channel, 18,000 km away.

Wave upon wave

In 1946, a tremor beneath the Aleutian Trench off the coast of Alaska, USA, was detected at the Hawaiian Volcano Observatory 3,700 km away. Within 20 minutes, the lighthouse at Scotch Cap on Unimark Island, Alaska, had been swept away by a tsunami measuring 30 m. Later that day, a tsunami caused by the same tremor hit the town of Hilo, on Hawaii, uprooting buildings and destroying bridges. Subsequent waves took the inhabitants by surprise as cars and boats were thrown into the air and the debris from the first waves was picked up and carried on by those that followed. The seventh wave was the biggest and most devastating of all as it destroyed a seafront hotel and buckled the railway line.

TSUNAMIS

SEISMIC SEA WAVES CAN REACH

The narrow bays along the shallow Hawaiian coastline did not help, as they funnelled the waves ashore, concentrating the force of their impact. In all, 159 people were reported dead or missing.

Death and destruction

Another tsunami crossed the Pacific Ocean with devastating effects in March 1964. Triggered by an earthquake measuring 8.5 on the Richter Scale, the tsunami hit in Prince William Sound, Alaska, USA. More than $100 million of damage was done and 122 people were killed. A wave that struck Whittier, Alaska, measured 31 m and destroyed two sawmills, a railway depot and a

Concepción, where 200 people were killed by a tsunami that struck within 15 minutes of the earthquake. The tsunami reached Hilo, on Hawaii, USA, 14 hours later, where it still measured almost 3 m in height. The tsunami's impact was so powerful in Hilo that parking meters were bent double under its force. In total, the damage cost $500 million to repair.

Crossing the Pacific

In November 1952, an earthquake off the coast of the Kamchatka peninsula in Russia, measuring 8.2 on the Richter Scale, produced a tsunami that travelled hundreds of kilometres across the Pacific.

some warning, and the Seismic Sea Wave Warning System, co-ordinated from Hawaii, USA, in the Pacific Ocean, has been set up to do just that. Other smaller organizations in Japan, Siberia and Alaska also monitor the build-up of waves. One successful example of their work came in 1994, when an earthquake measuring 7.9 on the Richter Scale was picked up 950 km from Tokyo off the Japanese coast of Hokkaido. A warning was relayed via television within four minutes and, although there were 200 minor injuries when the tsunami struck, loss of life and other serious consequences were averted as a result.

SPEEDS OF 1,100 KM/H

TSUNAMIS ARE HUGE WAVES OF WATER, SOMETIMES OVER 30 M HIGH AND 200 KM LONG. GENERATED FAR OUT AT SEA, THEY CRASH ONTO LAND AT INCREDIBLY HIGH SPEEDS, PICKING UP AND DESTROYING ANYTHING IN THEIR PATH

Prehistoric waves

According to current theory, a gigantic meteorite slammed into the Earth 65 million years ago. The colossal effect of its impact could have generated tsunamis up to 1,000 metres high. Geologists have recently uncovered strange rock formations in the Yucatán region dating back to this time. Huge boulders resting alongside shallow-water rocks and fragments of fossilized trees suggest violent and turbulent currents passed over the land. Archaeologists in Peru have also found evidence of giant tsunamis. Before about 900 BC, the major centres of Peruvian civilization lay along the Pacific coast, but these subsequently gave way to mountain cultures. A theory that a giant tsunami wiped out the coastal villages is corroborated by the discovery by archaeologists in the 1980s of damaged buildings layered with silt.

small harbour. Four hours after the original tremor, a wave measuring 4 m hit Crescent City, California.

Catastrophe in Chile

An earthquake which struck off the Chilean coast in May 1960 and measured 8.5 on the Richter Scale, contributed to the deaths of up to 2,300 people. The effects were most devastating in the area between Isla Chilóe and the city of

Buildings were destroyed and streets flooded on Midway Island, some 3,000 km from the original source of the wave.

Warning signs

A large tsunami is often preceded by the recession of water away from a shore or harbour, but such signals are unpredictable and cannot be relied upon. The study of earthquake patterns can provide

Glow wave

Survivors of a nocturnal tsunami have reported that the wave glows as it approaches. This is probably due to the presence of luminous algae that have been disturbed by the earthquake's tremors, and then collect at the crest of the wave. Marine algae frequently emit light when disturbed and these cause the wake of passing ships to glow.

DATA-BURST

WHAT CAUSES TSUNAMIS?
THERE ARE SEVERAL MAIN CAUSES, INCLUDING AN UNDERWATER VOLCANIC ERUPTION, EARTHQUAKES, SUBMARINE FAULT RUPTURE AND THE IMPACT OF COSMIC BODIES. NUCLEAR BOMB TESTS AT BIKINI ATOLL HAVE ALSO BEEN KNOWN TO CREATE TSUNAMIS.

HOW DO TSUNAMIS BREAK ON LAND?
THE SHAPE OF A COASTLINE HAS A GREAT EFFECT ON A TSUNAMI AS IT HITS. NARROWING BAYS AND INLETS WILL FUNNEL THE WAVES INWARDS, BUILDING THEM EVEN HIGHER.

HOW MUCH ENERGY CAN A TSUNAMI HAVE?
AN EARTHQUAKE-GENERATED TSUNAMI CARRIES BETWEEN ONE AND TEN PERCENT OF THE TOTAL ENERGY OF THE EARTHQUAKE ITSELF.

HOW FAST CAN THEY TRAVEL?
THE SPEED OF TSUNAMIS DEPENDS ON THE DEPTH OF WATER, WITH DEEPER

WATER CREATING FASTER TSUNAMIS. IN DEEP OCEANS, TSUNAMIS CAN REACH SPEEDS OF MORE THAN 700 KM/H AT DEPTHS OF UP TO 5 KM.

WHERE DO TSUNAMIS OCCUR?
AREAS PARTICULARLY PRONE TO EARTHQUAKE-TRIGGERED TSUNAMIS INCLUDE THE HAWAIIAN ISLANDS, JAPAN AND THE ALEUTIAN ISLANDS.

HOW HIGH CAN TSUNAMIS REACH?
TSUNAMIS IN THE OPEN OCEAN ARE ABOUT 1 M HIGH. AS THEY APPROACH THE SHORE, THEIR ELEVATION INCREASES SHARPLY AND HEIGHTS OF 30 M HAVE BEEN RECORDED.

WHAT IS A BORE?
A MASSIVE WALL OF WATER FORMED WHEN A TSUNAMI IS CONCENTRATED IN A BAY OR RIVER MOUTH. SOME ARE GENERATED TIDALLY, SUCH AS THOSE SEEN ON THE RIVER SEINE IN FRANCE AND THE SOLWAY FIRTH BETWEEN SCOTLAND AND ENGLAND.

LEFT: WRECKAGE TO HOUSES CAUSED BY A TSUNAMI IN HILO, HAWAII · RIGHT: ENGRAVING OF THE ROYAL MAIL SHIP, LA PLANTA, BEING STRUCK BY A TIDAL WAVE IN THE WEST INDIES IN 1867

Although still a relative mystery to scientists, El Niño is known to occur when normal east-to-west trade winds are reversed during an exchange of air masses between the Pacific and Indian Oceans. These winds, travelling across the Equator towards South America, heat up the water and air in their path, causing violent rainstorms along the way. The subsequent heat from the water fuels a climatic event which throws the global weather machine into chaos, prompting random and unpredictable changes in weather all around the world. These range from powerful hurricanes and unexpected twisters to record-breaking temperatures and freak floods.

Violent death

The 1997/98 El Niño is the most violent this century, far exceeding the 1982 phenomenon in terms of the death and devastation it has caused. So far, at least 4,000 people have been killed as a direct consequence of the freak floods, storms, twisters, droughts and other disasters delivered by El Niño, and the death toll is set to rise severely. It is also the most expensive El Niño in history, currently clocking-up global damages in excess of $20 billion.

Weird weather

In California, USA, inhabitants suffered torrential rains, fatal landslides and extremely violent twisters during 1997, and in the state of Florida a spate of twisters killed more than 40 people. Many states reported record snowfall levels in the winter of 1997/98. South America, and Peru in particular, has been one of the areas hardest hit by the current El Niño. Massive flooding, heavy rainfall and snow have destroyed much of Peru's farming potential,

whilst the fishing industry has collapsed as fishing boats unable to brave the stormy seas, lie dormant on the shores. Mudslides have left many homeless, and havoc has been wrought by unexpected snowstorms in the Peruvian Andes. In a normally dry region of northern Peru, Piura, extraordinarily heavy rainfall led to the creation of a 20,000-km^2 lake. Brazil provides a pronounced illustration of the extreme effects of El Niño: August 1997 saw the worst flooding in 30 years, yet

GLOBAL EL NIÑO DAMAGES

there was also a record-breaking heatwave in the same month, and still more torrential rainfall in October. There is a serious threat of drought in the Amazonian rainforest, and this has already resulted in massively destructive forest fires in March 1998.

Crop failures in Africa
In East Africa, more than 25 million people are at risk of starvation following El Niño-induced crop failure and floods; Kenya and Zimbabwe are especially hard hit. The secondary effects of the current El Niño have extremely serious implications because the severe weather conditions have knocked out

skies, sometimes covering an area equivalent to half the size of the USA. These dangerously high levels of pollution have led to an increase in breathing-related disorders, and the lack of clean water has caused over 250 cholera deaths. Food shortages seem inevitable in India as staple rice crops are under threat from an El Niño-induced 30% drop in the annual monsoon rains. Severe flooding in Burma has left more than half a million people homeless.

Drought in the Pacific rim
Up to 1 million people are in serious danger of starving to death in Papua New Guinea because of a drought that has raged for more

$200 million lost in livestock in New Zealand.

Shortening the day
The extreme power of El Niño has been demonstrated by a team of scientists from NASA's Goddard Space Flight Center. They have discovered that El Niño has actually caused a global slowing down of average day lengths. Since El Niño reverses trade winds, making them blow eastwards, this means that the atmosphere spins in the same direction as the Earth's rotation, west to east. The atmosphere takes some of the momentum out of the Earth's natural rotation, and so the time taken for a day increases

EXCEED $20 BILLION

EL NIÑO IS A GENERATOR OF EXTREMELY CHAOTIC AND COMPLEX WEATHER PHENOMENA. THE 1997/8 EL NIÑO EVENT IS THE MOST DESTRUCTIVE THIS CENTURY, AND ITS EFFECTS HAVE BEEN FELT ALL ACROSS THE GLOBE

crucial water and sanitation systems, resulting in a rise in cholera and typhoid outbreaks.

Smog in Asia
Indonesia has suffered the worst drought in 50 years. The resulting forest fires have spewed colossal smog and smoke clouds into the

than a year, producing terrible living conditions and extremely high levels of malaria and typhoid. In Australia, violent forest fires and drought have caused widespread havoc, resulting in huge crop and livestock losses, with an estimated $1 billion grain shortfall in Australia, and up to

slightly. Using a bank of radio telescopes, the scientists have demonstrated that the 1997/98 El Niño has slowed down the Earth's rotation by just under one-2,000th of a second per day. This means that, on average, each day is 0.4 milliseconds longer than it was prior to the start of the 1997/98 El Niño.

Ice escapade in Antarctica
In April 1997, a huge 120-km^2 chunk of ice broke off the coast of Antarctica, leaving behind it a vast frozen canyon. Thought to be a consequence of global warming brought on by the extreme effect of the 1997/98 El Niño, the giant Larsen B Ice Shelf is beginning to break up and may cause sea levels to rise by several metres. Scientists warn that this event is nothing compared with what the future might hold, dismissing it as just 'an ice cube'. They predict that in the next three years a chunk of ice the size of Northern Ireland could break off from the Antarctic, with dramatic global consequences. Experts fear that, left unchecked, global warming will cause sea levels to rise by 45 cm every 100 years. This, combined with stormy weather, could drown islands in the Pacific and flood the Nile delta.

DATA BURST

WHY THE NAME EL NIÑO?
EL NIÑO, WHICH IS SPANISH FOR BOY-CHILD, WAS THE NAME GIVEN BY PERUVIAN FISHERMEN TO THE STRONG WIND AND SEA CURRENTS WHICH THEY WITNESSED NEAR CHRISTMAS IN AN EL NIÑO YEAR. THE BOY-CHILD THUS REFERS TO THE BABY JESUS.

WHAT IS LA NIÑA?
LA NINA IS AN EFFECT OPPOSITE TO EL NIÑO, AND PART OF THE OSCILLATION THAT IS THE GLOBAL WEATHER MACHINE. IT IS AN ABNORMAL COOLING OF THE SEA WATER TEMPERATURE IN THE PACIFIC, OCCURRING AFTER AN EL NIÑO. ITS EFFECTS, FOCUSED ON THE WESTERN PACIFIC, CAN STILL BE WIDESPREAD AND DEVASTATING.

WHAT CAUSES EL NIÑO?
ALTHOUGH SCIENTISTS ARE CREATING COMPLEX MODELS OF HOW EL NIÑO OPERATES, THERE IS STILL SOME UNCERTAINTY AS TO EXACTLY WHAT TRIGGERS IT. MANY THEORIES, SUCH AS SUNSPOT ACTIVITY AND VOLCANIC THERMAL VENTS, HAVE BEEN PUT FORWARD. HOWEVER, THE SYSTEM IS TOO COMPLEX TO BE ATTRIBUTED TO A

SINGLE PHENOMENON. EL NIÑO IS CAUSED BY A COMPLEX INTERPLAY BETWEEN THE OCEAN AND THE ATMOSPHERE, AND AS YET IT IS IMPOSSIBLE TO SAY EXACTLY HOW THE INTERACTIONS FEED INTO EACH OTHER.

CAN EL NIÑO HAVE POSITIVE EFFECTS?
WHILE THE SHEER CHAOS AND DESTRUCTION EASILY OUTWEIGH ANY POSSIBLE BENEFITS, THERE CAN BE SOME USEFUL RESULTS. THE EASTERN USA COULD POSSIBLY EXPECT LESS VIOLENT HURRICANES DURING AN EL NIÑO EVENT, WHILE FISH THAT HAVE BEEN DRIVEN FROM THE COAST OF PERU COULD BE FARMED IN CHILE. OTHER MINOR BENEFITS COULD INCLUDE AN ENHANCED SKIING SEASON FOR THOSE AREAS WITH A GREATER ABUNDANCE OF SNOW.

HOW FREQUENT ARE EL NIÑOS?
EL NIÑOS CAN OCCUR UP TO 30 TIMES EACH CENTURY. HOWEVER, ONLY A VERY SMALL NUMBER OF THESE ARE LARGE AND POWERFUL ENOUGH TO CAUSE SIGNIFICANT DAMAGE ON A WORLDWIDE SCALE.

JARGON

EL NIÑO
SPECIFICALLY, A BODY OF WARM WATER THAT MOVES EASTWARDS DUE TO A REVERSAL OF TRADE WINDS BETWEEN THE PACIFIC AND INDIAN OCEANS

ENSO
[EL NIÑO/SOUTHERN OSCILLATION] THE NAME FOR THE COMBINED OCEAN AND ATMOSPHERE INTERACTION THAT CAUSES GLOBAL CHAOS

LA NIÑA
AN ANTI-EL-NIÑO, THIS BODY OF COOLER WATER IN THE PACIFIC OFTEN FOLLOWS CLOSELY AFTER AN EL NIÑO EVENT

NAO
[NORTH ATLANTIC OSCILLATION] AN EL-NIÑO-LIKE PHENOMENON CENTRED IN THE ATLANTIC

SOI
[SOUTHERN OSCILLATION INDEX] USED AS AN ATMOSPHERIC INDEX FOR EL NIÑO, THE SOI IS CALCULATED ON THE DIFFERENCE IN PRESSURE BETWEEN DARWIN AND TAHITI

SST
[SEA SURFACE TEMPERATURE] A CRUCIAL MEASUREMENT IN THE TRACKING OF EL NIÑO

TAO
[TROPICAL ATMOSPHERE OCEAN] A NETWORK OF BUOYS USED TO MONITOR EL NIÑO, SET UP BY THE TOGA PROGRAM

TELECONNECTION
A REMOTE CONNECTION BETWEEN CLIMATIC EVENTS. EL NIÑO CAUSES A NETWORK OF TELECONNECTED ANOMALIES TO BE DISPERSED THROUGHOUT THE WORLD

TOGA
[TROPICAL OCEANS AND GLOBAL ATMOSPHERE PROGRAM] SET UP IN 1985, THIS INTERNATIONAL PROJECT MONITORS ENSO EVENTS

Funny man Al
An unfortunate casualty of the 1997/98 El Niño phenomenon is an inhabitant of San Luis Obispo county in California, USA. Alfonso Niño, has been plagued with calls accusing him of playing havoc with the weather. Alfonso, better known as Al Niño, has a name with an uncanny resemblance to the warm water phenomenon in the eastern Pacific. Most of the callers are good-natured, although a few are seriously angry. Niño was once awakened at 2 am by an enraged, foul-mouthed woman complaining about the weather. Niño, a retired Navy man, replied in suitably nautical language. Later he said: "It's always something like, 'Why are you doing this?', and I say, 'Well, I didn't really have anything else to do. I thought maybe it would be kind of fun.' I usually joke around with them a bit."

LEFT: WATER FROM THE RIBERIA RIVER FLOODS THE CITY OF ELDORADO IN THE SOUTH OF BRAZIL'S SAN PAULO STATE ON JANUARY 24, 1997, LEAVING 13,000 PEOPLE HOMELESS

The 1982 El Niño

This was the most violent El Niño this century up until the 1997/98 outbreak. Some scientists suggest that in purely physical terms it was in fact stronger. Although the human and material cost was not as great, it was considerable, with total damages reaching US $10–15 billion and approximately 2,000 dead. One of the most severely hit areas was the west coast of California, which suffered a repeated onslaught of storms, giving way to widespread flooding, mudslides and the washing away of beaches. In contrast, the east coast saw a warm, wet spring. Violent El Niño-related phenomena such as drought, dust storms and forest fires affected huge areas of Africa, Australia and Indonesia.

Inca empire falls

In about AD 1500, there was reportedly a mass sacrifice of 80 people by the Incas. Research has suggested that the executions were carried out during a violent El Niño year by people who wanted to placate angry gods. El Niño may have contributed to the fall of the Incan empire as the onset of rain ensured food supplies for the horses of the conquistadors, who were fighting a long battle away from their native Spain. This was recorded in some of the first written documents about El Niño, scribed by explorers in 1567. The logbooks of the Spanish conquistador Francisco Pizarro noted increased vegetation in northern Peru in 1525–26, but the term El Niño was not used.

The Atlantic El Niño

While El Niño is triggered by a reversal of trade winds in the Pacific, in recent years there has been some research carried out on a similar phenomenon centred on the Atlantic Ocean. This is called the North Atlantic Oscillation, or NAO. When a high NAO is coupled with a mild winter, there can be chaos throughout many parts of Europe and Asia. The NAO can affect vine and olive crops in western Europe, sandstorms in the Sahara and the quality of fishing in northern Europe. It has been cited as the cause for heightened cyclone activity in the northern hemisphere, and has been considered a contributory factor in global warming. The North Atlantic Oscillation phenomenon has even been accredited with helping Hitler lose World War II. The logic behind this is that a negative NAO in the 1940s resulted in some extremely cold European winters during the war, and this may well have delayed Hitler's planned assault on France, and obstructed his attempted invasion of Russia.

J'ACCUSE EL NIÑO

SOME HISTORIANS BELIVE THAT EL NIÑO MAY HAVE HELPED TRIGGER THE FRENCH REVOLUTION. AN EL NIÑO EVENT IN 1787–88 BROUGHT WITH IT DEVASTATING CROP FAILURES, WHICH CERTAINLY CONTRIBUTED TO THE UNREST IN FRANCE DURING THE LATE 18TH CENTURY. SCIENTISTS AND HISTORIANS HAVE SUGGESTED A CONNECTION BETWEEN THE EL NIÑO PHENOMENON AND OTHER KEY EPISODES IN HUMAN HISTORY. FOR EXAMPLE, CROP FAILURE AND POOR WEATHER MAY HAVE ENCOURAGED THE SPREAD OF DISEASE, SUCH AS THE BLACK DEATH THAT STRUCK EUROPE IN THE MIDDLE AGES, OR THE OUTBREAKS OF MALARIA IN JAVA AND OTHER TROPICAL AREAS DURING THE 17TH CENTURY. ANOTHER CROP FAILURE THAT MAY HAVE BEEN EXACERBATED BY EL NIÑO WAS THE POTATO BLIGHT IN IRELAND IN THE MID 19TH CENTURY. A STRONG EL NIÑO IN 1845. MAY HAVE CONTRIBUTED TO THE CROP FAILURE, TRIGGERING THE TERRIBLE POTATO FAMINE IN IRELAND THAT YEAR.

EL NIÑO 2
1982 EL NIÑO LEAVES

Sealife suffers

As well as causing severe damage to natural environments and to human civilization, El Niño also affects lifeforms throughout the world. In addition to the obvious casualties of twisters, hurricanes and floods, El Niño has been a bane to many species of sealife. The cause of this is the abnormally warm water found near the Peruvian coast in an El Niño year. The warm water at the surface blocks the colder deep water, which is where many nutrients are to be found. As a consequence small fish, such as anchovies and sardines, are driven away from the warm ocean surfaces, and the many species of sealife that depend on them for their main food supply are left without any means of survival. Many birds and larger fish are either forced to move to other regions or are left to die. It is said that the gas from decaying sealife blackens the hulls of ships that pass through the Pacific.

Monitoring El Niño

Ice-core samples, tree rings, river flood data, corals, fish remains and marine sediments have all proved valuable resources for geologists and palaeontologists in reconstructing past El Niños, while historical documents have provided a good source of secondary and circumstantial evidence. However, El Niños can now be monitored with sophisticated equipment. Satellite images, for example, provide useful information about Pacific climatic variations. In addition, a network of 70 buoys has been placed as a matrix to measure varied ocean data such as sea surface temperature, wind and humidity. Although statistical surveys of past El Niños can be used to look for any emerging patterns, the sheer complexity of the phenomenon means that long-term forecasts will always be subject to the unpredictable character of El Niño.

Survival of the fittest

Research undertaken into the impact of El Niño on the native wildlife and vegetation of Australia has produced some fascinating results. It has been demonstrated that many animal species there have evolved to cope with the extreme variation and unpredictability of the weather caused by El Niño. For example, the red kangaroo and the long-haired rat are two species that have adapted to conditions where varied rainfall is likely. The fact that up to 30% of all Australian birds are nomadic may be a survival tactic inspired by El Niño. Plants have similarly adapted strategies to cope with El Niño, such as high levels of tolerance of drought, taller than average trees, and fire-resistant and fire-dependant plants. These evolutionary survival techniques mean that the flora and fauna of Australia can survive the severe droughts, forest fires and irregular rainfall brought about by El Niño.

LEFT: BEACH DWELLINGS AT MALIBU BATTERED BY AN EL NIÑO STORM, 1983 · RIGHT: A SECTION OF HIGHWAY ON THE WEST COAST OF AMERICA, WASHED AWAY BY THE 1981/82 EL NIÑO

2,000 PEOPLE DEAD

THROUGHOUT HISTORY THE DRAMATIC CLIMATIC CHANGES
BROUGHT BY EL NIÑO HAVE LEFT A TRAIL OF DRAMA AND
DISASTER IN THEIR WAKE, RANGING FROM REVOLUTIONS
AND FAMINES TO FLOODS, MUDSLIDES AND STORMS

Typhoon are strong tropical storms regionally specific to the north-west Pacific. They are classified by the 'hurricane-force' winds which blow at a minimum sustained speed of 118 km/h, but can sustain speeds approaching 320 km/h. Typhoons are named after the Chinese for great wind —'tai fung'—which was used to describe any violent storm originating in the China seas. It also derives from the Greek mythological monster Typhon, the father of storm winds.

Flying machine
A typhoon resembles a huge whirlpool, a gigantic mass of revolving moist air with a disc-like shape which can be tens of kilometres high and hundreds of kilometres wide. Fuelled by an incessant supply of latent heat released from condensation in ascending moist air, it is akin to a giant travelling heat engine. Frequently the engine 'lets off steam' in the form of heavy precipitation and violent winds which worsen as the centre of the storm draws nearer. Often this rain is torrential and causes severe flooding.

Hyperactive weather
The Philippines has more than its fair share of ferocious weather and extreme seismic action. Not only are there 200 volcanoes and fault lines generating at least five earthquakes a day, but the area is also besieged by some 19 typhoons every year, of which five are destructive. In the 10-year period between 1985 and 1995 a total of 215 storms, typhoons and tropical depressions hit the Philippines. In 1993, a record 32 typhoons blew through the islands, taking the alphabet of names beyond full circle, and killing 756 people. In 1995, typhoons caused damage to agriculture and infrastructure to the tune of approximately $5.1 billion. The super-typhoon Rosing was responsible for two-thirds of this damages bill, as well as the death of 700 people. Typhoon Ike, which struck on 2 Sept 1984 unleashed winds of up to 220 km/h, left 1,120,000 homeless and killed 1,363.

TYPHOONS

TYPHOON WINDS GUST AT

MANGLED MONGOLS - THE LEGEND OF THE KAMIKAZE

KAMIKAZE LEGEND REFERS TO THE 'DIVINE WINDS', OR TYPHOONS, THAT DISPERSED INVADING MONGOL FLEETS IN THE 13TH CENTURY. LEGEND HAS IT THAT WHEN KUBLA KHAN, THE GRANDSON OF GHENGIS KHAN, SENT A FLEET OF 900 SHIPS TO INVADE THE JAPANESE ISLAND OF KYUSHU IN 1274, A TYPHOON WHIPPED UP A STORM AND SANK MOST OF THE FLEET, FORCING THE REST TO RETREAT. UNDAUNTED BY SUCH MISFORTUNE, KUBLA KHAN SENT ANOTHER, EVEN BIGGER FLEET COMPRISING 400 SHIPS CARRYING 100,000 SOLDIERS TO INVADE KYUSHU IN AUGUST 1281. THIS TIME A TITANIC TYPHOON UNLEASHED ITSELF UPON THE INVADERS, WIPING OUT ALMOST THE WHOLE FLEET. THE UNLUCKY FEW WHO MADE IT ASHORE WERE SUMMARILY SLAUGHTERED BY THE WAITING JAPANESE TROOPS.

JARGON

ANTI-CYCLONE
AN AREA OF HIGH ATMOSPHERIC PRESSURE WHERE WINDS SPIRAL OUTWARD RATHER THAN INWARD

CYCLONE
A TROPICAL CYCLONE REGIONALLY SPECIFIC TO THE INDIAN OCEAN. SUCH CYCLONES, HOWEVER, ARE NOT NAMED

DIRECT HIT
WHEN A TYPHOON PASSES WITHIN 100 KM OF A TOWN OR CITY

SUPER TYPHOON
DESCRIBES TYPHOONS THAT SUSTAIN WINDS OF AT LEAST 240 KM/H (THE EQUIVALENT OF A CATEGORY 4 OR 5 HURRICANE ON THE SAFFIR-SIMPSON SCALE)

Deadly typhoon hits China
On 21 Aug 1994, China's eastern province of Zhejiang was devastated by Typhoon Fred. Travelling at 33 m/sec, Fred was the region's worst storm in 160 years. At the same time, floods besieged northern China and drought raged in the south and central regions. Floods claimed 4,300 lives in China in 1994, and Typhoon Fred killed at least 1,000 in a single city (Wenzhou). The airport at Wenzhou was closed as water rose to 1.3 m on the runway.

Fast and furious
Typhoon Paka blew through Guam, a US territory in the Pacific Ocean, on 17 Dec 1997, with sustained winds of 224 km/h and gusts of up to 320 km/h. Amazingly, out of a population of 150,000, only one injury was reported. However, Paka did destroy 20% of homes on the island, causing property damage in excess of $100 million. With the ruinous winds came considerable rain, giving rise to flooding and heightened storm surges. Some 1,400 people had to evacuate to higher ground as waves 12 m high engulfed low-lying areas.

SPEEDS OF 320 KM/H

RAGING TYPHOON WINDS CAN LASH THE NORTH-WEST PACIFIC COAST UP TO 35 TIMES IN ONE YEAR, CAUSING AN ONSLAUGHT OF FEROCIOUS STORMS, TIDAL WAVES AND RECORD FLOODS OFTEN LASTING FOR WEEKS AT A TIME

Record death toll
The cyclone of 12 Nov 1970 in East Pakistan (now Bangladesh) was one of the worst in recorded history. Between 300,000 and 500,000 people were killed by a combination of wind and water. Ferocious winds of up to 240 km/h and a tidal wave some 15 m high lashed the East Pakistan coast, the Ganges Delta, and several of the offshore islands.

Wayne's whirl
Typhoon Wayne lasted nearly three weeks, and in that time underwent two cycles of intensification and weakening, and made four major directional changes. Starting near the west Philippines coast on 18 Aug 1986, Wayne initially blew in the direction of Hong Kong. Two days later, it travelled through Taiwan and then subsided momentarily, apparently gathering momentum for its first U-turn, back towards the South China Sea. Another U-turn on 26 Aug took Wayne back in the direction of Taiwan. As Wayne weakened between 28 Aug and 3 Sept, it completed its third U-turn, heading back towards Hong Kong, and making landfall near Haikou on the island of Hainan and then reaching Vietnam on 6 Sept before finally dissipating.

Typhoon alley
This stretch of the western Pacific bordered by the Philippines, Taiwan and southern Japan possesses a combination of climatic conditions which allow the atmospheric heat engine to operate in the most effective way for typhoons to occur. Through this corridor, or 'typhoon alley', typhoons blow all year round, although they are most frequent between June and November.

DATA-BURST

HOW ARE THE SIZE AND INTENSITY OF TYPHOONS MEASURED?
INTENSITY IS A MEASURE OF EITHER MAXIMUM SUSTAINED WINDS OR CENTRAL PRESSURE. SIZE REFERS TO THE RADIUS SPANNED BY THE TYPHOON'S WINDS.

WHICH IS THE MOST POWERFUL TYPHOON ON RECORD?
TYPHOON NANCY WHICH STRUCK THE NORTH-WEST PACIFIC REGION ON 12 SEPT 1961 IS THOUGHT TO BE THE MOST INTENSE TYPHOON TO DATE, WITH A CENTRAL PRESSURE OF 870 MB AND ESTIMATED SURFACE SUSTAINED WINDS OF 85 M/SEC.

CAN TYPHOONS HAVE ANY POSITIVE EFFECTS?
THE RAIN FROM TYPHOONS HELPS THE WATER SUPPLY IN EAST ASIA, PROVIDING ESSENTIAL IRRIGATION FOR RICE PADDY FIELDS. TYPHOONS CAN PROVIDE RELIEF FROM THE OPPRESSIVE HEAT OF A LONG SUMMER.

IN SOCIETIES OF FAST PACE AND HIGH TENSION THEY CAN BRING A WELCOME DAY OF REST.

HOW LONG DO TYPHOONS LAST?
ONCE FORMED, TROPICAL CYCLONES CAN HAVE A LIFESPAN VARYING FROM A FEW DAYS TO A FEW WEEKS. OVER THE WESTERN NORTH PACIFIC AND THE SOUTH CHINA SEA, ONLY ABOUT HALF, ON AVERAGE, MANAGE TO ATTAIN TYPHOON INTENSITY.

IS THE ANNUAL NUMBER OF TROPICAL CYCLONES ON THE INCREASE?
THERE HAS BEEN NO SIGNIFICANT CHANGE IN THE TOTAL FREQUENCY OF TROPICAL STORMS OVER THE LAST 55 YEARS (1944–1998).

HOW POWERFUL ARE TYPHOONS?
THE MECHANICAL POWER GENERATED BY A TYPHOON IS IN THE ORDER OF 20 MILLION MEGAWATTS. IN ONE DAY, THIS EQUATES TO ABOUT 20 YEARS' SUPPLY OF ELECTRICITY FOR HONG KONG.

LEFT: VIEW FROM SHUTTLE OF THE EYE OF TYPHOON ODESSA AS IT SPINS 300 KM EAST OF THE JAPANESE ISLAND OF OKINAWA · RIGHT: MAP SHOWING TYPHOON ALLEY

Half the world's population depends for their survival on the seasonal reversal of winds, known as the monsoonal circulation. For six months of the year, the countries of South-east Asia are exposed to drought. Then, suddenly and violently, torrential rains burst forth to mark the start of the monsoon and the rainy season. The cause of the monsoon circulation lies in the unequal heating of the tropical continents and oceans as the overhead sun swings back and forth in its annual cycle between two hemispheres. Monsoons also occur in Africa but those in South-east Asia are the strongest, with greatest impact in India, Bangladesh, and Thailand.

Monsoon formation

The most extreme monsoon—the Indian—is formed in early summer. By June, humidity rises above 70%, leading to the torrential rain synonymous with monsoons. By October, northerly winds cover India, eventually bringing dry, sunny periods after the season of autumn rain. The West African monsoon, less severe than its Indian counterpart, is caused by the interaction of the south-westerly wind and the Harmattan which blows from the Sahara. A similar meeting of opposing wind systems causes the Malaysian–Australian monsoon. In May, gusty outflows of air from the Siberian anticyclone weather system are replaced by opposite south-westerly winds. The shallow monsoon stream formed between these weather systems hits the steep slopes of regions such as the Philippines where it is cooled and releases its moisture in heavy downpours of rain.

Intense downfalls

Monsoon rains are characterized by their extremity. Deluges release fierce downpours of rainwater. The town of Cherrapunji, near the border of Bangladesh, can claim to be one of the wettest places in the world. It is annually lashed by a 2,730-mm average of rain. In 1899, this town was soaked by 16,305 mm of monsoon rain during the month of July. In the same month in 1915, 897 mm of rain fell in just 24 hours.

MONSOONS

5,000 MM OF RAIN CAN FALL IN

SPEEDY WINDS

MONSOONS ARE RELIED UPON TO PROVIDE SEASONAL WATERING OF DRY LAND. IN DAYS GONE BY, THEY HAVE PROVIDED OTHER UNIQUE BENEFITS: DURING THE PERIOD OF SPANISH COLONIAL RULE IN THE PHILIPPINES, MERCHANTS DEPENDED ON MONSOON WINDS TO MAINTAIN VITAL LINKS TO THE OUTSIDE WORLD. THE WINDS BLEW THEIR TRADING SHIPS, SUCH AS THE *MANILA GALLEON*, ACROSS THE PACIFIC TO ACAPULCO IN NEW SPAIN IN THREE MONTHS—FIVE MONTHS LESS THAN THE VOYAGE USUALLY TOOK. AS A RESULT, GOODS WERE COLLECTED FROM ALL OVER THE PHILIPPINES TO BE SOLD IN MEXICO AND PERU, AND VITAL SUPPLIES OF FLOUR, OIL, WINE AND SALTED FISH BROUGHT BACK TO THE COLONISTS. IF THE SHIPS HAD FAILED TO RETURN, THE COLONIES WOULD HAVE FACED ECONOMIC RUIN.

Flood management

In India and Bangladesh water is a precious commodity. The River Ganges in India pours over 70,000 cubic metres of water per second into Bangladesh. The two governments negotiate with each other as to how this water supply should be used. If the massive influx is not carefully managed, the waters can kill. In this region of the world, 550 million people suffer from poor health and when the monsoon floods arrive, the water can spread diarrhoea and cholera. Farmers in Bangladesh also face the threat of their soil being washed away if they do not find ways to minimize the destructive effects of the rain.

JARGON

ANTI-CYCLONE
A WEATHER SYSTEM IN WHICH AIR SPIRALS SLOWLY AROUND A HIGH-PRESSURE CENTRE

EMBRYO MONSOON
A PART-MONSOON THAT DEVELOPS IN REGIONS AT LATITUDES TOO HIGH FOR TRUE MONSOONS TO FORM

HARMATTAN
A VERY DRY, DUSTY WIND THAT BLOWS OVER THE SAHARA WEST AND SOUTH-WEST TOWARDS THE AFRICAN COAST, CONTRIBUTING TO THE AIR PRESSURE THAT CREATES THE WEST AFRICAN MONSOON

LATITUDE
THE DISTANCE NORTH OR SOUTH OF THE EQUATOR, MEASURED IN DEGREES. ONE DEGREE OF LATITUDE IS ABOUT 110 KM

MONEX
REGIONAL INVESTIGATIONS INTO MONSOONAL WEATHER

MONSOON STATION
AN AREA, SUCH AS BOMBAY, WHERE THERE ARE SEASONS OF MONSOON WEATHER IN BOTH SUMMER AND WINTER

SUBTROPICAL JET STREAM
A STRONG, NEAR JET-FORCE WIND THAT FORMS AT HEIGHTS OF AROUND 15,000 M AND CARRIES WITH IT TYPICALLY MONSOONAL WEATHER

INDIA'S WET SEASON

MONSOONS BRING RAINY SEASONS TO DRY LANDS. THESE SQUALLY WEATHER SYSTEMS, WHICH LASH ASIA AND PARTS OF AFRICA, BRING TORRENTIAL RAINS AND HOWLING WINDS LEADING TO WIDESPREAD FLOODING

Sudden disaster

Some of the most spectacular rain clouds of the Indian monsoon occur over the Western Ghats, where 2,000–5,000 mm of rain falls during the monsoon season. Rains of this intensity can be disastrous. In Sept 1978 in the state of Bengal, India, around 1,300 people drowned and 1.3 million homes were destroyed when monsoons swelled rivers to

flooding point. A total of 15 million people were made homeless and the damage was estimated at a minimum of £6.7 million. An even worse monsoon tragedy hit Thailand in 1983. Flooding led to as many as 100,000 people contracting water-borne diseases. Around 15,000 people had to be evacuated from their homes and the total damage amounted to £264 million.

As part of one water management project, farmers gather silt from flooded and deforested regions once the rain has subsided and use it to create fertile banks where they can replant their crops.

Whirlwind romance

In India, the monsoon season is an integral part of culture and tradition. In Hindu myth, the god Indra did his people a great service

when he killed the dragon who prevented the monsoon from breaking. Without this, the land would have been subjected to continual monsoon downpours. As it is, the monsoon provides a temporary period of extreme weather. In India, this time of wild weather is the time for throwing caution to the wind: the monsoon season is traditionally a time for courtship.

DATA-BURST

WHERE DOES THE WORD MONSOON COME FROM?
THE WORD DERIVES FROM THE ARABIC WORD 'MAUSIN' WHICH MEANS SEASON. IT WAS ARAB GEOGRAPHERS WHO FIRST GAVE ACCURATE DESCRIPTIONS OF MONSOON CYCLES. A BOOK, WRITTEN IN 1554 BY SIDI ALI, ABOUT THE NAVIGATION OF THE INDIAN OCEAN, GIVES THE COMMENCING DATE OF EACH MONSOON AT 50 DIFFERENT PLACES. IT WAS AN ARAB PILOT WHO GUIDED THE PORTUGUESE EXPLORER VASCA DA GAMA FROM EAST AFRICA TO INDIA IN 1498.

WHAT IS A MONSOON FOREST?
A MONSOON FOREST IS AN AREA OF OPEN WOODLAND IN TROPICAL AREAS WHERE THERE IS A LONG DRY SEASON FOLLOWED BY A HEAVY DOWNPOUR OF RAIN. A MONSOON FOREST IS TYPIFIED BY TALL TEAK TREES AND THICKETS OF BAMBOO WHICH DROP LEAVES DURING THE DRY SEASON AND BUD LEAVES AT THE BEGINNING OF THE RAINY SEASON.

WHERE ARE MONSOONS MOST FREQUENT?
SOUTHERN ASIA HAS THE MOST FREQUENT MONSOONS, BUT THEY ALSO OCCUR IN WESTERN AFRICA, NORTHERN AUSTRALIA AND ALONG THE PACIFIC COAST OF CENTRAL AMERICA.

WHAT IS THE HIGHEST RECORDED MONSOON RAINFALL?
AT CILAOS ON RÉUNION ISLAND 1,870 MM OF RAIN FELL WITHIN A 24 HOUR PERIOD ON 15 MARCH 1952.

WHEN WAS THE WORST FLOODING CAUSED BY A MONSOON?
IN BANGLADESH IN 1988, TWO-THIRDS OF THE COUNTRY WAS FLOODED BY MONSOON RAINS MAKING 28 MILLION PEOPLE HOMELESS.

HOW DO WE KNOW ABOUT MONSOONS?
THE MONSOON EXPERIMENT BEGAN IN 1978 AS A SERIES OF INVESTIGATIONS AND OBSERVATIONS WITHIN PART OF THE GLOBAL WEATHER EXPERIMENT.

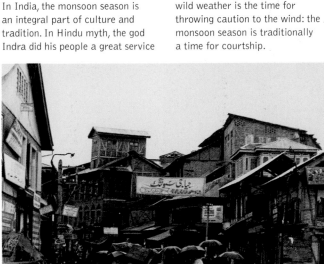

LEFT: TRAFFIC STRUGGLES THROUGH THE MONSOON FLOODWATER, TAMIL NADU, INDIA · RIGHT: PEDESTRIANS CROSS A BRIDGE TO THE OLD TOWN DURING A MONSOON, SRINAGAR, KASHMIR

Snow is a solid form of water that crystallizes in the atmosphere. Whereas some parts of the world are permanently snow-covered, others experience snowfall only intermittently. Snow can become treacherous in temperate regions where it can cause havoc to transport systems and threaten livestock. In these regions, the problem of snow is compounded because it often arrives in a blizzard and departs as an avalanche or in a sudden thaw. In places more used to snow, humans have found ways of utilizing its unique properties. Inuit tribes in the Arctic region, for example, use the insulating properties of snow to create their igloo homes.

White storm
A blizzard is a snowstorm where wind causes drifting on the ground and extremely poor visibility. The US weather service defines a

Chicago blanketed
The city of Chicago in the USA experiences snowstorms relatively frequently. A mammoth snowstorm took place there in 1967. Snow began to fall on Thursday 26 Jan and continued through to the early hours of Friday morning. Periodic snowfalls over the next 10 days caused havoc. The total accumulation of snow measured 58 cm and there were 2-m drifts. Cars, buses and planes all ground to a complete halt and schools and

Most brutal blizzard
Five hundred people died in a monumental winter storm that traversed the entire East Coast of the USA on 12 March 1993. A meteorologist described it as 'a storm with the heart of a blizzard and the soul of a hurricane'. Total damage amounted to $1.2 billion.

Snowy peaks
Snow falls over every continent in the world, but in areas of low latitudes it only falls on the tops

six-sided symmetry of every snow crystal in a pamphlet in 1611. Snow crystals come in an infinite variety of pattern and shape although they all form around a basic hexagonal symmetry. There are many different types: thin plates, hollow prismatic columns, needles, dendrites and stellars all result from complicated sequences of evaporation, condensation, sublimation and deposition. Temperature and humidity are the influencing factors that shape snow

75 TONNES OF SNOW

of high mountains. Snow lies on the ground whenever the air temperature is below 3°C. When air temperature is near this key figure, altitude can make a surprising difference to the weather. On 3 Nov 1958, rain fell on 34th Street in New York while guards on the top of the Empire State building were making snowballs. In latitudes of lower than 40°, snow falls wherever there are mountains high enough to project above the freezing level of the atmosphere. Among such mountains are Mt Fujiyama in Japan, (33°N); Mount Teide in Tenerife (28°N) and on the equator, Mt Kenya, which stands 5,199 m high.

Dry and wet snow
Dry snow is made up of very cold crystals that do not bond together and remain small. Dry snow is typical of continental land masses which are well removed from the sea. Particularly fine powdery snow can penetrate the smallest cracks, blowing under doors and around windows. Dry snow is the best for skiing because it does not clog under the surface. Wet snow, on the other hand, occurs at temperatures high enough to bond large snow flakes. Wet snow is ideal for making snowballs because the flakes bind together under pressure.

Crystal diversity
The Swedish historian Olaus Magnus (1490–1558) was the first man to study individual snow crystals, but it was the German astronomer Johannes Kepler (1571–1630) who described the

crystals. The nature of the nuclei on which the crystal forms can also affect their composition. Snow flakes may attain a size of several centimetres in diameter. At Bratsk, Siberia, in 1971, giant snowflakes measuring 30 cm were recorded.

Squeaky snow
As temperatures fall, so snow crystals become more resilient. Snow 'squeaks' when it is trodden on and the sound becomes sharper the lower the temperature falls. Sound travels faster in colder weather. During World War II, this fact helped the Russians predict the approach of the German troops in the 1941 offensive. The marching armies could be heard from a great distance because of the intense cold and plunging temperatures.

JARGON

AVALANCHE
AVALANCHES OCCUR WHEN A CHANGE IN TEMPERATURE CAUSES SNOW PARTICLES TO LOOSEN AND SLIDE DOWN HILL

CIRRUS CLOUD
THE TYPE OF CLOUD IN WHICH SNOW CRYSTALS CAN FORM

DIAMOND DUST
A GLITTERING, FALLING ICE CRYSTAL THAT OCCURS FREQUENTLY IN ANTARCTICA

SNOW BLINDNESS
VISION IMPAIRMENT BROUGHT ABOUT BY THE DAZZLE OF BRIGHT SUNLIGHT ON SNOW

SNOWLINE
THE LIMIT OF PERMANENT SNOW COVER, DEFINED BY ALTITUDE OR LONGITUTDE

---

blizzard as a storm with winds of more than 51 km/h and a visibility of less than 150 m. The term originated in the USA where blizzards are brought about every year by north-westerly winds rolling in from winter depressions. When blizzards strike, snow accumulates near obstructions, creating white sculptures that render visible the normally invisible behaviour of the wind. Snow collects and piles up against windward surfaces and traces aerodynamic flow patterns over slopes.

workplaces remained closed for several days. The Department of Streets and Sanitation estimated that a total of 75 tonnes of snow fell on Chicago during the storm. Some of the snow was sent south in empty rail cars as a present to children in Florida who had never seen snow before. Fatalities are usually uncommon in winter storms, but 60 deaths were attributed to the snowstorm in Chicago that year, mostly due to heart attacks brought on from shovelling the snow.

DATA-BURST

WHAT IS A WHITE-OUT?
A WHITE-OUT BLURS NORMAL PERCEPTION IN A SNOWSTORM. CLOUDS APPEAR TO MERGE INTO SNOW AND WITHOUT A VISIBLE HORIZON THE NORMALLY DISTINGUISHABLE CONTOURS OF THE LANDSCAPE DISAPPEAR. MULTIPLE REFLECTION FROM ICE CRYSTALS AND THE CLOUDS PREVENT SHADOWS FORMING, AND ALL SENSE OF DIRECTION AND BALANCE MAY BE LOST.

WHAT IS A CORNICE?
A CORNICE IS A WAVE-SHAPED SCULPTURE OF SNOW THAT PROJECTS OVER A VERTICAL DROP, SUCH AS A CLIFF OR A HOUSE WALL. IT IS FORMED BY VIOLENT EDDIES, SWIRLING WINDS THAT CARRY SNOW BACKWARDS INTO THE SIDE OF THE OBSTRUCTION AFTER BLOWING OVER THE TOP SURFACE.

WHAT IS GRAUPEL?
GRAUPEL IS THE GERMAN WORD FOR SOFT HAIL. IT IS SNOW THAT HAS PARTLY MELTED AND THEN REFROZEN, USUALLY TOSSED IN LAYERS OF DIFFERENT TEMPERATURE. IT FALLS TO THE GROUND AS COMPRESSED PELLETS OF ICE WITH A SOFT CORE.

WHAT ARE SNOW ROLLERS?
THESE ARE NATURALLY OCCURRING SNOWBALLS. THEY FORM WHEN SNOW FLAKES ARE DRIVEN ALONG THE GROUND BY THE WIND TO FORM GIANT CYLINDERS OR BALLS.

WHAT IS FIRN?
FIRN IS OLD COMPACTED SNOW. IT IS LESS WHITE THAN FRESH SNOW AND BECAUSE OF THE CLOSELY PACKED CRYSTALS, REFLECTS LESS LIGHT, MAKING IT LOOK LIKE PLASTER.

SURVIVAL IN THE SNOW

IN 1978 IN SCOTLAND, A BLIZZARD LASTED FOR 50 HOURS. THE SNOWFALL WAS SO RAPID THAT MANY PEOPLE WERE TRAPPED IN THEIR CARS AND THREE TRAINS WERE BURIED. A SALESMAN SURVIVED IN HIS VEHICLE ONLY BY POKING A STICK UP THROUGH THE SNOW TO MAINTAIN A FRESH AIR SUPPLY. HE MANAGED TO KEEP WARM BY WRAPPING HIMSELF IN THE PRODUCT HE WAS SELLING—LADIES TIGHTS. THE INSULATION OF SNOW COVER VARIES WITH ITS AIR CONTENT AND IS THEREFORE MOST EFFICIENT WHEN NEW. SHEEP CAN SURVIVE FOR SEVERAL WEEKS IN SNOW BECAUSE THEIR COATS INSULATE THEM AGAINST LOSS OF BODY HEAT. SNOW THEN MELTS NEAR THEIR BODIES TO FORM SMALL CAVES IN WHICH LAMBS ARE SOMETIMES BORN AND SURVIVE UNTIL THEY ARE RESCUED.

FELL IN 1967 CHICAGO STORM

BLIZZARDS AND SNOWSTORMS CAN TRANSFORM THE LANDSCAPE, BLANKETING THE GROUND WITH A COVERING OF SNOW. THEY CAUSE HAVOC TO TRANSPORT, REDUCING VISIBILITY AND MAKING ROADS TREACHEROUS

Freezes are dramatic drops in air temperature which can bring acute winter weather conditions, even during the summer months, with devastating consequences for harvests and livestock. They are initially caused by powerful volcanic eruptions that release dust into the air which can stay in the stratosphere for years. In time, this builds into a dense veil that the heat from the sun cannot penetrate. The causes of ice storms, in which huge lumps of ice fall from the sky, are far more mysterious. They have been variously attributed to tornadoes, whirlwinds, hurricanes and even passing aeroplanes.

Volcanic sun block
Benjamin Franklin was the first person to link volcanic eruptions and the occurence of freak freezes. He connected the unusually cold summer and winter of 1783 with a recent volcanic eruption in Iceland. He suggested that the smoke rising from the volcano created a 'dry fog' which veiled the impact of the sun and therefore lowered temperatures.

Java ash
When Mt Tambora erupted on the Indonesian island of Sumbawa, east of Java, in April 1815, the enormous explosion could be heard 3,000 km away. It created a blanket of ash and debris that covered an area of more than 500,000 km^2; everywhere within a radius of 500 km was plunged into darkness. However, the effects were also dramatic on a much larger scale: the enormous ash cloud prevented the heat from the sun breaking through the atmosphere. This contributed directly to freak freezes around the globe the following spring and summer.

FREEZES
3 MILLION IN CANADA

SKATING ON RIVERS

DURING THE 'LITTLE ICE AGE' IN THE 17TH CENTURY, THERE WERE SEVERAL DRAMATIC CLIMATE CHANGES . THE COLD SNAP AFFECTED MANY PARTS OF THE WORLD AND EVENTS THAT HAVE RARELY OCCURRED SINCE BECAME COMMONPLACE. FOR INSTANCE, ARCTIC SEALS COULD BE SPOTTED OFF THE NORTHERN COAST OF ENGLAND AND THE RIVER THAMES IN LONDON REGULARLY FROZE OVER. WALRUSES MIGRATED FROM NORTHERN TO SOUTHERN GREENLAND AND POLAR BEARS WERE ABLE TO WALK FROM ICELAND TO GREENLAND ACROSS PACK ICE. THE FREEZE DECREASED THE POPULATION OF BUTTERFLIES AND DEVASTATED GRAPE HARVESTS FOR MANY YEARS.

Deep freeze
The freak freeze of 1816 adversely affected much of Europe. Social unrest intensified as a result of crop failure. Two-thirds of Britain's total crop production was lost. In Paris, the imposition of a wheat tax led to riots, while in Ireland the typhus epidemic flourished in the extreme conditions, resulting in 50,000 deaths. Faced with massive wage cuts, East Anglian rioters marched through England in May 1816 wielding iron spikes and carrying banners proclaiming 'Bread or Blood'.

Summer snow
In the USA, church attendance rose dramatically during 1816. The cold freeze was thought to be an act of God. In the June of 1816, the region around Bennington, in Vermont, USA, was covered in snow. The leaves of the trees were blackened by the extreme cold and, in the town, snow drifts were higher than during any winter. The freeze inevitably destroyed crops, particularly the harvest of corn, the staple food of the region. Grain prices doubled, the price of oats springing from 50 cents to 92 cents that year.

Freak blizzards
Freezes and freak cold weather conditions often occur when weather systems collide. In March 1888 New York was subjected to freak blizzards that brought everything within a hundred-mile radius of the city to a standstill. This violent snowfall followed on from the warmest day of the year. This strange contrast of weather was created by two weather systems that collided on the Delaware coast. A mass of arctic air from Canada met a warm air mass from the Gulf of Mexico.

Canadian ice
A clash of weather fronts was also responsible for recent ice storms in Canada in 1998. These were the worst ice storms in the region for half a century. Over 10,000 federal troops were called in to alleviate the chaos. Three million people in New Brunswick, Quebec and Ontario were left without power. About 600 giant transmission towers collapsed and five days of freezing rain coated power lines with up to 10 cm of ice. The ice storm was probably caused by the

El Niño weather phenomenon, which had spawned two jet streams of air. The first ran along the border between Canada and the USA, while the second flowed across the southern states. When air streams clash, mixing cold and hot air, freak freezes can follow.

Frost sculpture
During an ice storm, ice gathers on the windward side of static objects. This creates a banner of feathery white ice, known as rime. Riming is common on hills which are consistently shrouded in cloud and mountain tops in winter periods. Trees, posts and telephone wires can gather such heavy ice banners that they bend or snap.

Killer icicles
Freak ice falls have caused some of the most bizarre deaths ever recorded. 'Bless my eyes/Here he lies/In a sad pickle/Kill'd by an icicle' is the inscription carved on a gravestone in Bampton, Devon, UK. It commemorates the unusual death of a parish clerk who was impaled by an enormous icicle that fell from the sky in 1776.

JARGON

ANEMOMETER
AN INSTRUMENT USED BY THE US WEATHER BUREAU TO MEASURE EXTREME COLD TEMPERATURES

DUST VEIL
A LAYER OF VOLCANIC DUST CARRIED AROUND THE GLOBE BY WINDS, IT ACTS AS A REFLECTIVE SHIELD BOUNCING BACK THE HEAT OF THE SUN, THUS ENCOURAGING FREAK LOW TEMPERATURES

LITTLE ICE AGE
A PERIOD OF PARTICULARLY ACUTE FREEZES

NAPOLEONIC WEATHER
FREEZING TEMPERATURES, OFTEN IN LATE SPRING, WHICH ARE NAMED AFTER THE FREAK EXTREME WEATHER THAT FOLLOWED TWO DECADES OF THE NAPOLEONIC WARS

RIME
FEATHERY RIMS OF ICE THAT GATHER ON WIRES AND TWIGS DURING AN ICE STORM

DATA-BURST

WHAT TRIGGERS FREAK FREEZES?
INTRICATE MECHANISMS OF WORLD WEATHER CAN TRIGGER DRAMATIC EXTREMES OF TEMPERATURE. A VOLCANO ON A SMALL ISLAND IN THE PACIFIC CAN CAUSE A FREAK FREEZE THROUGHOUT EUROPE. IF THE FORCE OF AN ERUPTION PROPELS HOT DUST INTO THE STRATOSPHERE, ABOVE THE RAIN CLOUDS, FREAK FREEZES OCCUR .

WHY DO ICE STORMS HAPPEN?
ICE STORMS ARE MYSTERIOUS IN ORIGIN. HUGE LUMPS OF ICE FALLING TO EARTH HAVE BEEN ATTRIBUTED TO TORNADOES AND HURRICANES. VIOLENT STORMS MAY SPIT OUT HAILSTONES LUMPED TOGETHER.

WHAT IS WIND-CHILL?
WIND-CHILL IS THE LOWERING OF THE STILL AIR TEMPERATURE DUE TO STRONG WIND. AT A WIND-CHILL TEMPERATURE OF −45°C, BARE SKIN WILL FREEZE IN 60 SECONDS OR LESS.

HOW MUCH FINANCIAL DAMAGE CAN FROSTS AND FREEZES CAUSE?
IN THE USA ALONE, ANNUAL CROP DAMAGE THROUGH FROST REACHES £1.1 BILLION, WHICH IS ABOUT $3 MILLION PER DAY. KNOCK-ON EFFECTS, SUCH AS THE CLOSURE OF TRANSPORT LINKS AND RETAIL CENTRES ADDS BILLIONS OF DOLLARS TO THE TOLL.

HOW DO SNOWSTORMS AFFECT DRIVING CONDITIONS?
ACCIDENTS INCREASE 200% WITHIN HOURS OF A SNOWSTORM. IN ILLINOIS, USA, IN THE FREEZING WINTER OF 1977-78, 24 PEOPLE TRAPPED IN CARS DIED FROM CARBON MONOXIDE POISONING.

RIGHT: PASSERSBY EXAMINE A SERIES OF HIGH VOLTAGE ELECTRIC TOWER PYLONS DAMAGED BY AN ICE STORM IN 1998 NEAR ST BRUNO, QUEBEC, CANADA

LEFT WITHOUT POWER

SUDDEN SNAPS OF ICY COLD WEATHER CAN CAUSE MAJOR DAMAGE TO CROPS, LIVESTOCK AND POWER LINES. ICE STORMS CAN KILL AND MAIM AND FREAK ACCIDENTS OCCUR WHEN ICICLES FALL SUDDENLY FROM THE SKY

EARTH'S LANDSCAPE REVEALED

8 38 72 106

PHENOMENAL PLANET

IN ALL ITS BEAUTY AND VARIETY

136 **170** **192** **220**

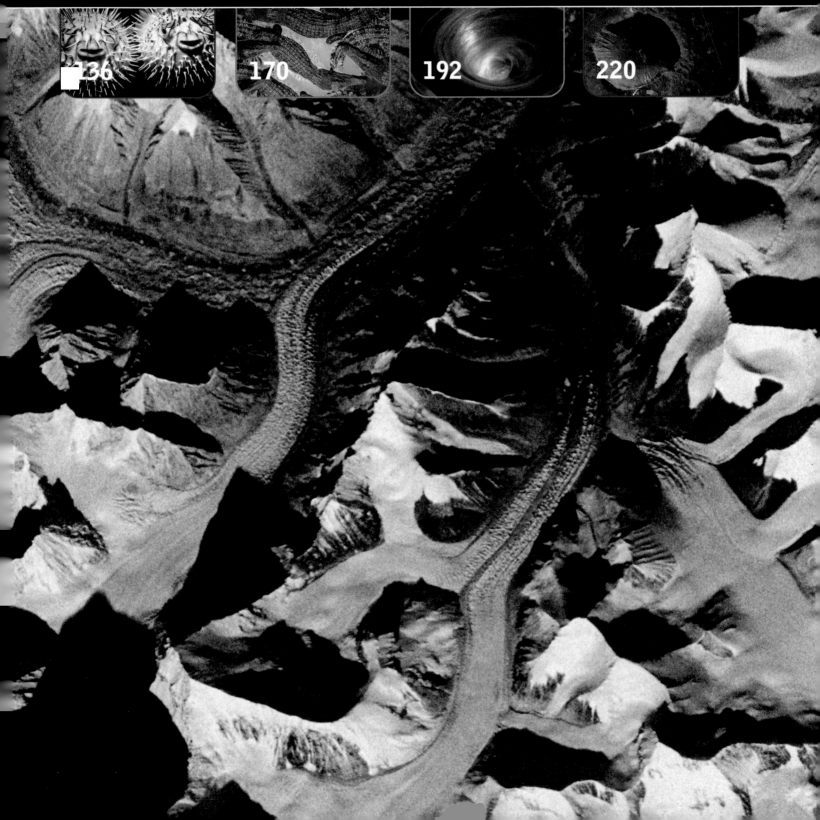

Around 5% of the Earth's land surface is officially termed desert. Deserts are dry, barren areas that are remarkable for their harsh conditions. They receive an average annual rainfall of 250 mm or less. In these arid areas, little vegetation breaks up the sparse, unrelenting landscape. The plants and animals that do manage to eke out an existence here only do so by adapting and evolving special characteristics to cope with the inhospitable environment. Although commonly assumed to be hot, deserts can also be very cold places. At night, with no cloud cover, temperatures plummet. Violent winds and sandstorms also prove hazardous.

A hostile home

Only plants and animals equipped to survive with very little water are able to thrive in a desert. Plants such as cacti, agaves and yuccas tend to be small and thorny. Their leaves have a small surface area, often with a waxy coating, in order to avoid loosing water. Some desert plants have long roots that can penetrate deep into the earth in search of water. Most desert animals are nocturnal or active during the cooler periods of dawn and dusk; many hide from daytime heat in the shade or in burrows. Small mammals extract the tiny amount of water they need from plant tissue while larger mammals store water by turning it into fat. The camel, for example, stores water in its humps.

Sculpting sand

The wind sculpts sand dunes into a variety of different shapes and sizes. The best known are *barchans*, crescent-shaped deposits that form in deserts where there is only one constant wind direction. These dunes are concave on the side that is sheltered from the wind, with horns pointing in the same direction as the wind. By contrast, *seifes* form when there are regular winds crossing from two points of the compass. 'Star dunes', with arms extending from a central peak, form when the wind changes direction frequently. Some banks of wind-blown sand can reach heights of 100 m.

DESERTS

DESERT REACH 54°C

BLISTERING DAYTIME HEAT AND FREEZING NIGHTS ARE TYPICAL OF DESERT REGIONS, CONTRIBUTING TO THE HARDSHIP OF LIFE FOR INHABITANTS OF AN ARID LAND WHERE SANDSTORMS CAN RAGE AT SPEEDS OF 110 KM/H

The Sahara
At 8,600,000 km², the Sahara is the largest tropical desert in the world, covering almost all of northern Africa. Only a third of the Sahara is covered by sand alone: it is this landscape that has given rise to a romantic image of rippling sand-blown dunes. The rest of the region is made up of mountains and stony plains. Intense heat, prolonged drought and mobile sandy soils make the desert area virtually uninhabitable for humans. Only 2.5 million people live in this huge expanse, around one person for every 2 km². However, since the discovery of oil in 1936, four-fifths of the desert is accessible by a new network of roads.

The Empty Quarter
The Arabian desert lies in the south of Saudi Arabia and is known as The Empty Quarter or *Rub al Khali*. It is the largest continuous sand desert in the world, covering 2,330,000 km², and is linked to another sandy desert in the north called the Nafud. Here, the sand dunes can reach heights of 100 m. Bedouin, who live by herding goats and camel, are the main inhabitants of this hot desert, where temperatures can reach 54°C.

The Mojave
The Mojave desert in California covers 0.5 million hectares. Swept by fierce wind eddies, the Eureka sand dunes rise 700 m from the desert floor. On the upper elevations of the Mojave grow Joshua trees—shrubs with curling stems that are named after the Old Testament prophet who raised his arms to God. This barren desert is populated only by the hardiest of animals: sidewinder snakes, lizards reptiles and coyotes.

Death Valley
Death Valley is located in south-east California, just east of the Amargosa desert. Lying 86 m below sea level, this narrow valley marks the lowest point in the continent of North America. Its 225-km long trough is only 10–24 km wide and receives an average of just 50 mm of rain per year. Temperatures of more than 49°C were recorded there on 43 consecutive days from 6 July 1917. The air is so dry that perspiration dries as soon as it forms, leaving salt on the skin.

Deadly heat
If a person spent a day in the Sahara desert in the full glare of the sun, without shade, water or clothing, their body temperature would reach 46°C. By the end of the day they would have lost 2–3.5 litres of water. By nightfall they would be dead.

Mirror mirages
Mirages often occur in hot deserts. Heated by intense sunshine, layers of warm air next to the ground can be trapped by cooler air above. Light then bends towards the horizontal line of vision, eventually travelling upwards. When the sky is the object of a mirage, the land is often mistaken for a lake of water.

Water havens
Oases are fertile spots in the desert which form in deep depressions in the sand. Here, the roots of plants are able to reach the watertable below and growth abounds. A small oasis will form around a single spring while others support large areas of irrigated land. The Souf oasis in the Algerian Sahara consists of closely planted trees that stop sand from encroaching on its centre while the al Kharijah oasis in the Libyan desert is fed by a large underwater lake. Two-thirds of the people living in the Sahara live around an oasis. When over-exploited, an oasis may not be replenished for 40,000 years.

Stinging sandstorms
One of the most terrifying features of the desert is the sandstorm. In March 1988, a vicious sandstorm hit Egypt, Cyprus, Syria and Jordan. It was an example of the seasonal Khamsin sandstorms which bathe the landscape in an eerie yellow light. Winds of up to 110km/h picked up tonnes of sand, hurling it into the air. Roads, ports and electricity and telephone networks all suffered as a result of the raging sandstorm. In Cairo alone, six died and 250 people were injured. Over 100 people were hospitalized in Cyprus suffering breathing difficulties.

Cold deserts
Deserts can be cold as well as hot. In the 'white desert' of Antarctica rain is unheard of, especially at the polar plateau which receives only 50 mm a year. In Iceland, for example, 37,000 km² is classified as barren desert.

LEFT: THE SAHARA IN NORTHERN AFRICA, THE WORLD'S LARGEST DESERT AT 8,600,000 KM², AS SEEN FROM OUTER SPACE

Mountains are relatively recent geological phenomena. They are almost always found in ranges, very rarely on their own, and most ranges form a part of one of the world's two major mountain belts: the Circum-Pacific System and the Alpine-Himalayan System. The mountains of the Circum-Pacific System include the Andes and the North American Cordillera, which includes the Rockies and Mount McKinley. All the ranges in the system were formed by the action of a chain of volcanoes which surrounds the Pacific Ocean and is known as the Ring of Fire. The Alpine–Himalayan, or Tethyan, System includes not only the Alps and Himalayas, but also the Caucasus Mountains and the Zagros and Bitlis mountains which lie in Turkey and Iran.

Mountain building

The process involved in mountain building, or 'orogenesis', occurs as a result of movement of the Earth's crustal plates. These continental and oceanic crusts jostle together like pieces of a giant jigsaw. Over millions of years, they squeeze and buckle as they grind and push against each other. There are three main types of mountain. Volcanic mountains form when lava and debris build up to form a dome around the vent of a volcano. Most of the Japanese mountains are formed in this way. Fold mountains occur when plates push together and the impact causes the rock to buckle upwards. The Appalachians in North America were thrown up by tectonic action. Block mountains

are formed when a block of land is uplifted between two faults as a result of compression and tension in the Earth's crust. When caught between a sandwich of shifting rock, a layer is forced up along the lines of the weak fissures.

Mount Everest

At 8,848 m, Mount Everest is the highest point on Earth and sits on the border between Tibet and Nepal. The 'Goddess Mother of the World', as it is known to local people, began forming when India collided with Asia about 40 million years ago. The Indian-Australian tectonic plate moved northwards at great speed (in geological terms) eventually smashing into the larger, heavier, Eurasian plate. This impact, which took place over millions of years, gave rise to what

are now called the Himalayan mountains. The ancient Tethys Ocean floor was propelled forward and up over the crumpled margin of the collision where it sits today. On the crest of Mt Makalau lie the youngest rocks of this ancient primeval seabed. Surveyors have called the Himalayas a 'horrible

mess' with strata piled up and squashed together. Deep fault lines have been found where material was first thrust up on collision and then pulled down by gravity. Today, the Himalayan-Karakoram range contains all 14 of the world's peaks which reach a height of over 8,000 m.

Still climbing higher

Over the past 30 million years, plate movement in the area has continued, pushing the Himalayas up still higher, while the forces of erosion have stripped away land in the river valleys below. At the higher reaches of Everest, oxygen is so sparse that climbers need apparatus to breathe. This lack of oxygen, as well as fierce winds and freezing temperatures, mean that no animals or plants can live there.

Bumper to bumper

The Western North American Mountains, unlike those in Eurasia, were not so much the result of a clash of equals but a confrontation between contestants of very different sizes. The evidence for this lies in the geological mosaic which makes up the mountain range. Altogether they are thought to contain 50 distinct rock types. Geologists have concluded that these terranes were originally

separate landmasses. Each landmass, when it collided with the North American plate, was folded and deformed like a car being smashed by a big truck.

Tallest and furthest

While Mt Everest may be the highest mountain in the world, it is not the tallest. When measured from its submarine base at 6,000 m in the Hawaiian Trough to its peak, Mauna Kea on the island of Hawaii, USA, is 10,205 m high. It is thus 1,357 m taller than Mt Everest, although only 4,205 m of it is above sea level. The record for the furthest summit from the Earth's centre belongs to the 6,267-m high Andean peak of Chimborazo.

Metal-rich Andes

Heat caused by the friction between tectonic plates in the Andes in South America has left the mountains rich in metallic ores. The deeper the Nazca ocean plate descends beneath the South American continent, plunging into the Earth's mantle, the hotter it gets. As temperatures rise, so minerals in the rock melt. These hot fluids rise up and then cool as they near the surface, leaving minerals in the veins in the rock. These include tin, copper, lead, zinc, silver and gold.

MOUNTAINS

14 HIMALAYAN PEAKS

HANNIBAL AND THE ELEPHANTS

ONE OF THE MOST AMBITIOUS MOUNTAINEERING EXPEDITIONS OF ALL TIME WAS UNDERTAKEN OVER 2,000 YEARS AGO. HANNIBAL, LEADER OF THE ARMIES OF CARTHAGE, DECIDED TO CROSS THE ALPS TO ATTACK THE CITY OF ROME. FIRST, HE TRANSPORTED HIS ARMY, INCLUDING 38 WAR ELEPHANTS, TO SPAIN, FLOATING THE ANIMALS ACROSS THE WATER ON RAFTS. AFTER CONQUERING SPANISH TRIBES, HANNIBAL AND HIS ARMIES BEGAN THEIR FAMOUS MOUNTAIN TREK. LOCAL TRIBES ATTACKED HIS ARMY AND LANDSLIDES AND AVALANCHES ADDED TO THE DEATH TOLL. BY THE TIME HE REACHED ITALY, MOST OF THE ELEPHANTS HAD DIED AND HIS ARMY WAS MASSIVELY DEPLETED. HE NEVER REACHED ROME.

RIGHT: THE HIMALAYAN MOUNTAIN RANGE IN NEPAL AS SEEN FROM A SATELLITE ORBITING THE EARTH

EXCEED 8,000 M

Rainforests are hot, humid places drenched with at least 1,800 mm of rain a year. The most extensive rainforests are in South and Central America, West and Central Africa, Indonesia, South-east Asia and tropical parts of Australia. Their characteristics vary according to location and climate, but all have fertile, often volcanic, soil which is what makes them so rich in plant and animal life. Tropical rainforest, located in a band around the Equator, is wet and hot all year round, with temperatures hovering around 30°C during the day, and falling to 20°C at night.

Life on three levels
The layered structure of rainforests enables countless types of plant and animal to survive in one habitat. In the highest layer, or canopy, flying squirrels and monkeys swing, glide and leap from branch to branch. The canopy trees have thick leaves to conserve water in the heat and a network of shallow roots to absorb nutrients from the rich soil. In the forest's dense middle layer, plants use the trunks of the towering trees for support. Here, ferns and orchids live and climbing plants called lianas grow up to 200 m by twining around tree-trunks to reach the sunlight. The animals of the twilight region on the forest floor feed on insects and fruit.

Water everywhere
The heaviest rainforest rain on record falls in Liberia, where it pounds the forest at the incredible rate of 400 mm per hour. In most rainforests 25 mm per hour of rain is not unusual. The stronger the

downpour, the larger the raindrops—at 100 mm per hour, the diameter of a raindrop is about 3 mm. If the soil cannot absorb the rain quickly enough during the deluge, the water may run off, taking soil away as it goes, causing a landslide. In Uganda's rainy season, 40% of rainwater is lost to run-off in this way, taking with it 80 tonnes of soil per hectare.

The disappearing Amazon
The largest surviving area of rainforest in the world is in the Amazon River Basin in Brazil.

This magnificent forest covers 6 million km²—40% of the country's land surface. In the Andean foothills in the west, the forest is 1,900 km wide, tapering to 320 km at the Atlantic coast in the east. This constantly hot and humid habitat is the most biologically diverse in the world, supporting millions of species of plants and trees, such as acacia, laurel, myrtle mahogany, cedar, palm, rosewood and Brazil nut. Animals include monkeys, jaguars, deer and tapirs. But the Amazon rainforest is disappearing rapidly, despite efforts by the Brazilian government to curb the destruction, as loggers move in and rip out the trees.

Mangrove forest
Cloaking a 260-km stretch of the Bay of Bengal, India, the mangrove forests of the Sundarbans are one of the last remaining strongholds of the Bengal tiger. These swampy forests are flooded with brackish water in places, so the mangrove trees build up tangled root systems above ground to absorb oxygen. The rivers and estuaries of the region are inhabited by crocodiles, and on the thick mud, peculiar goggle-eyed fish called mudskippers haul themselves out of the water and hop about in search of prey. The mangrove trees and shrubs grow to about 9 m— except for the black mangrove, which can reach 21 m—and have long, oval leaves with a thick, waxy surface and pale yellow flowers.

Co-habitation under the canopy
In the Congo River Basin in Zaire, dense rainforest stretches for 63,000 km². The forest's canopy is almost continuous, keeping the lower regions in almost unbroken darkness. This shadowy interior— a zone of tangled tree roots and scattered saplings—is home to Bantu-speaking and Pygmy peoples and supports more primates than any other rainforest. The monkeys and chimpanzees share their habitat with leopards, elephants and the forest giraffe, or okapi. Conditions are made even more difficult by annual rainfall of 1,900 mm and an average temperature of 31°C. In October and November, when the rainfall is at its highest, rivers often burst their banks, flooding the forest. One of these rivers, the Ituri, has been stained the colour of tea by leaves from the forest trees.

Monsoon forests of China
In the Chinese region of Kwangtung, the monsoon forests which have been decimated by agriculture are being regenerated. Oak and camphor are being planted to replace trees cleared by fire or harvested for fuel. These forests are home to spectacular birds, such as peacocks and silver pheasants, and snakes such as the Chinese and bamboo vipers and pythons which can grow to 7 m long, but the area's bears, panthers, rhinos and tigers have all but disappeared.

RAINFORESTS
50% OF ALL SPECIES

AMAZONIAN PEOPLES

THE RAINFOREST OF THE AMAZON REGION, BRAZIL, IS HOME TO ABOUT 600,000 PEOPLE WHO LEAD A TRADITIONAL LIFE HUNTING, FISHING AND FARMING IN THE FOREST. ONE OF THESE PEOPLES, THE YANOMAMI, LIVE IN HOUSES MADE OF THATCHED VINES AND LEAVES. THEY HUNT MONKEYS, DEER AND ARMADILLOS AND GROW PLANTAIN AND CORN, MOVING TO A

NEW PART OF THE FOREST WHEN THE SOIL IS EXHAUSTED. SCIENTISTS THINK THAT THE FOREST MAY HOLD CURES FOR MANY DISEASES, INCLUDING CANCER. THE AMAZONIAN INDIANS PERFECTED THE USE OF QUININE AS A TREATMENT FOR MALARIA AND DISCOVERED THE POISON CURARE, NOW USED AS A MUSCLE RELAXANT IN THE TREATMENT OF MULTIPLE SCLEROSIS.

RIGHT: RAINFOREST VEGETATION IN THE MIST · INSET: MIST FLOATS OVER THE TREETOPS AFTER A RAINSTORM IN AN ECUADORIAN RAINFOREST

LIVE IN RAINFORESTS

RAINFORESTS ARE DENSE AND COMPLEX ECOSYSTEMS.
LASHED BY AVERAGE RAINFALL OF 25 MM PER HOUR
AND ENDOWED WITH FERTILE, OFTEN VOLCANIC, SOILS,
RAINFORESTS ABOUND WITH ANIMAL AND PLANT LIFE

Badlands are barren, rocky areas, scarred by steep canyons and gullies and dotted with strange rock formations and protruding buttes. They have been eroded and shaped by the forces of nature in complex and intricate ways over millions of years, making badlands some of the world's strangest, most awesome landscapes. The process of erosion can turn the entire area into a wasteland, impossible to farm and home only to snakes, scorpions and lizards. Semi-arid conditions where rain falls in short, heavy bursts makes it almost impossible for soil and vegetation to take root. This inhospitable territory has the look of an alien or ancient world.

Hoodoos

Some badlands feature several different types of rock, often in multicoloured stripes. The forces of erosion wear away the different rock types at different rates. Where rock resistant to erosion lies on top of a layer of softer rock, the underlying rock wears away while the harder rock remains intact. The end result, which can be seen to spectacular effect in the Bryce Canyon, USA, is a pedestal rock, or hoodoo.

Badlands National Park

French-Canadians travelling across south-west South Dakota, USA, found that the deep gullies and desert conditions in the area were 'bad lands to cross'. Today, these original badlands extend to form a 5,200-km^2 national park. The treeless landscape is one of non-porous clay, sculpted into freestanding boulders and buttes and washed into gullies and saw-toothed divides. Temperatures rise and fall unpredictably here, helping to create a remote environment which is a haven for rare bald and golden eagles. But the barren appearance of the Badlands hides a fertile past: the National Park has yielded fossils of sabre-toothed tiger, mammoth, rhinoceros, camel and three-toed horse. Some believe that in prehistoric times the Park may have been covered with thick and lush vegetation which disappeared only when weathering processes gradually began to turn the area into badlands.

BADLANDS

BUTTES AND HOODOOS CARVED

BONE ZONE

THE BADLANDS OF ALBERTA, CANADA, ARE FAMOUS FOR THE NUMBER OF DINOSAUR FOSSILS THAT HAVE BEEN FOUND THERE. THIS BADLAND USED TO CONSIST OF A LOW SWAMPY LANDSCAPE WHICH PROVIDED PERFECT CONDITIONS FOR THE PRESERVATION OF BONES. HOME TO THE DINOSAUR PROVINCIAL PARK, THIS AREA HAS PRODUCED THOUSANDS OF INDIVIDUAL BONES INCLUDING SOME COMPLETE SPECIMENS SUCH AS THE TYRANNOSAUR COLLECTED IN 1997, ESTIMATED TO HAVE REACHED A LENGTH OF 8 M WHEN IT WAS ALIVE. IN 1996, PALAEONTOLOGISTS DISCOVERED THE COMPLETE SKULL OF A CENTROSAURUS APERTUS. AT 1.5 M LONG AND 1 M WIDE, THE SKULL PROVED TOO HEAVY FOR AN ATTEMPTED HELICOPTER LIFT AND WAS FINALLY REMOVED BY A GIANT TRUCK.

JARGON

BUTTES
SMALL, ISOLATED HILLS WITH STEEP SIDES

EPHEMERAL CREEKS
SMALL RIVULETS THAT COME AND GO WITH THE RAIN

GLACIAL ERRATICS
FREESTANDING BOULDERS

GULLIES
STEEP-SIDED, MINIATURE VALLEYS

HOODOOS
A COLUMN OF ROCK CARVED INTO FANTASTIC SHAPES BY THE WEATHERING PROCESS

MESAS
BIG FLAT-TOPPED NATURAL HILLS

BY WIND AND RAIN

INHOSPITABLE BADLANDS ARE ERODED AND SCULPTED INTO SPECTACULAR ROCK FORMATIONS OVER MILLIONS OF YEARS. ONCE THE HOME OF DINOSAURS, TODAY ONLY HARDY REPTILES CAN SURVIVE THE BARREN CONDITIONS

The Great Plains of Alberta
The Drumheller badlands in Alberta, Canada, were formed up to 80 million years ago by great rivers which flowed down from the Rocky Mountains carving deep, wide canyons in the region's sandstone. River deposits, left by retreating ice sheets at the end of the last ice age 13,000 years ago, have added to the area's jagged, rocky character. Heavy summer rains have carved the sandstone into amazing shapes, including natural arches and spectacular hoodoos on the Red Deer River. The most striking feature of the badlands are the multicoloured, flat-lying layers of exposed rock on the surrounding slopes. Referred to as the Horseshoe Canyon Formation, the sequences of strata reveal much about the area's past.

A land of the dead
Between the Himalayas and the Deccan Mountains lies India's most spectacular geological feature: the badlands of the Indo-Gangetic Plain, known locally as the 'land of the dead'. The plain itself is so flat that it rises only 95 mm per km, but the badlands area in the south-west of the plain, near the River Chambal, forms a stark contrast. Here, the desolate, jagged limestone scenery is typical of badlands. Wind and water have carved out gullies, boulders and tooth-like outcrops and made the region infertile. In summer the temperature rises above 40°C and less than 100 mm of rain falls in a year. The area is sinister not just in appearance but because these badlands are famous for being the hide-out of violent criminal gangs called dacoits.

The Dolomites
The steep, jagged limestone rock formations of the Dolomites in north-east Italy have been described as resembling 'a dead animal with its bones showing'. Called *calanchi* in Italian, these badlands are often afflicted by rock falls and landslides. The limestone has been eroded so quickly that debris has accumulated in gullies and ravines, partially filling-in valleys in some places and making exploration very difficult. Archaeologists studying the area have found a large number of fossils and ancient human artefacts. They have been able to build up a picture of the region over the last 5,000 years which shows that it was once inhabited by farmers whose sheep and goats destroyed the soil, setting off the process which culminated in the bleak appearance of the land today.

Spain's Sierra Nevada
Weathering and erosion over 3,000 years have created some spectacular badlands in south-eastern Spain. Rough outcrops and sheer rock faces characterize the high areas of the country's central plateau and some of its southern and eastern regions. Weather patterns stretching back thousands of years have shaped the badlands: very dry summers followed by stormy winters erode the crumbly soil of these regions and stop vegetation gaining a hold.

Life in badlands
The Red Creek Badlands in Flaming Gorge Country, Wyoming, USA, provide a home to a variety of adaptable wildlife. Golden eagles and prairie falcons swoop across the magnificent Tepee Mountains, 3,000 m high and containing the 50-million-year-old fossils of flamingo rookeries. Pronghorn antelope, mule deer and herds of wild horses raom the wild patches of rocky desert and rolling sand dunes which stretch across the open spaces between rock formations. Sharply eroded blood-red buttes and mesas are covered with the soft greens of juniper, pinyon and sage.

DATA-BURST

HOW ARE BADLANDS FORMED?
THROUGH A GRADUAL PROCESS OF EROSION AND WATER. THE BADLANDS OF DRUMHELLER ALONG THE RED DEER VALLEY, FOR EXAMPLE, WERE CARVED BY MELT WATER TORRENTS IN THE WAKE OF RETREATING ICE SHEETS 10,000 TO 15,000 YEARS AGO.

ARE BADLANDS STILL BEING ERODED?
YES. EROSION IS AN ONGOING PROCESS. FOR EXAMPLE, THE WHITE RIVER BADLANDS IN SOUTH DAKOTA, USA, ARE BEING WORN AWAY AT A RATE OF 2.5 CM PER YEAR.

HOW MUCH RAIN DO BADLANDS RECEIVE?
BADLANDS RECEIVE VERY LITTLE RAIN. INDIA'S LAND OF THE DEAD HAS ONLY 100 MM PER YEAR, WHILE IN THE SIERRA NEVADA IN SPAIN IT CAN RAIN LESS THAN 20 DAYS PER YEAR.

HOW DANGEROUS CAN BADLANDS BE?
AS WELL AS THE DANGEROUS

LIFEFORMS THAT CAN BE FOUND, SUCH AS VENOMOUS REPTILES, THE EXTREME HEAT CAN BE DEADLY. IN SOME PARTS OF THE WORLD, TEMPERATURES CAN REACH 40°C. IN ADDITION, THE LACK OF VEGETATION OR FOLIAGE MAKE BADLANDS PRONE TO LANDSLIDES WHEN RAIN DOES FALL.

WHAT ARE SPILLWAYS?
THESE CHANNELS CARVED INTO THE LAND CARRY AWAY SURPLUS WATER. THEY ARE OFTEN THE RESULT OF FLASH FLOODS RATHER THAN RIVER EROSION WHICH FORMS VALLEYS OVER A LONG PERIOD OF TIME.

WHO FIRST USED THE TERM BADLANDS?
'BADLANDS' IS A TRANSLATION FROM THE FRENCH—*LES MAUVAISES TERRES*. THE PHRASE WAS COÏNED BY 19TH-CENTURY FRENCH TRAPPERS AND TRADERS WHO TRAVELLED THROUGH THE DIFFICULT TERRAIN OF THE WHITE RIVER IN DAKOTA, USA.

LEFT: EERIE PEAKS MAKE UP THE STRANGE LANDSCAPE OF THE BADLANDS NATIONAL PARK, USA

WETLANDS
6% OF THE EARTH'S

Wetlands can be found on every continent except Antarctica, and in a wide range of climatic zones from the Tropics to the Arctic tundra. They cover up to 8.6 million km², or 6% of the Earth's surface. Some form naturally, while others are created to store water for domestic and agricultural purposes, such as paddy fields. Bordering between dry land and total water, and combining many useful features of both, wetlands are one of nature's most productive regions, home to a huge diversity of plant and animal life. The shallow waters and saturated soils enable matter to decompose slowly and lush hydrophyte plants to grow.

THE MARSH ARABS

AT THE CONFLUENCE OF THE TIGRIS AND EUPHRATES RIVERS IN SOUTHERN IRAQ LIES A UNIQUE NATURAL WILDERNESS. THE MARSHES TEEM WITH THOUSANDS OF SPECIES OF BIRDS, FISH AND ANIMALS. IN THIS LABYRINTH OF WATERWAYS LIVE 500,000 MA'DAN OR MARSH ARABS. THESE UNIQUE PEOPLE, WHO CAN TRACE THEIR ORIGINS BACK TO 3000 BC, ARE DESCENDANTS OF THE ANCIENT BABYLONIANS. THEIR LIFESTYLE HAS ALWAYS CENTRED ON AGRICULTURE: IN PARTICULAR, CULTIVATING RICE, WEAVING REED MATS, RAISING WATER BUFFALO AND FISHING. THE MARSH ARABS' DISTINCT CULTURE IS INEXTRICABLY LINKED TO THEIR ENVIRONMENT: THEIR DWELLINGS ARE MADE FROM PAPYRUS AND MUD, AND THEY TRAVEL BY REED CANOE. THIS FRAGILE EXISTENCE, UNTOUCHED FOR CENTURIES, IS NOW UNDER THREAT: SADDAM HUSSEIN IS DRAINING THE WETLANDS IN ORDER TO DRIVE OUT THE MARSH ARABS, SHIITE MUSLIMS WHO HE SEES AS POLITICAL ENEMIES. LARGE AMOUNTS OF TOXIC CHEMICALS HAVE BEEN DUMPED IN THE MARSHES AND A DAM HAS DIVERTED WATER. THE DROP IN WATER LEVELS HAS EXPOSED SOIL TO THE AIR, CAUSING THE REED BEDS TO DIE.

annually. During the 1970s, the Connecticut Department of Environmental Protection began the task of restoring 240 hectares of salt marshes. These coastal wetlands stretch 200 km along Long Island Sound. Once an important nursery and spawning ground for fish, they had been damaged by the creation of man-made dykes and ditches for hay cultivation. A large number of species, including fiddler crabs and snails, have since recolonized their natural habitat.

Wetlands down the drain
A huge area of 680,000 hectares around the delta of the River Danube in Romania was until

SURFACE IS WETLAND

BOGS, MARSHES AND SWAMPS ARE ALL AREAS WHERE WATER STANDS OR DRAINS SO SLOWLY THAT THE SOIL IS PERMANENTLY SATURATED. KNOWN AS THE 'KIDNEYS OF THE LANDSCAPE', WETLANDS REJUVENATE THE EARTH

JARGON

AQUIFER
A LAYER OF ROCK OR SOIL THAT HOLDS OR TRANSMITS WATER

HYDROPHYTES
PLANTS THAT HAVE BECOME ADAPTED TO WET CONDITIONS

MANGROVE
A TROPICAL TREE OR SHRUB THAT GROWS IN WETLAND MUD

POLDER
AN AREA OF LOW-LYING LAND RECLAIMED FROM A RIVER, SEA OR WETLAND

RICE PADDIES
THE PREDOMINANT FORM OF MAN-MADE WETLAND

RIPARIAN WETLANDS
WETLANDS RUNNING ALONGSIDE A RIVER OR STREAM

SEDGES
A GRASS-LIKE PLANT THAT FLOURISHES AND HELPS TO SUSTAIN WETLAND REGIONS

WETLANDERS
POPULAR NAME FOR THE PEOPLE WHO LIVE AROUND WETLANDS ALL OVER THE WORLD

Liquid riches
Wetlands supply clean water, help to control flooding and provide a home for a wide range of wildlife and fish. Inland marshes act like giant sponges, stabilizing shorelines and river banks by absorbing water run-off. Wetlands also lock up large amounts of carbon, often in the form of peat, thereby preventing it from entering the atmosphere as carbon dioxide—

the principal culprit in global warming. The lush and fertile conditions found in wetlands provide an ideal habitat for many birds—a third of all the USA's bird species, for example, live in wetlands. These boggy areas also serve to absorb and filter the pollutants that would otherwise degrade lakes, rivers and reservoirs. Cypress domes—small swamps with tall cypress trees at

the centre—act to eliminate waste carried in water. If fed domestic sewage, cypress domes will remove harmful nitrates, binding them up in mud and tree roots. In the past, wetlands were thought of as useless environments, but although they are now much depleted, these areas are increasingly being recognized as some of the Earth's fullest and richest ecosystems.

African swamps
The Okavango Delta in Botswana is one of the largest wetland areas in the world, extending over some 22,000 km² in the wet season. Its pattern changes from open water, papyrus reed beds, swamps and floodplains to countless small islands where trees can grow. This habitat is home to hippos, crocodiles, even elephants, together with various species of bird and fish. There is increasing pressure on the Okavango River for irrigation and industrial uses.

Reclamation in the USA
In the past 200 years, wetlands have been drained, filled and dammed to the extent that only half now remain intact in the USA. Laws have slowed wetland loss but 300,000 acres still vanish

recently covered by natural wetlands. In 1975, the Romanian dictator, Nicolae Ceausescu, set in motion a grand plan to convert part of the area for agriculture, fishing and forestry. Despite the creation of dykes around the delta, much of the reclaimed soil proved much too salty or sandy for cultivation. Water in the hastily created fishing lakes soon drained away. By 1989, 40,000 hectares of the delta had been ruined. One month after the area was reopened by the new Romanian government as an officially designated marshland, birds, fish and animals began to reappear. The Danube delta is now home to more than 110 species of freshwater fish and 320 birds.

DATA-BURST

WHAT AREA OF THE EARTH'S LAND SURFACE IS COVERED BY WETLANDS?
UP TO 8.6 MILLION KM³ OF THE EARTH MAY BE WETLANDS—MORE THAN THE SURFACE AREA OF AUSTRALIA.

IS THE CULTIVATION OF WETLANDS A MODERN PHENOMENON?
NO. ANCIENT CIVILIZATIONS, SUCH AS THE BABYLONIANS, EGYPTIANS AND THE AZTECS, ALL DEVELOPED AND CULTIVATED WETLANDS INTO UNIQUE SYSTEMS OF WATER DELIVERY.

WHAT ARE PADDY FIELDS?
THESE ARE THE PREDOMINANTLY MAN-MADE WETLANDS PREVALENT IN COUNTRIES WHERE RICE IS A STAPLE DIET. PADDY FIELDS FEED ABOUT HALF OF THE WORLD'S POPULATION.

WHAT ARE SEDGES?
GRASS-LIKE PLANTS THAT FLOURISH IN WETLANDS AND PLAY AN IMPORTANT PART IN SUSTAINING THEM, SEDGES ARE OFTEN THE FIRST COLONIZERS OF

SOIL IN A WETLAND REGION, AND THEY ENSURE THE CIRCULATION OF WATER. THEIR FRUIT, SHOOTS AND TUBERS PROVIDE NUTRITION FOR WETLAND CREATURES, WHILE OTHER SPECIES USE THEM FOR SHELTER.

WHAT ARE PEATLANDS?
MOST COMMON IN COOL TEMPERATE ZONES, THESE ARE BOGLAND AREAS WHERE PEAT HAS ACCUMULATED GRADUALLY, SOMETIMES OVER A PERIOD AS LONG AS 5,000 YEARS.

WHERE DO SALTWATER WETLANDS FORM?
IN COASTAL AREAS, ALONG SHORES WHICH ARE CALM AND PROTECTED.

WHAT ARE MANGROVE SWAMPS?
THEY ARE TROPICAL AREAS WHERE COASTAL MUDS HAVE BEEN COLONIZED BY MANGROVES. RICH HAVENS FOR A DIVERSITY OF LIFE, THEY HAVE BEEN DESCRIBED AS THE SALTWATER EQUIVALENT OF A RAINFOREST.

LEFT: ROWBOAT SINKING INTO BOGLAND · INSET: AERIAL VIEW OF A MARSH IN LOUISIANA, USA

A Russian term derived from the Finnish word 'tunturi', tundra literally means 'treeless heights'. It is used to describe any cold climate landscape that has some vegetation but no trees. These plants usually take the form of greenish-brown lichens, mosses, a few low-lying shrubs and spongy turf. Growth and regeneration are slow in this harsh habitat where the temperature is usually below freezing. However, a number of animals have adapted to life in the tundra—one of the few unspoilt regions left on Earth.

Frost top

Arctic tundra covers about one-tenth of the Earth's surface. The average temperature is below freezing and can plummet to -32°C, rising to 18°C in the brief summer months. The consistently low temperatures leave a layer of permanently frozen soil below the surface which can reach depths of 1,525 m. Above this level, the soil freezes and thaws as the temperature varies. Drainage is poor because the permafrost creates an impermeable barrier, while the cold prevents evaporation. The landscape is often waterlogged with bogs and lakes.

Arctic concerns

Because of the long, freezing winters, the cool summers and the lack of rain, vegetation in the Arctic tundra is sparse. The food chain is, therefore, extremely fragile and can be easily broken. Many of the plant and animal species are found in small numbers in limited areas and, if just one plant in the chain was to disappear, it would jeopardize the future of a

whole animal species further along the chain. Needless to say, the greatest threat to this sensitive survival process comes from human hands, which increasingly explore and exploit the region. Oil spills are a common hazard—the oil contaminates plants, poisons animals and fish and threatens the permafrost layer. The Inuit people who live in the region have found their place in the chain, but external intrusion can seriously affect their ability to hunt or fish for food, threatening their very existence.

Alpine tundra

Although cold and hostile, life in the alpine tundra is less severe than in the Arctic—winter temperatures tend not to fall below -18°C, but the surface soil freezes and thaws in a similar way. The alpine tundra generally begins on the slopes above a timberline of spruce and firs. The area is likely to be blitzed by snowstorms in the winter and heavy rain in the summer. Drainage, however, is good and shrubs thrive. Mountain sheep and goats are among the limited species of animals that live here.

Spotted tundra

Nearly half of the land covered by the former Soviet Union is underlain by a layer of permafrost, which can descend to depths of 1,400 m. In populated areas such as Siberia, houses have sunk into the ground as the heat they generate melts the soil far beneath. The landscape in such areas is known as spotted tundra, because it is characterized by hummocks and furrows created by thousands of years of thawing and freezing of the water trapped above the permafrost level.

JARGON

BOG
AREA OF PERMANENTLY WET GROUND WITH A PLANT COMMUNITY OF MOSSES, HEATHS AND RUSHES

INUIT
THE INDIGENOUS PEOPLE OF THE ARCTIC TUNDRA REGION

PERMAFROST
LAYER OF SOIL PERMANENTLY FROZEN BELOW THE LAND SURFACE

TUSSOCK
CLUMP OF GRASS OR GRASSLIKE PLANTS. THE SOIL LEVEL BELOW OLDER TUSSOCKS IS OFTEN HIGHER THAN THAT OF THE SURROUNDING GROUND, FORMING A SMALL MOUND

TUNDRA
FROZEN SOIL LIES

DATA-BURST

WHERE PRECISELY IS THE ARCTIC TUNDRA?
AT A LATITUDE BETWEEN 60 AND 70°, IT IS THE AREA AROUND THE ARCTIC COAST OF NORTH AMERICA, EUROPE AND ASIA AND THE COASTAL MARGINS OF GREENLAND.

HOW LONG IS WINTER IN THE TUNDRA?
IN THE ARCTIC TUNDRA, THE TEMPERATURE CAN REMAIN BELOW FREEZING FOR UP TO 10 MONTHS OF THE YEAR.

WHAT IS A PINGO?
THIS IS THE ESKIMO, OR INUIT, WORD FOR FROZEN MOUNDS FORMED BY WATER BENEATH THE SOIL SURFACE THAT EXPANDS AS IT FREEZES. IN WINTER, AS THE CORE OF ICE GROWS, IT PUSHES UPWARDS UNTIL IT RISES ABOVE THE SURFACE OF THE LAND. WHERE THE WATER SOURCE IS PARTICULARLY ABUNDANT, A PINGO CAN RISE TO BECOME A MOUND 60 M HIGH.

WHY ARE ANIMALS LIVING IN THE TUNDRA MOSTLY WHITE?
FOR CAMOUFLAGE AND WARMTH. WHITE HAIRS ARE HOLLOW, PROVIDING GREATER INSULATION.

WHY ARE TUNDRA INSECTS MOSTLY BLACK?
SO THAT THEY CAN ABSORB AND RETAIN AS MUCH HEAT AS POSSIBLE.

DOES IT RAIN IN THE TUNDRA?
RARELY IN THE ARCTIC—TYPICAL ANNUAL RAINFALL THERE IS LESS THAN 35 CM—BUT FREQUENTLY IN THE ALPINE TUNDRA.

DO BIRDS MIGRATE TO AVOID THE EXTREME TUNDRA WEATHER?
THE FEW BIRDS THAT LIVE IN THE TUNDRA THROUGHOUT THE YEAR INCLUDE THE GREAT SNOWY OWL AND THE PTARMIGAN. OTHER SPECIES SUCH AS THE CANADA GOOSE AND ARCTIC TERN FLY THOUSANDS OF KILOMETRES TO MILDER REGIONS TO NEST.

PLANT AND ANIMAL LIFE IN THE TUNDRA

IN A TUNDRA LANDSCAPE, THE GROUND IS TYPICALLY COVERED IN MOSSES, SEDGES AND COTTON GRASS. NEAR THE COAST, GRASSES AND RUSHES PREDOMINATE, YET FURTHER INLAND AND ALONG SANDIER STRETCHES, SOME FLOWERS AND PLANTS CAN SURVIVE. IT IS THOUGHT THAT THESE PLANTS DEVELOPED FROM CONIFEROUS FORESTS AND ALPINE AREAS AS THE CONTINENTS DRIFTED INTO COLDER, HIGHER LATITUDES

SEVERAL MILLION YEARS AGO. POLAR BEARS, ARCTIC WOLVES, FOXES, HARES AND WEASEL ALL LIVE HERE, AS DO REINDEER, CARIBOU AND MUSK OXEN. LEMMINGS ARE AN IMPORTANT SPECIES IN THE TUNDRA, BECAUSE THEY HELP IN THE FERTILIZATION PROCESS OF THE SOIL BY DEPOSITING MANURE AROUND THEIR BURROWS WHICH STIMULATE PLANT GROWTH BECAUSE OF ITS NUTRIENTS AND NITROGEN CONTENT.

LEFT: TUNDRA COLOURS ADORN THE AUTUMNAL LANDSCAPE AT DENALI NATIONAL PARK, ALASKA · RIGHT: TUSSOCKS IN THE TUNDRA, ALASKA'S ARCTIC NATIONAL WILDLIFE REFUGE

1,525M UNDERGROUND

BETWEEN THE FROZEN ARCTIC WASTELAND AND THE VAST
FORESTS OF NORTH AMERICA AND SCANDINAVIA LIES THE
TUNDRA—AN ENORMOUS, TREELESS, SPARTAN LANDSCAPE
HOME TO ONLY THE HARDIEST OF PLANT AND ANIMAL LIFE

Antarctica, which means 'opposite to the Arctic', lies almost concentrically around the South Pole. Twice the size of Australia, this continent is almost entirely blanketed by ice sheets. The plant and animal life that lives in this frozen wilderness is specially adapted to cope with the extreme cold that persists all year round. Thirty million cubic kilometres of ice covers the continent. Sea ice fringes the land mass, further extending the frozen landscape. This ice effects ocean currents and the sea level. Scientists are trying to understand how changes in its mass affect world ocean currents and climate.

Shrink and swell
Antarctica has been called the 'pulsating continent' because of the annual build-up and retreat of its icy coastline. Antarctica doubles in size during the winter months when seas freeze over. 'Pancake ice' gathers where free-floating discs of ice litter the sea. As winter deepens, they collect, crowding against each other. Eventually these plates cement into ice floes that buckle and ram against each other as they slide around icebergs.

This frosty lid, when it melts, is thought to produce much of the world's coldest, saltiest water. Sea ice covers much of the water surrounding Antarctica for at least 10 months of the year. Even during summer months, water under the ice receives less than 1% of surface sunshine.

Days by night
For four months of the year, Antarctica is plunged into total darkness. This is because the

Earth's axis is tilted 23.5° from a perpendicular position. As a result of this alignment, Antarctica, which lies at the bottom of the globe, is completely hidden from the sun during this portion of the year's seasonal cycle.

The coldest place
The world's lowest ever recorded temperature, -89°C, was taken at Vostok station in Antarctica on 21 July 1983. While temperatures of up to 15°C have been recorded

ANTARCTICA

ANTARCTIC TEMPERATURES

on the Antarctic peninsula, the average around the continent's edges is 0°C and, in the interior, between -20 and -35°C. Antarctica is much colder than the Arctic. This is partly because, at an average elevation of more than 2,000 m, it is also the world's highest continent. The wind chill factor is also significant as winds sweep across the barren landscape at up to 175 km/h. Rain here is almost unheard of, making this a giant ice-covered desert.

Before the ice arrived
The history of Antarctica can be traced back about 3 billion years to the Precambrian era when it was part of a giant continental

elsewhere in the world. In 1982, the first fossil of a mammal, a marsupial, was found on Seymour Island in the Weddell Sea. This fossil evidence proves that Antarctica's climate and terrain once supported many plants and animals. Coal has also been found in the Transantarctic Mountains, indicating that lush vegetation was once supported by a warm climate.

Discovery and exploration
Maori legend tells of a war canoe that sailed to the frozen ocean in AD 650 under the command of Ui-te-Rangiora. However, the mapping of Antarctica only started from the 1820s when the Russian explorer Fabian Gottlieb von

WHO OWNS ANTARCTICA?

THERE HAVE BEEN A SERIES OF DISPUTES ABOUT THE OWNERSHIP OF THE WORLD'S FIFTH-LARGEST CONTINENT. RECENT DISCOVERIES OF OIL AND GAS HAVE REVIVED DEBATE ABOUT THE FUTURE OF ANTARCTICA. THE FIRST HALF OF THE 20TH CENTURY WAS A COLONIAL PERIOD. BETWEEN 1908 AND 1942, SEVEN NATIONS DECREED SOVEREIGNTY OVER PIE-SHAPED SECTORS OF THE CONTINENT. BY THE MID 1950S, STATIONS HAD BEEN ESTABLISHED BY CHILE, ARGENTINA, BRITAIN, FRANCE AND AUSTRALIA. AN INTERNATIONAL GEOPHYSICAL YEAR IN 1958 SPURRED NATION STATES INTO DECIDING TO CO-OPERATE WITH EACH OTHER. IN 1959, 12 NATIONS SIGNED THE ANTARCTIC TREATY, PROMISING TO PRESERVE THE AREA FOR SCIENTIFIC RESEARCH, AND PUTTING ASIDE MILITARY AND STRATEGIC AIMS.

PLUMMET TO -35°C

ANTARCTICA IS THE LAST GREAT WILDERNESS ON EARTH. ALMOST ENTIRELY ICE-COVERED, IT IS PLUNGED INTO TOTAL DARKNESS FOR FOUR MONTHS A YEAR, WHILE THE SURROUNDING SEAS FREEZE OVER FOR TEN MONTHS

landmass called Gondwanaland. This ice-free ancient continent would have comprised most of today's southern hemisphere land masses. Africa and Australia probably broke apart from Antarctica some time between 180 and 160 million years ago. It is now known that Antarctica became isolated from the rest of the southern hemisphere at about the same time as mammals began to live in greater numbers

Bellinghausen first sighted the continent. Sled expeditions deep into the interior of Antarctica only began to take place at late as the 1900s. The area's severe climate continued to present insurmountable difficulties to those who sought to conquer it. When Denmark and Britain engaged in a competition to see who could reach the South Pole first, only Roald Amundsen's team survived the ordeal. The expedition

commanded by Robert F. Scott perished after they had reached the Pole on 17 Jan 1912.

Penguins and seals
The absence of mammalian predators makes Antarctica a haven for seabirds, and about 45 species live there. Penguins are distributed widely around the continent. Antarctic mammals are all marine and include seals, porpoises, dolphins and whales. Years of whaling and hunting for seals has led to the virtual extinction of the fur seal and the elephant seal, although numbers are now starting to recover.

Lichens and fungi
There are only about 800 species of plant that are able to survive Antarctica's extremely low temperatures. Many of the plant species are lichens, which grow on the darker-coloured rock that absorbs heat most readily. Other species include moulds, yeasts and fungi, algae and liverworts.

Global warming danger
Measurements taken over the past 20 years suggest that pack ice is now melting faster than it used to. This is one of the most obvious features of global warming. In

March 1996, an iceberg 200 m thick and measuring 78 km long by 37 km wide was calved from the Larsen Ice Shelf on the Antarctic peninsula. That same month, the Arctic peninsula of Blomstrandhaloya became an island for the first time because the ice that linked it with the Spitsbergen mainland melted. The melting of ice in the polar regions has an impact on sea levels all around the globe.

Perilous winter seas
Scientists only began to explore Antarctica's winter sea in 1974 when they examined ice flow at the edges of its reach. Only in 1986 did the first research ship, a German icebreaker named the *Polarstern*, venture deep into the sea. The trip was criticized as foolhardy and unnecessary: every ship that had gone in before had been trapped in the ice and the place was assumed to be a wasteland. However, the expedition found life in abundance. Since that pioneering journey, 10 other expeditions have risked the journey. Information collected so far has shown that the ice is vital for the proliferation of life throughout the south-east oceans. Algae provides a rich pasture for krill and tiny shrimp-like creatures which are the staple food for larger animals such as whales.

Lake Vostok
Lake Vostok is the largest of Antarctica's 70 underground lakes. It is more than 480 m deep and is thought to be between 2 and 15 million years old. Drilling here has led to the discovery of microbes previously unknown to science. Some have been revived after hundreds of thousands of years of preservation.

DATA-BURST

WHAT WOULD ANTARCTICA BE LIKE WITHOUT ICE?
THE AVERAGE ELEVATION WOULD BE ABOUT 450 M. IT WOULD CONSIST OF A SMALL CONTINENT AND ISLAND ARCHIPELAGO.

ARE THERE MINERALS IN ANTARCTICA?
MINERALS HAVE BEEN FOUND IN ANTARCTICA BUT FULL EXPLORATION IS DIFFICULT DUE TO THE FREEZING CONDITIONS. SOME COAL HAS BEEN FOUND IN THE TRANSANTARCTIC MOUNTAINS AND DEPOSITS OF IRON HAVE BEEN FOUND NEAR THE PRINCE CHARLES MOUNTAINS.

IS THERE OIL IN THE SEA SURROUNDING ANTARCTICA?
PETROLEUM HAS BEEN FOUND, MAINLY DURING DRILLING IN THE ROSS SEA BY THE *GLOMAR CHALLENGER* IN 1973. HOWEVER, AN AGREEMENT IN 1991

BETWEEN ALL THE ANTARCTIC TREATY NATIONS OUTLAWED THE COMMERCIAL EXPLOITATION OF MINERALS.

HAVE METEORITES BEEN FOUND IN ANTARCTICA?
THOUSANDS OF METEORITES HAVE BEEN DISCOVERED BY GEOLOGISTS BURIED IN THE ICE SHEETS OF THE CONTINENT. MOST OF THEM FELL BETWEEN 700,000 AND 10,00 YEARS AGO. ONE FOUND IN 1982 IS THOUGHT TO HAVE COME FROM THE MOON.

DOES THE ICE MELT?
ICE SHEETS AND GLACIERS 'CALVE' OR RELEASE ICEBERGS INTO THE SEA.

ARE THERE ACTIVE VOLCANOES IN ANTARCTICA ?
ACTIVE VOLCANOES CAN BE FOUND IN ELLSWORTH LAND AND MARIE BYRD LAND. MOST VOLCANIC ACTIVITY TAKES PLACE IN THE SCOTIA ARC.

LEFT: A SOLITARY BOAT CROSSES THE BARREN AND FREEZING WILDERNESS OF ANTARCTICA

Islands are either oceanic or continental. Oceanic islands form when undersea volcanoes spew out so much lava that the molten rock piles up as it solidifies and protrudes above the surface of the waves. Continental islands form when the sea rises and floods parts of a continental shelf, leaving high areas protruding above the water but totally separated from the mainland. The British Isles are continental, as are Java, Sumatra, Bali and Lombok; in fact, these Indonesian islands are really just the tops of underwater mountains, joined together by land during the last ice age, 35,000–10,000 years ago, when sea levels were lower.

Rising seas in the Maldives

Rising seas not only create islands, but also destroy them. In the Indian Ocean, the range of small islands known as the Maldives are being threatened by rising sea levels caused by global warming. The area's 1,800 low-lying coral islands, none of which are over 1.8 m high, are in imminent danger of disappearing beneath the slowly rising sea. This would spell disaster for the 250,000 people who inhabit 200 of the islands.

Birth of the Hawaii Chain

Perhaps the most familiar string of islands is the Hawaiian-Emperor series in the Pacific Ocean. They were formed around a hotspot—a site of extreme volcanic activity—60 km below the ocean floor. The chain, which comprises a series of eight major islands, the smaller Leeward Islands and about 30 submerged seamounts, is a stunning mountain-range rising a staggering 10 km from the sea bed. The islands date from 27 million years ago (Midway Island) to less than 700,000 years ago (Hawaii). They were formed when molten lava from the ocean floor rose above the hotspot, building up over many years until it finally burst through the surface. The islands, like Hawaii, continue to grow as long as they are still connected to the hotspot. However, the movement of the Pacific Plate means that the floor of the ocean traverses the hotspot at a rate of up to a metre per decade.

NEW TERRAIN

WORLDS'S NEWEST ISLAND

ARTIFICIAL ISLAND

KANSAI INTERNATIONAL AIRPORT IN JAPAN WAS CONSTRUCTED ON A PURPOSE-BUILT ARTIFICIAL ISLAND. IT WAS INITIALLY MEANT TO BE BUILT ON A FLOATING ISLAND BUT THIS WAS REJECTED ON THE GROUNDS OF THE HAZARDS OF EXTREME WEATHER CONDITIONS AND THE POTENTIALLY HIGH COSTS, ALTHOUGH IN THE END KANISA AIRPORT TURNED OUT TO BE THE WORLD'S MOST EXPENSIVE BUILDING PROJECT TO DATE. THE TOTAL REPORTED COST OF BUILDING THE AIRPORT, WHICH OPENED IN 1994, WAS £10 BILLION. THE PROJECT INVOLVED THE CONSTRUCTION OF A 1.75-KM-LONG INTERNAL STRUCTURE AND AN ARTIFICIAL ISLAND 5 KM FROM THE SHORE IN OSAKA BAY. THE ISLAND, WHICH IS 4.27 KM LONG BY 1.25 KM WIDE, WAS STABILIZED WITH A MILLION SAND PILES, AND TOOK FIVE YEARS TO COMPLETE.

OBSERVED IN 1995

FROM THE HUGE LANDMASS OF GREENLAND TO SMALL UNINHABITED ISLANDS IN THE PACIFIC OCEAN WHICH MEASURE JUST A FEW METRES ACROSS, THE EARTH'S ISLANDS WERE ALL FORMED IN ONE OF TWO WAYS

Eventually, the islands will be cut off from the source of their generation and then, with no lava build-up to replenish them, wind and sea erosion will begin to wear the islands down. They will ultimately collapse into one of the very deep trenches in the Pacific. Meiji, the oldest and most northerly seamount will be the first to disappear. Once it is free from the influence of the hotspot,

Hawaii will begin its own journey into oblivion. Yet, even as the current islands and seamounts begin to disappear, new ones are being formed above the hotspot. The result is an ongoing cycle of birth, death and rebirth.

Ancient mountains stand tall
The West Indian archipelago spans more than 3,200 km and has formed over many millions of

years. The shape and positioning of Cuba, Jamaica, Haiti, the Dominican Republic and Puerto Rico are determined by an ancient range of mountains which connected Central America to the Caribbean in Cretaceous times. Remnants of this mountain range include the Blue Mountains of Jamaica and the Duarte Peak in the Dominican Republic, which has the highest peak in the Caribbean standing at 3,170 m tall.

New life on new land
Islands can provide a unique opportunity for evolution because unfamiliar terrain allows the immigrant species to take on new roles. During their evolution, they may lose original features in favour of those which are more appropriate to the new environment, such as the development of flightless birds, for example the kiwi in New Zealand. Conditions of low competition can lead to a diversification of one species as it tries to fulfil a wide range of vacant roles. In this way, the tarweeds of Hawaii have evolved from plant to tree form. Charles Darwin's observations in 1835 on the Galapagos Islands— an archipelago of 19 rugged islands situated about 1,000 km

west of Ecuador in the Eastern Pacific Ocean—formed the basis for his evolutionary theories, which have informed our understanding of how new life forms develop.

Iceland's new neighbour
In geological terms, the island of Iceland is relatively young. It was formed when the North American and Eurasian tectonic plates moved apart. Volcanic action on the fault line belched out lava to produce a new crust and, about 65 million years ago, Iceland was born. But volcanic activity in the region was not at an end. Iceland itself has a number of active volcanoes and in 1967 a new island appeared off Iceland's southern coast. This island, called Surtsey, was forced 170 m above sea level—a massive 285 m above the ocean floor where the volcanic eruption took place.

High up in Oceania
The islands of the Pacific Ocean, sometimes called Oceania, are of both the continental type and the oceanic type. Many of the oceanic islands are actually large blocks of coral which sit upon volcanic bases. The smallest islands are coral 'atolls', the name for an island which is formed when flooding leaves only the highest point of land above water. The larger oceanic islands are usually small but very high, as they were forced up abruptly from the ocean floor by intense volcanic activity. The highest point of Hawaii, snow-capped Mauna Kea, was pushed 10,205 m above the sea floor by violent forces of this nature. These submarine upheavals are responsible for the formation of the world's newest island. Located in Tonga's Ha'apei group, halfway between the islands of Kao and Late, the island—so new that it has not yet even been named, was first observed on 6 June 1995.

Reminder of a forgotton land
Just off the coast of Cornwall, UK, between Land's End and the Isles of Scilly, lies a conical hill known as St Michael's Mount. This tiny island was formed when a rise in sea level cut the hill off from the Cornish mainland. According to legend, St Michael's Mount is all that remains of the lost country of Lyoness—a glorious and most prosperous land. When the sea rushed in and drowned this mythical domain, a lone horseman called Trevilian is said to have ridden out of the sea, mounted on a white horse.

DATA-BURST

HOW ARE ISLANDS FORMED?
BY ONE OF TWO MEANS: EITHER AS A RESULT OF VOLCANIC ACTIVITY OR BY RISING SEA LEVELS.

HOW BIG ARE CONTINENTAL ISLANDS?
THE TWIN PEAKS WHICH CROWN THE ISLAND OF HAWAII REACH HEIGHTS OF OVER 4,000 M. THEIR MOUNTAIN BASE, BIGGER THAN EVEREST, RISES FROM THE SEA FLOOR TO 10,205 M-HIGH.

WHAT ARE SEAMOUNTS?
THESE UNDERWATER MOUNTAINS ARE THE RESULT OF VOLCANIC ACTIVITY. NOT BIG ENOUGH TO PROTRUDE ABOVE THE WATER'S SURFACE, THEY USUALLY FALL SHORT WITHIN A FEW HUNDRED FEET. TO DATE, OCEANOGRAPHERS HAVE MAPPED OVER 2,000 SEAMOUNTS, MOSTLY IN THE PACIFIC OCEAN.

WHAT IS A BARRIER ISLAND?
A LONG, NARROW ISLAND, USUALLY MADE FROM SAND, PARALLEL TO THE MAINLAND AND SEPARATED FROM IT

BY A LAGOON. IT IS FORMED WHEN THE COAST IS ADVANCING SEAWARD AND WAVES BREAK FAR OFFSHORE. A CORAL REEF IN A SIMILAR POSITION IS CALLED A BARRIER REEF.

WHAT DO ISLANDS TELL US ABOUT THE ORIGIN OF SPECIES?
NEW ANIMAL AND PLANT SPECIES ARE MOST LIKELY TO ARRIVE ON AN ISLAND VIA THE AIR. SOME PLANTS HAVE SPECIAL STICKY SEEDS WHICH ATTACH TO THE FUR OR FEATHERS OF BIRDS OR MAMMALS, AND THE SEEDS OF FLESHY FRUITS MAY BE CARRIED LONG DISTANCES BEFORE THEY ARE EXCRETED AND CAN GERMINATE. BLUEBERRY, SANDALWOOD AND MINT PROBABLY ALL ARRIVED IN HAWAII THIS WAY. ANIMALS COMPETING FOR SURVIVAL RISE AND FALL IN DOMINANCE, DEMONSTRATING AN ONGOING BALANCE IN NATURE BETWEEN THE RATE AT WHICH NEW ORGANISMS COLONIZE AN ISLAND AND OLD ONES BECOME EXTINCT.

LEFT: AERIAL VIEW OF TWO OF THE GALAPAGOS, A GROUP OF OCEANIC ISLANDS ABOUT 970 KM FROM THE WEST COAST OF SOUTH AMERICA, FORMED AS A RESULT OF VOLCANIC ACTIVITY

CANYONS

THE DEEPEST GORGE

Canyons and gorges are dramatic plunging rock formations gouged out by the eroding flow of a river. Deep ravines and rocky crags are formed as the result of millions of years of water and wind erosion. Fast flowing water washes off rock, gradually widening walls and opening up cracks, while wind also scoops away soft rock. The best known canyons are to be found in the USA in the geological region known as the Colorado Plateau —a massive section of the continental crust that comprises some of the oldest rock that has been examined by man. The erosion that continues today began relatively recently in geological terms—only 10 million years ago.

WHO DISCOVERED THE GRAND CANYON?

THE OLDEST EVIDENCE OF HUMAN LIFE IN THE GRAND CANYON DATES BACK NEARLY 4,000 YEARS. TINY SPLIT TWIG FIGURINES DISCOVERED IN CAVES ARE THOUGHT TO BELONG TO THE EARLY NATIVE AMERICAN 'DESERT CULTURE'. THE FIRST EUROPEANS TO SEE THE BREATHTAKING LANDSCAPE ARRIVED IN 1540. ITS OFFICIAL 'DISCOVERY' WAS ATTRIBUTED TO TWO SPANISH PRIESTS, FRANCISCO GARCES AND SILVESTRE VELEZ DE ESCALANTE, IN 1776. MAJOR JOHN WESLEY POWELL, A ONE-ARMED VETERAN OF THE AMERICAN CIVIL WAR, WAS THE FIRST TO MAKE A PIONEERING JOURNEY THROUGH THE CANYON BY RIVER IN 1869. NAVAJO PEOPLES STILL LIVE IN THE REGION BUT THEY ARE DESCENDANTS OF TRIBES WHO ARRIVED ONLY IN THE 15TH CENTURY. THE ZUNI INDIANS, NOW IN NEW MEXICO, CLAIM THE AREA AS THEIR PLACE OF ORIGIN.

PLUNGES 2,400 M

CANYONS ARE DEEP ROCK VALLEYS AND GORGES CARVED OUT OF THE LAND BY MILLIONS OF YEARS OF RAIN AND WIND EROSION WHICH HAVE SHAPED THE ROCK INTO STEEP RAVINES, JAGGED CLIFFS AND DELICATE SPIRES

Rain-sculpted canyons
The process of canyon erosion takes place over millions of years. Because of the arid conditions that are often a feature of canyon lands, rain storms—when they come—often arrive violently and flash flooding is common. As there is very little vegetation, run-off is rapid and water collects in gullies and small washes, magnifying the power of water funnels in the

canyon. Canyons are continually deepening and being further scoured by the force of the elements. Rainwater penetrates weak joints and cracks until only thin 'fins' and 'needles' remain.

The biggest range
The Grand Canyon is the biggest and most varied of all the canyons in the USA. It lies in the north-west corner of Arizona, close to the

borders of Utah and Nevada. It became a national park in 1919. The park encompasses over a million acres of land, much of it high plateaus lying 150–275 m above sea level. The Colorado River itself is 446 km long and has many tributaries. At its deepest, the gorge measures 1,829 vertical metres from the river bed to rim. The trip from top to bottom, by foot or mule, is a two-day journey.

The continuing story
The forces of rain, snowmelt and tributary streams continue to shape the Grand Canyon. This erosion began 5–6 million years ago, only yesterday considering that some of the rock through which the canyon is carved is 2 billion years old. The different layers of limestone, sandstone, shale and granite all respond to erosion in different ways. Whereas some form slopes, others form cliffs. Rock types erode at different speeds, giving the canyon its varied shape and texture, and creating its characteristic 'stairstep' contour.

Bryce Canyon
Thousands of wind carved spires rise from the natural amphitheatre that is the Bryce Canyon National Park. The canyon, carved from the eastern edge of the Paunsaugunt Plateau in southern Utah, is surrounded by high elevation meadows. The high rim country is part forest, part grass while at lower, drier altitudes, juniper and pine predominate. Millions of years of wind and water erosion have etched the towering pink cliffs made up of strata of limestone, sandstone and mudstone. Their red and yellow colours are caused by iron oxides in the rock, while the purples and lavenders are the result of manganese.

Canyon de Chelly
The Canyon de Chelly National Monument, in north-eastern Arizona, occupies 339 km² and includes several hundred ancient cliff dwellings built at the base of red sandstone cliffs or in caves on the steep canyon walls. Many of these date from the 11th century, others from later Pueblo cultures. Modern Navajo Indian homes still occupy the canyon floor.

DATA-BURST

WHERE IS THE DEEPEST CANYON?
HELL'S CANYON IN OREGON, USA, IS DEEPER THAN THE GRAND CANYON. AT ITS MAXIMUM DEPTH IT MEASURES 2,400 M. WHEREAS THE LOWER ELEVATIONS ARE DRY AND BARREN, THE HIGH COUNTRY FEATURES TOWERING PEAKS AND ALPINE LAKES.

ARE THERE CANYONS UNDERWATER?
MANY OF THE EARTH'S MOST SPECTACULAR CANYONS ARE CUT DEEP INTO THE OCEAN FLOOR. THESE SUBMARINE GORGES ARE USUALLY V-SHAPED WITH STEEP ROCKY WALLS. THE MONTEREY CANYON IS THE LARGEST AND DEEPEST AND LIES OFF THE PACIFIC COAST OF THE USA.

HOW QUICKLY HAS EROSION TAKEN PLACE IN THE GRAND CANYON?
DIFFERENT ROCKS ERODE AT DIFFERENT SPEEDS. DEER CREEK IN THE GRAND CANYON GNAWS THROUGH SANDSTONE FORMED IN THE CAMBRIAN ERA AT A RATE OF LESS THAN 2.5 CM A

CENTURY. THE GRAND CANYON HAS ENTRENCHED APPROXIMATELY 1,8000 M AND WIDENED ITS WALLS BY 29 KM IN THE LAST 10 MILLION YEARS.

WHICH ARE THE OLDEST ROCKS FOUND IN CANYONS?
GRANITE AND VISHNU SCHIST, BOTH FOUND AT THE BOTTOM OF THE GRAND CANYON, ARE 2 BILLION YEARS OLD. ON TOP IS A LAYER OF SHALE, LIMESTONE AND SANDSTONE ALL IN EXCESS OF 300 MILLION YEARS OLD. THE NEXT LAYER, WAS FORMED IN THE MESOZOIC ERA, 66-245 MILLION YEARS AGO.

DOES TECTONIC MOVEMENT AFFECT THE FORMATION OF CANYONS?
THE FORMATION OF CANYONS IS ACCELERATED BY MOVEMENT IN THE EARTH'S CRUST. THE REGIONAL UPLIFT OF ROCK WORKS AGAINST EROSIVE FORCES TO DEEPEN THE CANYON. THIS ROCK UPLIFT INCREASES THE FLOW OF RIVERS WHICH ALSO ENHANCES THEIR CAPACITY TO ERODE.

JARGON

CANYON
A LARGE, RELATIVELY NARROW, STEEP RIVER VALLEY

HOODOOS
CANYON FORMATIONS OF SPIRES, PINNACLES, FINS AND TURRETS

MESA TOP
ISOLATED FLAT-TOPPED HILL WITH STEEP SLOPES

RAVINE
A STEEP VALLEY FORMED THROUGH THE EROSION OF AN UPLIFT OF LAND BY A RIVER

SAW-TOOTHED DIVIDE
RAGGED, SHARP-EDGED MINIATURE CANYONS

STAIRSTEP
STEPPED CONTOURS OF CANYONS FORMED WHEN SOFTER ROCK IN THE STRATA IS ERODED MORE QUICKLY THAN HARDER ROCK

LEFT: AGUA CANYON AT DAWN, BRYCE CANYON NATIONAL PARK IN SOUTHERN UTAH, USA · INSET: CAVE RUINS AT THE CANYON DE CHELLY IN ARIZONA, USA

Caves are underground chambers created by geological forces. These rock-formed spaces, carved away by the eroding power of underground streams and rivers, can be as mighty as cathedrals, filled with intricate features such as stalactites and stalagmites. Caves provided early human societies with natural shelter, and many still bear witness to the habitation of prehistoric man and preserve the earliest examples of primitive art. Caves remain places of fascination and exploration.

Cave creation
Primary caves develop when molten rock is still in the process of solidifying. Pockets of air are trapped in the lava flowing from an erupting volcano. As the lava cools, the rock hardens, leaving the cave's space. Most caves of this type consist of a single tube or tunnel that extends along the former lava field. Secondary caves are more common and develop after the rock has solidified. These are created by water erosion over a long period of time as chemicals in the water dissolve and erode the calcerous rock. This process, which occurs below the water table, gradually produces the honeycomb of passages that is characteristic of solution caves. As the water table drops, the cavities drain.

BELOW: REED FLUTE CAVE, GUILIN, CHINA

An unending labyrinth
The Carlsbad Caves in New Mexico provide a typical example of solution-created caves. This site is made up of a complex series of huge underground chambers that are linked by many tunnels and galleries. The full extent of the maze is still unknown but the explored portion measures 37 km long. The inter-connecting corridors took about 60 million years to form.

The biggest caves
The Sarawak Chamber, part of an extended cave system in the Gunung Mulu National Park on the island of Borneo, is the largest known cave in the world. It stretches for 700 m, with an average width of 300 m and a minimum height of 70 m, and was discovered and surveyed in 1980. The caves of Sarawak provide important information about humans' early inhabitation of South-east Asia. An expedition to

the Niah Cave in 1954 found tools dating back to 40,000 BC and a human skeleton from 38,000 BC. The cave was inhabited almost continually until the 19th century. Among its features are the 'boats of the dead', an ancient burial chamber, and the 'painted cave', so-called because the walls are made of red hematite, an iron-rich mineral oxide. Some 195 km of this immense cave system has been explored, but this is only an estimated 30% of the total area.

CAVES
LARGEST CHAMBER

Other caves in the park include the Deer Cave, a partially sunlit chamber 122 m high.

Church-like interiors

The Wyandotte Cave in Crawford County, Indiana, USA, contains 40 km of passages on five different levels. It is the largest of the Mississippian limestone caves and was probably inhabited during prehistoric times. Subsequently, it has been used by native American Indians. The cave's entrance is 60 m above the Blue River. Features include Rothrock's Grand Cathedral, an enormous chamber almost 500 m in circumference, and with a rock pile 52 m high at its centre called Monument Mountain. The Senate Chamber, an elliptical amphitheatre 43 m long and 17 m wide, houses the Pillar of Constitution. A column of white calcite made up of a stalactite and stalagmite, the pillar has a circumference of more than 20 m.

Subterranean life

While both the temperature and humidity can vary, all caves are very dark places. They support a range of specially-evolved animals and plants that can cope with life

FIRE-RED BISON FOUND IN THE DARKNESS OF A SPANISH CAVE

DISCOVERED BY A HUNTER IN 1869, THE ALTAMIRA CAVE IN NORTHERN SPAIN IS FAMOUS FOR PREHISTORIC PAINTINGS WHICH ARE THOUGHT TO BE 14,0000 YEARS OLD. ITS VESTIBULE HOUSED REMAINS INCLUDING CARVED ANIMAL BONES. THE HUGE 270-M DOME OF THE MAIN CHAMBER IS COVERED WITH DRAWINGS OF ANIMALS, MOST OF WHICH APPEAR TO BE BISON. EXECUTED IN VIVID REDS, BLACKS AND VIOLETS, OTHER ANIMALS DEPICTED INCLUDE WILD BOARS, HORSES AND SIMPLE HUMAN FIGURES, WHILE HUMAN HANDPRINTS ALSO DECORATE THE WALLS. IN MANY CASES, THE ARTISTS FOLLOWED THE NATURAL CONTOURS OF THE ROCK. THE DRAWINGS ARE SO COLOURFUL AND FRESH THAT AT FIRST THEY WERE DISMISSED AS FORGERIES: NOT UNTIL THE 20TH CENTURY WERE THEY ACCEPTED AS GENUINE.

without light. Most are colourless or white because the lack of light prohibits the development of a pigment. Perhaps the best-known cave-dwellers are bats, which often live underground in huge colonies. Each night, more than one million bats leave the Carlsbad cavern to feed in the nearby Pecos Valley. Because of the huge numbers, this exodus takes about four hours. In water-filled caves, fish which are pale, blind and no more than 10 cm

long are common. While they do have eyes, these have become obsolete in the conditions and the fish rely on their keen sense of touch to navigate and to feed. Luminous moss, known as Elfin Gold, covers the floor of caves in the northern hemisphere.

Secret hideaway

A vast and intricate network of caves zigzags under the city of Guilin, China. Stretching down for

some 240 m, the Reed Flute Cave, known locally as *Ludi Yan*, is the largest and most magnificent cave in Guilin. It is full of exquisite stalactites—constructed from limestone and crystal, they form in amazing shapes and different colours. Grass grows in abundance at the mouth of the cave and legend has it that local people built flutes from these reeds, and that the caves were used in ancient times as a refuge from war.

700 M LONG AND 300 M WIDE

Rock formations can be viewed as the final remnants of a geological battlefield. Scarred by the violent wounds of time and further shaped by erosion, rock is chiselled by nature into unusual shapes and forms. Some parts of the world boast awesome arches, towers, boulders and stacks that create an eerie landscape of incredible natural beauty.

Utah's natural arches
Landscape Arch in the Arches National Park and Kolob Arch in Zion National Park, both in Utah, USA, are the longest natural arches in the world, both spanning openings of some 94 m. Perhaps the most dramatic arch is Rainbow Bridge, also in Utah. Only 82.3 m long, it rises to a height of 88.4 m and, as it spans water, it is considered to be the longest natural bridge in the world. Landscape Arch, one of 1,900 natural arches in the Devil's Garden area of Arches National Park, is a reminder that the forces that created these amazing natural sculptures are still at work. Only 3.35 m wide at its thinnest point, the arch could collapse at any time under the force of its own weight.

The Giant's Causeway
On the tip of Northern Ireland lies a remarkable rock formation of hexagonal cliffs and columns, lashed by the crashing waves and spray of the Atlantic Ocean.Local mythology states that the structure was built by giants. In fact, this strange, irregular pavement was formed when lava, erupting beneath the sea, cooled rapidly as it hit the water, forming basalt. The hexagonal blocks of the Giant's . Causeway are 37–50 cm wide and up to 6 m in height, although one column is a massive 12 m wide. The columns of the Pleaskin Cliffs, part of the same formation, rise to a height of over 120 m.

Ayers Rock
In the parched and sun-baked Northern Territory of Australia lies the largest single rock in the world. Ayers Rock, or Uluru as it is known by Aborigines, is a lump of red sandstone that stands 335 m high and 9 km in circumference.

SCULPTURES

WORLD'S LARGEST NATURAL

This huge domed monolith, which projects from a flat plain, glows with vivid oranges and reds at sunrise and sunset. Ayers Rock is decreasing in size but not in shape. The continuous splintering of small flakes from its surface means that the rock is shedding skins of equal thickness all the time. It was named Ayers Rock by the deputy surveyor general, William Goose, who came upon the rock in 1873. But Uluru had been revered by indigenous Aborigine tribes for centuries. According to their tradition, every crevice, crack and indentation on the surface tells a story from the 'Dreamtime' when part-human, part-animal heroes inhabited the land.

ICICLES OF ROCK

THE WEIRD COLUMNS AND CONES OF ROCK FOUND HANGING FROM THE CEILINGS OR SPROUTING FROM THE FLOORS OF SOME CAVES ARE FORMED BY WATER ACTION. SUSPENDED FROM A ROCKY ROOF, STALACTITES USUALLY APPEAR EITHER AS THIN STONE STRAWS OR AS DOWNWARD-TAPERING CONES. BOTH TYPES FORM WHEN WATER WHICH CONTAINS DISSOLVED MINERALS DRIPS SLOWLY BUT CONTINUALLY FROM THE CAVERN CEILING. WHERE THESE DROPS HIT THE FLOOR OF THE CAVE, AN OPPOSITE GROWTH, CALLED A STALAGMITE, MAY GRADUALLY BUILD UP. AS LONG AS THERE ARE NO STRONG AIR CURRENTS IN THE CAVE, FRAGILE STONE-STRAW STALACTITES CAN HANG DOWN TO LENGTHS OF 50 CM AND IN SOME CAVES, THE TWO OPPOSING GROWTHS JOIN TOGETHER TO FORM A COLUMN.

JARGON

DOWNWARD-TAPERING CONE
A STONE STRAW THICKENED BY MINERAL DEPOSITS

EXFOLIATION
ONION SKIN WEATHERING WHEREBY A ROCK'S SURFACE HEATS AND EXPANDS, FLAKING OFF IN LAYERS

FROST WEDGING
JOINTS IN ROCK THAT HAVE BEEN WIDENED BY FROZEN WATER

IGNEOUS ROCK
ROCK FORMED WHEN VOLCANIC LAVA COOLS AND SOLIDIFIES

STONE STRAW
THIS FRAGILE THIN-WALLED STONE STRAW STALACTITE CAN REACH UP TO 50 CM IN LENGTH

ARCH SPANS 94 M

WHETHER CREATED BY SUDDEN EXPLOSIVE FORCES OR GRADUAL PROCESSES, THE EARTH'S NATURAL SCULPTURES ARE OFTEN OF SUCH BEAUTY AND ON SUCH A SCALE THAT HUMAN STRUCTURES PALE BY COMPARISON

The Devil's Tower
This tower of grey rock with a flat top and fluted sides lies in north-eastern Wyoming. The 263-m tower was formed when molten volcanic rock, pushing upwards inside the Earth, came to a layer of hard rock and stopped abruptly. Over millions of years, the surrounding rock has been eroded, exposing the plug of lava which once formed the volcano's core.

Monument Valley
Located on the border of south-eastern Utah and northern Arizona, Monument Valley contains some of the world's most dramatic rock formations. The large towers of sandstone, or buttes, which litter this 40-km valley are streaked with many coloured hues. To geologists, the rock formations are relics of prehistoric sand dunes, but to the Navajo Indian tribes who live on the reservation this remarkable landscape represents the work of supernatural powers.

Forest of Sweet Osmanthus
When rainwater comes into contact with limestone it dissolves minerals from the rock, starting a slow but sure carving process. In time, this process can sculpt tall spires, caves and labyrinths. In south-west China, the hanging hills of Guilin jut out above the surrounding plain like the teeth of a giant dragon. These needle-shaped pinnacles were created by water flows when the region was submerged 270 million years ago.

Yellowstone's rock terraces
Yellowstone National Park in Wyoming, USA, is the site of some spectacular rock terraces.

The stone forest at Guilin consists of 80 hectares of towering peaks of limestone, out of which sprout trees and shrubs. The vegetation is mainly osmanthus, after which Guilin—meaning 'Forest of Sweet Osmanthus'—is named. This area has long been an inspiration for Chinese poets and artists.

The process which created these formations began when water from thermal springs underground dissolved calcium carbonate from the surrounding limestone. The mineral-rich water, when heated by molten rock, rose to the surface. Here it cooled and the minerals were deposited in the form of giant sparkling steps around the thermal pools. As more spring water spilt over their edges, depositing minerals down the sides, these steps grew into huge columns.

DATA-BURST

HOW DO NATURAL SCULPTURES OCCUR?
THEY ARE THE RESULT OF ANCIENT GEOLOGICAL PROCESSES. SUCCESSIVE WAVES OF SEDIMENTATION LEAVE MULTI-COLOURED PLATEAUS AND MESAS OF SANDSTONE, LIMESTONE AND SHALE. VOLCANIC ACTIVITY CAN BLOW THE TOPS OFF MOUNTAIN PEAKS WHILE BUBBLES OF UPSURGING MAGMA CAUSE THE LAND ABOVE GROUND TO BLISTER.

WHAT ARE VOLCANIC EXTRUSION AND VOLCANIC INTRUSION?
EXTRUSION REFERS TO VOLCANIC LAVA THAT BURSTS THROUGH THE EARTH'S SURFACE AND QUICKLY SOLIDIFIES, WHEREAS INTRUSION OCCURS WHEN UNDERGROUND LAVA CANNOT ESCAPE.

HOW DOES EROSION SHAPE ROCK?
WIND-DRIVEN SANDS HELP MOULD THE ROCK BY ACTING AS ABRASIVE FORCES. EXTREME FLUCTUATIONS IN TEMPERATURE CAN CAUSE FRACTURES TO FORM IN THE STONE, PEELING AWAY SLABS FROM THE MAIN BODY. RIVERS ALSO SNAKE THROUGH GORGES AND CANYONS, SLOWLY CUTTING AWAY AT THE ROCK.

WHERE IS THE LONGEST STALACTITE?
THE LONGEST FREE-HANGING STALACTITE MEASURES 28 M LONG AND HANGS IN THE GRUTA DO JANELAO CAVE IN MINAS GERAIS, BRAZIL.

WHERE IS THE HIGHEST ROCK PINNACLE?
THE HIGHEST ROCK PINNACLE IS CALLED BALL'S PYRAMID NEAR LORD HOWE ISLAND IN THE PACIFIC OCEAN. IT STANDS AT 561 M TALL, BUT HAS A NARROW BASE AXIS THAT MEASURES JUST 200 M.

LEFT: SUNRISE LIGHTS UP THE DRAMATIC BUTTES, OR SANDSTONE HILLS, OF MONUMENT VALLEY, USA · RIGHT: ARCHES NATIONAL PARK, UTAH, USA

Dead zones are found in hot deserts and consist of salts that have accumulated in shallow saline lakes. Evaporation then produces a crust of varying hardness. Dead zones remain some of the few places of unspoilt wilderness in the world. These regions were once considered worthless because their lakes and seas contained water that was unable to sustain life, but these inhospitable and formerly uninhabitable areas are now being exploited by humans for their mineral wealth and natural beauty.

The Great Salt Lake
The Great Salt Lake in northern Utah, USA, is one of the largest inland bodies of salt water in the world. It is a remnant of the prehistoric freshwater Lake Bonneville, which was formed in the late Pleistocene period, around 30,000 years ago, and is very saline with a salt level far higher than any

it—the Bear, the Jordan and the Weber. Its surface area ranges from 2,460 km² to 6,200 km² and its depth from 5.4 m to 11 m.

An inhospitable home
The Great Salt Lake lies between extremely desolate stretches of sand and salt marshes. First accounts of it were given by fur trappers but it only appeared on maps in the 19th century when it was charted by the explorer Captain John C. Fremont in 1843.

The Dead Sea
At 397 m below sea level, the Dead Sea, or Salt Sea as it translates from Arabic and Hebrew, is the lowest body of water on Earth. This landlocked salt lake between Israel and Jordan is 80 km long and 18 km wide. It has such a high saturation of salt (30% in some areas) that it is impossible for bathers to sink. The sea originally dates back to the Pleistocene period, 10,000 to 2.5 million years ago, when its level was 215 m

survive in the Black Sea's upper levels because its lower levels are starved of oxygen. In the deeper levels, the water is saturated with dissolved hydrogen and sulphide, and only specially adapted bacteria can exist there. The Black Sea's saline level is nearly half that of most oceans. This is due to the fact that the region became isolated from the sea after structural upheavals split the Caspian Basin from the Mediterranean at least 58 million years ago.

DEAD ZONES
SALT SATURATION IN

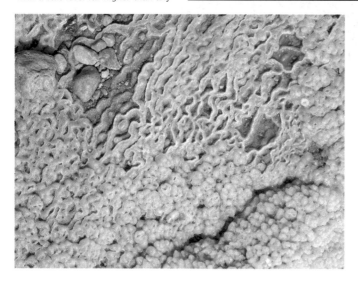

ocean. This is due to the rapid rate of natural evaporation, which is far faster than the rate of influx of water from its feeder rivers, and also because the lake has no outlet into the sea. When the outflow is cut off, this leads to a build-up of mineral deposits and a salt lake is then formed.

Gone with the flow
At one time, Lake Bonneville spread into what are now the neighbouring states of Idaho and Nevada and drained out through the Snake River and the Colombia River into the Pacific Ocean. However, during the inter-glacial and post-glacial periods, this flow was stemmed, the intake of fresh water dropped and the water level fell. The size and depth of the Great Salt Lake varies depending on the level of evaporation and the flow from the three rivers that feed into

Increasing awareness came in 1847 when the Mormons declared nearby Salt Lake City to be their 'promised land'. The lake is fed with 1.1 million tonnes of salt per year, and there are 5 billion tonnes of minerals dissolved in it, mainly salt (sodium and chlorine). Although table salt and potash have been extracted from the lake since the 19th century, it was considered too inhospitable for human habitation, and the few life forms that managed to survive did so only on the surrounding marshes, beaches and mud flats. Pelicans, herons, cormorants, terns and gulls are among the birds that do live there. In recent years, however, the area has been developed as a site for tourism and recreation, with water sports facilities and a wildlife preserve. The extraction of magnesium has been in operation since 1971.

higher than it is at present. It has since shrunk because heavy levels of sediment have been deposited at a faster rate than evaporated water has been replenished. The Dead Sea divides into two basins; the northern basin is more than three times the size of the southern one and far deeper (about 400 m). It is fed mainly by the River Jordan, but with no outlet, the inflow of water is balanced by a rapid rate of evaporation due to the hot desert climate and lack of rainfall. At its deepest levels the waters are so dense that they become fossilized.

Spa towns
The forbidding appearance of the Dead Sea is further enhanced by a thick mist that emerges above the lake when the heat evaporates the water. This evaporation process is estimated at around 1,4000 mm of water every year. No animal or vegetable life can exist in such conditions, apart from bacteria and some halophytes—plants that can survive in salty or alkaline soil. However, hotels are now springing up around the lake with tourists keen to take advantage of the water's health-giving properties.

The Black Sea
Situated in the south-east corner of Europe, separating the continent from Asia, the Black Sea covers 461,000 km² and is more than 2,210 km deep. The entire area has little coastal lowland and the deltas of just a few rivers push out to sea. Its largest feeder tributaries are the Rivers Danube, Dnieper, Dniester and Don. Sea life can only

JARGON

DELTA
LOW LYING PLAIN COMPRISED OF STREAM-BORNE SEDIMENTS DEPOSITED AT A RIVER MOUTH

HALOCLINE
A GRADIENT OF SALINITY

HALOPHYTES
PLANTS THAT GROW IN SALTY OR ALKALINE CONDITIONS

PLEISTOCENE PERIOD
A PREHISTORIC PERIOD THAT STARTED OVER TWO MILLION YEARS AGO

SALINE
NATURAL WATER IMPREGNATED WITH OR CONTAINING SALT

The vanishing Aral
The Aral sea, east of the Caspian Sea in Central Asia, is in the process of drying up. At one time it constituted the world's fourth largest body of inland water but change came when the flow of the Amu River was diverted for irrigation purposes. Since 1960, the level of the sea has dropped almost 3 m and its salinity has increased fourfold. The Aral has become too salty for fish to survive and the lake has shrunk to half its former size. Once prosperous fishing ports are now surrounded by barren land. The retreat of the shoreline has also exposed loose salt deposits mixed with man-made fertilizers and pesticides. Borne on fierce winds, this white toxic dust has caused health problems for humans and livestock—incidents of lung cancer and respiratory diseases in the region have increased dramatically.

LEFT: CLOSE-UP OF SALT CRYSTALS ENCRUSTED AROUND ROCK · RIGHT: THE DEAD SEA IN ISRAEL, THE LOWEST BODY OF WATER ON THE EARTH

DATA-BURST

WHY DOES SO MUCH SALT ACCUMULATE IN DEAD ZONE LAKES?
SALT ACCUMULATES TO SUCH A LEVEL BECAUSE IT HAS NO OUTLET. DEAD ZONES THEREFORE HAVE THE CHEMICAL CHARACTERISTICS OF AN OCEAN. BUT THEIR SALT LEVEL IS MUCH HIGHER THAN THAT OF OCEANS BECAUSE THE RATE OF EVAPORATION IS FAR GREATER THAN THE INFLUX OF WATER SUPPLY FROM FEEDER RIVERS.

WHY DOES THE DEAD SEA LIE BELOW SEA LEVEL?
THE DEAD SEA IS THE LOWEST BODY OF WATER ON EARTH. IT TAKES UP THE LOWEST PART OF A TRENCH 560 KM LONG. THE MEDITERRANEAN SEA ONCE COVERED SYRIA AND PALESTINE BEFORE THE FORMATION OF THE TRENCH WHICH TOOK PLACE AROUND 2 MILLION YEARS AGO.

WHY IS THERE NO SEA LIFE IN THE LOWER REACHES OF THE BLACK SEA?
PECULIARLY, OXYGEN ONLY DISSOLVES IN THE UPPER LEVELS OF THE WATERS OF THE BLACK SEA. AS A RESULT, SEA LIFE FLOURISHES IN THE UPPER REGION OF THE SEA BUT DEEPER DOWN, BELOW 70—100 M, THERE IS NO OXYGEN. THE LOWER PART OF THE SEA IS FILLED WITH A SATURATION OF DISSOLVED HYDROGEN SULPHIDE.

WHICH IS THE WORLD'S BIGGEST DEAD ZONE?
THE GREAT SALT LAKE IN UTAH, USA, IS THE SINGLE LARGEST INLAND BODY OF SALT WATER IN THE WORLD. ITS SIZE VARIES DEPENDING ON THE LEVEL OF EVAPORATION AND THE FLOW OF THE RIVERS THAT LEAD INTO IT. ITS SURFACE AREA HAS RANGED FROM A HIGH OF 6,200 KM^2 TO 2,460 KM^2.

AND THEY'RE OFF!

THE BONNEVILLE SALT FLATS IN NORTH-WEST UTAH, USA, ARE PART OF THE GREAT SALT LAKE DESERT. THIS 260-KM^2 BARREN STRETCH OF LAND WAS THE BED OF THE BONNEVILLE PREHISTORIC LAKE UNTIL THE WATER EVAPORATED LEAVING A VAST SMOOTH SURFACE—AN IDEAL PLACE FOR ATTEMPTED LAND SPEED RECORDS. MANY RECORDS HAVE BEEN SET HERE SINCE 1935, INCLUDING THE HIGHEST RECORDED SPEED FOR A WHEEL-DRIVEN CAR (696 KM/H ON 21 AUG.1991), SUPERSEDED IN OCT 1997 BY ANDY GREEN DRIVING THRUST SSC IN THE BLACK ROCK DESERT, NEVADA.

DEAD SEA CAN REACH 30%

DEAD ZONES ARE AMONG THE MOST DESOLATE PLACES ON EARTH. IN SUCH AN ENVIRONMENT, LIFE IS VIRTUALLY NON-EXISTENT, AND THOSE ORGANISMS THAT DO SURVIVE MUST ADAPT TO LIFE IN THE MOST AUSTERE CONDITIONS

The sea-bed accounts for two-thirds of the Earth's surface, but much of it has yet to be fully explored. As the mysteries of the deep are uncovered, many traditional theories about life are being challenged. Once thought to be a dead zone, unable to sustain life due to the absence of light, the great deep is now found to be populated by millions of creatures that have evolved alternative means of survival, particularly by feeding off the minerals that seep through or rise from the sea-bed.

The deepest deep
The deepest part of an ocean floor is known as the abyssal plain which lies at an average depth of about 3,800 m. On this deep ocean floor lies a layer of sediment made up of ooze—clays and fine wet muds—and silt that is formed from the decayed and decomposed remains of tiny sea creatures.

and had never been seen before. They estimate that there are 10 million as yet undiscovered species living on the deep sea-bed.

Mineral-rich habitats
It is only relatively recently that life has been examined on the ocean floor. Photosynthesis was thought to be the only means by which plants could sustain life, but cracks in the sea-bed have been found to emit nourishing gases and minerals which can support a rich

diversity of underwater life as storms and currents carry different species from place to place.

Mexican mussels
In the Gulf of Mexico, 140 km off the coast of Louisiana, USA, huge colonies of mussels have been found thriving on the sea-bed. They do not require light for photosynthesis but instead live off salt deposits laid down more than 150 million years ago. They also consume vast quantities of

by similar erosion processes to those on land, although marine action can speed up the process.

The deepest seas
Early explorations of the ocean floor were made from ships using a simple lead weight and line to estimate depth. Scientists today use sophisticated echo-sounding techniques—bouncing electronic waves off the sea-bed to measure vast distances. Remote-controlled submersibles that are capable of

THE GREAT DEEP
SEA-BED SMOKERS

Plumbing the depths
Our attempts to understand life at the bottom of the oceans have been greatly aided by the invention of the box corer. This stainless steel instrument plumbs the deepest areas of the ocean, cutting out measured chunks of mud as it makes contact with the sea-bed. By comparing samples and counting the number of life-forms present, scientists can piece together a much broader picture of life on the sea-bed. This technique, employed since the late 1960s, has led to the identification of many new species. A team of scientists working off the Atlantic coast in North America during the mid-1980s dug up 233 sample cores, each measuring 30 cm^2, over a 176-km long track. They found 90,677 animals belonging to 798 different species. More than half of these species were new to science

variety of lifeforms. In 1977, an American submersible first discovered 'smokers', tall chimney vents that belch out clouds of super-heated water as a result of volcanic activity. Chimneys of up to 50 m high build up from the minerals deposited by the hot water. Tube worms and clams are able to live around the necks of the chimney. In 1985, scientists exploring the Atlantic 3,000 km east of Miami at depths of more than 4,000 m discovered deep sea geysers. Underwater geysers have also been located in the Pacific Ocean and are now known to exist in mid-ocean ridges around the world. In many instances, geysers give off an infra-red glow because of the wealth of minerals they contain, and in some regions, copper, zinc, silver and gold have been successfully mined. Ocean turbulence also contributes to the

methane gas that seeps through the ocean floor. Other animals, such as tube worms, survive in a similar way. The Bush Hill colony off the Mexican coast contains worms more than 2 m long and 100 years old. They seek out hydrogen sulphide seeping through the sea-bed, which they collect in their gills. Bacteria then feed on this and the worms in turn feed on the bacteria.

Edible wrecks
Life deep under water may be sustained from the most unlikely sources. A species of deep sea worm was recently discovered clinging to the wreck of a French ship that sank off the coast of Spain. These worms had previously only been found thousands of kilometres away in parts of the sea-bed where they feed on the minerals emerging from the Earth's crust. The ship was carrying a cargo of copper, zinc, coffee beans and sunflower seeds. This proved to be a rich alternative supply of nutrients for the worms: as the beans and seeds started to rot, they gave off the same quality of sustaining hydrogen sulphide found around vents in the sea-bed.

Deep sea canyons
The sea-bed is far from flat and uniform. Many topographical features that occur above water are mirrored in the sea's depths. Trenches and canyons cut deep into many parts of the ocean bed and their features may be extreme—valleys tend to be narrow with steep-sided walls. They are formed

JARGON
BOX CORER AN INSTRUMENT USED BY SCIENTISTS TO TRAWL THE SEA-BED
COLD SEEPS CRACKS IN THE EARTH'S CRUST WHICH DISCHARGE PETROLEUM, METHANE AND VARIOUS OTHER HYDROCARBONS
SPEWING BLACK SMOKERS A COMMON NAME GIVEN TO DEEP SEA GEYSERS
VENTS HOT SPOTS ON THE DEEP SEA BED WHERE HEATED WATER IMBUED WITH MINERALS AND METALS PUSHES UP THROUGH CRACKS IN THE EARTH'S CRUST

descending to the very depths of the ocean record the variety of life on the ocean bed. The Marianas Trench, in the western North Pacific Ocean, plummets to depths of 10,911 m. Comparable in size to the Grand Canyon, it could hold 28 Empire State Buildings standing on top of each other. This arching depression stretches for more than 2,550 km. There is a smaller steep-walled valley on the side of the trench which was discovered in 1899. Called Nero Deep, it measures 9,660 m. Further record depths were measured in this vicinity in 1957 when a Soviet research ship sounded 10,860 m. On 20 Jan 1960 a US navy-operated submersible, the *Trieste*, made a record dive to 10, 740 m in the Marianas Trench. The son of the submersible's inventor, Jaques Picard, was on board.

LEFT: DEEP-SEA POGONOPHORA WORMS CONGREGATE AROUND A GALAPAGOS HYDROTHERMAL VENT · RIGHT: MATERIAL FROM A SMOKER IS TAKEN BY THE CANADIAN REMOTE VEHICLE, *ROPOS*

DATA-BURST

HOW MANY SPECIES LIVE IN THE GREAT DEEP?
ALTHOUGH ONLY 160,000 SPECIES HAVE BEEN NAMED SO FAR, AT LEAST 10 MILLION ARE BELIEVED TO LIVE IN AND AROUND THE MUD AT THE BOTTOM OF THE SEA.

WHY DO GASES AND OILS FORM ON THE DEEP SEA BED?
UNDER CERTAIN CONDITIONS, OIL AND GAS FORM FROM THE REMAINS OF DEAD PLANTS AND ANIMALS THAT ACCUMULATE ON THE SEA FLOOR. BACTERIA BREAK DOWN THE REMAINS INTO ORGANIC MATERIAL. MUD WASHED OFF THE LAND BY RIVERS FORMS LAYERS OF SANDSTONE WHICH COVER THE REMAINS. INCREASED PRESSURE FROM ACCUMULATING LAYERS OF ROCK TURNS THE ORGANIC REMAINS INTO OIL AND GAS.

WHERE ARE THE MAIN RIDGES AND TRENCHES IN THE SEA?
THE MAIN FEATURES OF THE OCEAN FLOOR FORM AT THE BOUNDARIES OF THE EARTH'S CRUST. TRENCHES FORM WHEN ONE PLATE PLUNGES BENEATH ANOTHER. VAST UNDERSEA MOUNTAIN RANGES FORM WHERE TECTONIC PLATES PULL APART.

WHAT IS A SUBMARINE CANYON?
A RIVER FLOWING OFF THE LAND AND INTO THE SEA MAY CARVE OUT A DEEP CANYON IN THE OCEAN FLOOR.

HOW HOT ARE SMOKERS?
SMOKERS, VOLCANIC VENTS IN THE SEA BED, CAN REACH TEMPERATURES OF 105°C. TUBE WORMS CAN LIVE ON SMOKER WALLS AT THIS EXTREME TEMPERATURE—HIGHER THAN ANY LAND ANIMAL CAN TOLERATE.

COLD WAR THAWS

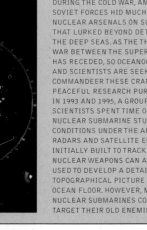

DURING THE COLD WAR, AMERICAN AND SOVIET FORCES HID MUCH OF THEIR NUCLEAR ARSENALS ON SUBMARINES THAT LURKED BEYOND DETECTION IN THE DEEP SEAS. AS THE THREAT OF WAR BETWEEN THE SUPERPOWERS HAS RECEDED, SO OCEANOGRAPHERS AND SCIENTISTS ARE SEEKING TO COMMANDEER THESE CRAFT FOR PEACEFUL RESEARCH PURPOSES. IN 1993 AND 1995, A GROUP OF MARINE SCIENTISTS SPENT TIME ON A NUCLEAR SUBMARINE STUDYING CONDITIONS UNDER THE ARCTIC ICE. RADARS AND SATELLITE EQUIPMENT INITIALLY BUILT TO TRACK AND GUIDE NUCLEAR WEAPONS CAN ALSO NOW BE USED TO DEVELOP A DETAILED TOPOGRAPHICAL PICTURE OF THE OCEAN FLOOR. HOWEVER, MOST NUCLEAR SUBMARINES CONTINUE TO TARGET THEIR OLD ENEMIES.

SUPPORT ANIMAL LIFE AT 105°C

FOR CENTURIES, THE BOTTOM OF THE SEA HAS SEEMED A DARK, COLD AND INHOSPITABLE PLACE. YET SCIENTISTS WHO PLUMB THE DEPTHS HAVE RECENTLY DISCOVERED AN UNEXPECTED DIVERSITY OF PLANT AND ANIMAL SPECIES

Coral reefs are the largest biological constructions on Earth. They harbour a diversity of marine species only bettered in number by the rainforest. A coral reef is a ridge or hummock formed in shallow ocean areas in the tropics. Reefs are made up of the skeletons of millions of individual coral polyps, some living, some dead. These polyps are small calcium-secreting organisms that divide and sub-divide at a prodigious speed. Their rate of growth depends upon the type of coral but it can amount to several centimetres a year. Polyps bind together, spreading upwards, eventually breaking the sea's surface to create coral islands.

reefs are restricted to shallow waters where temperatures reach 21°C (70°F). Reefs are always tropical in their distribution.

Darwin's atoll theory
The British botanist, Charles Darwin, was the first to put forward a theory explaining the creation of atolls. On his historic voyage around the Pacific from 1831–36, he recognized the different topographies of many tropical islands as stages in a

gave rise to theories of continental drift. These reefs began to develop in the Devonian period, 400 million years ago. They now form parts of mountain ranges, in the Guadelupe Mountains of Texas for example.

The Great Barrier Reef
Almost 3,000 individual coral reefs together comprise the Great Barrier Reef. The world's largest living structure, it first began to grow millions of years ago. While the present reef structure emerged

branched, some flat and plate-like, while others may form massive boulders. By day, a reef is alive with a spectacular diversity of fish species of all shapes and sizes, a spectrum made possible by the great range of feeding opportunities provided by the complex structure of the reef.

Warming risk
Islands initially formed by coral are under increasing threat from the effects of global warming. This

CORAL REEFS

AUSTRALIA'S GREAT BARRIER

Polyp growth
The coral polyp ranges in size from a few millimetres to tens of centimetres. Each individual polyp has tentacles for drawing food into its mouth. It constructs a stony limestone coral tube in which it lives. The growth of the colony of coral polyps is always upward towards the surface of the water. When one polyp dies, the skeleton it leaves provides the foundation on which the next polyp will grow.

Warm waters
The so-called 'paradise' islands of Bora-Bora, Taimanu and Pahia in the South Pacific offer the perfect environment for coral to form, with water at an ideal temperature for the coral polyps to thrive. Coral

familiar pattern. Atolls are round or horseshoe shaped structures with a central sheltered lagoon. Darwin proposed that these began as fringing reefs around small islands. The islands sank slowly enough for the coral's upward growth to keep pace with the rate of sinking until the necklace of coral was all that remained above sea level. Darwin's theories of coral island development have been widely accepted.

Historic coral
Reef structures provide a sensitive guide to environmental conditions over long periods of time. The discovery of ancient coral reefs in the rocks of continents which now lie well away from the tropics,

only relatively recently (about 15,000 years ago) it now extends for 2,010 km parallel to the north-east coast of Australia and covers an area of about 270,000 km². Some of the reefs surround small islands, rising just above the sea level; other islands rise to great heights, with Whitsunday and Magnetic Islands reaching a height of 1,000 m. Sea urchins, starfish and fish all graze on the Great Barrier Reef. The chewed debris is then deposited as fine coral sand.

Biological diversity
As many as 150 species of coral may be found on a single atoll or reef, each with a different ecological niche and structure. Some corals are delicately

is because they lie only just above sea level. The Ilhuru Islands, part of the Maldives in the Indian Ocean, are a coral-based area under particular threat. They lie a few metres above sea level. As the ocean warms, the rising water threatens to envelop the islands and their 250,000 inhabitants.

Dusk lovers
In Australia, coral growth has been so accurately measured that changes can even be recorded by the hour. It has been established that coral growth is most prolific around dusk, between 6 pm and 8 pm. Coral grows differently by night. Biologists have observed how during daylight hours, coral only grows in width, not length.

DATA-BURST

WHAT TYPES OF REEF ARE THERE?
THERE ARE THREE TYPES OF REEF: FRINGING REEFS, BARRIER REEFS AND ATOLLS. FRINGE REEFS ARE THE MOST COMMON. THEY EXTEND OUT FROM THE SHORE DIRECTLY, WHEREAS BARRIER REEFS ARE SEPARATED FROM THE COAST BY A LAGOON. ATOLLS ARE CIRCULAR REEFS THAT BEGIN AS FRINGE REEFS SURROUNDING A CENTRAL ISLAND. AS THE ISLAND SINKS, ALL THAT IS LEFT IS THE LOOP OF CORAL ATOLLS.

HOW OLD ARE CORAL REEFS?
SOME REEFS ARE VERY OLD. REEFS THAT HAVE DEVELOPED IN THE LAST 2 MILLION YEARS REMAINED ABOVE THE SEA AT THE TIME OF THE LAST GLACIATION. IN THE COURSE OF GLACIATION, THEY WERE ERODED. WITH THE RISE IN TEMPERATURES OVER THE LAST 10,000 YEARS, NEW CORAL GROWTH HAS DOMINATED THE 'SKULL' OF THE OLD CORAL FORM.

WHAT DO CORAL POLYPS FEED OFF?
POLYPS USE THEIR TENTACLES TO CAPTURE PLANKTON WHICH THEY HUNT BY NIGHT.

HOW DO ALGAE HELP CORAL GROW?
CORAL IS HOST TO ALGAE CELLS WHICH LIVE IN THEIR TISSUE. THESE ALGAE CELLS RECEIVE THE BENEFIT OF LIVING IN A PROTECTED ENVIRONMENT AND ALSO USE THE NITROGENOUS WASTES OF THE CORAL'S CELLS FOR THEIR OWN GROWTH. IN RETURN THE CORAL RECEIVES EXCESS CARBOHYDRATES PRODUCED BY THE PLANT CELLS. THIS TYPE OF MUTUALLY BENEFICIAL RELATIONSHIP IS CALLED 'SYMBIOTIC'.

HOW BIG IS THE BARRIER REEF?
THE BARRIER REEF EXTENDS 2,010 KM, PARALLEL TO THE AUSTRALIAN CONTINENTAL SHELF. ALONG THE COAST OF NORTH-EAST AUSTRALIA. IT IS SO BIG, IT CAN BE SEEN FROM THE MOON.

LEFT: ANEMONE AND CLOWNFISH SWIMMING IN CORAL REEF · RIGHT: ONE OF ALMOST 3,000 INDIVIDUAL CORAL REEFS THAT COMPRISE THE GREAT BARRIER REEF, AUSTRALIA

REEF DESTRUCTION

THE HUGE EXPLOSION OF TOURISM IN AUSTRALIA AND SOUTH-EAST ASIA HAS HAD A SERIOUS DETRIMENTAL EFFECT ON THE CORAL REEFS, BOTH BECAUSE OF POLLUTION AND THE ACTIVITIES OF DIVING, SWIMMING AND SAILING IN AND AROUND THE REEFS. COMMERCIAL FISHING AND THE COLLECTION OF CORAL AS SOUVENIRS ARE ALSO DESTRUCTIVE, AS IS THE EXTRACTION OF LIMESTONE FROM THE REEFS BY THE LOCAL PEOPLE FOR USE AS A BUILDING MATERIAL. THE ANIMALS THAT LIVE IN THE SEA AROUND A REEF CAN DO IRREPARABLE DAMAGE. THE CROWN-OF-THORNS STARFISH DEVOURS THE CORAL POLYPS AS PART OF ITS DIET, WHICH HAS DONE SIGNIFICANT DAMAGE TO ABOUT ONE-THIRD OF THE GREAT BARRIER REEF. FRUSTRATINGLY, THE STARfiSH SEEM TO THRIVE ALL THE MORE AS POLLUTION LEVELS IN THE AREA INCREASE.

JARGON

ALGAE
NON-FLOWERING, STEMLESS WATER PLANT THAT GROWS IN MUTUAL CO-OPERATION WITH CORAL

CORAL POLYPS
A CORAL ANIMAL RELATED TO THE SEA ANENOME

GUYOT
THE BASE STRUCTURE OF AN EXTINCT VOLCANO RUIN, THAT IS LEFT AFTER THE CORAL REEF THAT SURROUNDED THE BASE HAS SUBSIDED

LAGOON
STRETCH OF SALT WATER SEPARATED FROM THE OCEAN BY A SAND BANK OR CORAL REEF

REEF EXTENDS FOR 2,010 KM

CORAL REEFS ARE LIVING ROCKS BUILT BY MILLIONS OF TINY MARINE ANIMALS IN SHALLOW OCEAN AREAS. THEY GROW INTO THE LARGEST BIOLOGICAL CONSTRUCTIONS ON EARTH AND BECOME HOME TO A HUGE DIVERSITY OF LIFE

Icebergs are floating lumps of freshwater ice that have broken off a glacier. They occur in the spring and summer when sea and water temperatures rise. The great freshwater ice masses of Greenland and Antarctica melt around the fringes and blocks of ice 'calve' from the whole and float out to sea. Icebergs vary in size from small 'growlers' the size of a grand piano, to huge, towering white protrusions that rise 45 m above the water and extend many more below. As they move, these icebergs continue to melt and fragment. In the northern hemisphere, 10,000 icebergs are calved each year from the Greenland glaciers. They usually last two years but they may last up to a decade depending on size and how near the Pole they remain.

A floating danger

Most large icebergs show up on radar, but smaller growlers are visible only within a range of about 2 km when the sea is calm. Ice does not reflect sound very well and as a result the echo of sea waves can mask the presence of an iceberg. As icebergs float thousands of kilometres from their original position, they become an increasing threat to shipping, particularly since their cooling effect on the surrounding sea encourages foggy conditions. As they float and melt, they further subdivide, making it very difficult to keep track of them. International law demands that ships travel at slow speeds through iceberg waters. In addition, specialist international agencies

provide twice-daily reports as up to 300 icebergs travel along the Labrador Current, off the coast of Newfoundland, at any one time. In particularly dangerous conditions, coastguard planes fly from Argentia, Newfoundland, over the whole Grand Banks area. It is sometimes possible to destroy a particularly threatening iceberg using thermite, a mixture of aluminium powder and iron oxide that is ignited to produce a great deal of heat. This technique was first developed in 1929, while bombing, torpedoing, shelling and ramming have also been tried with limited success.

Sinking the unsinkable

The sinking of the *Titanic*, a British luxury passenger liner, on 15 April 1912 was the most famous tragedy

ICEBERGS

ICEBERG TRAVELS UP

to result from a collision with an iceberg. Ironically, the *Titanic* had been designed specifically to cope with the iceberg threat and its engineers had boasted that the ship was unsinkable. Its complex hull design contained 16 watertight compartments, four of which could be breached without the ship going

down. However, on its maiden voyage from Southampton, UK, to New York City, USA, it struck an iceberg 640 km off the southern coast of Newfoundland. Five compartments filled with water and 1,517 people died as a result. The disaster was compounded by the fact that a nearby ship failed to respond to the *Titanic's* SOS message, and by the insufficient number of lifeboats on board. A convention set up in London in 1913 to study the tragedy ruled that every ship should have lifeboat space for every person on board and that ships should remain in 24-hour radio contact. The International Ice Patrol was also set up to warn ships venturing into iceberg areas of a possible threat.

Pack ice

Pressure from inland geological movement ensures that the ice sheets of Greenland flow out towards the sea. As the area partially melts in spring and summer, so these giant sheets of ice are released into the sea forming huge floating masses of pack ice. At any one time, about a quarter of the world's oceans are affected by pack ice because the Arctic and Antarctic winters are only six months apart. Icebergs can travel

thousands of kilometres at speeds of up to 44 km per day. Some prove to be particularly resilient. Icebergs were spotted as far south as Bermuda in 1907 and 1926.

Antarctic drift

The Ross and Weddell Ice Shelves in Antarctica produce huge, flat-topped icebergs that are very different in size and shape from those produced by glaciers in the Arctic. In 1991, an iceberg 120 km long calved from the Weddell Ice Shelf and drifted dangerously across the shipping lanes between Antarctica and Argentina at a speed of 14 km a day.

PERIL AROUND THE GRAND BANKS

FROM THE EARLIEST JOURNEYS INTO THE NORTH ATLANTIC, ICEBERGS HAVE THREATENED SHIPPING. THE HISTORY OF NAVIGATION REVEALS MANY CASUALTIES OCCURRING AROUND THE VICINITY KNOWN AS THE 'GRAND BANKS'. A SHIP CALLED *THE LADY OF THE LAKE* SANK THERE IN 1833 WITH THE LOSS OF 70 LIVES. BETWEEN 1882 AND 1890, 14 PASSENGER VESSELS WERE LOST AND 40 DAMAGED DUE TO ICE. A LARGE NUMBER OF WHALING AND FISHING BOATS WERE ALSO LOST IN THIS PERIOD. HOWEVER, THE INTERNATIONAL ICE PATROL WAS ONLY FORMED AFTER THE LOSS OF THE *TITANIC* ON 15 APRIL, 1912. IT COLLIDED WITH AN ICEBERG SOUTH OF THE TAIL OF THE GRAND BANKS. FROM THAT TIME ONWARDS, SHIPS PATROLLED THE AREA AND AFTER WORLD WAR II AERIAL SURVEILLANCE BECAME THE PRIMARY ICE RECONNAISSANCE METHOD.

RIGHT: BLUE ICEBERG, ICE CONTE BAY, ALASKA, USA · INSET: LARGE ICEBERG PLATEAU FLOATING IN A CALM SEA AGAINST A STORMY SKY

TO 44 KM PER DAY

EVERY SUMMER, HUGE FLOATING BLOCKS OF ICE BREAK AWAY FROM GLACIERS. WITH ONLY ABOUT 10% OF THEIR MASS VISIBLE ABOVE THE SEA'S SURFACE, THEY CAN CAUSE HAVOC WHEN THEY FLOAT INTO SHIPPING LANES

FASTEST GLACIER

Glaciers are responsible for carving out and shaping much of the landscape that we see around us. Glaciers are large masses of ice that form in valleys. Snow collects in the hollows of a mountain and is then compressed into hard ice as more and more snow accumulates. This block then slips downhill under its own weight, grinding and scoring deep grooves in the rock floor. Rock fragments are carried away in the ice and scratch the valley floor by abrasion. During the last ice age, glaciers extended across a third of the Earth's surface, but today they cover just 11%. Glaciers are found in profusion only in Greenland and Antarctica.

DATA-BURST

WHAT ARE GLACIATED REGIONS?
GLACIATED REGIONS ARE THE PLACES ON THE PLANET WHERE GLACIERS FORM AS A RESULT OF PERMANENT SNOW COVER. GLACIERS FORM MAINLY IN THE POLAR REGIONS BUT ALSO IN HIGH MOUNTAINOUS AREAS SUCH AS THE HIMALAYAS IN ASIA, THE ALPS IN EUROPE, AND THE NORTH AND SOUTH AMERICAN MOUNTAIN RANGES.

HOW ARE MOUNTAINS SHAPED BY GLACIERS?
PYRAMIDAL PEAKS AND STEEP JAGGED SLOPES FORM WHEN A MOUNTAIN IS ATTACKED BY GLACIERS FROM SEVERAL SIDES. A SHARP RIDGE, OR 'ARETE', IS FORMED BETWEEN THE SIDES OF TWO GLACIERS. THE SCOOPED-OUT HOLLOW WHERE A GLACIER FORMS IS KNOWN AS A 'CIRQUE' OR 'CORRIE'.

WHAT ROCKS DO GLACIERS PICK UP AS THEY TRAVEL DOWN A MOUNTAIN?
GLACIERS PLUCK OUT FRAGMENTS OF ROCK FROM THEIR BASE AND SIDES AND CARRY THEM ALONG AS THEY SLIDE DOWN MOUNTAINS. THESE FRAGMENTS RANGE IN SIZE FROM FINE DUST TO HOUSE-SIZED BOULDERS. LARGE BULKY BOULDERS ARE CALLED 'ERRATICS'. BY EXAMINING THESE, IT IS POSSIBLE TO RECONSTRUCT THE DIRECTION AND MOVEMENT OF LONG-VANISHED GLACIERS.

WHICH GLACIER MOVES AT THE MOST CONSISTENTLY HIGH SPEED?
THE FRANZ JOSEF GLACIER FLOWS DOWN THE SOUTHERN ALPS OF NEW ZEALAND AT SPEEDS OF UP TO 7M A DAY. THIS RAPIDITY IS DUE TO HIGH TEMPERATURES AND HIGH SNOWFALL.

JARGON

CREVASSES
CRACKS IN GLACIERS

DRUMLINS
MOUNDS OF TILL ON VALLEY FLOORS OR TILL PLAINS

ESKERS
LONG RIDGES OF DEPOSITS ON LOWLANDS OR VALLEY FLOORS

GLACIOLOGY
THE STUDY OF ICE ON LAND

ICE SHEET
A GLACIER WHICH OCCURS ON FLAT LAND

KAMES
DEPOSITS WHICH APPEAR IN CREVASSES

NUNATAKS
ISLANDS OF LAND WHICH PROTRUDE THROUGH THE ICE. GREENLAND IS AN EXAMPLE OF A NUNATAK

RECRYSTALLIZATION
THE PROCESS WHEREBY SNOW TURNS TO ICE

SNOUT
THE END OR TAIL OF A GLACIER

SOURCE
THE FRONT SECTION OF A GLACIER

TILL
MATERIAL ON A VALLEY FLOOR THAT HAS BEEN DEPOSITED BY A MELTED GLACIER

TRAVELS 45 M A DAY

GLACIERS ARE HUGE RIVERS OF ICE THAT SCOOP OUT VALLEYS FROM MOUNTAINOUS TERRAIN. WHEN GLACIERS MOVE DOWNHILL, THEY PICK UP ABRASIVE MATERIAL, SCRATCHING AND SMOOTHING THE SURFACE OF THE LAND

Rivers of ice
Characteristically, a valley glacier is a few tens of kilometres long, a few hundred metres wide and several hundred metres thick. Glaciers deepen and widen the valley floor over which they travel, bulldozing away everything in their path. Glaciers often leave a wide tract in their wake. When glaciers retreat, for example at the end of the last ice age, they typically leave a U-shaped valley.

Speeding Giants
Glaciers can speed up in summer months when temperatures melt the ice on the underside providing lubrication as the glacier slips downhill. Other factors can influence the speed at which a

glacier travels: if the glacier has accumulated much debris in its base regions, the friction generated can slow down the flow of the ice. The central part of the glacier moves the fastest: in the case of an Alpine glacier on a shallow slope, speeds can amount to 100 m or so every year. The margins of a glacier are restricted by friction to speeds under of under 30 m each year.

Slow to flow
The Hubbard Glacier forms the longest glacial valley in North America. It extends for 150 km from the interior of Alaska to the Bay of Disenchantment and usually moves very slowly (about 5 cm per day). Early in 1986, however, it suddenly started to speed up,

covering 45 m a day for about one month. Because it was not melting as fast as usual, it blocked the Russel Fjord and the water behind it, fed by mountain streams, rose at a rate of about 30 cm a day. Thus, for a few months, what was previously a saltwater inlet became a freshwater lake. Porpoises, seals and sea lions all became trapped behind the glacier. Fortunately, the threat it posed to these animals receded as it eventually melted during the autumn of 1986.

Temperate signs
The Beardmore Glacier, in central Antarctica, descends 2,200 m from the South Polar Plateau to the Ross Ice Shelf. It lies between the Antarctic mountains known as Queen Maud and Queen Alexandra and, at 200 km long and 40 km wide, is one of the world's largest valley glaciers. Explorer Ernest Shackleton discovered the glacier while travelling towards the South Pole in 1908. The glacier contains petrified wood and fossils of ferns and coral, proving that the area was once a temperate region.

Mother of rivers
The largest glaciers are called continental glaciers, and it is these fields of ice that cover much

of Greenland and Antarctica. The largest icefield in the Rocky Mountains is the Columbia Icefield, on the border of British Columbia and Alberta in Canada. The glacier covers 500 km^2 between the summits of Mt Columbia (3,747 m) and Mt Athabasca (3,491 m). It is called 'the mother of rivers', because the meltwater flows 4,000 km from the Athabasca River all the way into the Arctic Ocean.

Alpine glaciers
While 99 % of all glaciers now surround the North and South Poles, they once covered much of the globe. In the last ice age, a kilometre of ice covered many areas that now have a temperate climate. Ice sheets extended over Northern Eurasia and North America. Some glaciers still remain in such areas, especially in the Himalayas and the Alps. The Aletsch Glacier, in Switzerland, is the largest and longest glacier in the Alps, covering an area of 171 km^2. Starting at the Aletschhorn, a mountain rising to 4,195 m, it extends southwards from the Concordia Platz to a nature reserve in the Aletsch Forest. Its meltwater feeds into the River Rhone.

GLACIERS ON MARS

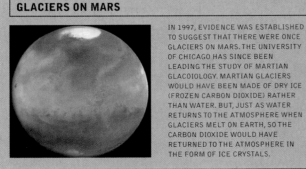

IN 1997, EVIDENCE WAS ESTABLISHED TO SUGGEST THAT THERE WERE ONCE GLACIERS ON MARS. THE UNIVERSITY OF CHICAGO HAS SINCE BEEN LEADING THE STUDY OF MARTIAN GLACOIOLOGY. MARTIAN GLACIERS WOULD HAVE BEEN MADE OF DRY ICE (FROZEN CARBON DIOXIDE) RATHER THAN WATER. BUT, JUST AS WATER RETURNS TO THE ATMOSPHERE WHEN GLACIERS MELT ON EARTH, SO THE CARBON DIOXIDE WOULD HAVE RETURNED TO THE ATMOSPHERE IN THE FORM OF ICE CRYSTALS.

LEFT: AERIAL VIEW OF THE PERITO MORENO GLACIER, SANTA CRUZ, PATAGONIA, ARGENTINA

HUMAN ACTIVITIES POLLUTE

GLOBAL DEVASTATION

AND SCAR EARTH'S LANDSCAPES

136   170   192   220

The establishment of pastoral agriculture by humans has ensured that areas cleared of trees have not been allowed to regenerate. Around 2,000 years ago, 47% of the Earth's surface was covered by forest. But two millennia of tree-felling and burning, firewood collecting, grazing by livestock and forest fires have reduced the world's forest cover to just 33%. Virgin temperate forest has been reduced to a collection of fragments. All over the world, from Alaska to Australia, deforestation is taking place. The main causes of deforestation today are clearance for agriculture and felling for the timber trade. In natural forests, out of every 100 trees felled, only one is commercially useful and for every 10 trees felled worldwide, only one is planted.

Trees in temperate regions
It took settlers only 200 years to destroy virtually all of the USA's old-growth native forests. Today, 30% of the land surface of the USA is forested, but, excluding Alaska, only 5% is covered by old-growth forest. In the countries of the European Union, deforestation reached its peak just over 100 years ago. Just 23% of the land area of the Union is now forested, but less than 10% of this—or 2% of the total area—is native, old-growth forest. In some European countries, re-afforestation keeps the total forest cover topped up: 30% of Germany is forest, 27% of France and 10% of the UK. These figures compare well with those of many tropical countries, but

represent a tiny proportion of the world's forests and pale into insignificance next to the huge coniferous forests of northern Russia. These Russian forests, lying between 55°N and the Arctic Circle, cover a total area of 1.1 billion hectares and form the largest forested area in the world.

Deforestation in the Tropics
Tropical forest once occupied 6% of the Earth's land surafce but now only about half of this remains. Although tropical countries are often blamed by the West for their rapid rate of deforestation, a far larger percentage of their land area is actually forested than in temperate countries—up to 60% in Malaysia, Indonesia and Brazil. But the story is not the same throughout the Tropics. In the

Dominican Republic, Jamaica, Mali and Ethiopia, the situation is even worse than in Europe, with just 10% of their territory covered by forest. In the Central American country of El Salvador, the level is just 5% and in Haiti, Somalia and Pakistan natural forests have all but disappeared.

DEFORESTATION
ONE TREE PLANTED

The Amazon rainforest
The largest remaining area of tropical forest in the world, Brazil's Amazon rainforest covers 6 million km². This amazing habitat contains an almost unbelievable diversity of plant and animal life—scientists estimate that 2,000 species can live in just one Amazonian rainforest tree. But the figures for its destruction are just as unbelievable: in 1989 alone, satellite imaging showed that 8% of the forest—or 404,000 km²—was destroyed. Of this, 30,000 km² was illegally burned by ranchers and farmers. This loss not only represents an irreversible depletion of valuable genetic resources but, through loss of carbon-dioxide-absorbing vegetation, may also help speed up the process of global warming.

Slash and burn
In the Amazon rainforest a traditional method of 'slash-and-burn' agriculture has been carried out for many years by indigenous people and landless peasants who have migrated from cities. Areas of the forest are cleared and farmed until they can no longer sustain crops; the soil is exhausted and land degenerates into scrub, or is sold to cattle ranchers. By this time the soil is so degraded that the

rainforest can never return. When forests are cleared in equatorial regions, the exposed soil is eroded by heavy rainfall and its nutrients are lost through leaching. What is left is barely able to sustain plantlife and within as little as five years, the soil can become exhausted, leaving a green desert where no crops can grow. On the island of Madagascar, between 1981 and 1990, forest cover was removed at a rate of 0.8% per year. As a result, rain erosion rendered the land utterly useless.

THE GREAT BEAR RAINFOREST

ON THE WEST COAST OF THE PROVINCE OF BRITISH COLUMBIA, CANADA, LIES A QUARTER OF THE WORLD'S REMAINING TEMPERATE RAINFOREST. THE GREAT BEAR RAINFOREST CONTAINS SOME OF THE TALLEST AND OLDEST TREES IN THE WORLD—SOME TOWER TO 100 M AND ARE OVER 1,500 YEARS OLD—AND PROVIDES A HOME FOR OVER 70% OF CANADA'S PLANT AND ANIMAL SPECIES. BUT THIS TREASURE CHEST OF BIODIVERSITY, WHERE PLANTS AND TREES GROW TWICE AS DENSELY AS IN TROPICAL RAINFORESTS, IS THREATENED BY COMMERCIAL LOGGING COMPANIES. WHILE THE WORLD'S ATTENTION HAS BEEN FOCUSED ON ITS TROPICAL RAINFOREST COUNTERPARTS, THE GREAT BEAR TEMPERATE RAINFOREST HAS SEEN ITS 353 TREE-COVERED VALLEYS REDUCED TO JUST 69. MOST OF THESE REMAINING VALLEYS, WHICH RUN DOWN TO THE PACIFIC COAST, ARE NOW THREATENED WITH DESTRUCTION AS A RESULT OF CLEARCUT LOGGING.

RIGHT: DEFORESTATION CAUSED BY SLASH AND BURN AGRICULTURE AT PARA, BRAZIL

FOR EVERY 10 FELLED

GLOBAL DEFORESTATION IS TAKING PLACE AT AN EVER INCREASING RATE. AN AREA OF RAINFOREST THE SIZE OF A FOOTBALL PITCH DISAPPEARS EVERY SECOND, AND OVER 170,000 KM² OF FOREST IS LOST EVERY YEAR

The process whereby fertile land is rendered arid is known as desertification. The problem has gained increasing awareness over the past 25 years as social change, especially population increase, has intensified the pressure to exploit land to the maximum. Around the world, an average of 100 km^2 of land becomes desert every day. Soil erosion, deforestation, the over-cultivation of land and changes in the climate have all helped to transform flourishing and fertile environments into barren landscapes. Traditional ecosystems have been irrevocably damaged. The situation is most severe in Africa, where successive droughts have prompted the dramatic southward spread of the Sahara.

Climate change
The spread of desert-like conditions is due to both human influence and changes in the climate. Changes usually occur slowly but the current rapid spread is thought to be caused by a combination of these two factors. The Sahel region in Africa has been subject to a succession of extremely severe droughts. Some meteorologists have speculated that these droughts were caused by an increase in greenhouse gases in recent years.

March of the Sahara
The Sahel is an area of Africa that borders the Sahara. Historically, it has always been prone to drought but conditions have deteriorated as a result of human intervention. The Sahara was once a fertile land of trees and grassland with fields of grain cultivated and harvested by the Romans. Between the 7th and 13th centuries, Ghana was one of the first great trading empires of western Africa. It was at its peak in the 11th century, at which point the

Muslim Almoravids arrived from the Sahara on a mission to convert the country to Islam. The Muslims introduced livestock into arid areas, and the process of desertification has continued ever since. Since the 1950s, there has been a huge growth in the population of the area, and the number of livestock has doubled. Tropical rain forests have been chopped down to make more room for urban development and the soil quality in the savanna grasslands has deteriorated, losing its intrinsic structure and ability to hold moisture. Cattle have been allowed to overgraze and land that was traditionally left to recover for up to 20 years between farming cycles is now re-used within only five years. Western technologies have contributed to the spread of desertification: water wells have been dug far too deep, disturbing the balance of the water table.

Extent of the problem
The Sahara Desert has spread southwards at a rate of about 5 km a year. In Mauritania, 75% of grazing land has been lost over the past 25 years. Throughout the 1980s, the surface area of Lake Chad, the largest lake in western Africa, shrunk from 17,800 km^2 to 3,900 km^2. The plant and animal life around its fringes has suffered as a result.

Soil erosion
Removing vegetation for firewood, intensive grazing of livestock and crop cultivation lead to breakdown in the soil-binding root systems of vegetation cover. When the soil has nothing to hold it in place it blows away in the wind. Shelter belts or windbreaks comprised of trees and shrubs can help cut down wind erosion. Rain, although infrequent, may also wash away the soil. If the top soil is blown or washed away, degradation of the land is most likely to be permanent as nutrients in the soil are depleted and soil productivity is diminished. A vicious circle exists: with no soil, there can be no crops; with no crops the land cannot retain moisture.

Peanuts in Niger
New agricultural techniques, introduced by the West into Africa have also led to desertification. In the 1920s, peanut production was introduce to central Nigeria. Seeds were distributed to local farmers by the colonial government who then liscensed private firms to set up a peanut marketing network. Crop production increased greatly until the 1970s when disease and lower prices halted the boom. A report in 1951 warned that production of the crop at the expense of bushland would cause severe soil erosion, but this advice went unheeded.

Barren lands
Desertification is not just a problem in hot climates. Large areas of Iceland are devoid of vegetation, making up a 5,000-km^2 barren zone. A further 37,000-km^2 is under threat. The overuse of the land in an extremely fragile and cold environment has contributed towards the problem in a country that is subject to violent volcanic eruptions. Volcanic soils consist of glass and crystalline materials and are naturally prone to erosion.

DESERTIFICATION
SAHARA DESERT HAS

DATA-BURST

WHO DISCOVERED DESERTIFICATION?
IN 1949, A FRENCH NATURAL SCIENTIST CALLED ANDRE AUBREVILLE FOUND THAT THE SAVANNA GRASSLANDS AND TROPICAL RAINFORESTS WERE BEING DAMAGED BY FARMING IN THE SAHEL REGION OF THE SAHARA. HE WAS THE FIRST TO USE THE WORD DESERTIFICATION TO DESCRIBE THIS PROCESS.

WHAT ARE THE RESULTS OF DESERTIFICATION?
THE WATER TABLE DECLINES AND TOPSOIL AND WATER IN THE AREA BECOME SALTY. SURFACE WATER BECOMES SCARCE. SOIL EROSION OCCURS AT AN INCREASED RATE AND PLANTS WITHER AND DIE. OFTEN THE RAINY SEASON IS SHORTER THAN IT SHOULD BE. THIS THREATENS CROPS SUCH AS MILLET WHICH REQUIRE

WATER UNTIL THEY ARE RIPE. DUE TO THE SHORTENING OF THE RAINY SEASON, OVER-USE OF THE LAND IS MORE PRONOUNCED. A CYCLE OF DESERTIFICATION THEN BECOMES INEVITABLE.

HOW MANY PEOPLE ARE THREATENED BY DESERTIFICATION?
WORLDWIDE, THE LIVELIHOODS OF A BILLION PEOPLE IN OVER 100 COUNTRIES ARE THREATENED BY THE SPREAD OF DESERTS.

HOW CAN WE HALT DESERTIFICATION?
FARMING METHODS SUCH AS TERRACING CAN REDUCE THE LOSS OF TOPSOIL AND STOP DESERTIFICATION. SOMALIA HAS BEGUN A MAJOR ANTI-DESERTIFICATION PROGRAMME THAT INCLUDES A BAN ON CUTTING DOWN TREES FOR USE AS FUEL.

UNDOING THE DAMAGE

DESERT RECLAMATION PROJECTS HAVE BEEN INITIATED ALL OVER THE WORLD. THE PROJECTS, ALTHOUGH PRIMARILY CONCERNED WITH TRYING TO REVERSE THE EFFECTS OF DESERTIFICATION, ARE ALSO CARRIED OUT IN ORDER TO MEET HUMAN NEEDS. EXAMPLES OF SUCH PROJECTS CAN BE FOUND IN THE SAHARA, KAZAKHSTAN, LIBYA, PAKISTAN AND THE NORTH AMERICAN DESERTS. ONE SUCCESSFUL

EXAMPLE IS IN CHURCHILL COUNTY, NEVADA, USA. HERE, RECLAMATION HAS TRANSFORMED MUCH OF THE ARID REGION INTO A RICH AGRICULTURAL AREA. IT NOW PRODUCES CROPS, POULTRY AND HONEY. HOWEVER, DESERTIFICATION IS A PROBLEM MORE PRONOUNCED IN POORER COUNTRIES AND ECONOMICS PLAY AN IMPORTANT ROLE IN THE SUCCESSFUL COMBATING OF ENVIRONMENTAL CHANGE. THE UNITED NATIONS SET UP AN ENVIRONMENTAL PROGRAMME IN 1972 FOLLOWING A HUMAN ENVIRONMENT CONFERENCE IN STOCKHOLM. THIS BODY ALSO DEALS WITH WATER ISSUES, DEFORESTATION, DROUGHT AND THE OZONE LAYER HOLE. HOWEVER, MANY PROGRAMMES, DESPITE THEIR GOOD INTENTIONS, HAVE FAILED TO STOP THE PROGRESSION OF DESERTIFICATION.

RIGHT: GHANZI VILLAGE SETTLEMENT IN THE STARK WASTELAND OF THE KALAHARI DESERT, SOUTH AFRICA

SPREAD 5 KM A YEAR

AS A DESERT REGION EXPANDS AND A ONCE-FERTILE
AREA BECOMES INCREASINGLY ARID, THE INDIGENOUS
PLANTS AND ANIMALS THAT ONCE THRIVED IN THE AREA
STRUGGLE FOR SURVIVAL AND EVENTUALLY DISAPPEAR

Forests are highly flammable ecosystems where outbreaks of fire on hot summer days are natural phenomena. Fire can be part of a regeneration cycle—for example, some species of eucalyptus need it to weaken their pods enabling seeds to be shed. In the African savannah, fires burn off the old vegetation allowing new green shoots to thrive, thus providing fresh grazing for the wildlife. But in extreme conditions, a forest fire can turn into an unstoppable inferno. In hot, dry areas of Australia, the Mediterranean, Chile, California and South Africa fire is an ever-present threat not just to forests, but to human life and property.

Burning inferno in Brazil
In January 1998, in the state of Roraima, northern Brazil, agricultural fires started by local farmers began to spread out of control in the oppressive heat. For three months they raged, turning 34,000 km² of savanna into a charred wasteland and destroying huge areas of rainforest. More than 1,300 fire-fighters, equipped with water-spraying helicopters, joined the struggle to control the flames. A detachment of 107 fire-fighters entered the rainforest reservation of the Yanomami Indians to prevent the flames from causing havoc in the tribe's villages. Rain finally arrived in March, two days after Kayapo Indian holy men flew in to the Yanomami reservation and performed a rain dance. After the previous six months of drought, an amazing 7 cm of rain fell in the first 12 hours of the downpour, extinguishing about 85% of the fires. But the devastation left by the fire was phenomenal, with an area of cultivated land and rainforest the size of England utterly destroyed.

Australia's worst fire season
In Australia, summer is the 'fire season' and 1998 was one of the worst on record. Forest fires hit the states of Victoria, Queensland, Tasmania and Western Australia, and in New South Wales 2,000 tourists had to be evacuated as more than 20 fires burned out of

FOREST FIRES

FIRES IN AUSTRALIA

control. Thousands of fire-fighters laboured to put out the fires, many of which were thought to have been started by electric storms. In Wingello State Forest, south-west of Sydney, fires were swept along by strong winds, travelling at speeds of up to 110 km/h. Three months of blazes saw homes engulfed by flames, forests destroyed and the outskirts of Sydney shrouded in smoke.

Smoke engulfs Indonesia
In the summer of 1997, farmers on the Indonesian islands of Sumatra and Java and in Kalimantan in Borneo, unwittingly started fires that were to rage out of control for months, and produce

---

THREE-PRONGED ATTACK

TO BRING A FOREST FIRE UNDER CONTROL, FIRE-FIGHTERS HAVE TO BREAK THE 'FIRE TRIANGLE' OF TEMPERATURE, OXYGEN AND FUEL. PLANES ARE OFTEN USED TO DRENCH THE FIRE WITH WATER THAT IS SOMETIMES TAKEN FROM THE SEA. ON THE GROUND, FIRE-FIGHTERS DOUSE THE FLAMES WITH HIGH-PRESSURE HOSES, REDUCING THE FIRE'S HEAT AND SATURATING THE TREES WHICH FUEL THE FIRE, MAKING THEM NON-FLAMMABLE. CHEMICALS ARE USED TO DEPLETE THE LEVEL OF OXYGEN AVAILABLE, MAKING THE FIRE BURN MORE SLOWLY AND REDUCING ITS POTENTIAL TO EXPAND. CONTROLLED FIRES ARE THEN IGNITED IN THE PATH OF THE BLAZE TO BURN OFF ITS FUEL SUPPLY, AND FIREBREAKS ARE CUT IN THE VEGETATION TO ISOLATE THE FIRE AND CONTAIN ITS DAMAGING EFFECTS.

JARGON

CROWN FIRES
FIRES WHICH SPREAD THROUGH THE UPPER BRANCHES OF A FOREST

FIREBREAKS
GAPS IN THE VEGETATION, SCOURED OUT BY BULLDOZERS, WHICH PROVIDE BOUNDARIES THAT THE FLAMES CANNOT CROSS. RIVERS, ROADS AND RAILWAYS ARE NATURAL FIREBREAKS

FIRESTORMS
THESE OCCUR WHEN THE AIR SURROUNDING A FIRE IS DRAWN INTO IT, BOOSTING THE OXYGEN SUPPLY

GROUND FIRES
THESE SLOW AND HIGHLY DESTRUCTIVE FIRES BURN BENEATH THE DEBRIS AND ARE HARD TO CONTROL

SURFACE FIRES
FIRES WHICH BURN THE DEBRIS ON THE FOREST FLOOR AND ABOVE

WETTING AGENTS
CHEMICALS SUCH AS SODIUM CALCIUM BORATE ADDED TO WATER TO IMPROVE ITS FIRE-FIGHTING CAPABILITIES

TRAVEL AT 110 KM/H

WHEN A FOREST FIRE RAGES OUT OF CONTROL IT CAN BURN TIRELESSLY FOR MONTHS ON END, IGNITING TINDER-DRY WOODLAND. FLAMES TRAVELLING AT SPEEDS OF UP TO 110 KM/H EAGERLY DEVOUR EVERYTHING IN THEIR PATH

a pall of smoke over the region so thick that it made life almost unbearable for the inhabitants. The farmers lit the fires to clear land for agriculture, but once the flames took hold they blazed through the root systems of rainforest trees, felling giant hardwoods and quickly spreading out of control. Fire-fighters were flown in from the USA, Australia and Malaysia to battle alongside

more than 8,000 Indonesian fire-fighters struggling to extinguish the raging fires.

Fire devastates Yellowstone
In the US states of Wyoming, Montana and Idaho—the location of Yellowstone, the world's first National Park—the summer of 1988 was the driest for 50 years. Temperatures soared to 32°C and wind speeds reached 160 km/h—

perfect conditions for forest fire. Since 1972, the National Park's fire policy was that any fire started naturally should be allowed to run its course unless it threatened human life. But the fires that raged in Yellowstone's forests during the summer of 1988 forced the abandonment of that policy: by July, when over 60 km² of land had been destroyed, it was clear that the flames had to be stopped. A huge team of 9,000 fire-fighters as well as botanists, meteorologists, and geographers, were brought in. Together they endeavoured to bring the blazes, some of which were moving at a rate of 19 km per day, under control. But by the end of the summer, 6,000 km² of forest had been destroyed. Only the September snows finally put an end to the summer's inferno.

Ash Wednesday
In the scorching Australian summer of 1983, temperatures of 40°C and 70-km/h winds in Victoria and South Australia caused some of the worst forest fires in their history. In mid-February the temperature reached its peak, and on Ash Wednesday forest fires broke out in 180 locations. The fires tore through grassland and eucalyptus

woodland, which was tinder-dry after the intense hot spell. Ten of the fires burned out of control, and in woodland areas the bark and leaves of eucalyptus trees went up like kindling. These burning scraps were picked up and blown around by the wind, creating spot fires which spread the blazes still further. The mainly wood-built town of Macedon on the outskirts of Melbourne, Victoria, was completely engulfed by fire. In total, 76 people were killed and 5,000 km² of land destroyed.

Out in Mongolia
In May 1997 scorching hot weather dried out large areas of forest in Mongolia, precipitating the onset of 72 separate forest fires, which ravaged 106 km² of land. In total, 25 people were killed in the blazes and 60 injured. Despite the efforts of 24,000 people to stem the spread of the fire, the end was finally brought about by heavy rainfall. But fires have blazed yet again—so far in 1998, 470 have been recorded.

Natural remedies
Although forest fires are a hazard to the environment, they can also have some beneficial effects. Over time, fallen trees and dead wood build up on the forest floor, providing a rich haven for funghi and insects and providing vaulable nutrients for trees. But young saplings struggle to push their way through the thick forest floor, and so fire is a welcome means of clearing it, providing new living space and regenerating the forest.

DATA-BURST

WHAT IS THE DEFINITION OF A FOREST FIRE?
IF A FIRE BREAKS OUT IN VEGETATION OVER 1.8 M HIGH, IT IS TERMED A FOREST FIRE. IT CAN SPREAD VERY FAST THROUGH HIGHLY FLAMMABLE MATERIAL, OFTEN OPERATING AT DIFFERENT LEVELS—ON THE UNDERGROWTH, SURFACE AND UPPER LEVELS OF THE FOREST.

ARE MOST FOREST FIRES STARTED NATURALLY?
NO, A SHOCKING 95% ARE STARTED BY HUMANS. ONLY 1–2% ARE CAUSED BY LIGHTNING STRIKES.

WHAT ARE THE NEGATIVE SIDE-EFFECTS OF FOREST FIRES?
POLLUTION IS A BIG PROBLEM. FIRES IN VICTORIA, AUSTRALIA, IN 1939 CAUSED AIR POLLUTION IN QUEENSLAND, MORE THAN 3,000 KM AWAY. FIRES ALSO AFFECT PAPER PRICES, AND REDUCE THE ANIMAL POPULATION LIVING IN FORESTS.

ARE THERE ANY POSITIVE EFFECTS?
YES, DISEASE CAN BE ELIMINATED BY FIRE, AND IT CAN HAVE A REGENERATIVE EFFECT ON CERTAIN PARTS OF THE FOREST.

CAN FOREST FIRES BE AVOIDED?
PRECAUTIONARY MEASURES CAN BE TAKEN. THESE INCLUDE FIREBREAKS, RECONNAISSANCE FLIGHTS IN SUSCEPTIBLE AREAS, CONTROLLED BURNING AND SATELLITE CHECKS.

HOW IS A FIRE EFFECTIVELY FOUGHT?
THE FIRE TRIANGLE—TEMPERATURE OXYGEN AND FUEL—HAS TO BE BROKEN. WATER AND CHEMICALS ARE SPRAYED FROM PLANES AND THE FIRE IS ATTACKED BY FIRE-FIGHTERS ON THE GROUND.

HOW LONG DOES IT TAKE FOR A FOREST TO RECOVER FROM FIRE?
IT TAKES ABOUT 300 YEARS FOR A FOREST TO RETURN TO NORMAL AFTER A BIG FOREST FIRE.

LEFT: FLAMES LICK THE TREES IN THE SCORCHING HEAT OF A FULLY-BLOWN FOREST FIRE

Dams are artificially-constructed structures that harness water to be used for irrigation, electric power generation and flood control. When they burst it is usually due to a combination of heavy rain or earthquakes, and faulty design. The majority of dams are solid constructions, built to last and unlikely to burst; the oldest dam still in use is a rock fill dam in Syria, dating back to 1300 BC. Embankment dams like the Nurek Dam in Tajikistan can reach up to 300 m high, but they are of ongoing concern to engineers who fear that the sheer weight of the water on land might activate restless seismic spots deep underground.

St Francis Dam disaster
Built in 1925–26 in the San Francisquito Canyon, the St Francis Dam reached 60 m high. The dam, which was designed to provide storage for 47 million m³ of water, failed catastrophically on its first filling. On 13 Dec 1928, the dam burst killing more than 450 people in the San Francisquito and San Clara River valleys. The greatest American engineering failure of the 20th century is now understood to have occurred due

to a combination of factors. These included excessive tilting when fully loaded, an absence of seepage relief in the sidewalls of the dam, and the partial reactivation of underlying mega-landslides from the palaeolithic era on which the dam was unwittingly constructed.

Message in a bottle
Eighty people lost their lives in Arizona, USA, when a forgetful messenger got waylaid in a bar. Two dams were built on the

Hassayampa River in the 1880s, and, in 1890, the run-off of water from the nearby Bradshaw Mountains was so heavy that the upper dam looked set to burst. A messenger was sent down to the lower dam to warn people of the immanent danger. However, he stopped at a bar on the way and one drink led to another. The upper dam duly burst and a 35-m-high wall of water shot down the river, carrying with it boulders and whole trees.

DAM BURSTS

35-M HIGH WALL OF WATER

BOUNCING BOMBS

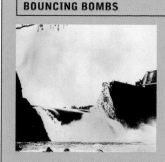

BRITISH DESIGNER AND ENGINEER SIR BARNES WALLIS WAS THE BRAINS BEHIND THE BOUNCING BOMB, WHICH WAS USED TO SUCH EFFECT AGAINST THE GERMANS DURING WORLD WAR.II. HE GOT THE IDEA OF BOUNCING BOMBS ACROSS THE SURFACE OF THE WATER FROM LORD NELSON, WHO HAD USED A SIMILAR TECHNIQUE TO FIRE CANNON BALLS FROM HIS SHIPS IN THE 18TH CENTURY. THE BATTLE OF THE RUHR BETWEEN MARCH AND JULY 1943 WAS CONCENTRATED ON GERMANY'S INDUSTRIAL HEARTLAND. ON THE NIGHT OF 16/17 MAY, THE RAF'S 617 SQUADRON CARRIED OUT THE FAMOUS 'DAMBUSTERS RAID' IN WHICH THEY USED WELLINGTON BOMBERS TO DESTROY THE MOHNE AND EDER DAMS IN GERMANY'S RUHR REGION. THE BOMBS WERE DESIGNED TO BOUNCE UP THE RIVERS AND THEN EXPLODE ON CONTACT WITH THE DAM WALL WHICH THEY DID TO GREAT EFFECT, PROVIDING THE ALLIES WITH A MAJOR TACTICAL ADVANTAGE. THE RESULTING FLOODS CRIPPLED INDUSTRY IN THE AREA AT A CRUCIAL STAGE OF THE WAR, SEVERELY WEAKENING ENEMY MORALE IN THE PROCESS.

JARGON

EMBANKMENT DAMS
EARTH-FILL DAMS, MAINLY USED TO BLOCK WIDE RIVERS

MASONRY DAMS
CONCRETE DAMS, USED TO BLOCK DEEP, NARROW GORGES

SKI-JUMP SPILLWAYS
OUTLETS IN THE MIDDLE OF A DAM WHICH ENABLE THE WATER TO SHOOT OUT

SLUICES
OUTLETS IN DAMS THROUGH WHICH WATER CAN PASS

TAILINGS DAM
BUILT BY PILING UP THE COARSE DEPOSITS OF THE SLURRY WASTE FROM INDUSTRIAL PROCESSES

RELEASED FROM DAM

CONSTRUCTED TO CONTROL MILLIONS OF TONNES OF WATER, DAMS CAN ALTER THE ECOSYSTEMS OF ENTIRE COUNTRIES. A DAM BURST HAS THE POTENTIAL TO CAUSE FLOODING, DEATH AND DAMAGE ON A CRITICAL SCALE

Dam burst in Bosnia

After a period of torrential rain in 1995 during war in Bosnia-Herzegovina, the Neretva River at Mostar burst a dam. French troop encampments nearby were flooded, military tents washed away and the soldiers had to be evacuated. Many homes were destroyed, but the Army successfully evacuated local people. Even after two of the three pedestrian bridges in the city were washed away, there were no human casualties. The only death occurred on a road out of Mostar, when an Italian police officer lost control of his jeep on the flooded road.

Toxic waste expelled from dam

Tailings dams are built up out of slurry and other by-products of industries like mills and mines. Notoriously unsafe, they often lack an engineered structure, and rely instead on upstream construction to try and prevent slurry from being washed downstream. These dams are particularly susceptible to the effects of seismic activity. In Saxony, Germany, a large uranium mill-tailings dam has been built on a geological fault line. It has been estimated that if the 1,800 m-long and 59 m-high dam were to burst, 30 million m^3 of slurries, including uranium and arsenic, would flow downstream into a local town. Such failure does occur with alarming frequency worldwide. On 24 April 1998, a lead-zinc dam failed near Seville, Spain, spewing out 4–5 million m^3 of toxic slurries into nearby Rio Agrio.

Secret flood

Some time between 1971 and 1973, Lake Klattasine in British Columbia, Canada, burst through a natural dam of rock and glacier debris. A total of 1.7 million m^3 of water from the lake flooded into surrounding valleys, and 2–4 million m^3 of rock and debris were carried along by the water. Nobody knows exactly when this occurred because the area is uninhabited and the event was not witnessed.

Gold diggers fined

When the Slimes Dam collapsed in February 1994, an avalanche of mud surged through Merriesprut, Virginia, USA, killing 17 people. The Virginia Regional Court fined Harmony Gold Mine $120,000 for its part in causing the disaster.

Raindrops keep falling

Twenty-seven counties in California, USA, were declared federal disaster areas in 1998 when the Anderson Dam in Santa Clara overflowed. As the state's average seasonal rainfall doubled, so nine out of ten of Santa Clara's dams either burst or were breached. The army was called in to build emergency dams. In Malibu alone, 1,500 people had to be housed in temporary shelters, and at least one million-dollar home was completely destroyed. The total cost in damages was estimated at $220 million.

DATA-BURST

WHICH DAM BURST KILLED THE MOST PEOPLE?
THE BANQIAO AND SHIMANTAN DAMS BURST ALMOST SIMULTANEOUSLY ONTO HENAN PROVINCE, CHINA, IN AUG 1975, KILLING 230,000 PEOPLE.

HOW BIG IS THE BIGGEST DAM?
IN TERMS OF VOLUME, THE BIGGEST DAM IN THE WORLD IS NEW CORNELIA TAILINGS ON TEN MILE WALSH, ARIZONA, USA. THIS EMBANKMENT DAM HAS A VOLUME OF 209.5 MILLION M^3. THE BIGGEST DAM IN THE UK IS THE GALE COMMON TAILINGS DAM AT CRIDLING STUBBS, N. YORKS.

WHAT ARE ARCH DAMS AND HOW EFFECTIVE ARE THEY?
ARCH DAMS USE THE PRESSURE OF WATER TO KEEP THEIR STRUCTURE INTACT. IN 1963 THE VAJONT DAM IN ITALY PROVED THEIR STRENGTH WHEN WAVES OVER 90 M HIGH SWEPT OVER IT, AND VERY LITTLE DAMAGE WAS CAUSED.

WHAT IS THE STRONGEST DAM?
IT IS THOUGHT TO BE THE SYANO-SHUSHENSKAYA DAM ON THE RIVER YENISEY IN SIBERIA, WHICH IS DESIGNED TO COPE WITH 18 MILLION TONNES OF WATER.

WHAT DAMAGES DAMS?
DAMS BUILT IN SEISMICALLY-ACTIVE AREAS MAY POSE PROBLEMS BECAUSE OF THE EFFECT OF EARTHQUAKES ON THE DAM'S FOUNDATIONS. FOR EXAMPLE, THE TOKACHI EARTHQUAKE IN 1968 DAMAGED 93 EMBANKMENT DAMS IN JAPAN. IN GENERAL, MASONRY DAMS ARE MORE SUSCEPTIBLE TO THIS TYPE OF DAMAGE, AS THEY DEPEND TOTALLY ON SOLID FOUNDATIONS.

CAN ANYTHING BE DONE TO PREVENT THIS TYPE OF DAMAGE?
TODAY, COMPUTERS ENABLE MODELLING OF THE DAM'S RESPONSE TO SEISMIC ACTIVITY. THIS TECHNIQUE WAS EMPLOYED SUCCESSFULLY AT THE GARIEP DAM IN SOUTH AFRICA.

LEFT: A HOME IN THE FOREGROUND OF THE ANDERSON RESERVOIR DAM SPILLWAY, CALIFORNIA, 9 FEBRUARY 1988 · RIGHT: THE BOULDER OR HOOVER DAM ON THE ARIZONA-NEVADA BORDER

Dams control the flow of a river so that water can be more effectively used and distributed. Large reservoirs and lakes emerge as the natural journey of the river is stemmed. Valleys are subsumed and flooded by the dam waters, often covering up towns and homes in the process. In this way, the construction of a dam can have far-reaching consequences for the ecology of a whole region. In certain parts of the world there is a threat of water in the reservoir becoming stagnant: bacteria, viruses and other chemicals that normally flow down a river and out to sea are no longer washed away. Several huge dam projects are currently under consideration and construction around the world and, while their benefits are obvious, lessons from the past indicate that the damaging effects of drowning a landscape should also be taken into account.

large numbers of Sudanese nomads were forced to return to Khashm al-Qirbah, in Sudan. Undoubtedly, the dam project has brought many benefits: it has proved effective in controlling the annual Nile flood and has improved irrigation. The local fishing industry has also benefited. The dam has made navigation of the Nile easier and produces huge amounts of hydro-electric power. However the cost to local people and the ancient landscape has also been immense.

species are also affected. Whereas some fight fast water currents in a river, others huddle in the calm. If the river environment changes, the fish migrate elsewhere or perish.

Indian unrest
In 1992, 400 protesters were nearly drowned when they demonstrated against the building of the Sardar Sarovar Dam in India. This massive scheme is still under consideration but it will involve the resettling of 100,000

the world. Work began in 1994 and the Three Gorges project will not be completed until 2009. Located at Sandouping village in Hubei province, the dam will be 170 m high and 1.6 km wide. The dam will be two-thirds the height of the Eiffel Tower and will contain enough concrete to build 12 standard dams. The huge walls must be strong enough to hold back the millions of tonnes of water and mud that the silty Yangtze River will wash up against the man-made

DROWNED LAND
2 MILLION CHINESE

Temples in the lake
An original dam was built at Aswan on the River Nile in Egypt between 1902 and 1907. It soon began to cause problems as the reservoir it created gradually submerged the island Qasr Anas al-Wujud on which stood several important ancient Egyptian temples. A new dam was therefore constructed in 1970 at a cost of £600 million and, while this reduced the direct threat of flooding to the temples, it did reveal that they had already suffered extensive damage. It also created Lake Nasser, which brought a new threat to the temples further south at Abu Simbel. The Egyptian government therefore decided to move the temples to a new, safer location at huge expense. The population also suffered severe displacement, with 50,000 Egyptians moving to the Kawm Umbu valley, 50 km away, while

People and power
The construction of the Theun-Hinboun Dam in Laos, South-east Asia, in 1998 has had a devastating effect on the local population. The dam provides a huge amount of hydroelectric power (some 210 megawatts), but the consequent flooding brought problems for the communities living nearby. The whole project cost about £150 million, but just £30,000 was set aside as compensation. The local economy was destroyed and fish catches declined by up to 90%.

Downside of dams
As well as the social upheaval that the building of a dam can bring, dams can also adversely affect the environment. Although they prevent flooding, this also means that soil downstream is not replenished. Fields become less fertile, even barren, on former floodplains. Fish

people and will flood more than 120,000 hectares of forest. However, it would also provide hydroelectric power, employment, irrigation and water for 5,600 villages and 130 towns located downstream. In this region in 1994, the cost of crop losses was put at £120 million because of the shortage of water. More than half of the directors of the World Bank voted to continue to fund the dam project in 1992, but building work was halted in 1993 by a court order after local people claimed they had not been consulted. Construction has since begun once again on the project.

Chinese giant
The largest dam in the world is proposed for the mighty Yangtze River in China. It is China's biggest engineering project since the Great Wall and the largest anywhere in

barrier. Upstream, the whole region will be flooded and nearly 2 million people will have to be resettled. The reservoir will flood 54,000 acres of farmland, 17,000 acres of forest, two cities and hundreds of smaller towns.

Yangtze dilemma
Partly as a result of protesters' objections, the World Bank decided to withdraw financial aid for the Three Gorges project in 1994. The Chinese are carrying on with the construction of the dam regardless. The dam is intended to control the monsoon floods which have killed thousands of people over the years. It will also provide 18,000 megawatts of electricity for the fast-developing Chinese nation-state. Opponents point out that sediment will have to be dredged regularly if the dam is to work, and that transportation problems are also inevitable, as the Yangtze River is a major shipping channel.

The damning of dams
The last decade has seen a marked change in public perception of the advantages that dams bring. This has led to pressure on power companies to improve their public policies. Federal law in the USA now requires such companies to give equal consideration to non-power factors (such as the environment) as part of their re-liscensing process. Older dams can outlive their economic usefulness and may become structurally unsafe. Repair bills can often be so high that removal proves cheaper than maintaining an old dam.

LEFT: LOCAL TOURISTS VISIT AN EXHIBITION WHERE A MODEL OF THE FUTURE THREE GORGES DAM IS DISPLAYED IN SANDOUPING · RIGHT: FLOODED EGYPTIAN TEMPLE AT PHILAE

DATA-BURST

WHO BUILT THE FIRST DAM?
BYZANTINE ENGINEERS USED ROMAN MASONRY TO BUILD AN ARCH-GRAVITY DAM IN AD 550. DAM BUILDING ONLY BEGAN IN EARNEST WHEN THE INDUSTRIAL REVOLUTION GAVE RISE TO THE NEED FOR WATER POWER IN THE 18TH AND 19TH CENTURIES.

WHAT IS A SPILLWAY?
A SPILLWAY IS THE MOST IMPORTANT AUXILIARY STRUCTURE OF A DAM. IT DRAINS AWAY ANY EXCESS WATER.

HOW DO DAMS RELEASE WATER FOR IRRIGATION?
DAMS HAVE MANY OUTLETS, CALLED SLUICES OR GATES, THAT ALLOW WATER TO BE CONTROLLED FOR IRRIGATION PURPOSES. SPECIAL GATES IN THE FORM OF STEPPED POOLS, LOCKS AND FISH LADDERS ARE BUILT INTO MANY DAMS TO ALLOW FOR THE UPSTREAM AND DOWNSTREAM PASSAGE OF MIGRATORY FISH, SUCH AS SALMON. SLUICES ARE ALSO USED TO DRAIN AWAY ANY SILT THAT MIGHT HAVE COLLECTED BEHIND THE DAM.

HAVE ANY DAM-BUILDING SCHEMES BEEN STOPPED FOR ENVIRONMENTAL REASONS?
YES. ONE OF THE BIGGEST DAM-BUILDING SCHEMES EVER ENVISAGED WAS TO HAVE BEEN BUILT IN BRAZIL AND COMPLETED IN THE YEAR 2010. IN ORDER TO MEET BRAZIL'S ENERGY DEMANDS FOR THE NEXT 20 YEARS, 136 HYDRO-ELECTRIC DAMS WERE TO HAVE BEEN BUILT. THIS WOULD HAVE ENTAILED FLOODING AN AREA THE SIZE OF THE UK AND DISPLACING 250,000 INDIANS FROM THEIR TRADITIONAL RAINFOREST HOME.

REBUILDING THE TEMPLES OF PHILAE

THE ANCIENT EGYPTIANS BUILT TEMPLES AT ABU SIMBEL AND ON PHILAE, OR TEMPLE ISLAND, PRECISELY BECAUSE THEY WERE ABOVE THE THREAT OF THE ANNUAL NILE FLOODS. THE EARLIEST KNOWN TEMPLE WAS BUILT BY THE SAITES IN 500 BC, ALTHOUGH THERE IS EVIDENCE OF CONSTRUCTION WORK THROUGHOUT THE PERIOD FROM 690 BC TO AD 565. WHEN THE DAMS WERE BUILT AT ASWAN IN 1902, THE WATER LEVEL INCREASED DRAMATICALLY. BETWEEN 1907-1912, THE DAM WAS HEIGHTENED AND FEARS WERE RAISED FOR ALL THE NUBIAN MONUMENTS. PHILAE WAS INUNDATED FOR PART OF EACH YEAR AND WHEN IT EMERGED FROM THE WATERS, THE RUINS ROSE FROM BLACK, SILT-LADEN SOIL. WHEN THE WATERS WERE AT THEIR HEIGHT, ONLY THE CAPITALS OF THE LOFTY COLUMNS COULD BE SEEN. WHEN ANOTHER DAM PROJECT IN THE 1960S THREATENED TO SUBMERGE THEM COMPLETELY, AN INTERNATIONAL APPEAL WAS LAUNCHED AND THE EGYPTIAN GOVERNMENT DECIDED TO MOVE THE TEMPLES BRICK BY BRICK. THIS COMPLEX RECONSTRUCTION TOOK PLACE IN 1980.

MOVE TO MAKE WAY FOR DAM

DAMS ARE BUILT IN ORDER TO CONTROL FLOODING AND GENERATE HYDROENERGY. BUT BY TAMPERING WITH THE NATURAL FLOW OF A RIVER, OTHER PROBLEMS ENSUE, CAUSING HUGE SOCIAL AND ENVIRONMENTAL UPHEAVAL

Global warming is the gradual increase in the Earth's temperatures. It is linked to an increase in carbon dioxide and other greenhouse gases in the atmosphere. These gases act like the glass in a greenhouse, reflecting heat from the sun back to Earth. One of the most worrying aspects of global warming, scientists believe, is that the increased temperatures could melt the Earth's glaciers and ice sheets, causing a significant rise in sea levels, and washing away entire areas of land. Already on the increase, they predict that by the year 2050 average global temperatures will have risen by 5°C and sea levels by 0.3 m.

Ice ages

For the past 2,300 million years, the Earth has been gripped by a continuous cycle of ice ages which have shaped the planet's rocks and climate, and had a profound effect on sea levels. About 125,000 years ago, the sea was 6 m higher than it is today; 18,000 years ago, it was 100 m lower than today. After the last ice age, seas began to rise again, reaching the current level 5,000 years ago. Scientists do not know what drives the cycle of ice ages, but they believe that global climate plays a significant role. If the Earth's temperature rises, it is possible that normal ice-age rhythms may be changed forever. The greatest worry is that rising temperatures will melt the Earth's mountain glaciers and the ice sheets of Greenland and Antarctica, causing seas to rise. But the evidence is confusing: scientists have found that the Greenland Ice Sheet is being formed as quickly as it is melting.

Less is known about the Antarctic Ice Sheet but some believe that the warm, moist air created by global warming may actually increase the amount of ice in Antarctica by causing an increase in snowfall.

Sea level changes

Sea levels, which are a measure of the amount of water in the world's oceans, can fluctuate as a result of global warming. The quantity of water increases as polar ice caps retreat and ice melts. In this way,

RISING SEAS

THE SEA HAS RISEN 15 CM OVER

WHEN 117 HEADS OF STATE—THE LARGEST NUMBER EVER GATHERED TOGETHER—MET AT A SUMMIT IN RIO DE JANEIRO, BRAZIL, IN 1992, GLOBAL WARMING WAS AT THE TOP OF THEIR AGENDA. IN ORDER TO TACKLE THE PROBLEM, THE 178 NATIONS THAT WERE REPRESENTED AT THE EARTH SUMMIT SIGNED A TREATY WHICH COMMITTED THEM TO REDUCING EMISSIONS OF CARBON DIOXIDE, METHANE AND OTHER GASES. THE PROBLEM THEY FACED WAS ONE OF ECONOMICS. POOR NATIONS AT THE SUMMIT WERE RELUCTANT TO ADOPT ENVIRONMENTALLY-SOUND POLICIES WHICH WOULD SLOW DOWN THEIR ECONOMIC GROWTH; AND THE RICHER NATIONS WERE NOT PREPARED TO PROVIDE THE MONEY TO HELP THE POORER NATIONS TO OVERCOME THIS PRACTICAL HURDLE.

JARGON

CFCs
CHLOROFLUROCARBONS ARE THE GASES PRODUCED BY REFRIGERATORS AND AEROSOLS WHICH CONTRIBUTE TO THE GREENHOUSE EFFECT

GLOBAL WARMING
THE RISE IN THE EARTH'S OVERALL TEMPERATURE WHICH OCCURS AS A RESULT OF THE GREENHOUSE EFFECT

GREENHOUSE EFFECT
THE WAY IN WHICH CARBON DIOXIDE AND OTHER GASES REFLECT HEAT BACK TO EARTH WHICH WOULD OTHERWISE BE REFLECTED INTO SPACE

RIAS
DROWNED RIVER VALLEYS

THE LAST 100 YEARS

RISING TEMPERATURES ARE HEATING UP THE EARTH'S SURFACE, MELTING HUGE GLACIERS AND ICE SHEETS AND CAUSING SEA LEVELS TO RISE BY 2 MM EACH YEAR—AS A RESULT MORE AND MORE LAND WILL BECOME SUBMERGED

changes in conditions in the polar regions can dramatically affect sea levels. The ice caps provide a delicate gauge of world climate. The melting of the whole Antarctic ice cap would result in a rise in sea level of 70 m. The melting of the Arctic would have less effect since most of the ice is floating, but the melting of the Greenland ice cap would alone induce a rise in sea levels of around 8 m.

Sea-level monitoring
Around the world, especially in areas vulnerable to coastal flooding, sea levels are continually monitored. In several Pacific Islands, including Papua New Guinea, Tonga, Fiji, Western Samoa and the Cook Islands, monitoring stations feed information into a surveillance project set up in 1993 and run by the Solomon Islands. Another

project, begun in 1991—the World Ocean Circulation Experiment— measures world sea levels, collecting data from 160 tide gauges. Countries as far apart as the UK, Korea, Greenland, Argentina, Russia, South Africa and the USA are involved. As part of the broader World Climate Research Programme, the project also studies the deepest oceans to try to work out the role of sea levels in changes to the Earth's atmosphere and climate.

Submerged cities
During the first century AD, rising seas reclaimed at least two ancient cities, submerging their buildings to form underwater archaeological sites. In the port of Pozzuoli, near Naples, Italy, the action of the nearby Solfatara volcano caused the land to sink and allowed the rising sea to submerge Roman temples and markets. Although most of the town's inhabitants moved to Naples, Pozzuoli is now a popular seaside resort with a population of around 80,000. On the western coast of Turkey, the Greek town of Assos met a similar fate, probably around the same time. The town, built by colonists from the nearby Greek island of Lesbos in the first millennium BC,

was constructed on terraced slopes and had a busy harbour. In the first century AD, however, the bustling port, along with part of the town's fortifications and a temple, were claimed by the rising sea. From then on, the town swiftly declined.

Rising seas and travel
The shortest sea route between China and India is the Strait of Malacca, which separates the island of Sumatra from Thailand and the Malaysian mainland. Throughout history, control of this 800-km strip of sea has been a prize keenly sought by trading nations. Over the centuries, the Arabs, British, Dutch and Portuguese have all struggled for control over this strategic waterway. The strait itself was formed when the sea rose at the end of the last ice age and submerged the Sunda Shelf to a depth of 200 m. This flooding not only created a short-cut to India, it also cut the island of Sumatra off from mainland South-east Asia. This affected the migration of people and animals which, in turn, helped to shape the course of evolution in the region.

Rising seas and local climate
The county of Cornwall, UK, has a climate quite different to that of the rest of the country. This is partly because of the rise in sea level after the last ice age, which drowned several local river valleys, including the Tamar, Fowey and Fal. The wet conditions caused by this sea-water intrusion have ensured consistently high rainfall and clement weather patterns ever since. The county's warm summers and mild winters provide lush grazing for livestock and are the perfect conditions for a wide variety of plantlife.

Sea-buried civilization
Archaeologists have found what could be one of the world's oldest buildings off the coast of Japan. It lies off Yonaguni, a small island south-west of Okinawa. The monument, a rectangular stone ziggurat, has been dated to at least 8000 BC when the land on which it was constructed was submerged by rising seas at the end of the last ice age. The earliest signs of human settlement in Japan have been traced to the 10th millennium BC. First discovered by divers 10 years ago under 60 m of seawater, locals initially thought the site was a natural phenomenon but if it is man-made, it presents evidence of a totally undiscovered civilization.

DATA-BURST

HOW MUCH HAVE THE SEAS RISEN OVER THE PAST 100 YEARS?
ESTIMATES BASED ON RESEARCH STUDIES PUT THE RISE AT 15 CM.

HOW MUCH COULD SEA LEVELS RISE IN THE NEXT 100 YEARS?
ESTIMATES SUGGEST THAT BY THE YEAR 2100 THE GLOBAL MEAN SEA-LEVEL MAY BE AS MUCH AS 0.6 M HIGHER THAN IT IS TODAY.

WHAT AREAS ARE UNDER RISK FROM A RISE IN SEA LEVELS?
LOW-LYING COASTAL AREAS AND SMALL ISLANDS, SUCH AS THE MALDIVES, WILL BE MOST AT RISK. OTHER SITES UNDER THREAT INCLUDE TOURIST BEACHES AND FISHING SITES AROUND THE GLOBE.

COULD RISING SEA LEVELS ADD TO EXISTING NATURAL PROBLEMS?
YES. EXPOSED COASTAL AREAS COULD BE MORE PRONE TO FLOODING DURING HURRICANES. THE EROSION OF

MANGROVE SWAMPS COULD RESULT IN THE LOSS OF NATURAL DEFENCES AGAINST TSUNAMIS.

COULD RISING SEA LEVELS AFFECT INLAND WATER RESERVES?
PERHAPS. SOURCES OF GROUND WATER COULD BE CONTAMINATED BY INCREASED SALINITY, RESULTING IN SHORTAGES OF FRESHWATER. IN PARTS OF INDONESIA MARSHY RURAL AREAS CLOSE TO THE COAST ARE HIGHLY SENSITIVE TO SEA LEVEL CHANGES.

WHAT PROBLEMS DOES GLOBAL WARMING CAUSE?
AN INCREASE IN GLOBAL TEMPERATURE MAY AFFECT AGRICULTURE, SPEED UP THE FORMATION OF DESERTS AND BEGIN TO DESTROY RAINFORESTS. IT MAY ALSO MAKE ORGANIC MATTER IN THE SOIL DECOMPOSE MORE RAPIDLY, RELEASING MORE CARBON DIOXIDE AND ACCELERATING THE WHOLE GLOBAL-WARMING CYCLE.

LEFT: THE RECENTLY DISCOVERED ZIGGURANT (A PYRAMIDAL, STEPPED TEMPLE TOWER) WHICH LIES BURIED DEEP UNDER THE SEA OFF YONAGUNI ISLAND, JAPAN

LAND SCARS

MINE LEAVES 800 M

Humans can and do cause great changes to natural landscapes. Activities such as open-cast mining can leave open wounds on the surface of the Earth. Massive concrete structures such as highways and interchanges, as well as trash islands, war trenches and pipelines, leave terrible scars on the landscape, and they can destroy or damage ecosystems which take centuries to return to their former state.

Wounded Earth
Surface mining and quarrying have littered the landscape with scars and caused serious environmental damage. Open-cast mining for peat, coal, limestone, chalk and

WIND TURBINES

DESPITE BEING CLEAN AND ENVIRONMENTALLY-FRIENDLY WAYS OF PRODUCING ELECTRICITY, WIND TURBINES HAVE ALWAYS BEEN AT THE CENTRE OF CONTROVERSY AS PEOPLE DEBATE HOW THEY SHOULD FIT IN TO THE LANDSCAPE IN AN AESTHETIC WAY. IN THE UK, THE COUNTRYSIDE COMMISSION HAS WARNED THAT ENGLAND'S COUNTRYSIDE IS BEING TURNED INTO A WINDPOWER WILDERNESS. ONE OF THE PROBLEMS IS THAT THE WINDIEST PLACES ARE OFTEN ON THE TOPS OF HILLS OR IN SPARSELY POPULATED AREAS WHICH ARE ENJOYED AS BEAUTY SPOTS. THERE ARE CURRENTLY 17 WIND ENERGY SITES NEAR AREAS OF OUTSTANDING NATURAL BEAUTY, WITH SEVEN MORE PLANNED ON HERITAGE COASTS. SOME TURBINES STAND TALLER THAN NELSON'S COLUMN WHICH IS 56 M HIGH, SPOILING VIEWS AND DOMINATING THE HORIZON. EACH WIND TURBINE REQUIRES A HOLE UP TO 300 M DEEP TO BE DUG. TO PRODUCE 10% OF THE UK'S ELECTRICITY, 30,000 TURBINES WOULD BE REQUIRED, COVERING AN AREA OF 3,000 KM^2.

exacerbated by the islands' close proximity to the Bering Sea, a renowned dumping ground for different kinds of hazardous waste, that includes mercury, mustard gas and detergents.

Pipelines across the Earth
The need to transport raw materials across vast distances has led to feats of engineering which can also leave terrible scars on the landscape. The Trans-Alaska Pipeline delivers oil from Prudhoe Bay on the North Slope to ice-free tanker terminals at Valdez, east of Anchorage—a distance of 1,285 km. The above-ground section of the pipeline is 615 km long, 122 cm in diameter, and carries 1.5 million barrels of oil a day. It is built on 120,000 piles which allow it to survive seismic and frost movements. On the North Slope, where the oil originates, industrial structures scar an otherwise beautiful landscape. When the oil industry set up in the region, huge bulldozers left tyre tracks which later filled with water. These have created vast parallel creeks and mini-rivers.

Albanian bunkers
Albania is littered with concrete bunkers, relics of the violence and wars which have scarred the land over the past 50 years. There are more than 850,000 bunkers in Albania, each large enough for one man. They were built by the country's Stalinist dictator, who feared invasion from every quarter. There are now more bunkers than houses, and since they are too numerous to move, people live above, around and in them.

WOUND IN THE EARTH

HUMANS HAVE IRREVOCABLY TRANSFORMED THE SURFACE OF THE PLANET; MAMMOTH ENGINEERING STRUCTURES, VAST OPEN-CAST MINES AND COMPLEX TRANSPORT INFRASTRUCTURES ALL LEAVE AN INDELIBLE IMPRINT

other minerals has gouged the surface of the land. Three millennia of copper mining on Cyprus has caused much degradation, while open-cast mining in Nauru has devastated the island. Phosphate mining in Oceania could result in nearly 80% of the land surface being reduced to coral pinnacles in a wasted landscape. During the 1960s, over 10,000 km^2 of the USA was disrupted by surface

mining and the figure currently stands at 23,000 km^2. Surface mines can actually be very deep— the Sungai Besi Tin Mine in Malaysia, for example, leaves an 800-m-deep wound in the Earth.

Trash islands
The disposal of human waste has always been a problem, and in recent years, the sheer quantities involved have produced unsightly

rubbish dumps of epic proportions throughout the world. Entire islands can become extended dumps, such as St Paul and St George in the Pribilof Islands, 500 km west of Alaska. During many years of fur seal harvesting, old rusting tanks, fuel lines and dump areas have accumulated, and the islands have become dangerous public health hazards. This problem is further

DATA-BURST

WHAT OTHER HUMAN NETWORKS PRODUCE UNSIGHTLY SCARS?
ELECTRICITY PYLONS, TRANSPORT SYSTEMS, RADIO AND TV RELAY STATIONS AND CELLPHONE RELAYS CUT UGLY SWATHES THROUGH PRISTINE LANDSCAPES.

CAN WIND TURBINES BE DISGUISED?
A LARGE GROUPING IN NÄSUDDEN, SWEDEN, HAVE BEEN PAINTED GREY TO MERGE WITH THEIR SURROUNDINGS. ANOTHER STRATEGY IS TO USE LARGER, SLOWER-MOVING TURBINES WHICH DO NOT STAND OUT AS MUCH.

WHAT PROBLEMS ARISE AS A RESULT OF MINING?
MINING CAUSES DEEP UGLY SCARS IN THE LAND, SPECIES AND HABITAT DESTRUCTION, DUST POLLUTION, FLOODING, UNSIGHTLY AND POTENTIALLY LETHAL SPOIL HEAPS, AS WELL AS INCREASED TOXICITY IN THE LAND THAT PREVENTS THE REGROWTH OF VEGETATION.

WHAT TRANSPORT SYSTEMS ARE MOST DAMAGING TO THE ENVIRONMENT?
THE MOST DAMAGING ARE HIGHWAYS WHICH CAN CAUSE SEVERE ENVIRONMENTAL DAMAGE AND LAND DEGRADATION. THESE MASSIVE ROADS ARE VERY STRAIGHT TO PREVENT UNNECESSARY VEHICLE BRAKING, AND SO THEY FREQUENTLY SLICE RIGHT THROUGH TERRAIN, INCLUDING HILLS, MOUNTAINS, VALLEYS, NATURAL LANDMARKS AND RAINFORESTS. IT HAS BEEN ESTIMATED THAT, IN THE USA, FOR EVERY KILOMETRE OF HIGHWAY CONSTRUCTED, AN AREA OF LAND EQUIVALENT TO 10,000 M^2 IS DEVASTATED IN THE PROCESS.

IS IT POSSIBLE TO CONCEAL CERTAIN SCARS?
THERE HAVE BEEN ATTEMPTS TO BLEND NEW RELAYS—AERIALS WHICH TRANSMIT TELEVISION AND MOBILE PHONE SIGNALS—INTO THE ENVIRONMENT. THESE INCLUDE DISGUISING THEM AS TREES.

LEFT: OPEN-CAST COPPER MINE CUTS INTO THE EARTH, CHUQUICAMATA, CHILE · RIGHT: ROW AFTER ROW OF ELECTRICITY PYLONS DOMINATE THE LANDSCAPE

The 20th century has witnessed more environmental damage as a result of war than any other. Developments in technology and science have been put to military use resulting in ever more sophisticated mechanisms for death and destruction. Modern weapons are capable of wreaking destruction on a massive scale. Damage from warfare comes in many forms: soil is eroded by tank and military movement while heavy bombing can lead to devastation of the landscape. With advances in nuclear and chemical weaponry, the effects of attack can be long-term. Modern warfare tests nature's powers of rejuvenation to the limit.

Light of a thousand suns

On 6 Aug 1945, a US aircraft dropped an atomic bomb over the Japanese city of Hiroshima. This unprecedented act heralded destruction on an altogether new scale, more lethal than that brought about by conventional warfare. Within a distance of 1 km from the hypocentre, everyone was killed instantaneously. Estimates of the death toll now amount to over 140,000. The bomb gave off a thermal flash of light and heat so intense that houses in the downtown area spontaneously combusted. It also caused a huge firestorm which killed thousands more on the ground. Everything within a 2-km radius of the hypocentre was completely burnt. Ruins melted together like lava as a result of being distorted in the intense heat. The view in all directions after the bomb had been dropped was of a flat scorched plain. The large amounts of radiation that fell on that day penetrated people's bodies, targeting and destroying their blood cells. The carcinogenic effects of radiation doses are still being felt by survivors today. A year after the explosion, only weeds grew in the ruins. News reports at the time estimated that the ground would be barren for the next 70 years. This has not turned out to be the case. A new modern city has been built on the site and park land now covers areas where once there was only rubble.

RUIN OF WAR

LANDMINES KILL AND MAIM

BOMB TESTING

DESPITE THE FACT THAT THE COLD WAR IS OVER AND THE THREAT OF NUCLEAR WARFARE HAS RECEDED, THE TESTING OF NUCLEAR BOMBS GOES ON UNABATED. IT CONTINUES TO CAUSE DAMAGE TO THE ENVIRONMENT. ON 5 SEPT 1995, FRANCE SET OFF THE FIRST IN A SERIES OF NUCLEAR TESTS AT MURUROA ATOLL, A CORAL ISLAND IN THE SOUTH PACIFIC. VIBRATIONS FROM THE UNDERGROUND EXPLOSION WERE DETECTED BY SEISMIC MONITORS AS FAR AWAY AS AUSTRALIA. ENVIRONMENTALISTS CLAIM THAT RADIOACTIVE MATERIAL IS RELEASED INTO THE OCEAN FROM THE DRILL HOLES IN WHICH THE BOMBS ARE BURIED. THEY CLAIM THAT THE STRUCTURE OF THE REEF ITSELF IS DAMAGED AS THE SIDES OF THE ATOLL WALLS FALL AWAY—THE RESULT OF FRICTION FROM THE BOMB'S BLAST. THE FRENCH GOVERNMENT'S ACTION CAUSED INTERNATIONAL OUTRAGE AND PROTEST DEMONSTRATIONS. THERE WERE WORRYING SIGNS OF AN ARMS RACE BETWEEN INDIA AND PAKISTAN IN 1998 WHEN BOTH NATIONS ENGAGED IN NUCLEAR TESTS. PUBLIC MORALE WAS RAISED BY THESE DISPLAYS OF NATIONAL VIRILITY, BUT IT MAY SOON BE UNDERMINED BY THE IMPOSITION OF INTERNATIONAL SANCTIONS.

JARGON

CONTAMINATION
RADIOACTIVE POLLUTION

HYDROGEN BOMB
IMMENSELY POWERFUL BOMB UTILIZING THE EXPLOSIVE FUSION OF HYDROGEN NUCLEI

HYPOCENTRE
THE POINT OF EXPLOSION OF A NUCLEAR ATOMIC BOMB

RADIATION SICKNESS
SICKNESS CAUSED BY EXPOSURE TO RADIATION, SUCH AS GAMMA RAYS

SCORCHED EARTH
THE MILITARY PRACTICE OF DESTROYING, USUALLY BY BURNING, THE LAND LEFT BEHIND AFTER A TROOP WITHDRAWAL

26,000 PER YEAR

AS WEAPONS OF MASS DESTRUCTION BECOME MORE POWERFUL, SO GLOBAL CONFLICT EXACTS AN EVER MORE TERRIBLE PRICE, TESTING THE POWER OF THE NATURAL WORLD TO REVIVE AND HEAL THE WOUNDS OF WAR

Radioactive waste
The legacy of the Cold War between the USSR and the USA is the huge amount of dangerous radioactive waste. Plutonium, a by-product in the production of nuclear weapons, lasts for 250,000 years. Safe storage of this deadly carcinogenic substance presents a long-term problem—countless future generations will live with its effects. Worldwide, only 20 nuclear power reactors have ever been decommissioned and stockpiles of old nuclear weapons will themselves eventually need dismantling. Often such complex and potentially dangerous procedures prove to be very costly.

Sitting submarines
Many of the decisions about what to do with the stockpile of nuclear devices that built up during the Cold War have not yet been made. Britain, for example, has 11 nuclear submarines that sit in the dockyards in Rosyth, Scotland. These submarines, which are well past their useful lifespan, each contain 850-tonne nuclear reactor cylinders and no-one is sure what kind of waste they contain. The decommissioning of Russian nuclear submarines is also a cause for concern. Russia has around 130 nuclear submarines laid up in scrapyards. Many hulls have been found to leak. On 10 Aug 1985, an accident in the naval shipyard near Vladivostok killed 10 people and contamination spread for 6 km.

Scorched earth
The Soviet invasion of Afghanistan in December 1979 was followed by Soviet occupation, withdrawal and a protracted civil war. These events have had a devastating effect on this central Asian country. The successive conflicts have reduced much of Afghanistan to wasteland, creating intense rural poverty. Mass urbanization has resulted as farmers have abandoned their land for work in the cities. The war has also led to the destruction of the country's transport infrastructure, which was all but eradicated by the relentless bombing of roads and bridges. Whole villages were flattened. A scorched earth policy initiated by Soviet troops has left much of the land unable to sustain life. Farmers who do use the land have to cope with the threat of landmines and unexploded bombs.

Gulf War legacy
The Iraqi invasion of Kuwait in 1990 and the subsequent Gulf War of 1991 brought environmental devastation to the Middle East. During the war, Kuwait's air, land and marine resources were degraded and the oilfields, on which the national economy depends, were largely destroyed. Even today, vast lakes of oil flood the land, poisoning birds and animals. There is also evidence of chemical warfare—millions of barrels of oil were dispersed into Gulf waters and set alight by Iraqi troops during the war, threatening the ecosystem across a far wider area. Fish have traditionally been an important source of food in Kuwait, but fisheries are now polluted and useless. Many similar problems affect Iraq, which also experienced devastating bombing campaigns. The landscape along the border with Saudi Arabia was particularly badly hit by the war. Roads, bridges, water treatment plants and factories were all completely destroyed during the intensive bombing campaign. Malnutrition is now rife throughout the country because of the destruction of agricultural land, depletion of livestock and the contamination of water supplies.

Land contamination
Every 22 minutes, someone somewhere in the world will become the victim of a landmine. It is estimated that 100 million such devices are lying in the soil of 68 countries, mostly developing nations. Landmines kill and maim 26,000 people every year. Angola alone has 5–12 million devices which were scattered over the land indiscriminately, hidden in roads, plantations, footpaths, even schools and homes. Long after conflict has ended, these landmines prohibit the tilling of soil and the grazing of animals. Farmers are therefore forced to over-graze and over-cultivate existing mine-free land which can lead to desertification. In Afghanistan and Cambodia, around 35% of the land is unusable because of millions of buried landmines. A worldwide campaign to ban the use of anti-personnel landmines is underway in an attempt to address the problem.

LEFT: SMOKE BILLOWS FROM BURNING OIL WELLS, KUWAIT, 1991 · RIGHT: A BOY HELPS HIS MOTHER FILL A SACK WITH SCRAP SALVAGED FROM THE WAR-TORN CITY OF KABUL, AFGHANISTAN

BIOTERRORISM
100 KG OF ANTHRAX

The misuse of potentially lethal bacteria and other micro-organisms can be traced back through the ages. Today, information about biological and chemical weapons can be easily accessed, making them available to a new group of people. Once the exclusive preserve of scientists and defence teams, biological and chemical weapons have been adopted by extreme factional and terrorist organizations who find them relatively cheap and easy to manufacture.

ranging from dry powder or liquid-slurry formations that cause diseases like Tularemia to Venezuelan equine encephalitis, and toxins such as paralytic shellfish poison. The USA also has weapons that can dispense airborne clouds of pathogenic microbes capable of causing mass destruction over large areas. These deadly machines exist in spite of a 1972 treaty signed by more than 70 countries which prohibits the production, stockpiling and development of biological agents.

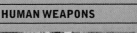

HUMAN WEAPONS

A PARTICULARLY GRUESOME EXAMPLE OF EARLY BIOTERRORISM OCCURRED DURING THE SIEGE OF CAFFA IN THE CRIMEA IN 1347. DURING THE SIEGE, THE MONGOLS THREW THE BODIES OF PLAGUE VICTIMS OVER THE WALLS OF THE DEFENDING GENOESE. AS GENOESE SHIPS TRAVELLED AROUND EUROPE, THE BACILLUS AGENT SPREAD REACHING EPIDEMIC PROPORTIONS, AND CONTRIBUTING TO THE OUTBREAK OF PLAGUE KNOWN AS THE BLACK DEATH, WHICH RAVAGED EUROPE KILLING BETWEEN ONE-THIRD AND ONE-HALF OF THE POPULATION.

MAY KILL 3,000,000

BOTH THE ABUSE AND MANIPULATION OF BACTERIA AND THE MIXING OF DEADLY CHEMICAL AGENTS CAN PRODUCE LETHAL COCKTAILS WHICH, IF DISPERSED, ARE CAPABLE OF CAUSING INJURY AND DEATH TO THOUSANDS OF PEOPLE

regeneration. A US Senate Committee investigating the cult found that although the attack on the Tokyo subway was a crude attempt at bioterrorism, the cult had the potential to do far more damage with over 40,000 members in Russia and Japan including hundreds of scientists hell-bent on instigating a war between Japan and the USA.

Chemical weapons
The USA and former Soviet Union have significant stockpiles of lethal chemical weapons including the nerve agents Sarin and VX and the liquid chemicals mustard gas, Lewisite and CS gas which can be loaded into artillery projectiles, bombs and missile warheads and detonated by an explosive charge, or sprayed from aircraft.

Biological warfare
Also known as germ warfare, this is defined as the military use of disease-producing agents. Official statistics released by the USA in the early 1970s revealed that the country's defences included extensive biological weapons,

Blowing in the wind
Air conditions during a bio-terrorist weapon assault have a major impact on the effectiveness of the manoeuvre. The US Office of Technology Assessment published a report in 1993 which hypothesized that on a clear and sunny day, with a light breeze, 100 kg of anthrax spores would cause 130,000 to 460,000 deaths over an area of 46 km^2, whereas an attack on an overcast day or night, with a moderate wind, would kill between 420,000 and 1,400,000, affecting an area of 140 km^2. If the attack occurred on a clear, calm night, the death toll would be in the region of a shocking 1–3 million within an area of 300 km^2.

Mass murder of Kurds
The most people killed in a single bioterrorist attack were the estimated 5,000 Kurds who died at Halabja, Iraq, in March 1988. When Saddam Hussein used mustard gas to prevent Iranian occupation, Iranian troops mistook fleeing Kurds for Iraqis and bombarded them with deadly hydrogen cyanide. Following this, the homes of tens of thousands of Kurds were razed to the ground, creating an uninhabited 'security' zone along the Iranian border.

Goddess-worship
On 20 March 1995 the nerve agent Sarin was released in a Tokyo subway by the Japanese cult Aum Shinrikyo, injuring 5,000 people and killing 12. Later that year, a further attack attributed to Aum Shinrikyo injured more than 300 people on a crowded train in Yokohama. The passengers were said to have experienced difficulty breathing and acute dizziness. Two days later, several people were admitted to hospital after they felt the effect of acrid fumes in a nearby shopping centre. Two Japanese men found guilty of carrying out the attack said that they were acting on orders from the cult's leader, Shoko Asahara. Asahara, a renowned maverick with numerous criminal convictions, founded the nihilistic cult in honour of Shiva, the Hindu goddess of destruction and

Failed fraudster
In March 1995, Larry Harris, a member of the white supremacist Aryan Nations Group managed to obtain some lethal organisms that cause bubonic plague. He used his professional credentials and a forged letterhead to get the deadly micro-biological samples from the American Type Culture Collection, Rockville, Maryland. Luckily, the ATCC became suspicious of Harris, and managed to retrieve the plague organisms unopened. There is no law in the USA against owning such substances, so Harris was prosecuted for mail fraud instead.

JARGON

ANTHRAX
A DISEASE OF CATTLE AND SHEEP THAT CAN ALSO KILL HUMANS

BOTULISM
A DISEASE CAUSED BY A TOXIN FROM THE COMMON FOOD-POISONING BACTERIA, CLOSTRIDIUM BOTULINUM

SARIN
A HIGHLY VOLATILE NERVE AGENT THAT IS A RESPIRATORY THREAT

SOMAN
A DANGEROUS NERVE GAS THAT CAUSES BOTH RESPIRATORY AND CONTACT HAZARDS

SPORE
A REPRODUCTIVE CELL OF MANY PLANTS AND MICRO-ORGANISMS

TULAREMIA
A PLAGUE-LIKE DISEASE THAT CAN BE INTRODUCED BY BIOTERRORISM

VX
A NERVE AGENT THAT IS HAZARDOUS AS A CONTACT POISON

DATA-BURST

IS THE POSSESSION OF KILLER GERMS ILLEGAL?
OWNERSHIP OF THE DEADLY SUBSTANCE THAT CAUSES BUBONIC PLAGUE IS NOT ILLEGAL IN THE USA. IN THE UK COMPANIES HAVE TO PROVE TO THE GOVERNMENT'S HEALTH AND SAFETY EXECUTIVES THAT THEY HAVE ADEQUATE FACILITIES WITH WHICH TO CONTAIN LETHAL PATHOGENS. PRIVATE INDIVIDUALS CAN OBTAIN THE SUBSTANCES IN THE UK, BUT THERE IS A LAW AGAINST TRANSPORTING, STORING, OR OBTAINING THEM BY FRAUD OR THEFT.

HOW MANY PEOPLE COULD DIE FROM AN ANTHRAX ATTACK?
A LIGHT AIRCRAFT CARRYING 100 KG OF ANTHRAX SPORES, EQUIPPED WITH A CROP SPRAYER, COULD KILL UP TO 3 MILLION PEOPLE.

WHAT EVIDENCE IS THERE OF A BIOTECHNOLOGICAL INDUSTRY?
LESS DEVELOPED COUNTRIES LIKE IRAQ ARE THOUGHT TO BE POURING MONEY AND RESOURCES INTO THIS AREA. BUT STATISTICS FROM THE USA ALSO GIVE CAUSE FOR CONCERN: THERE ARE 1,300 BIOTECHNOLOGY COMPANIES IN THE USA COMPARED TO 580 IN EUROPE. ONLY 25 YEARS AGO THERE WERE NONE AT ALL.

DO CHEMICAL AND BIOLOGICAL WEAPONS HAVE DIFFERENT EFFECTS?
YES, PLAGUE, BOTULISM AND TULAREMIA ARE THE MOST COMMON DISEASES BROUGHT ABOUT BY GERM WARFARE, WHEREAS CHEMICAL WEAPONS TEND TO AFFECT THE NERVOUS SYSTEM AND THE SKIN CAUSING RESPIRATORY PROBLEMS AND BLISTERING RESPECTIVELY.

LEFT: THE ANAEROBIC BACTERIA, CLOSTRIDIUM BOTULINUM, WHICH IS RESPONSIBLE FOR SERIOUS FOOD POISONING IN HUMANS, AND IS USED AS A BIOLOGICAL DEFENCE AGENT

POLLUTION 1
ALASKAN OIL SPILL

Environmental disaster comes in many forms. Industrial pollution occurs when no thought is given to the possible damaging effects of toxic substances on the environment or when existing safety standards are breached through accident or deliberate negligence. Potentially poisonous materials, such as crude oil, mercury and cyanide, have all been released in vast quantities into seas and rivers leading to the death of plant, animal and human life. Environmental damage is especially serious when it threatens the water supply as this can result in successive knock-on effects, damaging the whole balance of the delicate ecosystem.

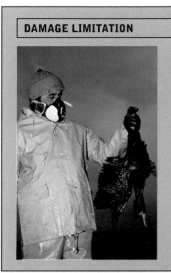

DAMAGE LIMITATION

AFTER AN OIL SPILL, NEARBY COASTAL AREAS EXPERIENCE A 'BLACK TIDE' WHERE THE OIL HAS COATED THE SEA'S SURFACE. CLEAN-UP OPERATIONS ONLY HAVE LIMITED SUCCESS AFTER SPILLAGE HAS TAKEN PLACE ALTHOUGH EFFORTS ARE USUALLY MADE TO PREVENT SLICKS REACHING THE SHORE BY USE OF 'BOOMS'. TRADITIONAL CLEANING TECHNIQUES HAVE INCLUDED VACUUMING, ABSORBING, BURNING, AND DISPENSING THE OIL. AFTER THE *EXXON VALDEZ* DISASTER, SHORELINES WERE SCRUBBED, ROCKS BLASTED WITH HOT WATER, AND FERTILIZERS APPLIED TO THE AFFECTED AREA. THOUSANDS OF PEOPLE VOLUNTEERED TO TRY AND CLEAN SEA BIRDS; ABOUT 300,000 PERISHED WHEN THEIR FEATHERS WERE COATED IN THE GLUEY, BLACK CRUDE OIL.

the casings erode, these old dumping sites now threaten to endanger life in the waters around them. The weapons were sealed in ships which were scuttled at depths of 6,000 m in four locations around Land's End, Northern Ireland, and two sites in the Hebrides. Nearly 120,000 tonnes of material, largely mustard gas and phosgene, lie on the sea-bed. Weapons dumps in the Irish Sea are thought to be responsible for the high levels of arsenic found in plaice caught at Liverpool Bay.

Changing sex
In recent times, concern has grown over a possible link between the presence of certain man-made

KILLS 300,000 BIRDS

HUMANS POLLUTE THE NATURAL ENVIRONMENT WITH A DEADLY VARIETY OF TOXIC SUBSTANCES AND CHEMICALS. WHEN OIL SPILLS INTO THE SEA, IT CONTAMINATES THE ECOSYSTEM, DISRUPTING THE DELICATE FOOD CHAIN

JARGON

CARCINOGEN
SUBSTANCE THAT CAUSES CANCER

DIOXIN
A SYNTHETIC COMPOUND MAINLY FORMED WHEN CHLORINE IS HEATED, AND FOUND IN SOME MANUFACTURING WASTES AND IN SOME HERBICIDES

IMPOSEX
INTERFERENCE IN THE GENDER CHARACTERISTICS OF PLANTS AND ANIMALS AS A RESULT OF CHEMICAL POLLUTION

PCB
POLYCHLORINATED BIPHENYLS ARE HYPOCARCINOGENS, DANGEROUS AS A SINGLE MOLECULE

TOXAPHENE
AN EXTREMELY TOXIC PESTICIDE

Alaskan tragedy
On 24 March 1989, the oil tanker, the *Exxon Valdez*, ran aground on the Bligh Reef in Prince William Sound in Alaska. The ship was carrying 1,264,155 barrels of North slope crude oil. About one-fifth of the total cargo, or 43 million litres, spilled into the sea. The oil came ashore on a 750-km long trajectory of islands known as the Kodiak Archipelago. Over 3,800 km of the shoreline was found to be heavily oiled. It took three years to clean up the coast at the cost of $2.1 billion. In that period, 300,000 seabirds, 2,650 sea otters and countless fish died as a result of the pollution.

Black day for Brittany
On 17 March 1978, the *Amoco Cadiz* supertanker, filled with 223,000 tonnes of crude oil, lost its entire cargo off Portsall in Brittany, France. The accident occurred during a storm in which the ship lost its ability to steer. A tug which attempted to tow the tanker off the rocks broke the ship in two. The oil slick covered more than 130 beaches with oil up to a depth of 30 cm. Over 30,000 seabirds died, along with 230,000 tonnes of crabs, lobsters, fish and other marine life. The area's prized

oyster beds were also damaged leading to loss of income for many local fishermen. The tanker belonged to the US-owned Amoco Oil Corporation. Although the vessel sailed under a Liberian flag, the US owners were eventually found guilty on several counts of negligence. In 1988, $85.2 million were awarded in damages to 90 Breton communities representing over 400,000 people.

New cleaning technology
The application of oil-eating microbes (or bioremediation) is an innovative new method of combating oil spillage. These microbes generate only natural by-products before dying or being eaten by other organisms. Another newly discovered technique involves the spraying of finely ground Australian clay, a substance formerly used in the commercial production of cat litter. Scientists have found that when sprayed on oil, this clay soaks up the spill, forming floating clumps that can later be gathered up.

Lake poisoning
A tanker carrying pesticides spilled its deadly cargo into the Sacramento River in an accident on 14 July 1991. The *Vapam*

chemical spill extended over many kilometres and killed everything in its path. A total of 100,000 rainbow trout were obliterated. Drifting more than 70 km over a period of three days, the chemical mass reached Shasta Lake, California's largest reservoir. The chemicals settled at the bottom of the lake where officials attempted to dilute the mass. Residents were evacuated after the accident and 200 were hospitalized for fume inhalation and skin irritation.

Cyanide and mercury
On 24 Aug 1995, President Jagan of Guyana declared an 88-km stretch of the Essquibo River a disaster zone. The banks of a pond holding the deadly poison, cyanide, had leaked into the river at the Omai Gold Mine. Tens of thousands of people were affected. The worst case of marine mercury pollution took place between 1953 and 1960 in Minimata Bay, Kyushu, Japan. A total of 43 people died, and 111 others were permanently injured when mercury waste leaked into the sea.

Underwater weapon dumps
In 1955, a number of chemical weapons were dumped off the British coast. As time passes and

chemicals found in the environment and hormone imbalances in some species of wildlife. Pollutants in the UK have caused a condition known as 'imposex' in river whelks: the females of the species acquire male characteristics that physically prevent them from laying eggs.

Poisoned polar bears
In 1998, scientists discovered deformed baby polar bears in the Arctic archipelago of Spitzbergen. The hermaphrodite cubs had both male and female sexual organs. Experts believe that a build-up of carcinogenic PCBs in the food chain are responsible. PCBs have long been linked with sex changes in animals but this finding marked the first in which such dramatic changes were found in mammals which, like humans, are at the top of the food chain. PCBs act as coolants in transistors, computers and nuclear submarines. Once dispersed in the enviroment, they slowly concentrate in polar regions.

LEFT: A SMALLER VESSEL ATTEMPTS TO OFF-LOAD CRUDE OIL FROM THE STRICKEN *EXXON VALDEZ* TANKER OFF PRINCE WILLIAM SOUND IN ALASKA ON 26 MARCH 1989

Long-term impact

The worst nuclear waste accident took place in 1957 when a nuclear waste container overheated causing an explosion at a complex at Kyshtym, Russia. Thousands of radioactive compounds were released and dispersed over an area of 23,000 km^2. More than 30 communities within a 1,200-km radius of the accident disappeared from the map of the USSR in the three years following the accident. About 17,000 people were evacuated. A 1992 report indicated that 8,015 people died over a 32-year period as a direct result of the radioactive discharges.

Chernobyl explosion

Unit 4 of the Russian Nuclear Reactor at Chernobyl exploded on 26 April 1986. The accident happened during a test designed to assess the reactor's safety margin. Reactor power rose to a peak of

and years that followed the accident many more people died as a result of the effects of the radiation and cancer-related illnesses. The magazine *USA Today* estimated the real death figure to be around 10,000. Following the blast, a 30-km 'special zone' was designated around the site and mass evacuation took place. High levels of radioactivity are predicted to exist in this zone for several centuries. Some areas around the former plant now report a total

neighbourhoods. The local hospitals were overwhelmed as upwards of 50,000 people sought medical attention. Breathing problems, eye irritations and blindness affected thousands. The lethal gas killed an estimated 6,300 people, making the disaster the single most devastating incident of air pollution ever. Investigations after the event established that understaffing and sub-standard safety procedures contributed to the calamity. In 1989, the company reached an

estimated 22,000 tonnes of chemical waste at the site of the Love Canal, a neighbourhood in Niagara Falls, New York. The waste included pesticides, dioxin and polychlorinated biphenyls. In 1953, the company sold the site to the local board of education and relieved itself of any future liability incurred because of waste on the site. A school was built on the site which was subsequently discovered to have been heavily contaminated. In 1984, it was the first place to

POLLUTION 2

6,300 PEOPLE DIED

100 times the design value and the subsequent explosion resulted in a fierce fire. Fifty tonnes of fuel, including contaminated plutonium and other highly radioactive materials, were ejected from the reactor and into the atmosphere. The amount of radioactive material, or fallout, that Chernobyl released was 10 times the amount experienced after the bomb explosion at Hiroshima in 1945. Prevailing winds blew the cloud of radioactive material towards Sweden. At first, the Soviet government was reluctant to impart any information about the accident—it was only when the Swedish government reported 10,000 times the normal amount of radioactivity in its air space that Moscow was forced to admit the scale and enormity of the disaster. The number of official deaths amount to 31, but in the months

absence of life after plants and animals were wiped out. The most contaminated regions affected were in southern Belarus, the northern Ukraine and southern Russia. Four million people live on contaminated ground and many children have been born with birth abnormalities as a result of the disaster.

Bhopal's deadly gas cloud

Bhopal, the capital of Madhya Pradesh state, India, was the scene of one of the worst industrial disasters of all time. In the early hours of 3 Dec 1984, about 45 tonnes of methyl isocyanate escaped from a Union Carbide insecticide plant. The gas formed a poisonous cloud that wafted over the city. Many people in the densely populated districts near the plant were killed instantly. More were killed later as a massive panic swept through the surrounding

agreement with the Indian government to make a settlement of £293 million to the victims and their relatives. This would help compensate some of the survivors of the catastrophe, many of whom suffered from numerous long-term ailments, including brain damage and chronic nerve disorder. The Bhopal factory never re-opened after the gas spillage, and the Union Carbide Corporation of the USA finally sold its 51% stake in Union Carbide India Ltd in 1994.

The poisoned Rhine

In 1986, firemen fighting a blaze at the Sandoz chemical factory works in Basel, Switzerland, flushed 30 tonnes of agricultural chemicals into the River Rhine, Europe's most heavily populated and heavily used waterway. The factory contained 850 tonnes of pesticides, dyes, fungicides and other toxic chemicals; 30 tonnes of this lethal cocktail entered the Rhine. Half a million fish died as a result and water supplies were cut off. Although nearby storage tanks containing the nerve gas chemical, phosgene, were undamaged, a high concentration of atrazine, a chemical which was not listed as being stored at the Sandoz factory site, was found. The incident aroused great public concern about the safety of chemical production. It took more than 10 years for the river to totally recover.

Toxic spill in the USA

Over an 11-year period, between 1942 and 1953, Hooker Chemicals and Plastic Company dumped an

be described by the Federal Government as an environmental disaster zone. The Environmental Protection Agency found levels of contamination to be 250 to 5,000 times the level deemed to be safe. In the lawsuits that followed, the former residents were awarded a compensation settlement of $20 million from the Hooker Company (then owned by the Occidental Chemical Corporation).

Black snow in Russia

The worst case of land pollution as a result of oil spillage occurred in the Komi region of Russia in 1994. From February to October, a burst pipeline spilled thousands of tonnes of crude oil across a huge expanse of pristine Arctic tundra creating a slick 18 km long. Estimates of the amount of oil lost range from 60,000 to 280,000 tonnes.

Disaster in Donana

On 27 April 1998 a chemical spill took place at the Donana National Park in Spain. One of the worst environmental disasters ever to happen in Europe, some 5—8 million cubic metres of toxic mud spilled from a waste dump at Aznalcoyar into the Guadiamar River. The river was blackened for 40 km to a width of some 200 m each side, killing thousands of fish. The black and viscous length of acid mud was loaded with hydrocarbons and was dumped by the Swedish-owned conglomerate, Boliden. As a result of eating dead fish, many other animals in the park were also affected by the river spillage.

LEFT: A STACK OF BARRELS CONTAINING TREATED NUCLEAR WASTE · RIGHT: FIREMEN IN PROTECTIVE CLOTHING CLEAN UP DEBRIS AT THE SANDOZ CHEMICAL FACTORY IN SWITZERLAND

DATA-BURST

HOW WIDESPREAD IS AIR POLLUTION?
POLLUTANTS STAIN THE AIR ON A MASSIVE SCALE. ESTIMATES SUGGEST THAT UP TO ONE IN FOUR PEOPLE WORLDWIDE IS BREATHING AIR WHICH IS DAMAGING TO THEIR HEALTH.

ARE THERE NATURAL SOURCES OF RADIATION ?
YES. RADON GAS EMANATES NATURALLY FROM ROCKS SUCH AS GRANITE. IN LARGE QUANTITIES IT CAN PROVE HAZARDOUS TO HUMAN HEALTH.

HOW SERIOUS IS THE WORLDWIDE WATER POLLUTION PROBLEM?
VERY. ONE-FIFTH OF THE WORLD'S POPULATION, 1.2 BILLION PEOPLE, REGULARLY DRINK POLLUTED DRINKING WATER. ONE PERSON DIES EVERY SIX SECONDS FROM DRINKING DISEASE-CONTAMINATED WATER.

ARE NUCLEAR AND CHEMICAL DISASTERS THE MAJOR CULPRITS IN WATER POLLUTION?
NO. AN ESTIMATED TWO-THIRDS OF WATER POLLUTION IS A RESULT OF AGRICULTURAL PRACTICES.

HOW QUICKLY IS HAZARDOUS WASTE PRODUCED?
INDUSTRIALIZED NATIONS PRODUCE LARGE QUANTITIES OF WASTE VERY QUICKLY. THE USA GENERATES ALMOST 420 TONNES OF HAZARDOUS WASTE EVERY MINUTE.

ARE THERE NATURAL SOURCES OF TOXIC GAS POLLUTION?
YES. IN 1991, MT PINATUBO ERUPTED, GENERATING 18 MILLION TONNES OF SULPHUR DIOXIDE—THE SAME AMOUNT THAT THE USA MANUFACTURES IN A YEAR.

ELECTRONIC GRAVEYARDS

COMPUTERS AND OTHER ELECTRICAL GOODS, SUCH AS REFRIGERATORS AND BATTERIES, ALL POSE A THREAT TO THE ENVIRONMENT IF THEY ARE NOT DISPOSED OF CAREFULLY. COMPUTERS COME COMPLETE WITH TOXIC AND CONTAMINATING MATERISLS SUCH AS CADMIUM, LITHIUM, LEAD, STRONTIUM, BATTERY ACIDS, HALOGENATED FIRE RETARDS AND OILS. EVEN MERCURY CAN BE LURKING IN OLDER EQUIPMENT. THE UK ALONE PRODUCES AN ANNUAL 900,000 TONNES OF DISCARDED ELECTRICAL GOODS. THE TOTAL ELECTRONIC WASTE PRODUCED BY THE WHOLE EUROPEAN UNION AMOUNTS TO 8 MILLION TONNES A YEAR. THIS WASTE RANGES FROM DISHWASHERS AND TELEVISIONS, TO FAXES AND HAND-HELD COMPUTER TOYS. A STUDY IN THE USA IN 1987 SUGGESTED THAT THERE WOULD BE 55 MILLION TONNES OF COMPUTERS TO BE LANDFILLED BY 2005. THE EUROPEAN COMMISSION IS DRAFTING A SERIES OF RECYCLING RULES. SOME OF THE LARGER MANUFACTURERS ARE ADOPTING A 'CRADLE TO GRAVE' SYSTEM WHEREBY GOODS ARE TRACKED IN ORDER TO ENSURE THEIR SAFE FINAL DISPOSAL. CURRENTLY ONLY A TINY PROPORTION OF THE TOTAL OUTPUT IS RECYCLED.

FROM LETHAL GAS IN INDIA

POISONOUS GASES AND NUCLEAR WASTE ARE INVISIBLE THREATS THAT INSIDIOUSLY CONTAMINATE A LANDSCAPE. RADIOACTIVE WASTE, ONCE SPILLED, IS IMPOSSIBLE TO CLEAN UP AND CAN LAST FOR SEVERAL CENTURIES

ACID RAIN

70% BLACK FOREST

An environmental problem that has attracted global attention, acid rain is caused by the emission of various pollutants into the air. Its most visible effect is the acidification of thousands of lakes and streams throughout North America and Europe. Scientists debate the extent of the problem, and politicians argue about who is responsible because acid rain crosses state, regional and international boundaries. What is certain is that acid rain in rivers, lakes and seas creates impossible living conditions for many organisms; it can have a detrimental effect on crop and forest yields; and it contributes to the deterioration of buildings.

HISTORY CRUMBLING AWAY

ACID RAIN'S RUINOUS ATTACK ON STATUES AND BUILDINGS IS BECOMING A WORLDWIDE PHENOMENON—FROM MICHELANGELO'S DAVID AND THE PARTHENON TO THE TAJ MAHAL AND THE STONE MONUMENTS ON THE BATTLEGROUND AT GETTYSBURG. SULPHUR DIOXIDE CAUSES THE FORMATION OF GYPSUM, A HEAVY BLACK DEPOSIT WHICH CLINGS TO THE SURFACE OF BUILDINGS. IN MEXICO, BLACK CRUSTS OF ACID DEPOSITS COAT SOME OF THE GREAT ARCHAEOLOGICAL TREASURES OF THE ANCIENT MAYA CIVILIZATION. TEMPLES, COLOURFUL MURALS AND HAUNTING MEGALITHS ARE BEING DESTROYED WHILE ANCIENT STUCCOS AND STONE INSCRIPTIONS ARE CORRODING AND CRUMBLING. POLLUTANTS FROM OIL REFINERIES AND TOURIST BUSES ARE THOUGHT TO BE THE CAUSE.

level can halt or disrupt their reproductive cycles. The Pennsylvania Fish and Boat Commission warn that acid rain poses a threat to over 8,000 km of streams that it stocks annually.

Elk poisoned by acid rain
Chemical emissions from British power stations have caused acid rain over Scandinavian countries, severely polluting the environment. Emissions have been linked to the death of the Scandinavian elk, the first grazing animal known to be affected by acid rain. Thousands of elk are likely to die from the effects of emissions over the past 50 years, even though targets for reductions in sulphur emissions have been met by British industry. In 1979, many European countries adopted a convention which bound them to reduce air-pollutant emissions although it set no targets. In 1983, after pressure from Scandinavia and Germany, 21 European countries made a commitment to reduce 1980 levels of emissions by 30% by 1993, although only 12 of them actually managed to reach this target.

Acid weapons
Burning oil wells, set on fire by Iraqi troops toward the end of the Gulf war, released enormous quantities of sulphurous gas into the atmosphere. This toxic mass was dispersed onto land when the rain came and when water was used to control the fires. Reports received between 2–31 March 1991 indicated that Kuwaitis were suffering an abnormally high degree of asthma, colds, burning eyes and sore throats. Acid rain had also caused corrosive damage to buildings.

Venus rising
The atmosphere of Venus continues to recover from an intense shower of sulphuric acid rain, according to images from the Hubble Space Telescope taken on 24 Jan 1998. The images, taken when Venus was about 113.6 million km from the Earth, reveal that the amount of sulphur dioxide in the atmosphere has declined by a factor of 10 since 1978 when the pioneer Venus Orbiter first flew. While the Earth is surrounded by water-vapour clouds, Venus is enshrouded by clouds of sulphuric acid. Scientists trying to explain the sulphur dioxide presence think that a gigantic volcanic eruption may have blasted the chemical above the clouds, causing acidic rain to pour down.

DAMAGED BY ACIDS

A FAR CRY FROM THE FRESH RAINFALL WHICH NURTURES AND REINVIGORATES THE LAND, THE DROPS OF POISON WHICH FALL IN AN ACID RAIN SHOWER ARE POTENTIALLY DEADLY, KILLING MANY ANIMAL AND PLANT LIFEFORMS

Forest and fields affected
Acid rain almost certainly contributes to a reduction in crop and forest yields because it leaches essential nutrients from the soil causing sensitive trees and plants to grow slowly or even die off. It also attacks the natural defences of trees. By eating away at the protective coating of their leaves, acid rain leaves them ill-prepared to cope with drought, a lack of nutrients or the possibility of attack from pests and diseases. Scientific reports suggest that there has been widespread forest damage as a consequence of high levels of acid rain in the north-eastern USA and Canada. In Europe, estimates suggest that as much as 70% of the Black Forest, situated on the eastern bank of the Rhine, has been damaged by pollution from acid rain.

Health hazard to humans
Acid rain can also cause problems to human health, usually affecting the respiratory system. Sulphuric and nitric acids cause asthma, dry coughs, headaches and eye, nose and throat irritations. Toxic metals dissolved in the rainwater can enter the food chain when they are absorbed in fruits, vegetables and in the tissues of animals, which in turn can be ingested by humans. For example, the accumulation of mercury in the organs and tissues of animals has been linked to brain damage, nerve disorders, and death. Aluminium leached from the soil causes kidney problems, and has recently been related to Alzheimer's disease.

Pennsylvanian problem
Pennsylvania receives one of the highest concentrations of acid deposition in the world. Studies in recent years have shown that the pH of rainfall in Pennsylvania averages 4.1 to 4.3, which is nearly 1,000 times the acidity of neutral water. When acids enter lakes and streams, the effects on aquatic life can be devastating. Organisms ranging from fish and frogs down to microscopic plankton cannot survive in highly acidic waters because the low pH

DATA-BURST

WHAT CAUSES ACID RAIN?
ACID RAIN IS CAUSED BY THE EMISSION OF POLLUTANTS INTO THE AIR. THE PRINCIPLE SOURCES ARE THE SMOKESTACKS OF FOSSIL FUEL POWER PLANTS, CAR EXHAUSTS AND OTHER INDUSTRIAL FACILITIES. THESE EMISSIONS CONTAIN SULPHUR DIOXIDE (SO2), THE MAJOR CONTRIBUTOR TO THE PROBLEM, AND NITROGEN OXIDE (NOX), WHICH COMBINE WITH OXYGEN AND WATER VAPOUR IN THE AIR TO FORM SULPHURIC AND NITRIC ACIDS.

HOW MUCH DAMAGE HAS ACID RAIN CAUSED TO FORESTS?
ACID RAIN HAS CAUSED EXTENSIVE DAMAGE TO AROUND 200,000 KM2 OF EUROPE'S FORESTS—AN AGGREGATE AREA THE SIZE OF BRITAIN, WHILE 67% OF BRITAIN'S TREES HAVE BEEN DAMAGED BY ACID RAIN.

WHAT FORM DOES ACID RAIN TAKE?
WHEN PRECIPITATION—SUCH AS RAIN, SLEET OR SNOW—CONTAINING DISSOLVED SULPHURIC OR NITRIC ACID FALLS TO THE GROUND, IT IS TERMED WET DEPOSITION OR 'ACID RAIN'. IF THESE ACIDS DESCEND AS SULPHATE OR NITRATE PARTICLES, IT IS CALLED DRY DEPOSITION.

HOW IS ACIDITY MEASURED?
THE AMOUNT OF ACIDITY IN WATER IS MEASURED USING THE PH SCALE, WHICH HAS 15 LEVELS (0-14). THE LOWER THE READING, THE MORE ACIDIC THE SAMPLE, WITH THE VALUE 7.0 BEING NEUTRAL. FOR EXAMPLE, 'PURE' RAIN, WHICH IS ONLY SLIGHTLY ACIDIC, HAS A PH OF 5.6, LEMON JUICE HAS A PH OF 2.0, AND BATTERY ACID HAS A PH OF 1.0. RAIN WITH A PH LOWER THAN 5.6 IS OFFICIALLY CONSIDERED TO BE ACID RAIN.

HOW DOES THE PH SCALE WORK?
THE SCALE IS LOGARITHMIC, WHICH MEANS THAT THERE IS A TENFOLD DIFFERENCE BETWEEN ONE NUMBER AND THE NEXT.

LEFT: HEALTHY TREES GROW ALONGSIDE SEVERAL WHOSE GROWTH HAS BEEN BLIGHTED BY ACID RAIN, IDAHO, USA

Smog, a cross between fog and smoke, is a form of air pollution that occurs in cities and other industrialized areas. The term was first coined in 1905 by H.A. Des Voeux, who used it to describe the atmospheric conditions above many British towns. In a report that he wrote on smog, published at a Manchester conference of the Smoke Abatement League of Great Britain in 1911, Des Voeux speculated that over 1,000 deaths in 1909 in Glasgow and Edinburgh were due to smog-related illness.

The big smoke
The growth of the city of London was achieved only at great cost to to its environment. As far back as the 13th century, concern about pollution prompted a commission to investigate the problem. Early forms of industry, such as brewers, dyers, lime burners and soap makers, covered the city with their

sources: industry switched from fossil to oil fuels while domestic coal fires were replaced by gas central heating systems.

Invisible poisons
Today, the smog that hovers over London is far less visible than it used to be. However, it is just as toxic. Modern day smog is full of carbon monoxide, nitrogen dioxide, ozone, benzines and aldehydes. It is caused not so much by the burning of coal as by traffic exhaust fumes.

automobile traffic. The stable weather conditions make matters worse: sunshine traps low-lying smog. Air warmed by the sun's rays acts as a lid, trapping the cooler air below. Meanwhile, the sun also heats the noxious vapours that rise from the traffic, factories and oil refineries. Despite spending millions of dollars, the city has not yet found a solution to the problem. As ozone production falls, so traffic congestion appears to rise. There seems to be little enthusiasm for

Old bangers
Motor vehicles cause around two-thirds of urban smog pollution. By concentrating efforts on the production of cleaner cars much can be done to reduce the problem. The USA may be one of the worst offenders but in 1975 it led the way with the introduction of catalytic converters, which are attached to car exhausts to reduce toxic emissions. These vital components for a cleaner engine did not start to appear in western

SMOG
LOS ANGELES GIVEN 148

emissions. In 1620, King James I complained about the soiling of St Paul's Cathedral. By 1784, the naturalist Gilbert White was able to record the 'dark plumes' rising above the city. Charles Dickens graphically evoked London's grey streets in his novels. The highest levels of pollution were found in the densely populated poorer districts of the East End. The problem of increasing pollution from industry was exacerbated by the low-lying land on which London was built. Despite the Smoke Abatement Act of 1853 and the Sanitation Act of 1866, the problem continued into the 20th century, when lethal smog caused thousands of premature deaths. The introduction of the Clean Air Acts in 1956 and 1968, which outlawed the burning of coal, greatly reduced the problem. Allied to this legislation, there were also important changes in energy

It can lead to asthma and bronchial and eye complaints. However, the variability of the London weather ensures that smog settles far less comprehensively than in some American cities where a full-scale photochemical smog develops and lingers for long periods.

Capital of the car
Los Angeles is the second-most densely populated city in the USA and is famous for its dangerously high levels of smog pollution. During the 1950s, the South Coast Air Quality Management District reported that the peak summer ozone concentrations in Los Angeles were 57 times above recommended levels and, as recently as 1988, there were 148 air-quality warnings broadcast in a single year. Smog is largely caused by the huge road network which carries an enormous amount of

moves to curb the number of cars in the city, although attempts to promote more environmentally-friendly vehicles have reduced carbon monoxide emissions slightly. In 1992, for the first time, the state of California did not exceed the carbon monoxide violation level.

Athens acts
In Athens, several drastic measures have been taken to improve the air quality conditions in the city. A retirement plan for old vehicles was put into effect in 1991, while a national inspection programme for the control of emissions from motor vehicles was initiated in 1994. Public transport systems were expanded while private vehicles were banned from the commercial centre of the city. A novel scheme for the use of cars was put into effect. The last number of the registration plate determined the days on which the cars could be used in the city centre. Odd numbers corresponded to odd dates in the calendar, even numbers alternated.

The summer of '88
One of the worst smog summers in history was recorded as recently as 1988. A heatwave in the USA exacerbated the problem—with temperatures regularly reaching above 90°C. In East Coast cities, smog warnings were repeatedly triggered. The head of the Los Angeles urban air-pollution agency warned that smog pollution would continue to present a serious public health hazard until more of the city's motorists 'radically changed their life-style'.

Europe until the late 1980s. Cars produced today emit 1% of the level of pollution compared to 1970 models. Experts now believe that 60% of smog is caused by just 20% of vehicles. The Clean Air Act of 1970 sought to cut automobile tailpipe pollution in the USA by 90%, but achieving that target is still a distant prospect. The invention of the electric car offers hope for a long-term solution, yet poorer parts of the world often cannot afford to implement Western pollution prevention measures. As the situation in the industrialized West begins to improve, so it deteriorates rapidly in other parts of the world.

JARGON

CATALYTIC CONVERTER
FITTED TO CAR EXHAUST SYSTEMS TO REDUCE TAILPIPE EMISSIONS

FINE SOOT
PARTICLES OF SOOT THAT PROVOKE ENVIRONMENTAL CONCERN, CAUSED BY INDUSTRIAL PROCESSES, AGRICULTURAL TILLING AND MOTOR VEHICLES

GROSS SOOT
CAUSED BY THE UNFILTERED BURNING OF COAL, THESE PARTICLES OF SMOG SATURATED THE AIR DURING THE EARLY YEARS OF THE 20TH CENTURY

NITROGEN DIOXIDE
AN ATMOSPHERIC GAS WHICH IS DERIVED MAINLY FROM VEHICLE EXHAUSTS

PEA-SOUPERS
POPULAR PHRASE USED TO REFER TO LONDON SMOG

PM10
THE TECHNICAL TERM FOR FINE SOOT

LEFT: A VIEW OF THE HOLLYWOOD FREEWAY SHROUDED IN SMOG, LOS ANGELES · RIGHT: AERIAL VIEW OF SMOG HANGING OVER LOS ANGELES AT SUNSET

DATA-BURST

WHAT TYPES OF SMOG ARE THERE?
THERE ARE TWO TYPES OF SMOG. THE FIRST RESULTS FROM A HIGH CONCENTRATION OF SULPHUR OXIDES IN THE AIR. THESE ARE THE RESULT OF THE BURNING OF SULPHUR-BEARING FOSSIL FUELS, SUCH AS COAL. SMOG CAN ALSO BE PHOTOCHEMICAL. THIS IS CAUSED BY NITROGEN OXIDES AND HYDRO CARBON OXIDES THAT ARE EMITTED BY CARS AND OTHER VEHICLES.

DO POLLUTANTS FORM SMOG?
YES. POLLUTION FROM CHIMNEYS PROVIDED AN ABUNDANCE OF DIRT PARTICLES ON WHICH CONDENSATION COULD TAKE PLACE. THE PEA-SOUPERS OF THE VICTORIAN ERA WERE SO NAMED BECAUSE THEY WERE COLOURED BY CHEMICAL POLLUTANTS. SMOG TODAY IS PRODUCED BY FINE VEHICLE SOOT. THE PARTICLES HAVE A DIAMETER OF 10 MICRONS OR LESS— HUMAN HAIR MEASURES ABOUT 75 MICRONS IN DIAMETER.

WHAT ARE THE HARMFUL EFFECTS OF SMOG?
SMOG REDUCES VISIBILITY AND COLOURS THE ATMOSPHERE WITH A LIGHT BROWNISH HUE. IT DAMAGES PLANTS, IRRITATES THE EYES AND CAUSES RESPIRATORY DISEASES THAT CLOG AND DAMAGE THE LUNGS, SUCH AS BRONCHITIS AND PNEUMONIA.

HOW HIGH IN THE AIR DOES SMOG LIE?
SMOG FUMES STAGNATE WHEN THEY ARE CAPPED BY A MASS OF HOT AIR. IN THIS WAY, LOW-LYING LAND MAKES A CITY MORE VULNERABLE TO SMOG. TRAFFIC FUMES IN LONDON HANG IN THE AIR AT AROUND 900 METRES.

LONDON'S PEA-SOUPER

LONDON'S FAMOUS 'PEA-SOUPER' SMOG WAS LARGELY THE RESULT OF THE WIDESPREAD BURNING OF COAL FIRES. ATMOSPHERIC CONDITIONS WERE SO BAD THAT VISIBILITY BECAME NEGLIGIBLE AND PEDESTRIANS EXPERIENCED DIFFICULTY FINDING THEIR WAY AROUND CITY STREETS. THE MOST INFAMOUS 'KILLER SMOG' OCCURRED IN 1952, BRINGING WITH IT THE MAXIMUM CONCENTRATION OF DIRT FROM SURROUNDING INDUSTRIAL AREAS. SULPHUR DIOXIDE COMBINED WITH WATER DROPS AND OXYGEN TO FORM SULPHURIC ACID. ALTHOUGH THE CERTIFIED CAUSES OF DEATH WERE USUALLY BRONCHITIS OR PNEUMONIA, AROUND 4,000 LONDONERS DIED AS A DIRECT RESULT OF RESPIRATORY ILLNESSES, MAINLY THE AGED AND THE ILL. THE RESULTING OUTCRY PROMPTED THE CLEAN AIR ACTS.

AIR QUALITY WARNINGS IN 1988

BROWN AIR HANGING OVER URBAN CONURBATIONS IS A SIGN THAT THE ATMOSPHERIC CONDITIONS ARE POTENTIALLY TOXIC. SMOG EXACERBATES ASTHMA AND CAN CAUSE RESPIRATORY DISEASES AND EVEN PREMATURE DEATH

Many forces affect our planet: volcanic eruptions, changes in solar irradiation and the erratic weather system known as El Niño have always had an impact on the temperature and conditions around the globe. But it is no coincidence that the 1990s have contained three of the hottest years since records began. For humans are now playing an unprecedented part in altering a balance that has been delicately maintained by natural means for thousands of years. Increasing industrial growth around the globe is severely damaging the ozone layer, a level of the stratosphere that shields the Earth from the sun's potentially lethal rays.

The ozone layer

The atmosphere is divided into several layers. Most ozone is concentrated in the stratosphere, between 10 and 50 km above the Earth. The ozone molecule contains three oxygen atoms, whereas the oxygen that we breathe contains two. In every 10 million air molecules, about two million are oxygen and just three are ozone. But these ozone molecules play a key role in absorbing the sun's radiation, especially the ultraviolet light called UVB, which has been linked to skin cancer, cataracts and marine and agricultural destruction. Chlorofluorocarbons found in everyday products such as refrigerators, solvents and aerosol cans, contain chlorine, which destroys ozone molecules faster than nature can create them. Some chlorine is created naturally, but about 85% in the stratosphere comes from CFCs and other widely-used industrial chemicals.

The hole over Antarctica

Humans produce about 750,000 tonnes of chlorine in various forms every year. In addition, volcanic eruptions release huge quantities of hydrogen chloride into the atmosphere. These gases create the extreme warming and cooling conditions that nature cannot completely overcome. Greenhouse gases, such as carbon dioxide and methane, heat the air in the troposphere—the layer of the atmosphere nearest to Earth—

GLOBAL CHANGE

THE OZONE HOLE IS THE SIZE

CONCORD DISCORD

CONCORDE AND OTHER SUPERSONIC AIRCRAFT DESTROY OZONE BY LEAVING A FOG OF SULPHURIC ACID IN THEIR WAKE. ORIGINALLY, IT WAS THOUGHT THAT NITROGEN OXIDE EMISSIONS WERE THE MAIN HAZARD PRESENTED BY AIRCRAFT, AND ENGINES HAVE BEEN DESIGNED FOR 20 YEARS WITH THIS IN MIND. HOWEVER, THE SULPHUR THREAT IS NOW TAKEN EQUALLY SERIOUSLY. BURNT SULPHUR IS EMITTED FROM THE CONCORDE EXHAUST SYSTEM AS SULPHUR TRIOXIDE, WHICH CONVERTS RAPIDLY INTO A FOG OF TINY SULPHUR DIOXIDE PARTICLES. CHLORINE POLLUTANTS DESTROY THE OZONE ON THE SURFACE OF THESE PARTICLES.

JARGON

CHLOROFLUOROCARBONS (CFCs)
CHEMICAL COMPOUND CONTAINING ONE FLUORINE ATOM, ONE CARBON ATOM AND THREE CHLORINE ATOMS. CFCs ARE THE GASES PRODUCED BY REFRIGERATORS AND AEROSOLS THAT CONTRIBUTE TO OZONE DEPLETION

OZONE
MOLECULE OF THREE OXYGEN ATOMS FORMED WHEN SUNLIGHT HITS AN OXYGEN MOLECULE

OZONE HOLE
THE EXTREME THINNING OF THE OZONE LAYER

OZONE LAYER
THE PROTECTIVE LAYER OF OZONE IN THE STRATOSPHERE

by the year 2000 and of methyl chloroform by 2005. Such targets are unlikely to be met.

Trees to the rescue

Trees are very effective in combating global warming—one single tree can remove about a tonne of carbon dioxide from the air during its lifetime. Some large industrial companies, ever aware of their public image, are major sponsors of tree-planting programmes. American Electric Power has recently purchased a jungle in Bolivia in an attempt to eliminate 58 millions tonnes of carbon dioxide over the next 30 years. The US government is also looking into ways of creating a carbon trading system, whereby companies that plant trees will earn credits which they can then 'sell' to companies that continue to pollute the atmosphere, boosting their profits in the process.

OF NORTH AMERICA

ALTHOUGH NATURE PLAYS A PART IN GLOBAL WARMING, HUMAN ACTIVITY IS ALTERING THE CONDITIONS OF OUR PLANET—THE RESULTANT HOLE IN THE OZONE LAYER IS A FRIGHTENING SYMBOL OF HUMANS' CAPACITY TO DESTROY

Destructive nature

Some scientists believe that nature itself is playing an increasingly destructive part in global change. One theory has it that the Earth is being warmed by increasing solar storms. The strength of the solar wind is thought to be linked directly to the strength of sunspot activity. These winds blow away cosmic rays which it is thought create their own protective clouds in the atmosphere, thereby exposing the Earth to more radiation from the sun. The impact of the weather system known as El Niño, and the eruption of Mt Pinatubo in the Philippines in 1991, have also been put forward as natural explanations for global warming in recent years.

while the chlorine leaking into the stratosphere cools the air above it. Such differentials create abnormally strong high-altitude winds, which help to make warmer areas on Earth warmer and colder areas colder. This is seen to most devastating effect in Antarctica, where the winter temperatures are being forced down by 6°C. The colder the temperatures, the faster compounds such as CFCs destroy

ozone molecules. The ozone hole was first identified in 1977 but only publicly disclosed in 1985. By the spring of 1993 a hole the size of North America had appeared over Antarctica. Scientists warn that the air in the stratosphere above the Arctic has been cooling in a similar way and the development of a similar hole, much closer to the major human populations, may be inevitable.

The Montreal Protocol

The Montreal Protocol on 'Substances that Deplete the Ozone Layer' was originally signed in 1987 but was substantially amended in 1990 and 1992. A landmark document, it heralds international agreement on how to protect the ozone layer. It stipulates that the production and consumption of CFCs and other harmful gases must be phased out

DATA-BURST

WHAT IS THE LOWEST RECORDED LEVEL OF OZONE?
BETWEEN 9 AND 14 OCT 1993, A LEVEL OF 91 DOBSON UNITS (DU), A MEANS OF MEASURING OZONE LEVELS, WAS RECORDED IN THE ATMOSPHERE OVER THE SOUTH POLE IN ANTARCTICA. SCIENTISTS CONSIDER 300 DU TO BE THE LEVEL NEEDED TO SHIELD EARTH.

WHEN IS OZONE DEPLETION AT ITS WORST?
SPRING IN ANTARCTICA (AUGUST AND SEPTEMBER) IS THE WORST SEASON FOR OZONE DEPLETION. DURING 1993, ABOUT TWO-THIRDS OF THE OZONE OVER ANTARCTICA WAS LOST IN LESS THAN TWO MONTHS.

WHAT THREAT IS POSED BY THE HOLE IN THE OZONE LAYER?
LESS PROTECTION FROM ULTRAVIOLET LIGHT WILL, IN TIME, LEAD TO HIGHER SKIN CANCER AND CATARACT RATES AND TO CROP DAMAGE. MARINE LIFE IS ALSO UNDER THREAT.

HAS ANYTHING BEEN DONE TO RESOLVE THE PROBLEM?
MORE THAN 140 COUNTRIES AROUND THE WORLD HAVE WOKEN UP TO THE DANGER AND HAVE AGREED TO PHASE OUT OZONE-DEPLETING SUBSTANCES. THIS ACTION, HOWEVER, COULD WELL PROVE TO BE TOO LITTLE TOO LATE.

WHAT EFFECT DOES THE PRODUCTION OF HARMFUL GASES HAVE?
IT WARMS UP GLOBAL TEMPERATURES. 1990, 1995 AND 1997 HAVE BEEN THREE OF THE HOTTEST YEARS RECORDED IN THE PAST 500 YEARS. CARBON DIOXIDE LEVELS IN THE ATMOSPHERE, FOR INSTANCE, ARE NOW AT LEAST 25% HIGHER THAN LEVELS BEFORE THE INDUSTRIAL REVOLUTION.

WHAT IS UVB RADIATION?
A HARMFUL FORM OF ULTRAVIOLET RADIATION WITH A WAVELENGTH BETWEEN 280 AND 320 NANOMETERS THAT IS USUALLY FILTERED OUT BY THE OZONE LAYER.

LEFT: THE OZONE HOLE OVER THE ANTARCTIC, COLOURED DARK BLUE · RIGHT: SATELLITE IMAGE OF INTENSE SOLAR ACTIVITY IN THE SUN'S OUTER ATMOSPHERE

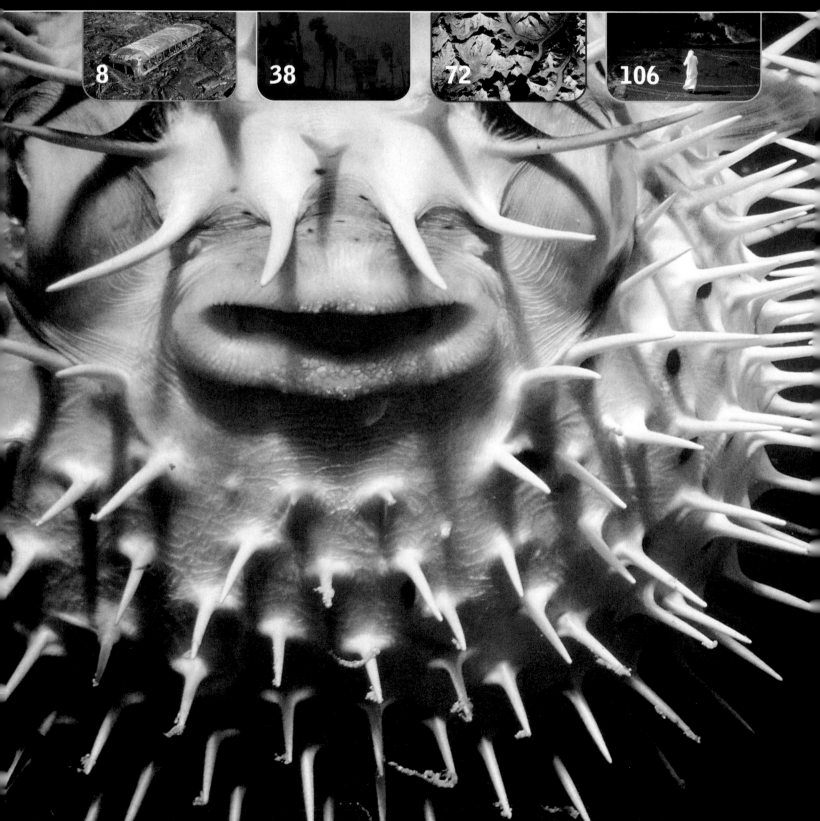

SURVIVAL STRATEGIES

THINGS ADAPT AND SPECIALIZE

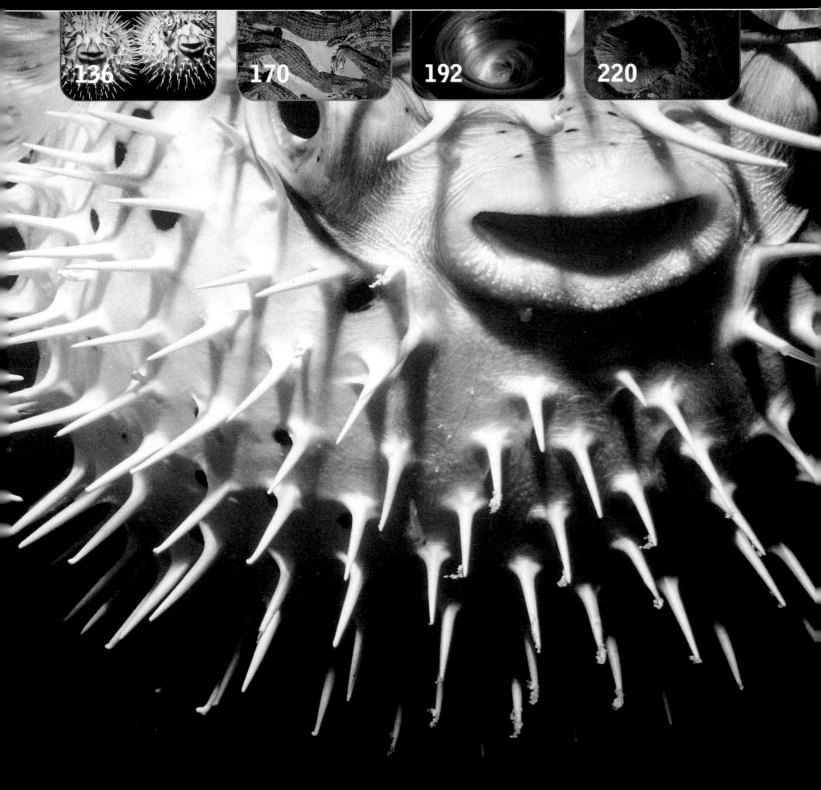

The strategies and techniques that predators use to catch their next meal are as varied as the predators themselves. Some, such as the cheetah, hunt alone; Others, such as wolves, join forces with other members of their group to hunt cooperatively. The tools at a predator's disposal also differ from species to species. Hawks rely on their incredibly sharp eyesight to spy potential victims while owls detect their prey using hyper-sensitive hearing.

Hawk-eyed

When it comes to sharp eyes, few predators can rival hawks. The hawk family birds include buzzards, eagles and kites. Hunting by day, these fast and agile birds of prey scan their surroundings from the air, sometimes taking a leisurely warm-up flight before scouring the ground for the tiniest movement. Once it has locked on to its target, a hawk may swoop suddenly or track its prey until the victim tires and the predator strikes, grabbing the prey in its sharp talons and ripping it apart with its powerful beak. Hawks are so fast that they can even snatch up rattlesnakes. Small mammals, birds and insects also fall victim to hawk air-strikes. These sharp-eyed raptors are found on all six continents where they nest either in trees or on marshland or cliffs. Some roam far and wide to find food, flying up to 500 km a day to scan the landscape. One species, the bat hawk, provides the ultimate testament to the incredible accuracy of hawk vision: it hunts only at twilight, locating and catching all its food within just half an hour.

Fastest land mammal

The cheetah is a stalker. It hunts alone in the morning or late afternoon, avoiding the intense midday heat of its African and Middle Eastern habitat. Its excellent eyesight enables it to spot prey—usually an antelope—at great distances. Then it waits, moving into position undetected by its victim before breaking cover and running its prey down with explosive speed. Incredible agility enables the cheetah to change

CHEETAH RUNS AT 100 KM/H

MAN-EATING TIGERS

TIGERS ARE CONSUMMATE PREDATORS. IN THE WILD, THEY STALK AND AMBUSH LARGE DEER. TIGERS OCCASIONALLY ATTACK HUMANS AND THE CAUSES OF 'MAN-EATING' BEHAVIOUR HAVE BEEN MUCH DISCUSSED. THE MOST LIKELY EXPLANATION IS THAT HUMANS FALL WITHIN THE NATURAL SCALE RANGE OF THE TIGER'S PREY. IN THE 19TH CENTURY TIGERS BECAME A POPULAR EXHIBIT AT ZOOS, ALTHOUGH THEY DO NOT RESPOND WELL TO A LIFE IN CAPTIVITY. IN THE UK IN 1850, ELLEN BRIGHT WAS KILLED BY A TIGER DURING AN OUTING TO AN ENGLISH MENAGERIE (ILLUSTRATED LEFT). ON 8 JAN 1998, A MEMBER OF THE CHIPPERFIELD CIRCUS FAMILY WAS SAVAGED BY ONE OF 12 TIGERS IN A CAGE IN FLORIDA, USA. THE TRAINER WAS MAULED AS HE PUT HIS FACE UP TO THE TIGER'S JAWS, SUFFERING A HUGE HEAD WOUND.

TO CAPTURE ITS PREY

A PREDATOR IS AN ANIMAL THAT CATCHES, KILLS AND EATS ITS PREY. WHEN SURVIVAL DEPENDS ON ACHIEVING THIS SUCCESSFULLY, EVERY SENSE MUST BE DEPLOYED IN THE TASK OF HUNTING WITH SKILL AND PRECISION

direction with the prey. Its sharp, non-retractable claws grip the ground and its strong, slender legs take it to speeds of over 100 km/h over short distances. Once it has caught its victim, the cheetah clamps its teeth on to its prey's throat to stop it struggling. Thanks to the arrangement of its teeth, the cheetah can still breathe while it subdues its victim in this throat-hold until the struggle is over.

Silent night-killers

Incredible night-vision is what makes owls such effective nocturnal killers. Their large eyes are positioned at the front of their head, maximizing perspective sight and enabling them to swoop with pinpoint accuracy on birds, small mammals and insects. Perching silently, an owl can scan its surroundings without changing position and alerting potential prey, thanks to highly adapted neck muscles which allow its head to swivel almost all the way round—through 270°. The shape of the head channels sound into the ears, which are positioned asymmetrically to locate the source of every sound perfectly. Even when the owl launches itself into the air to swoop on a victim, it makes almost no sound. This is because its flight feathers have a velvet-like covering which muffles the sound of the owl's wing-beat.

Team-work

Wolf packs hunt as a team. In the hostile habitats of the far north, grey, or timber, wolves work in packs of up to 25. Stalking downwind of their victim, the wolves suddenly give chase, bringing down animals much larger than themselves, like bison, caribou, elk and moose. The pursuit can last for several kilometres and often ends in a fearsome struggle. To weaken the victim quickly, the wolves target areas that will cause the fastest loss of blood—while the alpha wolf grips the animal's nose, the others rip at the flanks and throat. Once the animal has been felled and killed, the wolves tear open the belly and eat the protein- and fat-rich entrails. Wolf attacks can take place on ice, open ground or amongst vegetation. The pack is such a dedicated hunting unit that most prey stand little chance of survival. The largest wolf prey, moose, sometimes defend themselves by simply standing their ground against the pack. But if they eventually run, they are always chased and often killed despite their size.

Mongoose snake-killers

The mongoose is one of the fastest and most agile of all predators. This brave fighter, found in Africa, Asia and southern Europe, can grow to a metre in length and has short legs, a pointed nose, small ears and a long furry tail. It lives in burrows and feeds on birds, small mammals and reptiles, such as lizards. But it is against venomous snakes that this predator reveals its truly amazing ferocity. The mongoose jumps at the snake's head and, before its victim has time to bite, clamps its small teeth into the snake's skull and cracks the bone. Mongooses attack snakes so fearlessly that, traditionally, they were thought to be immune to snake venom. In fact this is not so; it is just their incredible speed and agility that makes these small mammals effective snake-killers.

JARGON

ALPHA WOLF
THE HIGHEST-RANKING MEMBER OF A PACK, WHICH FEEDS ON THE BEST MEAT AT A KILL

CARRION
THE CARCASSES OF DEAD ANIMALS

CREPUSCULAR
ACTIVE DURING THE TWILIGHT HOURS OF DAWN AND DUSK

DIURNAL
ACTIVE DURING THE DAY

NOCTURNAL
ACTIVE AT NIGHT

PERSPECTIVE VISION
ABILITY TO ACCURATELY DETERMINE THE RELATIVE POSITIONS OF OBJECTS

RAKING
A RAPTOR HUNTING TECHNIQUE IN WHICH THE BIRD FOLLOWS AN ANIMAL FROM THE AIR AND SWOOPS WHEN ITS VICTIM BECOMES TIRED

RAPTOR
A BIRD OF PREY

RETRACTABLE CLAWS
CLAWS THAT CAN BE COMPLETELY WITHDRAWN INTO SHEATHS IN THE PAW

TOP PREDATOR
ANIMAL AT THE TOP OF A FOOD CHAIN WHICH HAS NO NATURAL PREDATORS

DATA-BURST

WHAT IS THE MOST SUCCESSFUL MAMMAL PREDATOR?
AFRICAN HUNTING DOGS HUNT IN PACKS AND ARE SUCCESSFUL IN 50–70% OF THEIR ATTACKS, MAKING THEM THE MOST SUCCESSFUL MAMMAL HUNTER.

WHAT IS THE LARGEST KNOWN PREDATOR EVER TO HAVE LIVED?
A 18 MILLION-YEAR-OLD FOSSIL ALLIGATOR FOUND IN ROCKS ON THE BANKS OF THE AMAZON RIVER IS BELIEVED TO BE THE LARGEST PREDATOR EVER TO HAVE WALKED THE EARTH. AT 12 M LONG, WITH A 1.5-M-. LONG SKULL AND 10-CM TEETH, AND WEIGHING IN AT ABOUT 18 TONNES, THIS GIANT HUNTER WAS EVEN BIGGER THAN TYRANNOSAURUS REX.

WHICH BIG CAT IS MOST DANGEROUS?
SEVERAL OF THE BIG CATS CAN BE MAN-EATERS, INCLUDING LIONS AND LEOPARDS AND TIGERS. TIGERS ARE THE LARGEST OF THE CATS. THEY EMPLOY A 'STALK AND AMBUSH' STRATEGY. TIGERS USUALLY ATTACK DEER, BUT HAVE BEEN KNOWN TO KILL ELEPHANTS AND BUFFALO. HUMANS, UNABLE TO RUN VERY FAST, DO FALL PREY TO TIGERS ALTHOUGH USUALLY IT IS ONLY OLD OR INJURED TIGERS WHO BECOME MAN-EATERS.

HOW BIG IS THE AVERAGE PREDATOR?
TIGERS CAN GROW TO OVER 2 M LONG AND A METRE HIGH AND THEY WEIGH ABOUT 300 KG. WOLVES ARE MUCH THE SAME SIZE AS TIGERS, BUT LIGHTER AT ABOUT 80 KG. THE CHEETAH, A MORE NIMBLE BEAST, WEIGHS A MERE 55 KG AND STANDS AT JUST 80 CM TALL.

DO PREDATORS HUNT ON THEIR OWN OR COOPERATIVELY?
BOTH—THE CHEETAH AND TIGER ARE SOLITARY HUNTERS WHEREAS WOLVES ALWAYS HUNT IN PACKS. PELICANS GROUP TOGETHER TO DRIVE FISH INTO THE SHALLOWS BY FLAPPING THEIR WINGS IN THE WATER.

LEFT: A SNARLING PACK OF NORTH AMERICAN TIMBER WOLVES EAGERLY DEVOUR THEIR PREY

Predatory plants are those species that rely on other species of animal or plant in order to survive. While they inevitably derive some nutrients by means of photosynthesis, they also digest insects or draw nutrients from plants growing nearby. Those carnivorous species of plant that eat insects and small animals do so by a host of ingenious means. Those that rely on other plants for food do so more directly, by invading their territory or sucking nutrients directly from them.

Deadly designs
There are approximately 400 known species of carnivorous, or insectivorous, plants. While they vary greatly, all digest the prey that they trap by a process of chemical breakdown that is comparable with animal digestion. This ability to digest nitrogen-rich animal proteins means that they are often able to survive in hostile environments. Such plants do not feed exclusively on prey, however. As with other plants, they also create food by photosynthesis, the synthesis of organic compounds from carbon dioxide and water using light energy absorbed by chlorophyll.

Most carnivorous plants are small, often less than 30 cm tall, and the majority have green leaves and colourful flowers. The smallest of all tend to be those species that thrive in mossy regions surrounding bogs.

Trap-setters
Bladderworts are one of the few carnivorous plants to catch their victims under water. They have small pear-shaped leaves that feature a trapdoor, or valve. The chamber, or bladder, inside this trap is maintained by water tension, which flattens and curves the chamber's walls inwards. Tiny organisms, such as protozoans, crustaceans, worms and newly-hatched fish, become trapped on the bladderwort's leaves. The water then sucks the prey through the trap-door, which opens and closes in a split-second. It is still not clear whether the prey is then digested by enzymes produced by the plant or by bacterial action, but the end-product is harnessed to feed and nourish the plant.

PARASITIC MISTLETOE

THE MISTLETOE IS THE BEST-KNOWN PARASITIC PLANT. IT INVADES THE TISSUES OF A HOST TREE AND STEALS ITS NOURISHMENT. IT IS ESPECIALLY COMMON ON APPLE TREES AND IS AIDED IN ITS INVASION BY BIRDS, WHO EAT MISTLETOE BERRIES AND WIPE OFF STICKY SEEDS FROM THEIR BEAKS ONTO BRANCHES OF OTHER TREES. THERE ARE MANY VARIETIES OF MISTLETOE FOUND THROUGHOUT NORTHERN EUROPE, ASIA AND AMERICA. THE BERRIES ARE WHITE AND POISONOUS TO HUMANS, THE LEAVES OVAL OR LANCE-SHAPED AND AROUND 5 CM LONG. FLOWERS ARE YELLOW. THE MISTLETOE OBTAINS ITS FOOD AND WATER THROUGH THE CONNECTION IN THE BARK TO THE HOST TREE. SOME MISTLETOE PLANTS MAY EVEN FEED DIRECTLY OFF OTHER MISTLETOE PLANTS.

JARGON

CARNIVOROUS
MEAT-EATING

CHLOROPHYLL
THE GREEN PIGMENT FOUND IN MOST PLANTS RESPONSIBLE FOR LIGHT ABSORPTION

PHOTOSYNTHESIS
THE PROCESS BY WHICH GREEN PLANTS USE SUNLIGHT TO CONVERT WATER AND CARBON DIOXIDE FROM THE AIR INTO FOOD

SAPROPHYTES
PLANTS THAT TAKE SUSTENANCE FROM ROTTING PLANT MATERIAL

TRIGGER HAIR
HAIRS ON CARNIVOROUS PLANTS THAT DETECT INSECT PRESENCE

PLANT'S LIQUID POOL

KILLER PLANTS HAVE EVOLVED A VARIETY OF INGENIOUS TRAPS BY WHICH THEY CAN CAPTURE INSECTS AND FEED OFF THEIR FLESH. OTHER PLANT PREDATORS KILL BY MORE SUBTLE METHODS, SUCH AS COLONIZING A HOST

After swallowing an organism, it takes about 30 minutes for the bladderwort to discharge the water and reset the trap. On dry land, butterworts capture insects using sticky glands on the leaf surface. The leaf rolls up to trap and digest the prey, before unrolling again when digestion is complete.

Sticky tentacles

The Sundew family of plants are widely distributed in tropical and temperate regions. They are bedecked with nodding, five-petalled pink and white flowers. The roundish, reddish leaves measure less than 2.5 cm in diameter and are covered with gland-tipped hairs. These exude a sticky nectar that attracts insects. The insects are trapped by the plant's flexible tentacles on the upper part of the leaves. The leaves fold and the prey is then digested by enzymes secreted by the tentacles before the leaf reopens again. Sundews lure midges, gnats, mosquitoes and other tiny insects. The digestion process can take up to a week.

Venus fly-trap

The Venus fly-trap is found primarily along the coastal plains of North and South Carolina in the USA. A member of the sundew family, it grows on the edges of ponds and wet depressions. The blade of each leaf has two lobes that are hinged to one another like jaws. These jaws have nectar glands and bright-red digestive glands. Insects become trapped on the spine-like teeth along the margins. On the middle lobe of each leaf, there are three pressure-sensitive hairs which, when touched, send a chemical message that triggers the jaws to close. The insect, having landed in search of nectar, then becomes engulfed and is digested over several days. The leaf, which tends to be between 8 and 15 cm long, can only complete three or four trappings before it dies.

Drowning in nectar

Pitcher plants capture prey by a variety of means. Some have tubular leaves that resemble a trumpet or an urn. They have stiff, downward-pointing hairs around the entrance and smooth, greased surfaces beyond. Insects are attracted to the entrance by nectar-secreting glands that may then extend inside the trumpet. As the insect follows the nectar path, it falls deeper inside and, because of the smooth surface, is incapable of retracing its steps. Eventually, it falls into a liquid pool at the bottom of the leaf where digestion then takes place.

Territorial combat

Honeysuckle and ivy are the best-known territorial plants. They grow in a diverse range of conditions and invade the territory of other plants, shutting out the light for the plant underneath. Despite, or perhaps because of its intrusive nature, the honeysuckle plant has long been a symbol of love and protection. The scent is meant to encourage erotic dreams. When placed over a door, honeysuckle is meant to keep out fevers and those with ill-intent. Ivy, on the other hand, is associated with death and decay, perhaps because it requires a structure to support it, such as a crumbling wall or a dead tree. Ivy is associated with the gods of wine, Bacchus and Dionysus, and used to be hung outside inns as a sign that good wine was drunk within.

DATA-BURST

WHAT IS A CARNIVOROUS PLANT:
ONE SPECIALLY ADAPTED TO CATCH AND EAT INSECTS. THERE ARE AROUND 400 DIFFERENT SPECIES OF CARNIVOROUS PLANT.

WHY HAVE SOME PLANTS BECOME CARNIVOROUS?
SOME PLANTS FEED ON FLESH BECAUSE THEY LIVE IN AREAS WHERE THE SOIL IS POOR IN NITRATES. IN ORDER TO OVERCOME THIS DRAWBACK THEY BECOMING CARNIVOROUS, DIGESTING THE PROTEIN IN THE BODIES OF THEIR VICTIMS.

DO PREDATORY PLANTS RELY SOLELY ON THEIR PREDATORY SKILLS?
NO. THEY ALSO GATHER NUTRIENTS BY MEANS OF PHOTOSYNTHESIS, LIKE ORDINARY SPECIES. HOWEVER, THE MINERALS THEY EXTRACT FROM THEIR PREY COULD MEAN THE DIFFERENCE BETWEEN SURVIVAL AND EXTINCTION.

WHAT INSECTS DOES A VENUS FLY-TRAP CATCH?
ANTS, SPIDERS AND FLIES ARE ITS USUAL PREY BUT IT MAY ALSO CAPTURE OTHER SMALL ANIMALS SUCH AS SNAILS AND SLUGS.

WHERE ARE THE LARGEST CREATURES TRAPPED BY PITCHER PLANTS?
THE LARGEST PITCHERS ARE FOUND IN MALAYSIA AND BORNEO. AFTER HEAVY RAIN, THE PITCHERS' HOLLOW JUGS FILL WITH RAINWATER AND ARE LARGE ENOUGH TO DROWN BIRDS AND EVEN SMALL MAMMALS.

LEFT: VENUS FLY-TRAP LEAF SNAPPING SHUT ON A CAPTURED DAMSELFLY · RIGHT: PITCHER PLANTS, WHICH OBTAIN THEIR NUTRIENTS FROM DISSOLVED INSECTS AND ANIMALS

Examples of cannibalism in the animal world are not hard to find. Alligators in Florida must reach a length of at least 2 m before they are safe from the appetites of larger alligators, and wide-mouth frogs have been known to choke while eating larger members of their own species.

The black widow spider
One of the most notorious cannibals of the animal kingdom is the female black widow spider. This small venomous spider, found in the Americas, Africa, southern Europe and south-western Asia, has a body no bigger than a grape. It lurks in dark corners of fields and woods, under logs and stones or in rubbish bins. The female has earned her name and gruesome reputation from her habit of eating the male of her species after mating. The male is only a quarter of the size of the female and when he enters her web to mate, he may well not leave again. To the female, the male is just another food item and if she is hungry after mating she grabs the male, wraps him in silk, punctures a hole in his body, injects digestive juices to dissolve his organs and then sucks out the soupy innards—just as she does with other small creatures she catches. If the male is lucky he escapes the web before the female can entrap him. For one black widow species, however, escape is not an option. The male redback spider, or Australian black widow, always pays the ultimate price for continuing his line. When he enters the female's web to mate, he flips his body over, presenting his abdomen to the female's jaws. While he mates, she feeds. Barely alive, the male leaves the web, the first stage of mating complete. When he returns to the web to complete the process he once again flips over, but this time the female binds him in silk to be eaten later.

Tiger among insects
The male praying mantis also has a cannibalistic mate. These large, slow-moving insects, usually found in tropical forests, are superbly camouflaged: perching motionless, they are easily mistaken for a twig,

CANNIBALISM
FEMALE BLACK WIDOW EATS

leaf or flower. But when they strike at an insect their accuracy is deadly—earning them the description 'tiger among insects'—and their huge jaws crunch the prey up with ease. It is these jaws that the male mantis must dodge while he mates, and many do so successfully so that only a third of matings end in cannibalism. For the female, a male of her species might well be the largest meal she will ever eat and will boost the food reserves she needs in order to raise her young.

Genetically-determined appetite

In certain conditions, the young of the tiger salamander boost their start in life by eating their brothers

Cannibals of Aldabra Island

Lying in the Indian Ocean, 400 km off the east coast of Africa, Aldabra Island is home to two cannibalistic species: a giant tortoise and the world's largest lizard, the Komodo dragon. About 150,000 giant tortoises live on Aldabra, growing to sizes of up to 1 m and weighing in at a hefty 200 kg, thanks partly to their habit of eating anything that they can digest—including each other. The reason for this behaviour—very unusual among tortoises which are normally vegetarian—is thought to be the lack of pasture on the island. As a result, the tortoises readily feed on dead members of their own species and

MALE AFTER MATING

IN THE ANIMAL WORLD CANNIBALISM CAN MEAN THE DIFFERENCE BETWEEN LIFE AND DEATH. IT NOT ONLY PROVIDES A GOOD MEAL, BUT IT ALSO REDUCES THE NUMBER OF POTENTIAL RIVALS FOR FOOD AND TERRITORY

and sisters. Every tiger salamander egg has a genetic blueprint which determines whether it will feed on plankton in the water in which it hatches, or will turn into a cannibal. The cannibals all have large heads, while the plankton-eaters have small heads. If the water in which the salamanders hatch is shallow, or conditions are crowded, more of the young have large heads and develop special mouthparts which help them to eat their fellow hatchlings.

have even been known to eat the tents of campers. The other giant of Aldabra, the Komodo dragon, may also owe its huge size to its cannibalistic habits. This giant lizard, which grows to lengths of over 3 m, eats mice, birds and even animals as large as pigs and deer. But its droppings show that it also eats small specimens of its own kind. It is this behaviour that differentiates it from other lizards and may explain why it is the largest lizard in the world.

The struggle for supremacy

When the dominant male in a pride of lions gets old, young males begin to attack him in an attempt to claim his supreme position. Eventually, the aging ruler gives in and moves away from the pride to die alone. This leaves the females and cubs without protection. Young males fight between themselves in order to determine which one will inherit control of the pride.
To assert his complete power, the winner kills and eats the cubs

fathered by his predecessor, making a special show of devouring the male cubs who would otherwise have grown up to challenge him. His savage behaviour also ensures that the females in the pride, bereft of their young, will immediately mate with him.

Better the devil you know

A protected species in its native Australia, the Tasmanian devil is a ferocious terrier-sized marsupial that attacks, kills and eats other small mammals including its own species. Its jaws are powerful enough to consume a dead sheep in its entirety. Just a metre long and rather a slow-moving animal, the Tasmanian devil becomes agitated when threatened, often screaming and becoming very aggressive. In the ensuing battle, frequently with another Tasmanian devil, the animals will fight to the death, the winner then devouring the remains of its opponent. Only one out of 10 Tasmanian devils survive into adulthood.

DATA-BURST

WHERE DOES THE WORD CANNIBAL COME FROM?
IT DERIVES FROM THE SPANISH NAME FOR A WEST INDIAN TRIBE OF CANNIBALS CALLED THE CARIB.

WHAT ARE THE ADVANTAGES OF CANNIBALISM?
SURVIVAL AT ALL COSTS IS THE GOAL OF EVERY SPECIES AND CANNIBALISM NOW MAY ENSURE PLENTIFUL FOOD LATER: BROWN BEARS EAT THE CUBS OF OTHER BEARS, EVEN WHEN THERE IS A RIVER FULL OF FISH, IN ORDER TO REDUCE THE COMPETITION FOR TERRITORY IN THE FUTURE.

WHY DO CAPTIVE ANIMALS RESORT TO CANNIBALISM?
POPULATION CONTROL IN AN ENVIRONMENT OF A LIMITED SIZE IS OFTEN THE REASON FOR CANNIBALISM IN CAPTIVE ANIMALS. GUPPIES LIVING

IN AN AQUARIUM REGULARLY EAT MANY OF THEIR OFFSPRING TO STOP THE TANK BECOMING OVERCROWDED. HAMSTERS IN CAGES MAY EAT THEIR OWN YOUNG IF THREATENED BY THE PRESENCE OF HUMANS.

WHY DO SOME ANIMALS CHOOSE CANNIBALISM?
AN ANIMAL OF THE SAME SPECIES PROVIDES A GUARANTEED SOURCE OF NUTRIENTS—OFTEN CANNIBALISTIC ANIMALS GROW LARGER AND STRONGER AND LIVE LONGER THAN NON-CANNIBALS.

WHAT OTHER ANIMALS ARE CANNIBALISTIC?
THE BEETLE IS A BRUTAL CARNIVORE AND ITS LARVAE ARE CANNIBALISTIC; SHREW EAT THEIR OWN SPECIES WHEN FOOD SUPPLIES ARE LOW, AS DO SLUGS AND BROOK TROUT.

MAD COWS EAT EACH OTHER

CANNIBALISM IS KNOWN TO CAUSE THE SPREAD OF SERIOUS DISEASE AMONG CERTAIN SPECIES. THE FORE PEOPLE OF PAPUA NEW GUINEA TRADITIONALLY ATE THE BRAINS OF THEIR DEAD. THIS PRACTICE SPREAD A DISEASE CALLED KURU. SINCE THE DECLINE OF HUMAN CANNIBALISM IN THE REGION, INCIDENCES OF KURU HAVE FALLEN. IN MODERN TIMES, ENFORCED

'CANNIBALISM' OF SOME FARM ANIMALS SPREADS DISEASE. THE FARMING PRACTICE OF FORCE FEEDING ANIMALS WITH BONE MEAL CONTAINING SPINE AND BRAIN MATTER FROM LIVESTOCK CARCASSES IS KNOWN TO SPREAD DISEASE, SUCH AS SCRAPIE IN SHEEP AND BSE IN COWS. SINCE IT WAS FIRST IDENTIFIED IN THE UK IN 1986, THERE HAVE BEEN 171,367 REPORTED CASES OF BSE IN COWS. ALTHOUGH MUCH LESS COMMON, BSE HAS BEEN KNOWN TO PASS TO HUMANS—VIA THE CONSUMPTION OF BEEF—IN THE FORM OF CREUTZFELDT-JACOB DISEASE (CJD). IN RESPONSE TO THE CJD SCARE IN 1996 THE EUROPEAN PARLIAMENT IMPOSED A BAN ON THE SALE AND EXPORT OF BRITISH BEEF. THE BAN, WHICH GREATLY ANGERED BRITISH FARMERS AND THE PUBLIC, WAS ORIGINALLY CONTESTED BY THE BRITISH GOVERNMENT.

LEFT: BLACK WIDOW SPIDER WITH MAMMOTH EGG BALL · RIGHT: A KOMODO DRAGON, THE LARGEST LIZARD IN THE WORLD

If an animal relies on the flesh of other animals in order to survive, it must have an attack system that can overcome its prey's defences. Some of these systems are truly remarkable, enabling the tiniest of creatures to feed off prey much larger and more powerful than themselves. It is often the smallest and most harmless-looking animals that have the most deadly attack systems.

Deadly seashell
Cone shells are familiar to most people as holiday souvenirs. In fact this deadly marine snail possesses one of the most powerful poisons known to man. Once the cone has located its prey on the sea floor, it harpoons its victim and injects its fast-acting poison. Fish die instantly, and a human injected by one of the more deadly specimens can die an agonizing death.

Vampiric fish
Certain species of fish are known to have vampire tendencies. In 1994 a tiny transparent fish, about 1 cm long, was discovered in Brazil. This fish, as yet unnamed, uses the same attack strategy as the vampire bat—it makes a tiny incision in the gills of larger fish and sucks out the blood. It is also known to wriggle into the orifices of other animals, including humans, and lodge itself there with two hooked teeth.

Venomous arachnids
Scorpions have changed little in design for millions of years. They vary in size from just a few cm long to the huge tropical emperor scorpion of West Africa which can grow to 29 cm long and can weigh up to 60 g. All scorpions have a long, curved tail, armed with a highly venomous stinger, but the scorpion does not always use this to kill prey. Waiting motionless until its victim comes within striking distance, the scorpion suddenly runs up and grabs its prey with its pincers. If the victim is small, the scorpion simply holds on to it while it eats. If it is large, the scorpion uses its sting, injecting venom so potent it can kill a human—over 5,000 people die each year from scorpion stings.

Electric shock tactics
The electric eel found in South American rivers, and the electric ray or torpedo fish found in warm ocean waters all over the world, have special organs made of muscle and nerve tissue which can emit a pulse of electricity which they use to stun their prey. In the electric eel these organs are located in the tail and can emit a shock of up to 650 volts—enough to stun, but not kill, a human. This slow-moving, grey-brown fish has a cylindrical body up to 3 m long. The torpedo fish, a circular smooth-skinned fish, varying in size from 30 cm to 2 m, has its electric organs in the main part of its body. It can produce shocks of up to 220 volts and uses its electric pulses for defence and prey location as well as for attack.

DATA-BURST

WHAT IS THE WORLD'S MOST VENOMOUS SNAKE?
THE FIERCE SNAKE OF QUEENSLAND, AUSTRALIA IS THE MOST VENOMOUS LAND SNAKE IN THE WORLD. ONE SPECIMEN WAS FOUND TO CONTAIN ENOUGH VENOM TO KILL 250,000 MICE. NO HUMAN FATALITIES HAVE EVER BEEN REPORTED.

HOW DOES SNAKE VENOM KILL?
SOME VENOM CONTAINS TOXINS WHICH CHANGE THE CHEMISTRY OF RED BLOOD CELLS, OTHERS STOP BLOOD FROM CLOTTING, CAUSE THE VICTIM'S HEART TO SEIZE, OR ATTACK THE NERVOUS SYSTEM. THE STRATEGY FOR DISPENSING VENOM ALSO VARIES. VIPERS HAVE LONG, HOLLOW FANGS WHICH THEY PLUNGE INTO THEIR VICTIMS TO INJECT THE POISON. OTHERS PRODUCE VENOM IN SALIVARY GLANDS. THE AFRICAN BLACK-NECKED COBRA SPITS ITS VENOM AT THE EYES OF ITS PREY, CAUSING BLINDNESS. THIS SNAKE IS ACCURATE AT OVER 2 M.

WHAT IS THE MOST DANGEROUS SPECIES OF SCORPION?
THE TUNISIAN FAT-TAILED SCORPION IS THE MOST VENOMOUS SPECIES. IN NORTH AFRICA, THIS SCORPION IS RESPONSIBLE FOR 80% OF STINGS AND 90% OF DEATHS

WHAT IS THE STRANGEST FORM OF ATTACK?
THE ARCHER FISH PREYS ON INSECTS. LURKING UNDERWATER NEAR THE RIVERBANK, IT WAITS UNTIL IT SEES A SUITABLE VICTIM ON AN OVERHANGING BRANCH. THEN IT SHOOTS A PELLET OF WATER UP TO 1.5 M INTO THE AIR, KNOCKING THE INSECT OFF THE BRANCH INTO THE WATER WHERE THE FISH GULPS IT DOWN. THIS BIZARRE TECHNIQUE IS MADE POSSIBLE BY GROOVES ON THE ROOF OF THE FISH'S MOUTH. THE FISH SIMPLY PRESSES ITS TONGUE AGAINST THESE GROOVES, CLOSES ITS GILLS, AND WATER SPURTS OUT IN A POWERFUL AND ACCURATE JET.

thing in the water, regardless of its size. They are capable of stripping flesh from bones within a matter of minutes thanks to their sharp, triangular teeth and powerful jaws. In 1981, when a passenger boat capsized off the coast of Brazil, 300 people were devoured by a group of piranhas.

ANIMAL ATTACK
EEL EMITS ELECTRIC

VAMPIRE BAT

THE FICTIONAL VAMPIRES OF HORROR FILMS MAY BE THE STUFF OF NIGHTMARES, BUT IN THE NATURAL WORLD THERE ARE ANIMALS THAT DO FEED ON THE BLOOD OF LIVE VICTIMS. IN SOUTH AMERICA, A SMALL, SHY BAT THAT GROWS TO JUST 8 CM LONG IS ONE SUCH ANIMAL. NAMED FOR ITS BLOOD-SUCKING HABITS, THE VAMPIRE BAT FEEDS AT NIGHT. IT USUALLY ATTACKS ITS VICTIMS AS THEY SLEEP, MAKING A TINY INCISION WITH ITS RAZOR-SHARP TEETH AND LAPPING UP THE BLOOD THAT OOZES FROM THE WOUND. VIRTUALLY ANY MAMMAL OR BIRD, INCLUDING CATTLE AND POULTRY, CAN FALL VICTIM TO THE VAMPIRE BAT, AND EVEN HUMANS HAVE WOKEN UP TO FIND THAT THEIR BLOOD HAS BEEN SUCKED. CHEMICALS IN THE SALIVA STOP THE WOUND FROM CLOTTING SO THAT THE BAT CAN DRINK ITS FILL. THE SALIVA CAN CARRY RABIES, SO THE BITE HAS DEADLY POTENTIAL.

RIGHT: AN EMERALD TREE BOA BARES ITS POISONOUS FANGS, READY TO ATTACK

Snake attack
Snakes vary in size from 12 cm to the mighty python which can reach 9.5 m. Snake attack systems vary, but all snakes locate their food with a highly specialized mechanism called the 'Jacobson's organ'. This sensory receptor, located in the roof of the mouth, receives and analyzes chemical traces picked up in the air by the snake's forked tongue. This is why snakes continually flick their tongues out—they are literally tasting the air for potential prey.

Flesh-eating fish
Found in eastern and central South America, piranhas can grow to a maximum length of 60 cm. The reason why these relatively small fish are an object of terror is the efficiency of their attack system. Piranhas feed in groups and are attracted to the scent of blood. They will attack any living

Military strategy
Chimpanzees have been observed to hunt in highly organized groups of up to 20. These groups invade neighbouring chimpanzee communities to take over their territory and reduce competition for food, as well as to hunt. These raids are carried out with military precision. The chimps group and regroup to exchange information and send spies ahead and high into the trees to check for danger. While the attacking party moves in, strict silence is maintained unless communication is absolutely necessary. But once the chimps fall on their rivals, the noise becomes deafening. The aggressors make howling and screaming war cries and beat their enemy to death with breathtaking ferocity. Not only is this attack system highly effective, it is also thought to reinforce bonds between males in the attacking group.

SHOCK OF 650 VOLTS

VAMPIRE TEETH, DEADLY POISONS, STEALTH, BRUTE STRENGTH, ELECTRIC SHOCKS, FORCE OF NUMBERS AND SKILLFUL PRECISION—ALL ARE EXAMPLES OF ANIMAL ATTACK SYSTEMS REFINED OVER MILLIONS OF YEARS

DEFENCES
BEETLE CAN RELEASE

A successful defence mechanism can be the difference between life and death—and not just once. Predators learn by experience which species to avoid. Animals that protect themselves with poison are often brightly coloured to advertise to predators that eating them will cause sickness. Once a predator has had a bad experience, it learns to be more cautious next time. Other animals use colour, or even sound, to warn predators that they are quite capable of defending themselves.

thanks to one simple defence system: a shell. This tough, plated armour is so effective that its design has changed little over the past 200 million years. Turtles cannot retract their limbs or head into the shell—instead, tough eyelids protect the eyes against attack. This defence system is so impenetrable that killer whales and large sharks are the only predators that bother to tackle turtles. The other danger to turtles comes from motorboat propellors which can cut right through the shell.

NOW YOU SEE ME, NOW YOU DON'T

SOME CREATURES HAVE INGENIOUS MEANS OF SELF-DEFENCE: CHAMELEONS CAN CHANGE COLOUR FROM BRIGHT GREEN TO DARK BROWN TO BLEND WITH THEIR SURROUNDINGS. CHUCKWALLA LIZARDS DASH INTO A CREVICE WHEN THREATENED WITH ATTACK. HERE, THEY PUFF UP UNTIL THEY FIT THE GAP SO SNUGLY THAT EVEN THE MOST DETERMINED PREDATOR CANNOT GET TO THEM. THE AUSTRALIAN FRILLED LIZARD OPENS OUT A HUGE FLAP OF SKIN AROUND ITS HEAD IN ORDER TO DETER PREDATORS BY LOOKING BIGGER AND MORE SCARY.

HOT GAS UP TO 100°C

SOME ANIMALS EMPLOY THE MOST EXTRAORDINARY TACTICS TO DEFEND THEMSELVES AND TO CAUTION POTENTIAL ATTACKERS—FROM BLUFFING, MIMICRY AND DISGUISE, TO OFF-PUTTING SMELLS AND DEADLY POISONS

A pound of flesh

Lizards use a variety of inventive systems to protect themselves from predators. In an extreme defence measure, some sacrifice part of their body to save their own life. When attacked, a lizard can shed its tail and run off while the predator is distracted by the wriggling body-part. For the lizard, no long-term harm is done as the tail eventually grows back, but for the predator the tail can prove unpalatable due to parasites which live in its tissue.

Protective armour

Turtles are quiet, non-aggressive marine animals that can live safe from predators for up to 80 years

Prickly protector

The spiky skin of a hedgehog is enough to deter any predator, but it could also inflict a nasty prick on the hedgehog's own young. This is why hedgehogs have soft undersides. Their young, which are born with soft, rubbery spikes that lengthen and sharpen as they grow, can suckle without danger. To gain full protection when threatened, therefore, a hedgehog must roll itself into a tight ball, tucking its snout into its furry belly.

Hot air

The bombardier beetle has an ingenious means of defence. In its abdomen, it stores two harmless chemicals. When threatened, the

beetle squirts the chemicals, along with an enzyme, into a special chamber. Then the beetle unleashes its secret weapon. In the chamber, a chemical reaction takes place which releases a gush of hot gas— up to 100°C—from the beetle's anus. This makes a popping sound which startles predators. The beetle can turn the gas on and off 500 times a second until the predator is deterred.

Frog defences

The poison-arrow frogs of South and Central America produce some of the deadliest poisons known to man. Eating one of these frogs can induce hallucinations, convulsions, nervous system failure and a narrowing of the blood vessels which can be fatal. All frogs have poison glands in their skin, but these particularly deadly poison-arrow frogs (so called because people native to the forests where they are found use their poison to tip their arrows) advertise the potency of their toxin by their bright blue, green, orange or yellow colouring.

The art of imitation

Not all animals that advertise their defence systems with colour are quite what they seem. The South American coral snake is a very dangerous venomous snake striped in black, red and yellow. The false coral snake has almost identical stripes but is very rarely venomous.

In the same way, the bright colours and spots of the inedible ladybird are imitated by the Philippine roach in order to minimize its chances of being attacked.

Taking flight

One group of fish has an ingenious way of escaping predators in the sea—they take to the air. By building up high speeds in the water and then moving up to the surface, flying fish can leap up to a metre clear of the waves and glide through the air at speeds of 15 km/h on their outstretched, rigid fins, leaving their pursuer behind. This system can backfire as fish are often found on the decks of boats, where they have landed.

Playing dead

For some beetles, the perfect defence system is to not look like a beetle at all. The body of one African species looks like a clump of dead moss and its antennae look like twigs. Some weevils put off predators by falling off twigs when threatened as if they are dying. They fold their wings next to their bodies to make themselves look like a seed or piece of soil. Most predators do not favour eating victims that are dead, so weevils often emphasize the illusion of dying by dropping great distances.

Deathly puffers

Pufferfishes have the singular ability to inflate themselves into a balloon shape by swallowing water. Some have distinctive round markings on their sides or back which look like the eyes of some threatening creature when they are inflated. Their bodies are also covered with thorny spikes, which stand out on inflation, providing a formidable defence against attack. To top it all, the organs and fluids of pufferfishes are highly poisonous to humans—if consumed, a small amount can kill a person. Despite this, pufferfishes are considered a great delicacy in Japan.

DATA-BURST

DO SOME ANIMALS PERFORM DEFENCE ROUTINES WHEN NOT IN DANGER?
YES. FOR SOME ANIMALS, SHOWING OFF THEIR DEFENCE SYSTEM CAN BE A MATING RITUAL. MALES SOMETIMES PUT ON AN IMPRESSIVE DEFENCE DISPLAY TO LURE FEMALES.

HOW STRONG IS A TURTLE'S SHELL?
THE SHELL OF THE BOX TURTLE CAN SUPPORT A WEIGHT 200 TIMES GREATER THAN ITS OWN BODY— EQUIVALENT TO A HUMAN SUPPORTING TWO LARGE ELEPHANTS ON ITS BACK.

HOW DO CHAMELEONS CHANGE COLOUR?
CHAMELEONS CAN ALTER THE DISTRIBUTION OF PIGMENTS IN CELLS CLOSE TO THE SURFACE OF THEIR SKIN. IF THE PIGMENT IS CONCENTRATED WITHIN THE CELLS, THE CHAMELEON

IS PALE IN COLOUR; IF IT IS DISPERSED WITHIN THE CELLS, IT IS DARK.

WHAT IS THE FURTHEST A FLYING FISH CAN FLY?
THE LARGEST SPECIES, WHICH CAN GROW TO 50 CM, CAN FLY 200 M IN A SINGLE GLIDE. THEY GENERALLY MAKE A SERIES OF CONSECUTIVE GLIDES LASTING 30 SECONDS IN TOTAL.

CAN DEFENCE SYSTEMS PREVENT FURTHER ATTACK?
YES, BECAUSE A PREDATOR SOON LEARNS IF AN ANIMAL IS INEDIBLE AND IT WILL BE CAUTIOUS NOT TO REPEAT A BAD EXPERIENCE. SKUNKS, FOR EXAMPLE, HAVE A DISTINCTIVE BLACK AND WHITE COLOUR SCHEME TO IDENTIFY THEMSELVES TO POTENTIAL PREDATORS WHO, SO WARNED, WILL THEN AVOID THEM.

LEFT: THIS VENEZUELAN POISON-ARROW FROG USES ITS BRIGHT COLOUR TO WARN OFF POTENTIAL PREDATORS · INSERT: CLOSE-UP OF A PAIR OF INFLATED SPINY PUFFERFISHES

For many plants, it is true to say that attack is the best form of defence. Cacti rely on their prickly spines to ward off animals, while nettles sting the animals that are likely to eat them. Other plants use chemical deterrents: they protect themselves by being poisonous. Plants can be both poisonous to touch and to ingest and can even produce airborne allergies. Some varieties of plant are extremely toxic: just 10 berries of the white bryony plant are enough to kill a child.

Toxic shock

Hemlock, especially the root and fruit, is extremely toxic, causing paralysis of the central and peripheral nervous systems. Only a very small dose of its poison is enough to kill. Its botanical name, *Conium maculatum*, comes from the Greek *konos*, meaning spinning top, a reference to the delirium caused by its poison. Hemlock is the plant said to have been used to poison the Greek philosopher Socrates. It is a species native to Europe, western Asia and North Africa. If it grows in sunshine, its poison becomes even more virulent. The plant, which can grow up to 2 m high can be identified by its small white flowers and by the distinguishing purple spots on its leaves. It also emits a nauseating smell.

Witches' brew

Every part of the aconite plant is virulently toxic. The plant is named after Aconitus Hill where, according to the Greek legend,

Hercules fought Cerberus, the three-headed watchdog of the gates of Hell. It was from the mouth of Cerberus that the white poison is supposed to have spurted. This poison was used to add a deadly tip to the points of arrows and javelins. The plant was banned by the Roman Emperor Trajan in AD 117 in an attempt to curtail the huge number of murders being committed using its poisonous leaves. Common throughout Europe, aconite is found mainly in woodland and scrub areas, along water courses or on rich mountain pastures. It has hooded mauve-blue flowers. If consumed, the poison provokes a violent attack on the central nervous system. Even if its leaves are rubbed on the body, its poison can produce delirium.

PLANT ATTACK
HEMLOCK CAN CAUSE

Fatal attraction

Belladonna was used by 16th-century Italian ladies as a beauty aid: dropping the juice of its berries into the eyes would make them sparkle. It is still used today to dilate the pupils of the eyes to facilitate medical examination. In large doses, however, belladonna is

highly toxic. Also known as deadly nightshade, it is said to have been used with aconite by witches to induce the illusion of flight. It thrives in arable fields, refuse tips and gardens, and has dull purple flowers and small black berries.

Stinging nettles

Many of the most successful weed species are plants with well developed defences against herbivores. In addition to preventing the plants from being eaten, these defences also inhibit animal movement. The common stinging nettle employs sophisticated stinging hairs that act like hypodermic syringes. They inject an irritant liquid into the skin of any animal that gets too close. The stinging hair of a nettle has a rounded bulbous end that breaks off at the slightest pressure. The ingredients of the irritant include formic acid, acetlcholine and histamine.

Prickly encounter

Many plants eschew chemicals and poisons and simply rely on purely physical defences. Holly has hard spines formed at the margins of its leaves, while the thistle is heavily protected with a whole armoury of sharp spines that protrude from its

A BRUSH WITH DEATH

THE POISON IVY PLANT IS POISONOUS TO TOUCH. DIRECT CONTACT IS LIKELY TO CAUSE DERMATITIS, A SEVERE INFLAMMATION OF THE SKIN. THIS POWERFUL POISON MAY LEAVE RESIDUES ON PEOPLE OR ANIMALS THAT COME INTO CONTACT WITH THE PLANT. THE POISON IS STILL DANGEROUS IF CLOTHING IS WORN CONTAINING SUCH RESIDUES A YEAR AFTER ORIGINAL CONTACT. THE PLANT

STORES ITS POISON IN THE RESINOUS JUICE OF THE DUCTS OF LEAVES, FLOWERS, FRUITS AND BARK OF STEMS. THE LEAVES OF THE PLANT CAN BE HAIRLESS, GLOSSY, TOOTHED OR LOBED. THE PLANT IS NATIVE TO NORTH AMERICA WHERE IT GROWS IN ABUNDANCE. A LESS COMMON TYPE OF POISON IVY IS KNOWN AS POISON OAK. THE TWO SPECIES BELONG TO THE CASHEW FAMILY.

RIGHT: CLOSE-UP OF THE PRICKLY SPINE FORMATIONS FOUND ON SOME SPECIES OF CACTUS

JARGON

CLADODES
LEAF-LIKE STEMS

DERMATITIS
INFLAMMATION OF THE SKIN

HISTAMINE
CHEMICAL RELEASED IN THE PRESENCE OF AN ALLERGEN, SUCH AS POLLEN, WHICH CAUSES AN ALLERGIC REACTION

PHYTOTOXICOLOGY
THE STUDY OF POISON IN PLANTS

URUSHIOL
THE POISON WITHIN POISON IVY

head. Both the blackberry and rose have curved thorns that run along the length of their stems.

Cacti spines

The leaves of the cactus have evolved into sharp spines. These help to protect the plant from predators and also minimize water loss. Also known as stem succulents, cacti have swollen, fleshy, leaf-like stems, called cladodes, which store water. These stems are covered in spines or barbed bristles. There are about 1,650 species of cacti, all of which have adapted to arid climates. Mexico is host to the most species.

DEATH IN 30 MINUTES

PLANTS PROTECT THEMSELVES AGAINST HUNGRY HERBIVORES BY DEVELOPING AN ARMOURY OF SPINES AND THORNS. THESE DETERRENTS ARE OFTEN MATCHED BY THE NATURAL CHEMICAL WEAPON OF PLANTS: POISON

Many animals have senses that are far more developed than those belonging to humans. Animals acquire the senses that will best ensure the survival of their species. A nocturnal animal, for example, may evolve an acute sense of hearing as this provides a better way of measuring distance at night than a sense of sight. Other animals use several super-senses in conjunction in order to give them a crucial advantage. Sharks, for instance, have acute senses of both smell and vision.

to 200 pulses per second when it attacks. Using this extremely specialized system, bats can catch up to two flies per second.

On the scent

The animal with the most highly developed sense of smell is the European freshwater eel, which is able to detect key chemicals at a ratio of one part in every 3 million. This ability helps it to travel thousands of kilometres across the Atlantic Ocean in order to find its ancestral spawning grounds in the

EAGLE-EYED

BIRDS OF PREY, ESPECIALLY EAGLES, ARE RENOWNED FOR THE POWER OF THEIR EYESIGHT. THE ACCURACY OF THEIR BINOCULAR VISION ENABLES THEM TO SPOT SMALL ANIMALS FROM

GREAT HEIGHTS AND SWOOP WITH PINPOINT PRECISION TO SNATCH UP THEIR VICTIMS. PAIRED EYES GIVE A WIDE FIELD OF VISION: TWO VIEWS OF AN OBJECT ARE PUT TOGETHER TO FORM A THREE-DIMENSIONAL IMAGE. THIS IS IMPORTANT IN JUDGING DISTANCE AND THE SPEED OF MOVING OBJECTS. BIRDS OF PREY HAVE EYES PLACED WELL FORWARD ON THEIR HEADS TO GIVE THEM A LARGE OVERLAP BETWEEN TWO POINTS OF VIEW. THE OSPREY CAN SPOT A MOVING SALMON AT A HEIGHT OF 30 M BEFORE SWOOPING DOWN TO CATCH IT.

FEMALE AT 11 KM

SOME ANIMALS HAVE AMAZINGLY ACCURATE SENSES THAT GIVE THEM THE EDGE IN THEIR STRUGGLE FOR SURVIVAL. FINELY-TUNED SENSES OF SMELL, SIGHT AND HEARING CAN HELP THEM TO LOCATE AND ENSNARE THEIR PREY

JARGON

CHEMORECEPTORS
ORGANS USED TO DETECT CHEMICALS SECRETED BY ANIMALS OF THE SAME SPECIES

ECHOLOCATION
A SYSTEM OF DISTANCE MEASURING WHICH WORKS BY BOUNCING SOUND OFF OBJECTS—IN THE SAME WAY AS SONAR

ELECTRORECEPTORS
ORGANS USED TO DETECT ELECTRICAL ACTIVITY

OLFACTORY
RELATING TO THE SENSE OF SMELL

PHEROMONES
CHEMICALS SECRETED BY AN ANIMAL TO TRIGGER A RESPONSE IN ANOTHER INDIVIDUAL OF THE SAME SPECIES

THERMORECEPTORS
ORGANS USED TO DETECT HEAT

Sonar bats

Some bats use a finely-tuned supersense called echolocation to navigate and find prey during the hours of twilight and darkness when they are active. They emit short, high-frequency pulses of sound, normally beyond the hearing range of humans. When these pulses hit objects, they bounce back to the bat and are picked up by the animal's large ears. The returning pulses enable the bat to build up a 'sound picture' of its surroundings. The system is so accurate that flying bats can avoid wires as thin as 0.08 mm in diameter. When a bat is searching for food, it sends out about 10 sound pulses per second. This rises

Sargasso Sea. Some predatory mammals also boast a powerful sense of smell. A polar bear can detect a dead seal from 20 km.

Moth perfumery

Many animals use smell during courtship and mating. To attract males, female moths release pheromones so potent that, in one experiment, a female attracted 100 males in a six-hour period. The males have chemoreceptors on their antennae that can detect a single molecule of the female's chemical. The male emperor moth can trace a female's scent at a range of 11 km—even though the female carries less than 0.0001 mg of the pheromone.

Snouting armadillo

Armadillos use their developed sense of smell to discover and eat their insect prey. Armadillo brains have a well developed olfactory section which enables the animals to sniff out termites that lie as deep as 12 cm underground.

Bloodthirsty sharks

Sharks can detect blood in seawater at a concentration of just one part of blood per 10 million parts of water. Once they have located their prey, they often circle it before attacking from below. But chemical location is not the only technique sharks use when hunting. They are also highly sensitive to water-borne sound waves, enabling them to detect any movement in the water which could signify the presence of potential prey.

Heat-seeking snakes

Snakes such as pit vipers and rattlesnakes hunt their prey by sensing their heat emissions. Thermoreceptors below and in front of their eyes are so sensitive to heat that these snakes can strike accurately at their prey without using their eyes at all. If an animal is present for just half a second within a 0.5-m vicinity of the rattlesnake then the surrounding temperature will be raised by 0.002°C. The snake is able to record this subtle change in temperature and is alerted to the presence of the animal.

Whisker touch

Mice have collections of sensory hairs, or whiskers, arranged on either side of their snouts. Each whisker is extremely sensitive to touch. These hairs connect with a specialized collection of neurons in a mouse's brain. Foraging at night in complete darkness, a mouse is able to gather detailed information about its habitat through these finely-tuned touch receptors.

Clicking birds

Some birds that live in huge colonies in dark subterranean caves, such as swiftlets, navigate in the same way as bats. They emit clicking noises at lower frequencies than bats—about six per second. These clicks are audible to the human ear.

Magnetic bees

It was only in 1995 that scientists gained an insight into the extraordinary sensitivity of bees to the Earth's magnetism. Tiny magnetic iron oxide crystals in the abdomens of honeybees enable them to orientate themselves by the Earth's magnetic field.

DATA-BURST

HOW IS HUMAN HEARING DIFFERENT FROM THAT OF ANIMALS?
THE HUMAN EAR AMPLIFIES SOUND 18 TIMES. THIS IS QUITE SUFFICIENT FOR OUR NEEDS, BUT RATS NEED MUCH SHARPER HEARING TO SURVIVE. THE SOUNDS THAT THE KANGAROO RAT HEARS ARE AMPLIFIED 100 TIMES— LOUD ENOUGH TO PICK UP THE MOVEMENT OF A SNAKE'S SCALES.

HOW DO FISH HEAR UNDERWATER?
FISH HEAR IN MUCH THE SAME WAY AS WE DO EXCEPT THAT THE FISH EAR LACKS THE AIR-FILLED CHAMBER OF THE MIDDLE EAR. MANY SPECIES OF FISH HAVE CALLING SOUNDS IN ORDER TO ATTRACT MATES.

HOW DO ANIMALS SEE IN THE DARK?
NOCTURNAL AND DEEP-SEA ANIMALS NEED TO BE ABLE TO SEE IN DIM LIGHT.

THEIR PUPILS TEND TO BE VERY LARGE AND A REFLECTIVE LAYER, KNOWN AS TAPETUM, SITS BEHIND THE RETINA. THIS REFLECTS LIGHT BACK INTO THE RETINA, MAXIMIZING ABSORPTION. IT IS THE TAPETUM THAT IS RESPONSIBLE FOR THE EYE-SHINE THAT MANY NOCTURNAL ANIMALS EMIT WHEN CAUGHT IN A CAR'S HEADLIGHTS.

WHICH ANIMALS HAVE THE KEENEST SENSE OF SMELL?
MAMMALS, ESPECIALLY ANIMALS SUCH AS RABBITS AND DOGS, HAVE PARTICULARLY SENSITIVE NOSES.

WHY DO SOME ANIMALS DEVELOP A SENSITIVE SENSE OF SMELL?
ANIMALS WITH A VERY DEVELOPED SENSE OF SMELL USE THEIR NOSES TO DETECT FOOD, FIND MATES AND SENSE THE DANGER OF PREDATORS.

LEFT: GREATER HORSESHOE BAT, REMARKABLE FOR ITS ABILITY TO 'SEE' USING ULTRASOUND

ENDURANCE 1

CAMELS GO WITHOUT

The amazing ability of some animals to endure extreme temperatures, survive great journeys or bear weights many times greater than their own is due to the adaptations their predecessors have made. These physical modifications, which have developed over generations, equip animals perfectly to endure the difficult environments in which they have to live. Staying airborne for four years, for example, is a simple matter for the common swift, thanks to a physical make-up which enables it to eat, drink, sleep and mate on the wing. Camels and polar bears both have special means to cope with scorching heat and freezing cold.

ANIMALS DOMESTICATED FOR THEIR ENDURANCE

SINCE THE FIRST WOLVES WERE DOMESTICATED THOUSANDS OF YEARS AGO, HUMANS HAVE USED DOGS FOR THEIR ENDURANCE AS WELL AS FOR COMPANIONSHIP. SOME OF THE HARDIEST BREEDS ARE THE ALASKAN MALAMUTE AND THE SIBERIAN HUSKY. BOTH ARE INTELLIGENT, MAKING THEM EASY TO TRAIN, AND HAVE THICK COATS TO PROTECT THEM FROM SEVERE COLD. MALAMUTES HAVE EVEN BEEN TAKEN ON ANTARCTIC EXPEDITIONS. THEIR LARGE SIZE AND GREAT STRENGTH MAKE THEM IDEAL FOR PULLING SLEDGES OVER SNOW AND ICE. MULES—THE OFFSPRING OF A MALE ASS AND A FEMALE HORSE—ARE ALSO USED FOR THEIR STRENGTH. STANDING ABOUT 150 CM TALL, THESE ANIMALS HAVE A THICK HEAD AND STURDY MUSCULAR BUILD. FIRST USED AS BEASTS OF BURDEN IN ASIA MINOR 3,000 YEARS AGO, MULES ARE STILL VALUED TODAY FOR THEIR ABILITY TO COPE WITH ROUGH AND STEEP TERRAIN. THE ARABIAN HORSE IS VALUED NOT FOR ITS CARRYING CAPACITY, BUT FOR SPEED AND STAMINA. IT WAS FIRST BRED FOR THESE SPECIFIC QUALITIES IN THE 7TH CENTURY AD AND HAS FORMED THE BLUEPRINT FOR HORSE-BREEDING TO THE PRESENT DAY.

dehydration without suffering any ill effects. The single hump of the Arabian camel, or dromedary, and the double hump of the Bactrian camel store fat which can keep the camel alive when food is not available and can be converted into water. Their broad feet enable camels to walk easily on soft sand and double eyelashes and sealable nostrils protect their eyes and nose during sandstorms. They can survive on the thorny desert plants which other animals could not endure. These remarkable adaptations have made camels extremely useful as desert pack animals. When water is made available after a long journey, camels can drink 100 litres within a matter of minutes to replenish their body's supply.

WATER FOR 17 DAYS

FROM BIRDS THAT FLY FOR 26,000 KM WITHOUT TOUCHING LAND TO TINY ORGANISMS THAT CAN BEAR 100 TIMES THEIR OWN BODY WEIGHT, THE TESTS OF ENDURANCE FACED BY SOME ANIMALS EXCEED HUMAN CAPACITIES

Weightlifters

Some of the most remarkable load-bearers of the animal kingdom are some of its smallest members. Ants have two sets of jaws: one for chewing and one for carrying. Many species forage alone and have to carry prey over seven times their own body weight. One species, which measures only 3 mm long, has been observed dragging prey 10 mm in length, such as locusts, to its nest. This would be equivalent to humans carrying a small car in their teeth over a distance of 8 km. The trapdoor spiders of North America and Japan can endure weights up to 40 times their own while defending their burrows from intruders. But perhaps the strongest of all are the rhinoceros beetles, which can carry up to 100 times their own body weight.

Highs and lows

Jumping spiders have been found at altitudes of 6,500 m on Mount Everest, but it is birds that endure the highest altitude of any animal. In December 1967, a pilot spotted 30 whooper swans on their way from Iceland to Northern Ireland flying at an altitude, confirmed by radar, of over 8,230 m. The highest-flying bird on Earth, however, is the Ruppell's vulture which can soar at altitudes of 11,000 m. In November 1973, one of these birds, identified from feathers retrieved afterwards, collided with an aircraft at 11,277 m over the Ivory Coast. At the other extreme, tusk shells—marine molluscs with a tapering shell which houses a foot for digging—are found in ocean waters at depths of up to 4,000 m, often buried in the sea- bed. The deepest-living fish, the brotulid, has been found in the Puerto Rican Trench in the Atlantic Ocean at depths of an incredible 8,300 m.

Hot and hardy

Camels inhabit scorching desert regions in Africa and Asia where they can survive without water for up to 17 days. These phenomenally hardy animals can lose 25% of their body weight through

Cold and hungry

The polar bear survives in icy Arctic conditions thanks to its remarkable coat and a 10-cm layer of insulating fat. Each of the coat's hairs is a clear, hollow tube which channels heat from the sun to the skin. The coat is white to provide the polar bear with perfect camouflage on the drifting ice sheets of Canada, Greenland, Norway, Russia and Alaska. Underneath the white fur, however, lies a thick black skin which absorbs the sun's rays. The bear's head is small to minimize heat loss, but the long snout contains large membranes that warm and moisten the freezing dry air before it reaches the lungs. The bear's large feet are covered in fur to stop it slipping on the ice. After the ice has melted in the summer the polar bear lives for some eight months without food. Gorging on seals from April to July, the impregnated females can increase their body fat by 50% or more. They build up a thick layer of fat around the thighs and rump which will provide additional calories when food is scarce. The massive polar bear—weighing up to 750 kg and standing 1.5 m at the shoulder—is a strong swimmer, living up to its scientific name *Ursus maritimus* or 'sea bear'. It often swims over 150 km from land or ice, searching for its main prey: seals.

Great journeys

Migrating birds travel long and difficult journeys, often in search of food not available in one region. Ducks, geese, swans and swifts migrate across Europe, while the golden plover flies the 3,9000 km from Alaska to Canada each year.

DATA-BURST

WHAT ANIMAL CAN ENDURE THE GREATEST G-FORCE?
THE CLICK BEETLE JACK-KNIFES ITS NIMBLE BODY INTO THE AIR TO EVADE PREDATORS, WITHSTANDING A G-FORCE OF 400 IN THE PROCESS. ONE BEETLE WHICH WEIGHS ONLY 40 MG CAN JUMP TO A HEIGHT OF 30 CM, ENDURING A PEAK BRAIN DECELERATION OF 2,300 G BY THE END OF THE LEAP.

WHAT ARE THE HIGHEST AND LOWEST TEMPERATURES ANY ORGANISM CAN ENDURE?
HUMANS CANNOT WITHSTAND BODY TEMPERATURES ABOVE 40°C OR BELOW 30°C BUT SOME PROKARYOTIC BACTERIA CAN LIVE IN POOLS AT TEMPERATURES ABOVE 90°C AND OTHER SINGLE-CELLED ORGANISMS CAN BE FROZEN TO −183°C, THE TEMPERATURE OF LIQUID OXYGEN, AND THAWED OUT AGAIN WITH NO ILL-EFFECT.

WHAT IS THE LONGEST RECORDED BIRD FLIGHT?
THE RECORD GOES TO A COMMON TERN WHICH WAS RINGED IN FINLAND IN JUNE 1996 AND RECAPTURED SEVEN MONTHS LATER AT ROTAMAH ISLAND, VICTORIA, AUSTRALIA IN JAN 1997. IT HAD TRAVELLED AN AMAZING JOURNEY OF 26,000 KM.

WHAT IS THE LONGEST JOURNEY MADE BY AN INSECT?
A MONARCH BUTTERFLY TAGGED AND RELEASED NEAR ONTARIO, CANADA, IN SEPT 1986 WAS LOCATED IN JAN 1987 ON A MOUNTAIN NEAR ANGANGUEO, MEXICO, 3,432 KM AWAY.

WHAT IS THE LONGEST JOURNEY MADE BY A FISH?
THE EUROPEAN EEL LIVES IN FRESHWATER FOR 15 YEARS THEN UNDERTAKES A SIX-MONTH JOURNEY OF UP TO 6,400 KM IN ORDER TO REACH THE ATLANTIC OCEAN.

LEFT: LEAFCUTTER ANTS CARRYING A SECTION OF LEAF ALONG A TREE TRUNK

In the world's most extreme habitats—its arid, rocky deserts, its freezing polar wastes and its barren mountain tops—animal and plant life is scarcely possible. But a few of the toughest plant species do manage to survive. Specially equipped to cope with the most adverse conditions that the Earth can produce, they provide a reminder of the resilience of life.

High altitude

Plant life is scarce at high altitudes due to low temperatures and barren soil. In the northern Andes in Colombia and Ecuador, alpine meadows called *paramo* contain grass and herbaceous plants. Some of these plants, called frailefones, can grow to 4–6 m. In the southern *paramo*, rough grasses, cushion and rosette plants, shrubs and cacti survive. The Alps support a range of hardy plants called pulsatillas. The key to the survival of these plants is their thick, long, woody rootstocks that penetrate deep into the sparse soil and gravel. The plants open their leaves for a short period of activity during the early spring thaw, producing enough food to see them through the winter. Once the flowers are pollinated, they produce fuzzy seeds with tufts of hair to carry them in the wind.

Hardy lichens

The Earth's polar regions are some of the most barren of all, where only 10 mm of rain falls each year and the soil is always frozen. Only in the six months of

DATA-BURST

WHY DO PLANTS IN ARID CONDITIONS HAVE SUCH LONG ROOTS?
THE LONG ROOTS MAXIMIZE THE PLANT'S ABILITY TO CAPTURE WATER; MORE WATER IS AVAILABLE UNDERGROUND THAN IN THE AIR.

WHY DO ALPINE PLANTS OFTEN HAVE HAIRY LEAVES AND BRIGHT FLOWERS?
THE HAIRS ON THE LEAVES OF ALPINE PLANTS, SUCH AS EDELWEISS AND FRAILEFONES, HELP TO CONSERVE MOISTURE AT HIGH ALTITUDES WHERE AIR IS VERY DRY. THE FLOWERS ARE BRIGHT TO ATTRACT THE FEW INSECTS THAT ARE ACTIVE HERE IN EARLY SPRING. IF THE FLOWERS MISS THEIR CHANCE AND ARE NOT POLLINATED, THE PLANTS CANNOT PRODUCE SEEDS.

HOW MUCH LIFE IS THERE IN THE ANTARCTIC?
ONLY 4% OF THE LAND AREA OF THE ANTARCTIC CAN SUSTAIN LIFE FORMS, BUT THE FOSSIL RECORD SHOWS THAT BEFORE THE POLES FROZE 4.5 BILLION YEARS AGO, BOTH THE ANTARCTIC AND THE ARCTIC MAY HAVE BEEN TEMPERATE REGIONS WITH FORESTS.

WHY DO MANY DESERT PLANTS HAVE NO LEAVES?
THE LARGE SURFACE AREA MAY BE GOOD FOR PHOTOSYNTHESIS, BUT BIG LEAVES LOSE A LOT OF MOISTURE TO THE ATMOSPHERE THROUGH TRANSPIRATION. IN DRY DESERT CONDITIONS, THIS WOULD LEAD TO DEHYDRATION AND DEATH.

JARGON

FLORA
THE PLANTS OF A SPECIFIC AREA

PHOTOSYNTHESIS
THE PROCESS BY WHICH GREEN PLANTS USE SUNLIGHT TO CONVERT WATER AND CARBON DIOXIDE FROM THE AIR INTO FOOD

SUCCULENTS
PLANTS, SUCH AS CACTI, WHICH REDUCE WATER LOSS BUT CONTINUE PHOTOSYNTHESIS BY STORING WATER IN SPECIAL TISSUES AND RECYCLING IT

TRANSPIRATION
EMISSION OF WATER FROM PLANTS INTO THE SURROUNDING AIR

ENDURANCE 2
CACTUS SURVIVES ON

summer sunshine, when snow meltwater is available, can the flora of these regions emerge. In the Arctic, temperatures rise above freezing for only one month a year. But this is enough for 1,000 species of ferns and flowers, 850 species of fungi, 300 liverworts and around 2,000 algae to flourish. Perhaps the hardiest of all the Arctic's plants are the lichens. These tiny plants can survive on barren rocks, nourished by the occasional bird dropping. In the

Antarctic, around 400 species of lichen survive, along with snow algae which colour the coastal landscape red, green and yellow.

Fertile deserts

Desert plants have to face scorching sun and lack of water. In the Arabian Desert plants spring into action at the first sight of rain—seeds, buried for months in the dry gravel soil, germinate and send up shoots within hours. Mustard, pea, daisy, caper, iris and milk-weed plants turn the normally barren plains green with their hastily produced shoots and blooms. Along with these seasonal plants, hardy shrubs survive, yielding fragrant frankincense and myrrh. The desert carrion flower of southern Africa has no leaves, just spine-tipped stems which store rainwater and protect the plant from grazing animals. At the tips of these stems the plant produces odd, star-shaped flowers. Patterned in yellow and red to imitate rotting flesh, the flowers give off a foul stench like carrion to attract flies which pollinate the flowers, enabling the plant to reproduce.

Spiky cacti

Succulents are the true specialists of arid regions. The most amazing of all is the miracle plant which can live for 1,000 years. Also called the 'living fossil', this plant, found in the deserts along the southern shore of South Africa,

consists of two huge leaves which grow out flat to the sand in opposite directions from a low woody stem. These leaves can be up to 3 m long and over 1 m wide. The plant gains water from sea fogs, driven inland by winds from the Atlantic—these same winds disperse the plant's seeds across the hot desert sands. There are a total of 1,650 known cactus species. Many of these can be found in the arid deserts of Mexico, including Button cacti which live on drops of moisture from beneath the desert rocks, and protect themselves from hungry animals by looking just like stones. One cactus which inhabits the totally arid Atacama Desert in Chile never receives any rain, only the damp mist from the Pacific.

Action beneath the surface

Using extremely long roots to get to any available water is a survival strategy common to the most resilient of desert plants. In the sandy Arabian Desert, the long, deep roots of sedge plants are so substantial that locals use them for firewood. The banana plant has an underground stem that sustains it safely through the dry season. This stem sends out a sturdy shoot that consists of thick leaf stalks, arranged one inside the other, and ends in an oblong leaf blade. When the rain comes, this shoot finds the water and a flower stem emerges from its centre.

LIVING WITHOUT LIGHT: THE RAFFLESIA

IN THE SEMI-DARKNESS OF THE GROUND-LEVEL ZONES OF INDONESIA'S RAINFORESTS LIVES ONE OF THE STRANGEST PLANTS ON EARTH: THE RAFFLESIA. A TOTAL PARASITE, THIS AMAZING PLANT SURVIVES WITHOUT THE NEED FOR SUNLIGHT—AN ABSOLUTE MUST FOR OTHER PLANTS WHICH RELY ON LIGHT FOR PHOTOSYNTHESIS. INSTEAD, THE RAFFLESIA SENDS UP SHOOTS FROM GROUND LEVEL, SEEKING OUT THE ROOTS OF CLIMBING JUNGLE VINES. ONCE THE RAFFLESIA'S SHOOTS HAVE LATCHED ONTO A VINE, THEY PENETRATE ITS ROOTS, TAPPING INTO

ITS FOOD AND WATER SUPPLY. THE RAFFLESIA EVEN RELIES ON THE VINE TO HELP IT REPRODUCE. ITS OWN HUGE FLOWER ACTUALLY BURSTS OUT OF THE VINE AND OPENS UP TO EMIT A STINK LIKE ROTTEN FLESH IN ORDER TO ATTRACT THE FLIES THAT SPREAD ITS POLLEN. BUT EVEN THE CLIMBING VINE IS NOT SELF-SUFFICIENT. IT RELIES, IN TURN, ON A TALL RAINFOREST TREE FROM WHICH TO GAIN ITS NOURISHMENT. SO THE RAFFLESIA, DOWN ON AT THE FOREST FLOOR, IS SUSTAINED BY A PROCESS OF PHOTOSYNTHESIS THAT GOES ON AROUND 40 M OVERHEAD.

DROPS OF MOISTURE

EVEN IN THE MOST BARREN OF ENVIRONMENTS, SOME PLANTS CAN EKE OUT AN EXISTENCE. SURVIVING ON THE BARE MINIMUM OF NOURISHMENT AND MOISTURE, THESE LIFE-FORMS DISPLAY QUITE ASTONISHING ENDURANCE

PARASITES
HUMAN TAPEWORM

A parasite is an organism that lives on or within another organism upon which it is dependent for survival. Some of the world's most successful lifeforms, parasites have developed a wide variety of special techniques and tools to help them grow and reproduce at the expense of their host. They have discovered ways of resisting the harsh environments of host bodies, making them some of the most hardy and ingenious creatures known to humans.

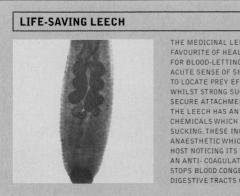

LIFE-SAVING LEECH

THE MEDICINAL LEECH WAS ONCE A FAVOURITE OF HEALERS, WHO USED IT FOR BLOOD-LETTING. THE LEECH'S ACUTE SENSE OF SMELL ALLOWS IT TO LOCATE PREY EFFECTIVELY, WHILST STRONG SUCKERS ENABLE SECURE ATTACHMENT TO ITS HOST. THE LEECH HAS AN ARRAY OF CHEMICALS WHICH FACILITATE BLOOD-SUCKING. THESE INCLUDE AN ANAESTHETIC WHICH PREVENTS THE HOST NOTICING ITS PRESENCE AND AN ANTI-COAGULATION AGENT WHICH STOPS BLOOD CONGEALING IN THE DIGESTIVE TRACTS OF THE LEECH.

JARGON

HOST
CREATURE THAT ACTS AS HABITAT AND FOOD SOURCE FOR A PARASITE

NEMATODE
ROUNDWORM PARASITES, FOUND IN VIRTUALLY EVERY KIND OF HABITAT

PROGLOTTID
AN INDIVIDUAL SEGMENT OF A PARASITIC WORM

TREMATODE
A CLASS OF FLATWORMS THAT OFTEN INHABIT THE GUT

CAN GROW TO 22.9 M

PARARSITES CAN BE BOTH LIFE-SAVERS AND DESTROYERS: LEECHES ARE USED FOR BLOOD-LETTING AND MAGGOTS FOR WOUND-CLEANING, WHILE TAPEWORMS FEED OFF THE HUMAN GUT AND HOOKWORMS SUCK HUMAN BLOOD

Bloodsucking blackfly
Blackflies are some of the most threatening of insect pests. Found mainly in the temperate northern hemisphere, they kill tens of thousands of domestic animals every year, and have also been known to kill children. They often appear in massive bloodsucking hordes, causing death by suffocation when thousands get caught in a creature's bronchial tubes. Blackflies have very short mouths, and so have to rasp a hole through their victim's skin. The insect feeds for several minutes from the blood that trickles from the hole. The bites, often painless at first, become increasingly distressing.

Maggot attack
Both humans and animals can be attacked by maggots, but the Congo floor maggot is known to be exclusively parasitic on humans. This maggot is found throughout tropical Africa, in regions close to permanent human habitats. The larvae hide under floor mats during the day, and at night they suck human blood by puncturing the skin with mouth hooks. Fortunately, their bites are not known to transmit disease, and are only mildly irritating.

Medicinal maggots
A large number of flies deposit their larvae in the decaying flesh of dead animals. They are also attracted to dead tissue in living animals. This, coupled with the fact that their excrement has anti-bacterial properties, has led humans to use them extensively as medicinal aids. They have been used to remove dead tissue and clean wounds for centuries. In the 1930s and 1940s, maggots were widely used in hospitals in the USA. The practice declined following the development of antibiotics, but since 1989, clinical trials have been underway to test the ability of maggots to clean infected and gangrenous wounds. Between five and eight disinfected maggots are placed on the wound, which is then covered with gauze and a dressing.

Tapeworms
Tapeworms are amongst the giants of the parasite world. Living in the intestinal tracts of their hosts, they consist of a chain of segments, with a head at one end containing suckers—rings containing powerful hooks or rows of spines which attach to the host. The tapeworm can have 3–4,000 segments, and can shed more than one million eggs per day. When ingested, tapeworms attach themselves to the mucous membrane of the host's intestine where they grow into their adult forms. Most tapeworms are ingested through the mouth; once established in the intestine, their larvae can spread into the host's stomach and other organs. Tapeworms can grow to enormous sizes: the biggest is the broad fish tapeworm, which is found in fish and creatures that eat fish, including humans. It usually grows to a length of 10 m, with certain specimens known to have been more than 18 m long. Some tapeworms can live up to 25 years within a host's body. Medical literature reports a case of one woman who carried a total of 143 worms.

The beef tapeworm
One particularly common large parasite in humans is the beef tapeworm. Its average length is 4.5—6 m, but specimens have been known to reach 22.9 m. Its body can have up to 1,000 segments, known as proglottids. Each segment can contain as many as 80,000 eggs. A human host probably excretes about nine of its segments daily. This means that approximately 720,000 eggs are dispersed every day. The segments lost by the tapeworm are constantly regenerated. The tapeworm can live up to 25 years, which means that in its lifetime, its human host will potentially excrete 6,570,000,000 eggs.

Hookworms
The hookworm is a dangerous human parasite. It can cause extreme damage through the sheer amount of blood it sucks, resulting in haemorrhage, anaemia and loss of vitality. Hookworms are generally chunky worms, about 1 cm in length. They have cavities which contain ridges of cutting teeth. In humans, they live in the small intestine, where they feed on blood and tissue juices. As well as gorging themselves, hookworms are continually laying eggs, and they can produce between 5,000 and 10,000 daily, which are passed out in the faeces. A hookworm is capable of laying eggs constantly for five years, generating 18 million offspring.

DATA-BURST

WHAT PROPERTIES DO PARASITES HAVE IN COMMON?
PARASITES HAVE THE ABILITY TO INFECT, TO ESTABLISH THEMSELVES IN A HOST AND TO TRANSMIT OFFSPRING TO DIFFERENT HOSTS.

ARE PARASITES VISIBLE TO THE HUMAN EYE?
ONLY 30% OF PARASITES ARE VISIBLE TO THE HUMAN EYE. THE MAJORITY ARE MICROSCOPIC ORGANISMS SUCH AS VIRUSES, BACTERIA AND FUNGI.

CAN TAPEWORMS BE USED BENEFICIALLY?
NOT REALLY, BUT SOME PEOPLE HAVE INGESTED THEM TO HELP THEM LOSE WEIGHT. THIS PRACTICE, HOWEVER, IS DANGEROUS BECAUSE A TAPEWORM CAN SPLIT INTO MANY SEGMENTS WHICH FORM INTO MANY TAPEWORMS.

WHAT MAJOR DISEASES ARE CAUSED BY PARASITES?
PARASITES CAUSE A NUMBER OF FATAL DISEASES INCLUDING MALARIA AND BUBONIC PLAGUE. MALARIA PARASITES ARE TRANSMITTED BY MOSQUITOES AND ARE RESPONSIBLE FOR 3 MILLION DEATHS EACH YEAR.

DO HOSTS HAVE MECHANISMS WITH WHICH TO ATTACK PARASITES?
YES. THERE ARE SEVERAL BIOLOGICAL STRATEGIES AVAILABLE, INCLUDING INFLAMMATORY TISSUE RESPONSES AND THE PRODUCTION OF NATURAL ANTIBODIES BY THE IMMUNE SYSTEM. THE BODY'S ATTEMPT TO EXPEL PARASITES CAN LEAD TO OVER-SENSITIVE IMMUNE SYSTEMS WHICH RESPOND EVEN WHEN NON-HARMFUL SUBSTANCES ARE PRESENT. THIS IS KNOWN AS AN ALLERGIC REACTION.

LEFT: THE LARVA OF A ROUNDWORM PARASITE EMBEDDED IN MUSCLE MAGNIFIED 400 TIMES

The task of detecting, hunting and killing prey can be too much for some animals. Capturing and killing other animals can be highly dangerous activities, with no guaranteed meal at the end of many hours of exertion. To avoid this, some species have become scavengers and carrion feeders—creatures that live off dead animals. The art of scavenging can be sophisticated, employing techniques such as mimicry, stalking and hiding.

Stealing by stealth
There are many ways for animals to find food without having to hunt. A primary method is piracy, the 'hi-jacking' of food by covert means. Strategies include 'area-copying', which entails searching the same area as a successful predator or forager; 'following', whereby a successful animal is stalked by another in its search for food, sometimes usurping the food before the original animal has a chance to get to it; and 'snatching' or violently grabbing food from the mouth or claws of another animal. Piracy often occurs in larger colonies of animals when the group return to the same feeding grounds again and again.

The piracy arms race
Piracy as a food-scrounging strategy has resulted in an 'arms race' between species as they try to remain one step ahead of the competition. This is vital, since some animals can lose a large proportion of their spoils: cheetahs lose more than one-tenth of their kill to other carnivores. Victims of piracy have developed methods to counter the pirates, including evasive techniques, retaliation and a certain level of toleration.

Bones to pick
Hyenas are opportunistic animals. These predatory beasts hunt in large packs of around 10–30 individuals but they also feed off the remains of animals that other predators have killed. They have evolved and adapted in ways that aid them in their scavenger lifestyle. Hyenas have large heads with high boney crests which serve as the attachment for a massive jaw muscle. Because of the huge size of their jaws hyenas have one of the strongest bites of any carnivore. Their strong bone-crunching teeth enable them to break down large carcasses and chew though tough hide. In order to cope with this unwieldy diet, their digestive systems are particularly robust. Hyenas can ingest the hard tissue that other carnivores cannot. The toughest items that they cannot dissolve, such as hooves and antlers, are expelled by regurgitation. Brown and striped hyenas are smaller and less massively built than the spotted hyena and feed on eggs and fruits as well as carrion and larger prey.

Wheeling vultures
Vultures present a familiar image of the scavenger. These large birds, with wingspans of up to 3 m, feed on carrion, excrement and human litter. Occasionally, they have been known to feed off living animals, such as lambs, which are unable to defend themselves. Adaptations have helped vultures to succeed in their scavenger lifestyle. They use their strong hooked beaks to rip up carcasses and facilitate easy rending of the flesh. A vulture's head and neck are free of feathers that would become clogged with blood and be difficult to keep clean. Vultures are able to walk more easily than many birds and have excellent eyesight to aid them in their search for food. Their large wings enable them to soar and glide for hours at a time using minimal energy. Once a carcass has been spotted on the ground, many vultures may converge around a body at the same time.

Nature's undertakers
The sexton beetle belongs to a group of insects which are popularly known as 'burying beetles'. They detect dead bodies through their acute sense of smell, and upon arriving at the scene they may have to fight off other beetles for possession of the carcass. Often working as a pair, one of each sex, they quickly attempt to bury the body out of sight of other potential scavengers by scrubbing away at the soil underneath the corpse until it sinks into the land. They have even been known to cut off the limbs from corpses to aid a speedy burial. As a body is buried in the soil by the beetle, it is compacted; the entire process can take between three to ten hours, depending on the type of soil. Once the body has been buried, the female creates a brood chamber underground where she lays her eggs. Once they hatch and develop, the young beetles are able to feed off the buried carcass until they are ready to travel to the surface where they will begin the cycle all over again. By burying the corpses of small mammals, such as voles, shrews and mice, these beetles can be effective in helping to clean up the countryside.

SCAVENGERS

SCAVENGERS SNATCH UP TO

DATA-BURST

WHAT ARE PRODUCER/SCROUNGER RELATIONSHIPS?
THESE ARE INTERDEPENDENT RELATIONSHIPS IN WHICH ONE SPECIES, THE PRODUCER, GATHERS FOOD BY DIRECT MEANS AND IS THEN EXPLOITED BY ANOTHER SPECIES THROUGH SCAVENGING, SCROUNGING OR PIRACY.

DO PRODUCERS HAVE ANY DEFENCE AGAINST SCROUNGERS?
YES. AS WELL AS DIRECT ATTACK, PRODUCERS MAY SEEK TO REGAIN LOST FOOD THROUGH USURPATION AND BY EMPLOYING SOME OF THE STRATEGIES THAT HAVE BEEN USED UPON THEM BY THE SCROUNGERS.

WHAT KINDS OF BIRDS PRACTISE PIRACY?
BIRDS OF THE ORDER *FALCONIFORMES* (E.G. HAWKS, FALCONS, EAGLES) AND *CHARADRIIFORMES* (E.G. GULLS, WADERS) DISPLAY THE HIGHEST LEVELS OF PIRACY.

WHAT MAMMALS PRACTISE PIRACY?
MAINLY THE SCAVENGER/PREDATOR SPECIES. FOR EXAMPLE, LIONS OBTAIN NEARLY ONE-SIXTH OF THEIR FOOD BY PIRACY, AND HYENAS OBTAIN MORE THAN ONE-QUARTER.

DO INVERTEBRATES PRACTISE PIRACY?
YES. IT IS WELL KNOWN IN DIPTERAN FLIES AND WEB-BUILDING SPIDERS.

HOW ARE PIRATES CHARACTERIZED?
THEY OFTEN HAVE A FLEXIBLE DIET, WITH A RANGE OF FEEDING STRATEGIES AND THE ABILITY TO MOVE QUICKLY AND WITH AGILITY.

WHAT OTHER STRATEGIES DO SCAVENGERS EMPLOY?
SOME IMITATE THE STRATEGY OF SUCCESSFUL HUNTERS IN ORDER TO FIND FOOD; OTHERS MIMIC THEIR BEHAVIOUR OR APPEARANCE, WHILE SOME RESORT TO SCROUNGING AND SNATCHING FOOD.

RIGHT: HYENAS DEVOUR THE CARCASS OF A ZEBRA ON THE AFRICAN SAVANNA · LEFT: CAPE VULTURES SWOOP DOWN TO FEED FROM A GIRAFFE'S CARCASS

Snapping turtle

The common snapping turtle has developed the ability to sniff out dead animals. It is able to detect corpses and rotting flesh and eats carrion, small birds, and fish. Its jaw has a powerful hooked beak, like a bird of prey, which it uses to dissect its meals. Its worm-like tongue is used to lure unsuspecting fish and ducklings into its open mouth. It lives in stagnant ponds and swamps and uses algae for camouflage in murky waters. On occasion, these turtles have been known to attack swimmers. Humans have exploited the turtle's scavenger skills by using them to help sniff out human bodies in bogs, lakes and swamps.

FOOD FIGHT

PUFFINS ARE LOCKED IN AN ONGOING WAR OVER FOOD WITH GULLS AND SKUAS. BOTH HAVE DEVELOPED SOPHISTICATED TECHNIQUES FOR THE FIGHT: SKUAS CHASE PUFFINS WHEN THEY ARE MOST LIKELY TO DROP FOOD—FAR AWAY FROM THE COLONY OR WHEN THEY ARE FLYING LOW. TO DEFEND THEMSELVES, PUFFINS CIRCLE HIGH OVER THEIR NESTS, THUS AVOIDING THE WAITING SKUAS. SKUAS TRY TO TARGET LONE PUFFINS, SO PUFFINS BRINGING IN FOOD HAVE LEARNT TO FLY WITH OTHER, NON-FOOD-CARRYING, PUFFINS IN ORDER TO LESSEN THEIR CHANCES OF BEING ATTACKED. GULLS LURK ON SLOPES NEAR PUFFIN BURROWS WAITING FOR THE RIGHT MOMENT TO ATTACK, SO PUFFINS OFTEN NEST IN STEEP ROCK FACES WHERE GULLS FIND IT MUCH MORE DIFFICULT TO REACH THEM.

JARGON

AREA-COPYING
SEARCHING FOR FOOD IN THE SAME AREA AS A PREDATOR THAT HAS BEEN SUCCESSFUL

FOLLOWING
STALKING ANOTHER ANIMAL IN ITS SEARCH FOR FOOD

KLEPTOPARASITES
FOOD PIRATES

SNATCHING
VIOLENTLY GRABBING FOOD FROM THE MOUTH OR JAWS OF ANOTHER ANIMAL

USURPATION
SEIZING FOOD FROM A SUCCESSFUL PREDATOR BEFORE IT HAS A CHANCE TO GET TO IT

A TENTH OF A CHEETAH'S KILL

IN THE COMPETITIVE ANIMAL KINGDOM MANY ANIMALS RESORT TO EXTREME MEANS TO OBTAIN FOOD, FROM SCAVENGING ON LITTER TO HOARDING DEAD CARCASSES AND SNATCHING FOOD FROM THE MOUTHS OF OTHERS

Symbiosis is the intimate association of different species. Many animals collaborate with organisms from different species because such cooperation means mutual survival. Symbiotic relationships can be amicable and mutually beneficial, as is the arrangement between the cleaner fish and its host, or they can be more sinister, as is the enslavement of some ants by their fellows.

Ant slavery

A small number of ant species are known to pillage, plunder and enslave other ants. Found in the northern temperate zone, there are four genera known to be slave-makers. Their victims tend to be eggs or larvae snatched from defending workers trying to save their colony. Most of the spoils are eaten, but those that are not are given work that would normally have been done by workers of the invading species. The enslaved ants' workload increases all the time, and in some cases, the slave-owners become wholly dependent on their slaves to the extent that they cannot even feed themselves. Ant slavery can lead to changes in the social structures of colonies— workers from colonies may disappear altogether as slaves are brought in. It has been observed that some ants, when reduced to slavery, can kill their own queen causing the demise of the colony.

Cleaner fish

Certain animals groom or clean others, helping to remove parasites. These lifestyles are mutually beneficial; hosts benefit by having parasites removed, while groomers get a ready source of food. Over 40 species of fish are known to be cleaners, as well as several crab and shrimp species. A wrasse is a small brown fish which cleans a number of other species, including the opaleye, blacksmith, black sea bass and sunfish. When they are being cleaned, they adopt a motionless position, sometimes remaining perfectly still upside down, as the wrasse cleans. The cleaner is granted immunity from attack, even when it cleans inside the mouth of large predatory fish.

SYMBIOSIS

CLEANER FISH ARE IMMUNE

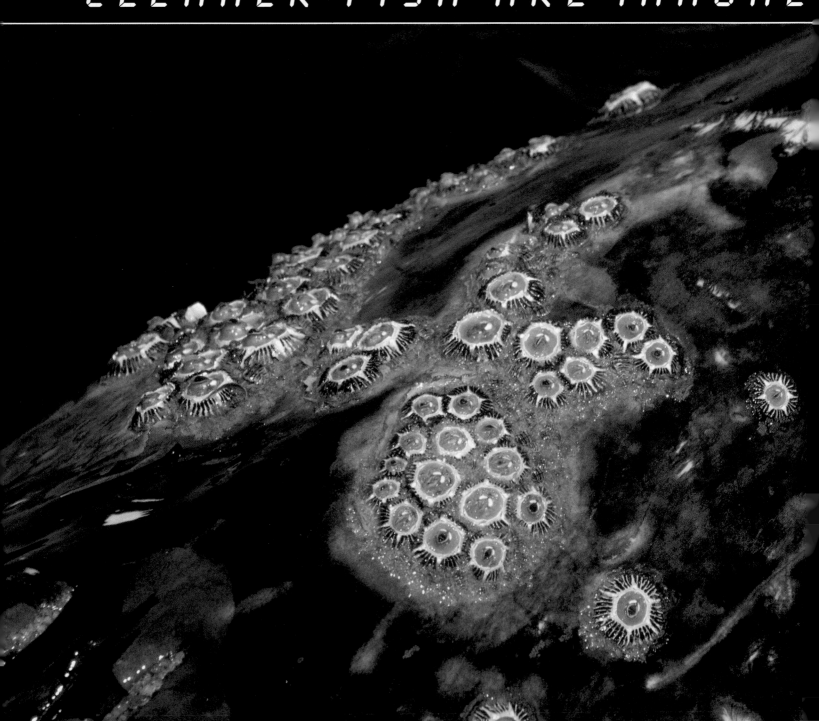

Marine fraudsters

Some non-cleaner fish have exploited the immunity that cleaners seem to enjoy. For example, several cleaner fish have elaborate dances and display sequences which they use to advertise their services. One such cleaner, the Labriodes, moves its posterior up and down as a signal to a passing fish that might need cleaning. The blenny fish has learnt to imitate the size, shape and colour of this fish, and has even copied its dancing techniques in its efforts to attract a fish who wishes to be cleaned. But the blenny is really a fraud: a fin-eater, its true motive is to capture and kill the fish.

SAFE HAVENS

WHILE SOME CREATURES HAVE CAMOUFLAGE OR OTHER STRATEGIES TO INCREASE THEIR CHANCES OF SURVIVAL, OTHERS RELY ON THE PROTECTION OF FELLOW CREATURES. THERE ARE MANY EXAMPLES OF PROTECTIVE ASSOCIATIONS, ESPECIALLY IN THE SEA. SEA-URCHINS PROVIDE IDEAL SHELTERING ENVIRONMENTS FOR SOME CREATURES. THE URCHINS HAVE LONG, DELICATE BUT NEEDLE-SHARP SPINES WHICH ARE POISON-TIPPED. THIS MAKES THEM VERY DIFFICULT TO APPROACH, A USEFUL FEATURE WHICH HAS LED SHRIMP FISH AND CLING FISH TO SEEK PROTECTION THERE. AS THEY ARE LONG AND THIN THEY ARE ABLE TO FLOAT HEAD FIRST BETWEEN THE SPINES OF THE URCHINS, THUS AVOIDING THE UNWELCOME ADVANCES OF PREDATORS.

other large fish, sharks, whales and turtles. Several remoras can be found on a single host. The suction-disc is under the direct control of the remora, so it can easily break free of its host. Remoras often hitch a ride to the host's feeding ground, and then break free to share in a meal to which they have conveniently been transported. Humans have utilized remoras' special skills by tying a fishing line around a live remora's tail to catch turtles and other marine life. Remoras do have some beneficial uses as they often take part in grooming, thereby ridding their host of unwanted parasites.

Close companions

Symbiosis between birds and mammals is one of the most familiar and enduring symbols of species interdependence, and no bird highlights this better than the oxpecker. The two species, the red-billed and the yellow-billed oxpecker, live on the bodies of large mammals in the African savanna. These mammals include rhinos, hippos, giraffes, cattle and antelope. The birds grip tightly with strong claws to the hides of their hosts, eating parasites such as ticks and flies. The bird-mammal symbiosis works well most of the time, but the working relationship between the two does occasionally break down—the mammals can get irritated by the persistent pecking of the birds, while the oxpeckers have been known to worry at skin wounds and peck the flesh of their hosts. On occasion, the oxpeckers roost overnight on their host in order to avoid the trouble of finding a new mammal to peck in the morning.

FROM HOSTS' ATTACK

WHETHER HITCHING A RIDE ON THE BACK OF A WHALE OR CLEANING EDIBLE PARASITES FROM THE HIDE OF A HIPPO OR RHINO, CREATURES THAT DEVELOP SYMBIOTIC RELATIONSHIPS DEPEND ON ONE ANOTHER FOR SURVIVAL

Marine hitchhikers

Several animals use others as a form of transportation. Hitching a lift on another creature is often a useful way of expanding the territory a species can occupy. Hitchhikers have also been known to rely on the movements of hosts to generate water currents from which food can be gleaned. Barnacles are well known for hitchhiking. They usually attach to

non-living hard surfaces, such as driftwood, but they are also known to attach to animals such as whales. One species, which has transverse ridges in the valves of its shell, actually grows into the host's upper skin, literally screwing itself to the whale, resulting in visible scars on the host animal. Others choose large eels, ships' hulls, turtles, manatees, lobsters, sunfish, sea-snakes and even the

teeth of sperm whales as their hosts. Barnacles are highly-adapted to the hitchhiking life, possessing specialized funnels to gather in water from which they extract food.

Suction powered

The remora genus is perhaps the best known of hitchhiking fish. It has a powerful suction disc at the top of its head which it attaches to

DATA-BURST

WHAT ARE THE BENEFITS OF SYMBIOTIC RELATIONSHIPS?
THERE ARE MANY ADVANTAGES. FOR EXAMPLE, MIGRATING HERDS OF DIFFERING SPECIES CAN FIND SAFETY IN NUMBERS THROUGH GALLOPING TOGETHER. SYMBIOSIS CAN, ON OCCASION, PROVIDE FOOD FOR ONE PARTNER WHILST PROTECTING THE OTHER FROM HARMFUL ATTACK BY A PARASITE.

CAN SYMBIOSIS BE HARMFUL?
MINOR DAMAGE CAN BE CAUSED BY OVER-ENTHUSIASTIC CLEANERS OR BY OVER-VIGOROUS ATTACHMENT TO THE HOST. IN EXTREME CASES, PARASITES WILL BECOME DOMINANT, GROWING AND THRIVING AT THE EXPENSE OF THEIR ORIGINAL HOST.

DOES SYMBIOSIS EXIST WITHIN SPECIES?
ALTHOUGH NOT STRICTLY SYMBIOTIC, ALTRUISTIC BEHAVIOUR HAPPENS ALL THE TIME BOTH BETWEEN AND WITHIN

SPECIES—FROM CARING PARENT-CHILD RELATIONSHIPS TO LOOK-OUTS, PATROLS AND GROUP HUNTING EXPEDITIONS.

DOES SYMBIOSIS EXIST BETWEEN PLANTS AND ANIMALS?
YES. MANY PLANTS DEPEND UPON INSECTS AND SMALL MAMMALS TO POLLINATE THEM, IN RETURN FOR WHICH THEY HAVE ACCESS TO NOURISHING NECTAR.

DOES INTERDEPENDENCE EXIST BETWEEN HUMANS AND ANIMALS?
YES. ONE MODERN EXAMPLE IS THE GUIDE DOG LEADING THE BLIND. HOWEVER, MANY OTHER HUMAN-ANIMAL RELATIONSHIPS BORDER ON THE VERGE OF EXPLOITATION.

WHAT IS A SYMBIONT?
A CREATURE THAT FORMS AN INTERACTIVE RELATIONSHIP WITH AN INDIVIDUAL FROM ANOTHER SPECIES TO THEIR MUTUAL BENEFIT.

LEFT: BARNACLES FIRMLY ATTACHED TO THE SKIN OF A LARGE GREY WHALE • RIGHT: A CLEANER SHRIMP CLEANS THE ARM OF A BLUE STARFISH

Almost all animals communicate, though their reasons for doing so vary enormously. They may be establishing and maintaining hierarchies within a group, expressing feelings of hunger or guiding each other to food or nesting places. Communication can take many forms, such as visual displays, sound production or the release of chemicals. Sound signals can be used when animals are out of sight of each other to warn of an approaching danger. The messages conveyed by facial signals vary widely between species: a chimpanzee displays insecurity and fear when it bares its teeth whereas a tiger is issuing a threat.

Sounds of the deep
Whales, porpoises and dolphins belong to the order of mammals called Cetacea. All have complex vocal communication systems. Dolphins live in groups, or 'schools', which may include up to

300 animals. Members of the group communicate with each other by means of pulsing high and low-pitched sounds. The low-pitched sounds include barks, whistles, screams and moans, and are audible to humans. The high-pitched sounds, which use sound wave frequencies that are inaudible to humans, are used for navigation. Whales and porpoises use a similar communication system to dolphins. The finback whales produce a long, drawn out sound which is thought to enable them to communicate with each other over distances of 850 km.

Sign language
The use of language is one of the main differences between humans and animals. Some animals are

THE DANCE OF THE HONEYBEE

WHEN A BEE DISCOVERS A SOURCE OF FOOD IT RETURNS AT ONCE TO THE HIVE WHERE IT COMMUNICATES THE NEWS TO ITS FELLOW BEES BY DANCING. INFORMATION ABOUT THE LOCATION AND QUALITY OF THE FOOD IS EXPRESSED BY THE LENGTH AND EXCITEMENT OF THE DANCE. THE DANCE'S RHYTHM DENOTES THE LOCATION OF THE FOOD. IF THE FOOD IS NEAR THE HIVE, THE BEE PERFORMS A 'ROUND' DANCE; IF IT IS MORE THAN 80 M AWAY, IT PERFORMS A 'TAIL-WAGGING' DANCE. IF THE FOOD SOURCE IS PARTICULARLY GOOD, THE BEE WILL MAKE EXCITED SOUNDS. THE DIRECTION OF THE FOOD SOURCE IS MEASURED IN RELATION TO THE SUN. IF THE SUN IS OBSCURED BY CLOUDS, THE BEE MEASURES THE AMOUNT OF LIGHT IN THE SKY AND ADJUSTS THE DANCE ACCORDINGLY.

COMMUNICATION

CHIMPANZEE UNDERSTANDS

advanced enough to be able to use one sound to warn of the approach of a snake, another for a lion. But no animal can use language as humans can: to communicate an abstract concept. Attempts to teach human languages to animals, particularly to chimpanzees, have met with little success as chimps cannot form the range of sounds necessary. However, recent attempts to teach sign language to these most intelligent of mammals have proved more successful: one female chimp called Washoe has learned to use some 150 signs and understand over 300. But does the chimp know the meaning of the words or is it just responding to a stimulus for which it has previously been rewarded? There is evidence which suggests that chimpanzees are capable of communicating with each other by using concepts, not just noises. The trainer of a chimp

knifefish produce electricity at levels higher than average creatures. The knifefish, so-called because it is shaped like a knife-blade, uses low voltages to locate its prey—a useful talent in the murky waters of the Amazon. From recent research it appears that knifefish talk to each other by changing frequencies, stopping and starting electricity production very rapidly—rather like morse code. Similarly, electric eels can communicate their presence to other eels through electric pulses. Males make the loudest and most frequent emissions, while females respond with shorter bursts. This allows a male to correctly identify the female.

Birdsong anthems
About half of the world's birds are able to use their vocal cords to produce the sounds by which they

DATA BURST

WHAT IS BIOLUMINESCENCE?
THE PHENOMENON WHEREBY ORGANISMS EMIT LIGHT. SOME CREATURES, SUCH AS FIREFLIES, CUTTLEFISH, CRAYFISH AND GLOW-WORMS EMIT AND RESPOND TO THIS LIGHT, USING IT TO COMMUNICATE.

WHICH ANIMALS USE VISUAL DISPLAYS WHEN APPROACHED BY PREDATORS?
A GREAT MANY INSECTS, PARTICULARLY MOTHS, MANTIDS AND GRASSHOPPERS USE THEIR WINGS TO PRESENT STARTLING DISPLAYS WHENEVER THEY ARE APPROACHED BY POTENTIAL PREDATORS.

HOW DO BIRDS COMMUNICATE WITH EACH OTHER IN THE FOREST?
THEY USE HIGH-FREQUENCY SOUND BECAUSE IT PENETRATES OR CIRCUMVENTS OBSTACLES BETTER THAN LOW-FREQUENCY SOUND.

HOW DO ANIMALS COMMUNICATE THEIR TERRITORIAL CLAIMS?
MANY ANIMALS USE SCENT TO COMMUNICATE, ESPECIALLY WHEN MARKING OUT THEIR TERRITORY. CATS RUB THE LEGS OF THEIR OWNERS TO LEAVE A TRACE OF THEIR PERFUME WHILE RHINOS STAMP IN THEIR OWN FAECES TO SPREAD THEIR SMELL WITH EACH STEP THEY TAKE.

not only varies in pitch, volume and structure, but can change from day to day.

Squid semaphore
Some animals communicate their mood by visual means. In the deepest and darkest parts of the ocean live squid whose tentacles glow like strings of fairy lights. The eyes belonging to squid and

Language of wolves
Animals that live in complex societies will often develop sophisticated sign-systems to help them survive in harmony. Wolves, amongst the most socially complex of carnivorous mammals, have several means of conveying messages. Amongst the strongest and fiercest of dogs, they have a special status language which can determine rank without the need for pack infighting. This involves a series of facial expressions, tail positions and other gestures that convey which is the top dog. Wolves also use effective communication prior to hunting. Before setting out on the hunt, wolf packs may engage in a series of gestures, including circling around each other, rubbing noses, wagging tails and vocalising. These movements and howls may be the wolves' way of deciding where to hunt, what strategy to use or which route to take.

300 DIFFERENT SIGNS

ANIMALS COMMUNICATE WITH EACH OTHER, NOT ONLY THROUGH VISUAL DISPLAY AND BY MAKING A VARIETY OF SOUNDS, BUT ALSO BY SENDING ELECTRICAL SIGNALS, RELEASING CHEMICALS, EVEN CHANGING THEIR SHAPE

called Lucy received the following request from her: "Roger tickle Lucy". The trainer replied: "No, Lucy tickle Roger". After a pause, the chimp tickled the trainer.

Electric code
All creatures generate electricity, but usually at very low levels. Species such as electric eels and

communicate. The main reasons for sound production are to enable a male bird to attract a mate, to establish and maintain its territory and to warn of danger. Each species has its own calls, ensuring that within a large group of birds only members of its own species will be contacted. The nightingale's song is one of the most complex: it

octopus are as highly developed as some mammals and they use them to observe each other in the murky depths. These molluscs can change colour at will. When angry or sexually aroused, they will pulse with vivid bands of colour. Some octopuses can alter the texture of their skin, raising small bumps or sprouting finger-like projections.

Defensive postures
Mammals that feel threatened by predators can make themselves seem larger, louder and more frightening. A wolf's fur will rise all the way along its arched back, while an elephant will trumpet, flapping its ears away from its body, like giant flags.

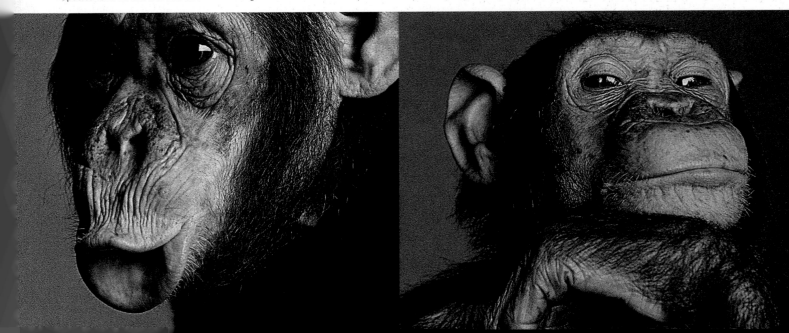

Animals gather together in swarms for a specific reason: swarming is a migration strategy which ensures that, whatever the losses along the way, a large proportion of a species will reach its destination. It also constitutes a devastating hunting strategy: with all the members of a swarm aiming at a common goal, their force can be irresistible. This phenomenal force can not only cause great damage to crops, it can even endanger human life.

Plagues of locusts
Locusts are a type of grasshopper, common in hot countries, which migrate in huge numbers and can devastate crops. The most damaging species of all is the desert locust which is found in Africa. Vast numbers of these creatures can gather and fly in huge swarming towers up to 1,500 m in height. Massive swarms or 'plagues' of this proportion are almost impossible to stop. Spraying the swarm from the air with powerful insecticides can reduce numbers but even this measure cannot prevent the extraordinary damage locusts inflict on crops. Not all locusts swarm; in fact, scientists believe that locusts are by nature solitary creatures which spend their lives moving about slowly and munching vegetation in small amounts, just like grasshoppers. It is only when there is a shortage of food or when their habitat becomes overcrowded that locusts cluster together in huge numbers. The insects become nervous and more active and enter

what is known as their 'gregarious phase'. When their metabolic rate reaches fever-pitch, the locusts rise up in a massive swarm to seek food sources elsewhere.

Side-stepping army
Located in the Indian Ocean, 1,400 km north-west of Australia, Christmas Island plays host to one of the most remarkable sights in nature. At the start of the rainy season, this tiny tropical island of only 135 km² witnesses the mass migration of hundreds of millions of red crabs. After spending the dry season burrowed in the ground all over the island's rainforests, the crabs crawl in their millions across

the island to the sea. During their urgent march, they push forward through all obstructions. They are run over on roads and even march through houses that lie on their migration route. For about a week, the island is carpeted with a moving red mass. Once the crabs have reached the shore and fed, they return to the forest to mate. The females then have to make the journey once again in order to lay their eggs in the sea.

SWARMS
1.5 MILLION ANTS

Bullying bees
Most of the 20,000 species of bee are solitary insects which do not swarm. Social bees, such as the honeybee, which live in nests or hives, may swarm as part of their lifecycle or as a defence against intruders. Like all bees, social bees feed on the pollen and nectar of flowers. They produce a substance called royal jelly in their salivary glands which is fed to potential queen bees. When these new queens hatch, they fight until only one is left. The victor then attacks and drives out the old queen. It is at this point that some of the bees in the colony swarm, flying out to follow the defeated queen and set up a new colony somewhere else. Researchers in Japan have discovered that honeybees will also swarm to protect their colony from hornets. These insects can kill honeybees in a hive at a rate of 40 per minute. When a hornet is detected, bees cluster around the hive in order to defend it from attack. Swarms of up to 500 bees surround the attacker in a dense ball. This swarming creates a temperature of 47°C in the 'ball of bees'—a heat which kills the hornet but leaves bees unharmed.

Sting attack
In 1957, during a scientific experiment in Brazil, a dangerous subspecies of the African honeybee was accidentally released. Ever

since, this species of killer bee has been moving north at about 400 km per year, reaching Mexico during the 1980s and Texas and California in the 1990s. It is not just their increased swarming tendency that makes these bees so deadly, but also their aggressive instinct. When one bee stings a human, it leaves behind a scent which causes other swarm members to follow suit. In 1992, a man in Panama who swatted a single bee, was stung to death by the swarm over a five-hour period.

Armies of ants
Army or legionary ants lead a nomadic life, constantly moving in columns as much as 10 m wide through the tropical forests of Central and South America. The marching swarm can number as many as 1.5 million. Insects, spiders and lizards are all devoured by the swarm as it progresses, while at the edges of the marching column some creatures get picked off by birds. The ants never establish a permanent base—one study showed that they travel in a 36-day cycle, marching for 16 days then resting for 20 days while the queen lays her eggs. When the larvae hatch, the ants pick them up and carry them as the colony moves on once again. By working together the ants can kill their prey much more quickly than if they hunted alone.

THE EARTH'S LARGEST BIOMASS

OF ALL THE ANIMALS VISIBLE TO THE NAKED EYE, KRILL FORM THE GREATEST BIOMASS. THESE, SHRIMP-LIKE CRUSTACEANS ARE FOUND EVERYWHERE UNDERWATER FROM THE OCEAN SURFACE TO DEPTHS OF 2,000 M. THEY SWARM IN SUCH HUGE NUMBERS THAT THEY CAN EVEN BE SEEN FROM SPACE. IN THE ANTARCTIC OCEAN THERE CAN BE UP TO 20,000 KRILL PER CUBIC METRE OF WATER AND FROM JANUARY TO APRIL IN THE ATLANTIC, EACH CUBIC METRE OF WATER CAN CONTAIN AS MUCH AS 20 KG OF KRILL. THESE TINY CREATURES, WHICH THRIVE IN SEAS WITH

TEMPERATURES AS LOW AS -1.5°C, FORM THE STAPLE DIET OF SOME OF THE GIANTS OF THE SEA. THE BLUE WHALE AND FIN WHALE MIGRATE TO THE AREAS WHERE KRILL CAN BE FOUND IN LARGE QUANTITIES, AND SCOOP THE KRILL UP IN THEIR MOUTHS. IN THE COURSE OF JUST A FEW MINUTES THEY CAN STRAIN AS MUCH AS A TONNE OF KRILL OUT OF THE WATER USING THE MESH-LIKE POCKET IN THEIR HUGE MOUTHS. BIRDS AND FISH ALSO FEED ON KRILL, BUT THESE REMARKABLE CREATURES CAN EVADE THEIR MANY PREDATORS BY SWIMMING AT GREAT SPEED.

RIGHT: SALLY LIGHTFOOT CRABS SCATTER OVER BLACK ROCK · INSET: RED CRAB MIGRATION CAUSES MANY PUNCTURED TYRES ON CHRISTMAS ISLAND IN THE INDIAN OCEAN

MARCH TOGETHER

SOME ANIMALS TAKE THE PRINCIPLE OF SAFETY IN NUMBERS TO EXTREMES, GATHERING IN THEIR MILLIONS TO FORM IMMENSE SWARMS. THE COMBINED STRENGTH OF SWARMING ANIMALS CAN PRODUCE KILLER PLAGUES

MIGRATION
GREY WHALE SWIMS

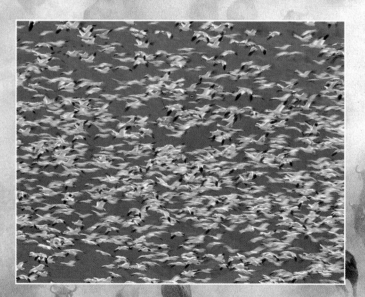

To survive, many animals must travel from one habitat to another. Migrating animals, which range from individual trekkers to herds of millions, demonstrate an amazing sense of direction which enables them to chart their route over long distances and sometimes even between continents. These arduous journeys, often through severe weather and difficult terrain, test the animal's stamina and endurance to the limit.

Butterfly marathon

Creatures many times smaller than humans undertake journeys that would make even the hardiest traveller weary. The North American monarch butterfly is one

JUMPING AGAINST THE FLOW

SALMON ARE FAMED FOR THEIR AMAZING JOURNEYS. BEGINNING LIFE IN CLEAR RIVERS, THEY MAY SPEND A NUMBER OF YEARS THERE BEFORE VENTURING OUT INTO THE WIDE OCEANS WHERE THEY CAN REMAIN FOR UP TO FIVE YEARS, MATURING AND SUSTAINING GROWTH. FINALLY, THEY ARE READY TO MAKE THE EPIC JOURNEY BACK TO THE WATERS OF THEIR BIRTH SO THEY MAY BREED. THEY HOME IN ON THEIR PARENTS' SPAWNING SITE, OFTEN TRAVELLING THOUSANDS OF KILOMETRES JUST TO GET TO THE RIGHT ESTUARY. THEY THEN HAVE TO NAVIGATE THEIR WAY UPSTREAM, SWIMMING AGAINST THE CURRENT AND PERFORMING SPECTACULAR LEAPS TO NEGOTIATE UPWARD GRADIENTS. IF THE RIVER IS LONG, THIS PHASE OF THE JOURNEY MAY BE AS MUCH AS 4,000 KM.

California to finish their journey in Mexico. This journey from the Arctic Circle to the subtropics is the longest undertaken by such a mammal. Having spent the winter months courting, mating or calving, the grey whales head north again in the spring. It is on the return journey that mothers teach their young how to navigate using coastal landmarks to pilot their way home.

Long haul flight

Flocks of birds flying south for the winter are a common sight. The distances travelled by these birds are truly astounding. Arctic terns are truly global voyagers; every autumn, they leave their summer breeding grounds in the Arctic for the Antarctic before making the long return leg of the journey back to the Arctic to breed again. This round trip, which circumnavigates the globe, is in the region of 30,000–40,000 km. The actual routes taken by the terns vary, with some favouring an Atlantic crossing via the bulge of west Africa, while others prefer to travel down the west coast of the Americas. Many other birds make epic migratory journeys. The tiny blackpoll warbler travels from North to South America in only 80 hours. The short-tailed shearwater is born on the south coast of Australia, yet travels as far as the Arctic Ocean to mature. It will then travel back to Australia to breed. The whole cycle spans some 35,000 km and can last for years.

Natural compasses

Some migrating animals have a magnetic sense rather like an in-built compass, which helps them to find their way during migration. A barnacle goose, for example, can orientate itself by determining the angles made by the Earth's lines of magnetic force as its body travels through them. Most migrating birds use this sixth sense of magnetism, and so they find it hard to navigate in times of high sunspot activity when many magnetic storms rage across the globe.

Starling experiment

Starlings migrate from the eastern Baltic in a south-westerly direction, resting briefly in the Netherlands to winter in England. Most migrate in groups with older experienced birds guiding the young. In one study to test the navigating skills of starlings, adults were removed from the group. The flocks were disorientated and ended their journeys in France and Spain.

10,000 KM A YEAR

ANIMALS CAN TRAVEL IMMENSE DISTANCES ACROSS CONTINENTS WHEN THEY NEED TO FIND NEW HABITATS FOR FEEDING OR BREEDING. THESE INCREDIBLE JOURNEYS TEST THE STAMINA OF AN ANIMAL TO THE VERY LIMIT

such creature. They are dispersed throughout North America east of the Rocky Mountains. As the parent butterflies die away, a new generation in eastern North America travels thousands of kilometres south to California and New Mexico towards the end of summer. Being highly sensitive to frost, the monarch butterflies have been known to make round trips of 8,000 km to avoid the cold north.

They embark in groups of only a few individuals, but these merge into larger and larger groups as they continue to fly southwards. They travel during the day, preferring to rest in trees during the night. Having endured the epic journey, they rest in a state of slumbering stillness for up to five months in their overwintering sites. This makes them easy targets for a whole range of predators. Those

that survive mate as spring approaches. They then begin their long journey back to the north, but this time they are alone.

Stampeding bison

Seasonal climatic changes can trigger a mass migration as mammals seek suitable weather for feeding and breeding. One of the great migratory journeys in the past used to be the annual trek of the North American bison. In the springtime, tens of millions of these creatures headed off in search of new pastures. The bison gave birth as they migrated, the young becoming part of the moving herd only a few hours after being born. However, over-hunting has terminated this once-epic journey. The North American caribou is one large herbivore that still makes an annual migration. Winters are spent in the forests of Alberta, Saskatchewan and Manitoba in Canada, while in the spring the animals migrate northwards.

Whale journey

Arctic grey whales are incredible aquatic migrators. They travel up to 10,000 km south on an annual basis to breed. Hugging the western coast of America, they travel past British Columbia, Washington and

DATA-BURST

WHY DO ANIMALS MIGRATE?
THEY MAY BE SEEKING SUITABLE BREEDING GROUNDS OR GRAZING TERRITORY, OR THEY MAY BE ESCAPING HARSH SEASONAL CLIMATES FOR MORE MODERATE HABITATS.

HOW MUCH ENERGY DOES AN ANIMAL USE IN ITS EPIC JOURNEY?
IT DEPENDS ON THE MEANS OF MIGRATION. ESTIMATES BASED ON RESEARCH SUGGEST THAT 1 G OF FAT STORED AS FUEL CAN TAKE A 100 G CREATURE 15 KM BY LAND, 54 KM BY AIR AND 154 KM BY SEA.

HOW DO BIRDS FIND THEIR WAY ON THEIR MIGRATIONS?
EVIDENCE SUGGESTS THAT BIRDS DO NOT USE VISUAL LANDMARKS TO GUIDE THEM ON LONG JOURNEYS. INSTEAD THEY USE THEIR BODY CLOCKS WHICH ARE INFLUENCED BY LIGHT AND DARKNESS. THE RELATIVE POSITION OF THE SUN IN THE SKY ALSO PLAYS AN IMPORTANT ROLE IN ESTABLISHING

FLIGHT DIRECTION. AS WELL AS USING SOLAR NAVIGATION, MOST BIRDS CAN ALSO NAVIGATE WHEN THE SUN IS HIDDEN BEHIND CLOUDS BY ORIENTATING FLIGHT RELATIVE TO THE EARTH'S MAGNETIC FIELD.

HOW DO ANIMALS SUCCEED IN UNDERTAKING SUCH STRENUOUS LONG DISTANCE JOURNEYS?
BIRDS ARE AIDED ON THEIR WORLDWIDE FLIGHTS BY THERMAL WINDS WHILE FISH CAN MAKE USE OF OCEAN OR TIDAL CURRENTS. MANY ANIMALS STORE UP TO 50% OF THEIR BODY WEIGHT AS FAT TO PROVIDE THEM WITH ENERGY FOR THE JOURNEY.

WHICH ANIMALS MIGRATE TO BREED?
MANY SPECIES. SEA TURTLES TRAVEL A GREAT DISTANCE TO REACH THE SANDY BREEDING BEACHES FREE FROM PREDATORS ON ISOLATED ISLANDS. AMPHIBIANS, SUCH AS FROGS AND TOADS, RETURN TO THEIR OWN SPAWNING GROUNDS TO BREED.

LEFT: MIGRATING BUFFALO CREATE A CLOUD OF DUST AS THEY GALLOP ACROSS OPEN LAND · INSET: MIGRATING GEESE IN FLIGHT

Animals are introduced to new areas by a variety of means—some deliberate, others accidental. Pest control is often the motivation for deliberate introductions, but it is a strategy that can backfire. Sometimes the new species will run riot amongst native wildlife, sometimes it will not survive at all. Only very adaptable animals will flourish in a new environment and some adapt so well that they evolve with great rapidity and actually create a new species.

Rabbits down under

When a farmer brought 24 European rabbits to Australia in 1859, he could have had no idea of the devastation these small mammals would bring to the continent. Unchecked by the predators and parasites that keep their numbers under control in their native European habitat, the

was introduced to Australia. But the use of this disease, which causes high fever, skin tumours and kills rabbits within 2–4 weeks, has been fought by animal rights campaigners who believe it to be an inhumane method of control.

The cane toad

The lesson of the European rabbit did not protect Australia from a second species introduction nightmare. In 1935 the cane toad was brought to Australia from

Tenacious termites

Termites are not endemic to the UK, but have been accidentally introduced from mainland Europe and other parts of the world on ships. There are over 2,000 species of termite worldwide. Only 10% of these species are destructive, but their reputation as a serious pest comes from the fact that they are swarming insects. Because of this, they can quickly infest wooden structures, nesting in and eating their way through them, making

native animals for food and can cause considerable damage to grain crops.

Battle of the squirrels

If an introduced species fills the same ecological niche as a native species, the new arrival can often take over completely. In the UK, the red squirrel is suffering this very fate. Its rival is the American grey squirrel which was introduced to the UK by landowners during the 19th century. The grey squirrel

INTRODUCTIONS
300 MILLION RABBITS

newly arrived rabbits bred at a lightning pace. They soon began to overrun the country, burrowing into the ground, eating crops and destroying the bark of young trees. Bred from the first 24 individuals, there are currently around 300 million rabbits in Australia. Their effect on endemic plant and animal life has been disastrous. In Western Australia alone, 50 species of plant have become extinct since the arrival of rabbits, and the rare platypus has fallen dramatically in number, unable to compete with the rival rabbit species which burrows into its riverbank habitat. Even though other introductions, such as pigs and sheep, have contributed to the damage to native species, it is rabbits that have taken most of the blame. In 1950, in a desperate effort to reduce the numbers of rabbits, the deadly rabbit disease myxomatosis

Central America to control pests such as cane beetles in the sugar plantations of Queensland. But these huge poisonous toads fed not only on beetles, but also on native reptiles and amphibians. Australian predators, which might have kept cane toad numbers down, have no immunity to the toad's poison—unlike the toad's natural predators in Central America. The toxin released from glands on the toad's shoulders also makes waterways poisonous for native Australian animals. Found mostly on the east coast of Queensland, the cane toad is gradually making its way south into New South Wales and east into the Northern Territory. Here, the wetlands of Kakadu National Park—one of Australia's most spectacular wildlife habitats—will provide ideal conditions for this introduced amphibian to thrive.

avoidance measures vital. They can survive long periods of dryness, which equips them to endure long sea voyages, transported in shipping crates, wooden parts of boats, and wooden cargo such as furniture. In southern England in 1998, one woman found that the wood of her conservatory was being eaten by termites which had reached the UK in this way. These insects cannot survive in northern parts of the UK because temperatures are too cold, but with global climates becoming warmer, scientists fear that northern latitudes will now be affected by termite infestation. This will make anti-termite measures, such as fumigation and insecticide treatments for wood products, increasingly necessary in the future, even in cooler areas.

Escaping the hunter

The fur of the nutria, a large South American rodent, has long been highly valued. Fur-hunting during the 19th century nearly eradicated the species in its native habitat but its introduction for fur breeding in Europe had disastrous consequences. Captive animals both escaped and were deliberately released into the wild where they soon became a pest. Today, these huge web-footed rodents, which can grow up to 1 m in length, are found from the Baltic Sea to the Alps. They live along pond and river banks where their burrowing habits damage the soil and interfere with drainage systems in canal banks—particularly in Holland. Nutria also compete with

is larger, more aggressive and more adaptable than the red, and has literally driven its smaller relative out of its native habitat. Now the red squirrel is one of Britain's most endangered species, with only about 160,000 surviving in isolated colonies. Other factors, such as the clearance of native forests in Scotland and their replacement with sitka spruce plantations, have also contributed to the red squirrel's decline, but the role of the grey squirrel has been devastating. The problem is so great that the government's Joint Nature Conservation Committee has suggested that in order to boost numbers of native red squirrels, their introduced grey rivals should be humanely poisoned or shot. Meanwhile, red squirrels are being reintroduced to the areas where they have died out over the last 50 years.

LEFT: THE CANE TOAD WAS IMPORTED TO AUSTRALIA TO CONTROL SUGAR CANE PESTS · RIGHT: THE RABBIT WAS INTRODUCED TO AUSTRALIA IN THE 19TH CENTURY

DATA-BURST

WHAT ARE THE DANGERS OF SPECIES INTRODUCTION?
APART FROM THE DISRUPTION TO NATIVE ECOSYSTEMS, INTRODUCED SPECIES CAN BECOME INBRED DUE TO THEIR ISOLATION. THEY CAN ALSO SOMETIMES INTERBREED WITH LOCAL SPECIES TO CREATE HYBRIDS, THREATENING THE SURVIVAL OF BOTH ORIGINAL SPECIES.

HOW SOON COULD GREY SQUIRRELS REPLACE RED SQUIRRELS IN THE UK?
UNLESS SWIFT ACTION IS TAKEN, THE RED SQUIRREL WILL BE EXTINCT IN BRITAIN WITHIN A DECADE.

WHAT IS THE MOST SUCCESSFUL SPECIES INTRODUCTION?
THE INTRODUCTION OF STARLINGS TO BOTH AUSTRALIA AND THE USA. IN 1890, JUST OVER 100 STARLINGS WERE SET FREE IN NEW YORK. THE USA NOW SUPPORTS SOME 150 MILLION BIRDS, ONE-THIRD OF THE WORLD'S STARLING POPULATION.

WHICH ANIMALS ARE MOST AT RISK FROM INTRODUCED SPECIES?
ISLAND DWELLERS ARE ESPECIALLY AT RISK IN THE MODERN WORLD AS THEIR ECOSYSTEMS ARE MORE UNIQUE AND ARE THEREFORE MORE VULNERABLE TO INTRODUCTIONS FROM THE WORLD OUTSIDE. HALF THE WORLD'S ENDANGERED SPECIES OF BIRDS, FOR EXAMPLE, COME FROM ISLANDS.

WHICH IMMIGRANTS SPECIES ARE THE MOST DESTRUCTIVE ?
WHEN RATS BECOME ENDEMIC THEY ARE IMPOSSIBLE TO WIPE OUT. OFTEN THE ONLY SOLUTION IS TO REMOVE NATIVE CREATURES TO SAFER AREAS.

CAPTURE AND CONSERVATION

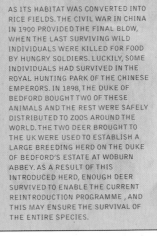

SPECIES INTRODUCTION DOES NOT ALWAYS HAVE DAMAGING CONSEQUENCES – IT CAN IN FACT COMPRISE A VITAL PART OF WILDLIFE CONSERVATION. PÈRE DAVID'S DEER BECAME EXTINCT IN THE WILD IN 1900, BUT IS NOW BEING REINTRODUCED TO ITS NATIVE HABITAT IN THE SWAMPY PLAINS OF NORTHERN CHINA. THE DECLINE OF THIS SPECIES OF DEER BEGAN SEVERAL HUNDRED YEARS AGO AS ITS HABITAT WAS CONVERTED INTO RICE FIELDS. THE CIVIL WAR IN CHINA IN 1900 PROVIDED THE FINAL BLOW, WHEN THE LAST SURVIVING WILD INDIVIDUALS WERE KILLED FOR FOOD BY HUNGRY SOLDIERS. LUCKILY, SOME INDIVIDUALS HAD SURVIVED IN THE ROYAL HUNTING PARK OF THE CHINESE EMPERORS. IN 1898, THE DUKE OF BEDFORD BOUGHT TWO OF THESE ANIMALS AND THE REST WERE SAFELY DISTRIBUTED TO ZOOS AROUND THE WORLD. THE TWO DEER BROUGHT TO THE UK WERE USED TO ESTABLISH A LARGE BREEDING HERD ON THE DUKE OF BEDFORD'S ESTATE AT WOBURN ABBEY. AS A RESULT OF THIS INTRODUCED HERD, ENOUGH DEER SURVIVED TO ENABLE THE CURRENT REINTRODUCTION PROGRAMME , AND THIS MAY ENSURE THE SURVIVAL OF THE ENTIRE SPECIES.

BRED FROM 24 INDIVIDUALS

WHEN HUMANS RELEASE AN ANIMAL SPECIES TO A NEW ENVIRONMENT, THE RESULTS ARE OFTEN UNPREDICTABLE. TRANSFERRED SPECIES CAN SPREAD LIKE WILDFIRE WITH DEVASTATING CONSEQUENCES FOR NATIVE WILDLIFE

FROM EVOLUTION TO EXTINCTION

LIFE AND DEATH

THE CYCLE OF LIFE CONTINUES

In 1859, Charles Darwin proposed a convincing case for the evolution of species. This revolutionary theory was based on his study of finches made while he was visiting the Galapagos Islands in South America. He found that similar species of finch existed in slightly different forms between neighbouring islands. He also studied fossil records and noted how species could alter and change over long periods of time. These observations led him to theorize that species gradually but continuously adapt to suit the environment around them. Darwin speculated that the reason animals produce more offspring than can be expected to survive is that only those with the correct adaptations will be successful—the survival of the fittest.

Spring of life

Planet Earth was formed about 4.5 billion years ago. Just how life was created out of the inanimate Earth is still a mystery. Some scientists believe that biopoiesis (literally, 'the making of life') provides the answer. According to this theory, molecules in the sea and in mud pools on the newly formed Earth used energy from the sun and water to join together in complex groups. After many millions of years, these molecule groups were able to reproduce by splitting apart. They eventually evolved into blue-green algae—the first form of life. Some scientists believe that this process goes on even today, with molecules coming together to create new forms of

life. Others argue that conditions on Earth are no longer suitable for this process to occur. Some biologists have recently suggested that life on Earth originated in hydrothermal vents on the ocean floor. These pockets of hot water are full of nutrients and minerals and are home to countless bacteria. These bacteria can live without oxygen, relying instead on chemicals to create the substance of life. This particular type of chemosynthesis is the most primitive to be found on Earth and may hold the key to the origin of life itself.

Fossil evidence

The most compelling evidence for the course of evolution from Earth's beginnings to the present day is provided by fossil records.

EVOLUTION

FIRST LIFEFORMS 3.5

The earliest life on Earth, blue-green algae, has been found in fossilized form in rocks dating back 3.5 billion years. The first known animals were small worm-like creatures which appeared 700 million years ago. Animals with skeletons did not evolve until about 570 million years ago and

the first animals with backbones appeared 170 million years later—about 400 million years ago. Mammals, the most evolved of all the species, only began to roam the Earth 200 million years ago.

Explosive spurt

An amazing evolutionary explosion took place 590 million years ago. Known as the Cambrian explosion, fossils of this period testify to a staggering burst of new lifeforms—some of them bizarre in appearance. The richest evidence for this evolutionary spurt is found at a site called the Burgess Shale on the flank of Mount Stephen, British Columbia, Canada. This layer of rock, 60 m long and 2.5 m thick, has yielded fossils of over 120 animal species from the time of the Cambrian explosion. At least 20 of the fossils are of creatures so weird in form that biologists have been unable to place them in any known category. They include an animal called Amiskwia, a worm-like swimmer with lateral fins, a paddle at one end and a bulbous head complete with tentacles. Other strange-looking creatures found in this rock include Hallucigenia, a caterpillar-like creature with outlandish shoulder spines, and Dinomischus, a stalked

animal which looks like an unopened daisy. This creature had a set of petal-like tentacles around its head which captured particles floating in the surrounding water.

Living dinosaurs

The first crocodilians, known as protosuchia, emerged along with mammals about 200 million years ago and lived at the same time as dinosaurs. Since then, crocodile design has altered little. Modern crocodiles display features that are the same in fossil dinosaurs—namely, certain openings in their skull and the arrangement of their teeth. One of the reasons why crocodiles have evolved so little is that their habitat of tropical swamps and marshes has remained fundamentally the same. This is not to say that crocodiles have been immune to the processes of evolution. At the beginning of their history, these reptiles evolved considerably from short-snouted animals to the long-snouted forms of today. This change took place over the course of several million years, but once crocodiles became perfectly suited to their environment, there was no need for further change. Crocodile design remains a success: those in the Nile can live up to 100 years.

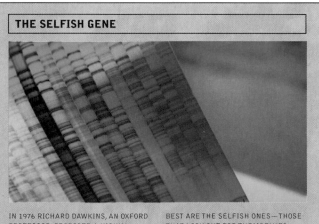

RIGHT: OVERHEAD VIEW OF CROCODILES CROWDED TOGETHER IN A POOL

BILLION YEARS AGO

EVOLUTION EXPLAINS THE AMAZING DIVERSITY OF LIFE ON EARTH IN TERMS OF THE ADAPTATION OF SPECIES TO THEIR ENVIRONMENT—A SLOW PROCESS OF NATURAL SELECTION THAT TAKES PLACE OVER BILLIONS OF YEARS

MATING RITUALS
DIVORCE RATE OF

The many different types of courtship ritual found in the animal kingdom serve several vital purposes. First of all, they ensure that an animal is mating with the correct species, thus avoiding the danger of hybridization. Secondly, they help animals either to choose a lifelong partner or to select the best possible mate for a single season. For some animals, such as birds of paradise, a lengthy courtship is followed by a mating process which lasts only a few seconds. For others, mating takes the form of an elaborate ritual to confirm that each partner knows that the other has only mating in mind—and is not out for a quick meal or to grab territory.

FAITHFUL MATES

ALBATROSSES PAIR FOR LIFE AND ARE COMPLETELY FAITHFUL TO THEIR CHOSEN MATE, BUT HUMANS ARE INADVERTENTLY BREAKING UP THESE STRONG BONDS. WHEN THE FEMALE HAS LAID HER EGGS, SHE LEAVES THE MALE TO GUARD THEM WHILE SHE GOES OFF TO FISH AT SEA. TRAGICALLY, IN RECENT YEARS, JAPANESE TUNA

TRAWLERS HAVE CAUGHT MANY FEMALES DURING THEIR FISHING EXPEDITIONS. THE MALES WAIT IN VAIN ON THE NEST FOR THEIR MATE TO RETURN. THEIR WIDOWER STATUS MAKES OTHER MALES AGGRESSIVE TOWARDS THEM AND THE SCARCITY OF FEMALES MEANS THAT MALES MUST COMPETE VIOLENTLY FOR A MATE.

rate' is less than 1%. These swan marriages strengthen over several years. Swans choose their partner at about two and a half years old and usually spend their first few years feeding together, spending time in each other's company and looking for a suitable home in which to breed. Only then do the swans mate for the first time. Taking it slowly makes sense for swans: these long-lived birds must ensure that conditions are absolutely right before they make the commitment of producing and protecting offspring.

Low-down cheat
The male pied flycatcher is a less than devoted partner. Once he has gained himself a territory and attracted a female, he mates with her and waits for her to lay her eggs. At this point about 15% of male pied flycatchers desert their partner, acquire another territory and attempt to woo a second mate. About three-fifths of these attempts are successful and the male mates again and waits for his new partner to lay her eggs. Once she has done so, the male abandons her once again, returning to his first mate to help her bring up her young. For the second female, all may not be lost. She sometimes succeeds in inducing a new male to pair up with her and unwittingly look after his predecessor's young.

Man-eaters
For male spiders of the Araneae family, mating rituals are extremely perilous. The female spiders are much larger than the males, and regard their mate as a convenient meal. So the males perform rituals to avoid being eaten. Some waggle their legs at the female from a safe distance and approach only when it is clear she has mating, not eating, in mind. Others vibrate the female's web from a corner before entering in a way that makes it obvious they are mates, not prey. Some even tie the female down with silken threads or hold her mouth closed during mating, while others distract her attention with the gift of a fly.

Keeping a harem
Lions are just one of the species for which the right to mate belongs to only one male within a group. The dominant male maintains control of a 'harem' of females, and retains the sole right to mate with them. If a rival male wishes to challenge the ruling male, he must fight him to the death to gain the supreme position.

SWAN LESS THAN 1%

BIRDS OF PARADISE DANCE, CRICKETS SING, FIREFLIES FLASH, BOWERBIRDS HOARD AND STAGS FIGHT. FANTASTIC FEATS, COLOURFUL DISPLAYS AND BIZARRE DEEDS ARE UNDERTAKEN WITH ONLY ONE AIM: TO ATTRACT A MATE

Birds of paradise
The most elaborate and colourful mating rituals are performed by the 40-odd species of bird of paradise which inhabit the island of Papua New Guinea in the Pacific Ocean. Many birds of paradise dance at night and so their rituals remain a secret. Females have to choose their mate from a selection of males which perform in groups 30 m up in the rainforest trees. The ritual proceeds in several stages. First, the males dance flamboyantly, revealing their attractive plumes. Some puff up their neck feathers like umbrellas; others, such as the long-tailed Astrapia bird—make short flights, trailing out their long streamers as they fly. After showing off, the males bow their heads to the female and the female then lands on the perch of her chosen male.

The pair jump up and touch one another, flapping their wings and play-fighting in their excitement. The birds separate after mating, and the female then raises the young on her own.

Worldly goods
Male bowerbirds found on the western tip of Papua New Guinea chew rainforest leaves into a paste and use it to bind together orchid and maypole branches into a thatch-roofed bower. Once the male has built his bower—which can measure over 1.5 m across—he collects attractive objects to place in it in order to entice the female. These may include shining beetle wings, fruit, flowers, acorns and leaves. All the objects will be of a particular colour, depending on the species of bowerbird. For nine months the male hoards his treasures, heaping them into piles around the entrance to his bower, ready for the mating season. When the females are ready to mate, they choose their partner by selecting the most impressive bower.

Life-long bond
Swans are well known for their stable long-term monogamous relationships. Pairs stay together for up to 15 years and the 'divorce

DATA-BURST

WHY DO SOME MALE ANIMALS FIGHT?
SOME MALES GO TO EXTREME LENGTHS TO ATTRACT A MATE WITH THEIR SUPER-MASCULINITY. STAGS, SAGE GROUSE AND BABOONS ALL SHOW OFF THEIR STRENGTH AND CONDITION TO FEMALES WHICH THEN CHOOSE TO MATE WITH THE MOST DOMINANT ONE.

WHY IS THERE OFTEN A GAP BETWEEN COURTSHIP AND MATING?
WHERE BOTH SEXES HELP TO BRING UP THE YOUNG, THE GAP EXISTS SO THAT OFFSPRING FROM PREVIOUS ENCOUNTERS WILL BE APPARENT.

ARE THERE ANY SPECIES WHICH MATE IN A PARTICULARLY UNUSUAL WAY?
BLACK-HEADED GULLS ARE HIGHLY TERRITORIAL. THEIR DARK FACE MASKS STIMULATE AGGRESSION IN OTHERS OF THE SPECIES DURING DISPUTES. WHEN IT COMES TO MATING, THE GULLS MUST AVOID BECOMING AGGRESSIVE SO THEY 'FACE AWAY' IN ORDER NOT TO LOOK AT EACH OTHER'S FACE MASKS.

WHAT IS A LEK?
TAKEN FROM THE SWEDISH WORD MEANING PLAYGROUND, A 'LEK' IS A COMMUNAL AREA WHERE MALES GO TO DISPLAY DURING THE MATING SEASON. THESE MATING GROUNDS ARE USED BY SPECIES AS DIVERSE AS BULLFROGS, FLIES, BATS, BIRDS, EVEN ANTELOPE. AS THE MATING SEASON BEGINS, THE MALES GATHER AT A LEK AND CALL THE FEMALES IN A CHORUS. WHEN THE FEMALES ARRIVE THE MALES PERFORM SPECTACULAR DISPLAYS IN ORDER TO IMPRESS THEM.

WHAT ARE PHEROMONES?
PHEROMONES ARE AIR-BORNE CHEMICAL MESSAGES USED BY THE FEMALES OF SOME SPECIES TO ATTRACT MALES.

DO FEMALES INSTIGATE MATING?
SOME SPECIES, SUCH AS THE DOMESTIC DOG OR HAMSTER, EMIT A SPECIAL ODOUR WHICH CAN LURE MALES FROM AFAR.

LEFT: BIRD OF PARADISE PREPARES TO START MATING RITUAL · INSET: BIRD OF PARADISE PUFFING UP ITS NECK FEATHERS IN A COLOURFUL AND ELABORATE DISPLAY

Different animals produce and protect their offspring in a variety of different ways. Insects, fish, amphibians and reptiles lay huge numbers of eggs in order to increase their offspring's chances of survival into adulthood. After laying their eggs, these creatures tend to leave their young to fend for themselves. Mammals and birds usually take the opposite approach. They produce only a few offspring, but spend a considerable period of time nourishing their newborns, even educating them for adult life. Bringing up their young in a larger group is often the best way for mammals to protect their offspring from danger.

Turtle D-day

The green turtle goes to some remarkable lengths to mate and lay eggs. These marine reptiles live in warm shallow waters off the coasts of central America, Africa, Australia and Asia. Every year both males and females travel great distances to reach their mating beaches. In an amazing feat of endurance and navigation, turtles living off the coast of Brazil swim 2,080 km to get to their breeding beaches on Ascension Island, a tiny area of land just 13 km by 9 km which lies in the middle of the Indian Ocean. Once there, the turtles mate in the water and a few nights later the female hauls herself on to the beach. She scoops out a pit in the sand where she lays a clutch of up to 100 round white eggs before returning to the sea. She nests at intervals of 12–14 days, producing up to 11 clutches. This huge number of eggs is vital to ensure the survival of the species. When the young hatch they must quickly crawl down the beach and into the water. But their chances of reaching it are slim: lizards, snakes and seabirds simply snap up an easy meal as the young turtles struggle to reach the sea. Once in the water, sharks lurk. Only a few survive the ordeal and grow into adult turtles.

Catching the tide

The most unusual reproductive strategy of any fish is that of the grunion. Three or four nights after

NEW LIFE

MALE PENGUIN INCUBATES

a full moon when the spring tide is at its highest, grunions enter shallow water and swim in the surf so that they are swept up on to the beach. Once stranded on dry land, the females partially bury themselves in the sand and shed their eggs for the males to fertilize externally. The next large wave sweeps the fish back out to sea and buries the eggs in the sand. Two weeks later, at the return of the next high tide, the surf disturbs the eggs; they hatch and the young fish are dispersed. If the water does not disturb them, the eggs can wait up to a month for the next high tide to reach them. They must remain in a state of suspended animation until a wave can free them.

THE RED KANGAROO

WHEN A BABY RED KANGAROO IS BORN IT IS A STAGGERING 30,000 TIMES SMALLER THAN ITS MOTHER. WEIGHING ONLY 28 G, THE TINY KANGAROO CLAMBERS OVER THE ROUGH FUR ON ITS MOTHER'S BELLY TO REACH HER POUCH. ONCE THERE, THE YOUNG GRABS A NIPPLE IN ITS MOUTH AND STAYS PUT FOR 190 DAYS, FEEDING ON ITS MOTHER'S MILK AND NEVER RELEASING ITS GRIP ON THE NIPPLE UNTIL IT HAS GROWN BIG ENOUGH TO LEAVE THE POUCH. TO MAKE SURE HER YOUNG IS BORN AT THE BEST POSSIBLE TIME, THE FEMALE KANGAROO CAN HOLD A FERTILIZED EGG IN HER WOMB IN A STATE OF SUSPENDED ANIMATION FOR SEVERAL MONTHS. THIS ENABLES HER TO MATE AT ANY TIME OF YEAR BUT POSTPONE THE BIRTH UNTIL ENOUGH RAIN HAS FALLEN TO PRODUCE GRASS FOR FEEDING.

JARGON

FRY
NEWLY HATCHED FISH

GESTATION
THE GROWTH AND NOURISHMENT OF A FOETUS IN A WOMB BETWEEN CONCEPTION AND BIRTH

OVIPAROUS
PRODUCING EGGS WHICH HATCH OUTSIDE THE BODY

OVOVIVIPAROUS
PRODUCING EGGS WHICH HATCH INSIDE THE BODY; THE FEMALE THEN GIVES BIRTH TO THE YOUNG

PARTHENOGENESIS
REPRODUCTION FROM AN UNFERTILIZED EGG WITHOUT THE NEED OF A MALE FOR FERTILIZATION

EGG ON TOP OF FEET

FOR ALL ANIMALS, REPRODUCING IS THE MOST ESSENTIAL TASK THAT THEY MUST COMPLETE IN THEIR LIVES. SOME ANIMALS GO TO EXTRAORDINARY LENGTHS TO ENSURE THAT THEIR YOUNG GET OFF TO THE BEST POSSIBLE START

Penguin protectors

Parent emperor penguins have to endure the harshest climate on Earth to bring their young into the world. They breed during the Antarctic winter when the average temperature is around -20°C and where winds reach speeds of up to 200 km/h. After spending January and February feeding at sea, the penguins return to the ice to mate. The female lays her single egg in mid-May—the start of the southern winter—and returns at once to sea. For nine weeks of the bleakest conditions on Earth, the male emperor penguins each incubate their egg on top of their feet. During this time they do not eat, and by the time the egg is about to hatch, each male has fasted for 110–115 days and has lost up to 45% of his body weight. Only now does the female return to take over the last few days of incubation and allow the male to return to the sea to feed.

Maternal fathers

Seahorses reverse male and female roles. Looking after eggs and young is the job of the male for several creatures known to science, but the seahorse takes it one step further: the male actually becomes pregnant. During the mating season, which begins in May, the female lays 300–500 eggs into a 'brood pouch' on the male's abdomen. The male fertilizes the eggs and then incubates them in this pouch during June and July. The eggs hatch in August and September and the male 'gives birth' to the tiny seahorses, releasing them from his brood pouch into the sea.

Sibling-eating salamanders

The female Alpine salamander produces up to 60 eggs, all of which are internally fertilized by the male. But she only gives birth to 1–4 young. This is because the embryos of the first few eggs to be fertilized feed on the other developing eggs, devouring their own siblings inside their mother's body. These embryos also feed on their mother's blood; special blood cells, which nourish the growing embryos, are produced by her reproductive system.

DATA-BURST

WHAT IS THE LONGEST MAMMAL GESTATION PERIOD?
THE ASIAN ELEPHANT HAS AN AVERAGE GESTATION PERIOD OF 609 DAYS, BUT SOMETIMES AS LONG AS 760 DAYS—OVER TWO AND A HALF TIMES THAT OF HUMANS.

WHICH MAMMAL HAS THE SHORTEST GESTATION PERIOD?
SEVERAL MARSUPIALS, INCLUDING THE VIRGINIA OPOSSUM OF NORTH AMERICA AND THE WATER OPOSSUM, OR YAPOK, OF SOUTH AMERICA, SHARE THE RECORD WITH AN AVERAGE GESTATION PERIOD OF JUST 12–13 DAYS ON AVERAGE. OCCASIONALLY GESTATION CAN LAST EIGHT DAYS.

WHAT IS THE LARGEST KNOWN MAMMAL LITTER?
ONE TAILLESS TENREC, A SMALL HEDGEHOG-LIKE MAMMAL FOUND ON THE ISLAND OF MADAGASCAR, GAVE BIRTH TO 31 YOUNG IN A SINGLE LITTER, OF WHICH 30 SURVIVED.

WHAT MAMMAL HAS THE EARLIEST PREGNANCY?
THE FEMALE LEMMING OF SCANDINAVIA CAN BECOME PREGNANT WHILE SHE IS JUST 14 DAYS OLD.

WHICH ARE THE MOST PROLIFIC KNOWN DOMESTIC ANIMALS?
IN AN OFFICIAL TEST FROM AUGUST 1978 TO AUGUST 1979, A WHITE LEGHORN CHICKEN LAID 371 EGGS IN 364 DAYS AT THE COLLEGE OF AGRICULTURE, UNIVERSITY OF MISSOURI, USA. A TABBY CAT NAMED 'DUSTY' FROM BONHAM, TEXAS, USA, PRODUCED 420 KITTENS DURING HER LIFETIME.

CAN ANY BIRD FLY IMMEDIATELY AFTER HATCHING?
THE CHICKS OF THE AUSTRALIAN BRUSH TURKEY HATCH OUT FULLY EQUIPPED WITH ADULT FEATHERS. THEY ARE TOTALLY INDEPENDENT FROM THEIR PARENTS AND CAN FLY FROM THE MOMENT THEY HATCH.

LEFT: A CLUTCH OF EGGS STORED UNDERNEATH A SEA TURTLE'S TAIL · RIGHT: THE MALE SEAHORSE FERTILIZES THE EGGS IN A 'BROOD POUCH' BEFORE RELEASING THEM INTO THE SEA

Metamorphosis is a visible change in form or major transformation of structure during the lifecycle of an animal. Instead of reaching adult form by simply growing and changing gradually, species that metamorphose undergo intermediate stages during which they can be radically different from the adult in both appearance and behaviour. These changes serve a useful purpose in the battle for survival.

From worm to wing

Butterflies and moths provide the most clearly visible example of complete metamorphosis. The earthbound caterpillar could not be more different from the winged adult that takes flight from the chrysalis, the protective cocoon which the larvae spin around themselves. One key link remains: the adult feeds on the same plant species as it did when it was a caterpillar.

The paradoxical frog

On the way from egg to adult all frogs metamorphose, passing through a kind of re-enactment of the evolutionary history of amphibians—from a fish-like tadpole stage, through a number of intermediary forms to a creature equipped for life on land. Most frogs increase in size when they change from a tadpole to a froglet, but not the paradoxical frog. This unusual frog lives in marshes near the large rivers and lagoons of Trinidad and the Amazon Basin, Brazil. It starts life as a gigantic tadpole usually measuring up to 16.8 cm, but sometimes up to 25 cm, with large eyes and a high dorsal fin. It then shrinks to become an adult frog only 5.6 cm in length—three times smaller than its earlier form. This remarkable shrinking, which has no obvious advantage, affects not only the frog's body: even its vital

FIVE-FINGERED STARFISH

ADULT STARFISH LIVE ON THE OCEAN FLOOR WHERE THEY REPRODUCE BY RELEASING LARGE NUMBERS OF EGGS AND SPERM INTO THE WATER. THE FERTILIZED EGGS HATCH INTO MINUTE LARVAE THAT THEN FLOAT IN THE SEA WITH PLANKTON. AFTER THIS PERIOD THEY METAMORPHOSE INTO THEIR ADULT FORM WHEN THEY BECOME RADIALLY SYMMETRICAL AND SINK TO THE SEA BED. THEIR BODIES CAN UNDERGO FURTHER CHANGES IF NECESSARY. IN RESPONSE TO INJURY, STARFISH CAN SHED THEIR LIMBS AND REGROW NEW ONES. SOME STARFISH CAN EVEN REPRODUCE BY DIVIDING IN TWO, THEN GROWING NEW LIMBS ON EACH SEGMENT TO FORM TWO NEW ANIMALS. SPONGES ALSO HAVE THE ABILITY TO REGENERATE: IF THESE PRIMITIVE ANIMALS ARE REDUCED TO THEIR COMPONENT CELLS. THE CELLS CAN CLUMP TOGETHER TO BUILD SEVERAL NEW SPONGES.

JARGON

CHRYSALIS
THE COCOON IN WHICH A CATERPILLAR PROTECTS ITSELF WHILE IT UNDERGOES METAMORPHOSIS (PUPATES)

ENDOPTERYGOTES
INSECTS, SUCH AS BUTTERFLIES AND BEES, WHICH UNDERGO COMPLETE METAMORPHOSIS, PASSING THROUGH LARVAL AND PUPAL STAGES BEFORE ADULTHOOD

EXOPTERYGOTES
INSECTS, SUCH AS GRASSHOPPERS AND DRAGONFLIES, WHICH UNDERGO INCOMPLETE METAMORPHOSIS, GOING THROUGH A 'NYMPHAL' STAGE DURING WHICH THEY ARE SIMILAR TO THE ADULTS

MORPHOLOGY
THE CHANGE IN FORM OR FUNCTION OF THE ORGANS OF THE BODY

METAMORPHOSIS
JEWEL BEETLE TAKES

organs, such as the heart and gut, are reduced to a more compact size during metamorphosis.

The Suriname toad

The tadpoles of the Suriname toad, an amphibian native to Brazil and the Guianas, gain a remarkable head start in life. The male and female mate acrobatically underwater and once the female's eggs have been fertilized by the male, he pushes them onto a patch of spongy tissue on her back. Here, each egg sits in a tiny depression and is protected by a lid of tissue while it incubates. When the egg hatches, the tadpoles do not disperse as they do in other

species; instead, they remain in their incubating chambers, safely protected from predators until the onset of metamorphosis. After 80 days, they emerge from the female's back as miniature versions of the adults.

The 17-year-old cicada

One of the longest periods of metamorphosis in the animal kingdom is that of the periodic cicada. Also known as the 17-year cicada, this insect undergoes a process of metamorphosis that takes 17 years. Native to northern parts of the USA, this insect is similar to the 13-year cicada of the southern part of the country.

Both species hatch from eggs as nymphs which burrow into the ground where they feed by sucking the juices of plant roots. During their years underground, they undergo five moults before emerging above ground as an adult. These adults can grow to lengths of up to 26 mm. But the periodic cicada's life in the sunshine is short-lived: it survives for only four weeks, during which time it mates in order to start the long cycle all over again.

Jewel beetles

The jewel beetle makes the lifecycle of the periodic cicada seem like a hurried affair. This

insect, named for its bright colouring as an adult, lays its eggs under the bark of trees. The newly hatched young tunnel into the tree and feed on the wood. But wood has very little nutritional value, so the larva has to eat its way through an incredible amount before it emerges as an adult. If the tree in which the larva is feeding is cut down, the beetle continues to feed and grow inside the wood. Even if the wood is then made into furniture, the larva keeps on munching. Jewel beetles have been known to emerge, metamorphosed into adults, from pieces of furniture 20 or even 40 years after the furniture was made.

Sole fish eyes

Plaice and sole seem flattened from top to bottom, but are really flattened sideways and swim on their sides. The young fry are a normal symmetrical fish shape, but after just a few weeks' development, one eye moves to the other side of the head and the mouth twists round. The fish then sinks to the sea-bed and lies on its side, developing an undulating swimming style.

Shedding skins

Moulting does not only occur during metamorphosis: many animals shed their old skins in order to grow. Snakes and other reptiles literally crawl out of their skins. These land-living vertebrates produce keratin—a hard, water resistant protein—in the outer skin layer. As keratinization causes many cell components to degenerate and eventually die, the layer of keratinized cells is shed from time to time. Birds and mammals slough off small pieces of keratinized skin almost continually. Most dust found in homes is actually powdered skin.

DATA BURST

WHAT TRIGGERS METAMORPHOSIS?
THE TIMING OF CHANGES INVOLVED IN METAMORPHOSIS IS CONTROLLED BY HORMONES IN THE ANIMAL'S BODY. SEASON, DAY LENGTH AND TEMPERATURE ALSO PLAY A PART IN TRIGGERING THE CHANGE, AS DOES THE ANIMAL'S OWN GROWTH AND AGE.

HOW MUCH DO INSECT LARVAE GROW?
BEFORE ITS FINAL TRANSFORMATION INTO ITS ADULT FORM, AN INSECT LARVA CAN INCREASE IN WEIGHT BY AS MUCH AS 1,000 TIMES.

HOW LONG DOES METAMORPHOSIS TAKE?
DEPENDING ON THE ANIMAL, THE CHANGES INVOLVED IN METAMORPHOSIS CAN TAKE ANYTHING FROM A MATTER OF DAYS TO 40 YEARS IN THE CASE OF ONE PARTICULAR JEWEL BEETLE.

WHAT ARE COMPLETE AND INCOMPLETE METAMORPHOSIS?
WITH COMPLETE METAMORPHOSIS THERE IS A CLEAR DISTINCTION BETWEEN THE VARIOUS STAGES OF AN ANIMAL'S DEVELOPMENT—FROM EGG TO LARVA TO PUPA TO ADULT. THE PROCESS BY WHICH THE YOUNG ANIMAL RESEMBLES THE ADULT AND CHANGES GRADUALLY THROUGH MOULTING OR SHEDDING IS KNOWN AS INCOMPLETE METAMORPHOSIS.

WHAT CREATURES UNDERGO COMPLETE METAMORPHOSIS?
TYPICALLY, FLIES, WASPS, BEETLES, BUTTERFLIES AND MOTHS UNDERGO COMPLETE, OR HOLOMETABOLOUS, METAMORPHOSIS.

WHAT CHANGES OCCUR DURING METAMORPHOSIS?
PHYSICAL CHANGES ARE ACCOMPANIED BY SHIFTS IN THE PHYSIOLOGY, BIOCHEMISTRY AND BEHAVIOUR OF THE ORGANISM.

DO HUMANS UNDERGO METAMORPHOSIS?
YES, ALTHOUGH THE CHANGES ARE OFTEN NOT AS PHYSICALLY DRASTIC AS IN CERTAIN OTHER SPECIES. PUBERTY, WHEN THE REPRODUCTIVE ORGANS DEVELOP FULLY, PROBABLY MARKS THE MOST DRAMATIC PHYSICAL SHIFT IN THE HUMAN LIFECYCLE

BELOW: A POLAR ADMIRAL BUTTERFLY IN THE THREE STAGES OF METAMORPHOSIS: THE CATERPILLAR MUTATES INTO A CHRYSALIS OUT OF WHICH THE FULL-WINGED ADULT EMERGES

40 YEARS TO METAMORPHOSE

METAMORPHOSIS RADICALLY ALTERS THE APPEARANCE OF SOME ANIMALS THROUGH A SERIES OF TRANSFORMATIONS, RANGING FROM THE BUTTERFLY WHICH STARTS LIFE AS A CATERPILLAR, TO THE FROG WHICH SHRINKS AS IT GROWS

Animals build their homes for different purposes. While some, such as wasps and beavers, build to protect themselves and their young from predators, others, like spiders, build to catch prey and store it for future consumption. Spiders can spin their webs in a matter of minutes while beavers may take generations to complete a large dam. Teamwork is often a great advantage in a large building project and many social animals instinctively work together to pull off their impressive feats of construction.

Thatched homes

Social weavers are small African birds with yellow and black plumage. They live together in large colonies and construct a huge canopy over a 'tree house' which can contain up to 300 chambers. Hanging upside-down from branches, the birds weave palm leaves into a thatch which can be up to 8 m wide and 1.5 m high. Beneath the thatch, each chamber is occupied by a pair of nesting birds and is entered from ground level. The thatch serves to keep the nests dry from the heavy tropical rain while their small chambers are inaccessible to predators such as hawks.

Spiders' lairs

Spiders' webs come in a huge range of designs but they are all made of the same remarkable building material: silk. The fine silken strands that spiders produce from special organs on their abdomens are sticky and amazingly strong and elastic. The most common type of webs are orb webs, which trap insects that fly into them by accident. The vibrations caused by the captive alerts the spider, which can move over its own web without getting entangled. The basic construction of an orb web starts with a single line of silk which floats on the wind until it becomes attached to something solid. The spider then moves along the thread, releasing more and more silk and sometimes dropping down to anchor the web to a branch or to the ground. The construction of an average-sized orb web of about 1.5 m diameter takes about an hour. When the web is complete, the spider withdraws to a nearby twig holding a single thread from the web. If this thread

STRUCTURES
AVERAGE ORB WEB

moves, the spider knows it has a victim and enters its web to bind the insect, often leaving it in a silk coffin for days before eating it.

Wasps' nests

Wasps are supreme builders, constructing their nests in trees or the lofts of buildings. Labour is strictly divided; worker wasps are responsible for building and maintaining the nest, using chewed wood and plant material mixed with saliva. They are helped in the initial construction by the queen, who then installs herself in a special cell in order to produce young. It is the job of sterile female wasps to defend the nests. They go to great lengths to protect the complex paper-like construction which hangs from a branch or rafter. This is why humans are most often stung near nests. Inside the nest's 100 or so cells, the wasps congregate to exchange information about food sources and to feed the queen and larvae insects and spiders they have caught. Different wasp species use different designs for their nests, but all entrances face the ground to stop rain getting in.

Beaver dams

Perhaps the most ambitious building projects in the animal kingdom are the dams of beavers. These huge constructions, often built and maintained over generations, actually change the landscape. The purpose of the dams is to provide the beaver with protection from predators and a place in which to live and feed.

Building is a full-time job— beavers spend nearly all their waking hours working on their dam. They gnaw at small trees to fell them, then float logs up to 2.5 m in length down to their dam site, where they shore up the construction with sticks, stones and mud. The finished dam has two levels: a lower level for feeding on wood and plants and an upper level for sleeping. The dam often encloses a private pond for the beaver of up to 100 m². In the middle of the pond, the beaver may construct an island of sticks and mud up to 2 m high containing a network of tunnels where it will be safe from predators.

House-proud husband

In spring male sticklebacks build cocoon-like nests, binding together leaves and aquatic algae. The cocoon can be up to 40 mm in diameter with an opening at both ends and is attached to plants or rests at the bottom of the lake. When the male has completed his nest, the female lays her eggs in it and, once he has fertilized them, the male defends the nest to the death, chasing even the female away. As the eggs develop, he swims around the nest fanning fresh water over the eggs.

TERMITE MOUNDS

IN MANY PARTS OF THE TROPICS, TINY TERMITES CONSTRUCT HUGE MOUNDS UP TO 10 M HIGH IN WHICH THEY LIVE IN SOCIAL COLONIES. THE TOWERING MOUNDS ARE OFTEN DOME-SHAPED WITH A TAPERED SUMMIT AND ARE MADE OF SOIL, CLAY AND BITS OF WOOD GLUED TOGETHER WITH TERMITE SALIVA AND EXCREMENT. THE NEST OFTEN EXTENDS BELOW GROUND LEVEL AND AT ITS CENTRE IS THE CHAMBER OF THE QUEEN. WITHIN THE MOUND, THOUSANDS OF TERMITES MOVE AROUND IN AN INTRICATE NETWORK OF CHAMBERS AND TUNNELS, OFTEN DEMOLISHING AND REBUILDING WALLS. THE EXTERNAL WALLS ARE HARDER THAN THE INTERNAL ONES, AND GIVE NO CLUE TO THE FRENETIC ACTIVITY WITHIN. SOME TERMITE SPECIES BUILD THEIR NESTS IN TREES RATHER THAN ON THE GROUND, CONSTRUCTING THEM FROM A MIXTURE OF WOOD AND SALIVA WHICH MAKES A MATERIAL LIKE PAPIER MACHÉ WHICH PROVIDES GOOD PROTECTION FROM THE ELEMENTS. TO GET TO THESE TREE-HOUSES, THE TERMITES BUILD RAMPS FROM THE GROUND.

RIGHT: YOUNG ADULT WASPS EMERGING FROM CELLS, SURROUNDED BY LARVAE · INSET: FINE SILKEN STRANDS WOVEN BY A SPIDER TO FORM AN INTRICATE WEB

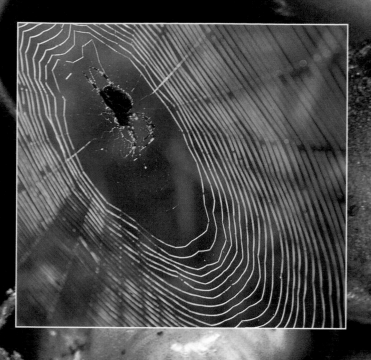

IS SPUN IN 1 HOUR

SOME ANIMALS GO TO GREAT LENGTHS TO BUILD COMPLEX DWELLINGS WHICH CAN BE AS MASSIVE IN SCALE AS THEY ARE INTRICATE IN CONSTRUCTION. ANIMALS WHO LIVE IN SOCIETIES OFTEN WORK TOGETHER TO BUILD THEIR HOMES

SOCIETIES
400 MILLION PRAIRIE

Many animals lead a solitary life, only contacting others of the same species when they wish to mate, but other animals, such as lions, ants and baboons, live together in social groups. Within these groups, strongly defined hierarchies are established and maintained. There are advantages and disadvantages to living in a society of other animals. Although fellow animals in the group act as sentries to warn of potential danger, a large group of animals is an attractive target for predators.

Bushtit cooperatives
Ornitholgists used to think that bushtits bred in pairs and functioned without societies, but recent research has shown that breeding groups cooperate to build the nests—complex structures made of spiders' webs and feathers which take up to two months to construct—to provide food for the young and to guard against predators. Most of the helpers are males, and it has been suggested that they are demonstrating their eligibility to a potential mate.

ANTS NEST

ANTS ARE OUTSTANDING IN THE NATURAL WORLD FOR THEIR HIGHLY ORGANIZED COOPERATIVE SOCIETIES AND THE WAY IN WHICH THEY WORK TOGETHER TOWARDS A COMMON GOAL. THERE ARE SOME 8,000 SPECIES OF ANT, WHICH USUALLY LIVE IN UNDERGROUND NESTS. ANT SOCIETIES HAVE VERY COMPLEX AND RIGID HIERARCHIES MADE UP OF THREE CASTES: QUEENS, MALES AND WORKERS. THE QUEEN LAYS THE EGGS, THE MALES MATE WITH THE QUEEN AND THE FEMALE NON-REPRODUCTIVE WORKERS TAKE CARE OF THE NEST.

DOGS IN ONE COLONY

MANY ANIMAL SPECIES HAVE EVOLVED HIGHLY COMPLEX RULES AND HIERARCHIES WHICH ENABLE THEM TO LIVE TOGETHER IN LARGE COOPERATIVE GROUPS IN WHICH EVERY INDIVIDUAL HAS ITS OWN STATUS AND FUNCTION

Penguin colonies
Penguins live together in enormous colonies, especially in Antarctica, where hundreds of thousands can gather. At the beginning of the breeding season penguins always return to the same colony, the same nest and nearly always to the same partner. There is no hierarchy in a penguin colony and because of the abundance of food and the strong ties formed between pairs, there is little fighting between the males. Penguin societies best display their cohesive solidarity during a violent storm: the entire colony stands crushed tightly together in a huge crowd called a 'huddle', their backs to the storm, sharing the communal warmth.

A helper male enjoys other advantages: it has been observed that while the legitimate male is away searching for food, the helper male takes the opportunity to breed with the female. Cooperation within bushtit society extends to females too: they can contribute eggs to a nest that is already built, or distribute their eggs in a number of different nests, thus ensuring that at least some of them will reach maturity.

Baboon troops
Baboons are big, powerful monkeys which live in large groups—known as 'troops'—on the open savanna and lightly forested regions of Africa. The troops are tightly

organized societies, led by two or more dominant males and females. A dominant male, while often having the last say in a confrontation, is always accompanied by a female. If a male attacks a female, which happens frequently, other females high in the hierarchy will come to the victim's aid, screaming at the attacker. Males at the top of the hierarchy will cooperate with each other to keep the lower males in their place, but in general, males move from troop to troop, attempting to rise up the new troop's hierarchy, while females inherit their mother's rank and remain with the same troop throughout their lives. This permanence of the females has given rise to the conjecture that female baboons are at the centre of the group's structure.

Lion prides
Lions are the only large cats to live in groups, or 'prides'. The pride consists of several generations of lionesses—all of them related to one another—their cubs, and one or two males who are the dominant members of the group. The males are not related to the females but come from other prides. Their role is to mate with the females and to protect the pride from attack by outsiders; males seeking to take over a pride will often attack the cubs and even eat them. A pride's territory is

defined by the amount of prey in the area; it may be only 20 km² or, when game is scarce, as large as 400 km². The lionesses do most of the hunting, but the dominant males take their fill of the meat before the rest of the pride. Small groups form within the pride, and tend to remain together during the day unless hunting or eating are taking place, when the groups join together again.

School politics
Dolphins are amongst the most sociable of all animals. They live together and form enduring societies, called 'schools'. Their social cohesion helps them to navigate more successfully since each animal's sound-wave radar system contributes to the groups' spatial awareness. As well as being part of dolphin play, somersaults, leaps and spins serve the useful function of identifying the position of other dolphins. Within the group, dolphins develop kin relationships; mother-child relationships are very strong, and they often travel in subgroups, while bachelor males may also form subgroups. Mating dolphins form strong relationships, and will pair off together and mate throughout the year.

DATA-BURST

WHAT IS THE LARGEST KNOWN ANIMAL COLONY?
THE BLACK-TAILED PRAIRIE DOG BUILDS HUGE COLONIES. ONE FOUND IN 1901 HAD 400 MILLION INDIVIDUALS AND COVERED 61,440 KM².

ARE THERE WAYS IN WHICH ANIMAL SOCIETIES MIRROR HUMAN ONES?
YES. MANY ASPECTS OF ANIMAL LIFE CAN BE FOUND IN HUMAN CULTURES. FOR EXAMPLE, PENGUIN CHICKS ARE GROUPED TOGETHER IN NURSERIES AFTER BIRTH, AND CHIMPANZEES HAVE GANGS OF RIVAL MALES WHO DEFEND TERRITORIES JEALOUSLY.

ARE THERE EXAMPLES OF ANIMALS MAKING USE OF EACH OTHER?
ONE SPECIES OF AFRICAN ANT, TAPINOMA, EMPLOYS AN UNUSUAL METHOD OF ENSLAVEMENT: THE

QUEEN ANT ALLOWS HERSELF TO BE DRAGGED INTO THE NEST OF THE TAPINOMA ANT. HERE THE USURPER DECAPITATES THE OTHER QUEEN AND LAYS HER OWN EGGS. SHE THEN FORCES THE ORIGINAL ANT TO TAKE CARE OF HER EGGS.

CAN ANIMALS SHOW THEY RESPECT EACH OTHER'S FEELINGS?
IN LABORATORY EXPERIMENTS, SOCIAL ANIMALS SUCH AS MONKEYS WILL STOP PRESSING A LEVER FOR FOOD IF THEY CAN SEE THAT IT ADMINISTERS A SHOCK TO ANOTHER MONKEY.

ARE THERE ANIMALS WHO EXIST TO HELP THE GROUP AS A WHOLE?
WORKER BEES ARE NOT REALLY INDIVIDUALS BUT EXTENSIONS OF A GROUP; THEY CANNOT REPRODUCE AND ONLY EXIST TO HELP THE SPECIES.

JARGON

CASTES
DIFFERENT CLASSES WITH THEIR OWN FUNCTIONS AND RESPONSIBILITIES WITHIN ANIMAL SOCIETIES

MATRIARCHAL SOCIETY
A SOCIETY DOMINATED BY FEMALES

PATRIARCHAL SOCIETY
A SOCIETY DOMINATED BY MALES

PRIDE
AFRICAN LIONS LIVE IN FAMILIES OR PRIDES RANGING FROM 3–30 INDIVIDUALS

TROOPS
A TROOP OF BABOONS CONSISTS OF ON AVERAGE 25 TO 30 ANIMALS, AND OCCASIONALLY AS MANY AS 200

LEFT: A COLONY OF KING PENGUINS CLUSTERED TOGETHER ON THE ANTARCTIC ICE

DISEASE

EBOLA KILLED 80%

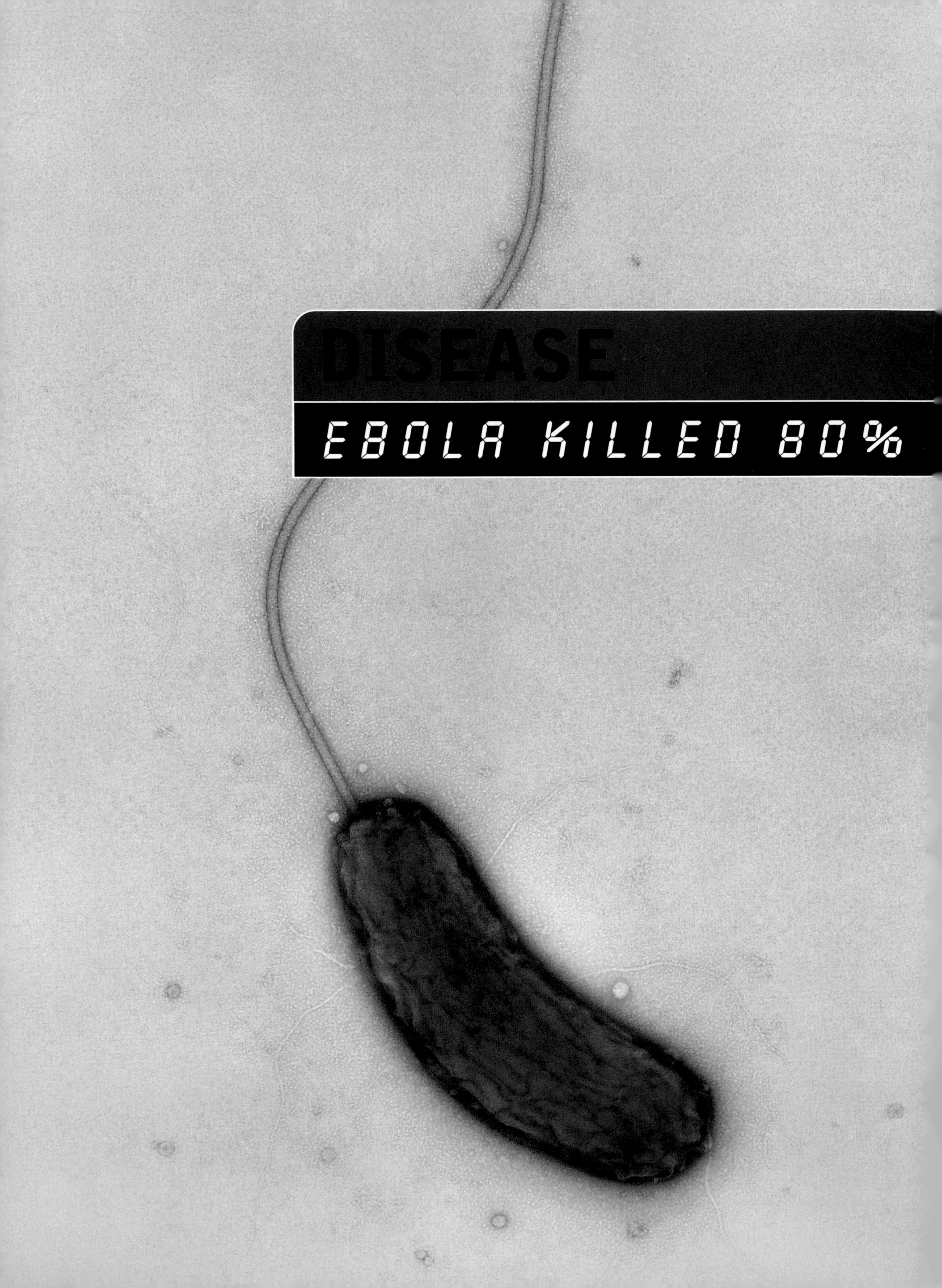

The lives of all living animals are potentially under threat from tiny killers. Bacteria and viruses, some of the smallest lifeforms known to humans, kill millions each year. Animals often become the unwitting hosts to these killer germs, allowing them to spread through populations at an alarming rate. If the spread is uncontrollable, mass epidemics and plagues are the result.

The Black Death
The Black Death originated in Asia in the 11th century, reaching Europe in 1347, where it raged for four years and killed as many as 66 million people. A mixture of bubonic and pneumonic plague, it

DUTCH ELM DISEASE

CAUSED BY A FUNGUS AND FIRST DISCOVERED IN HOLLAND, THIS DISEASE CAUSES ELM TREES TO WILT, TURN DULL GREEN OR YELLOW AND FINALLY CRASH TO THE GROUND. YOUNG ELMS CAN DIE WITHIN A MONTH, WHILE MORE MATURE TREES TAKE UP TO TWO YEARS TO DIE. DESPITE CAMPAIGNS TO STOP THE SPREAD OF THE DISEASE, IT IS PROVING IMPOSSIBLE TO CONTROL. THIS IS

PARTLY BECAUSE THE FUNGUS CAN SPREAD BETWEEN TREES UP TO 50 M APART ALONG THEIR ROOTS, WHICH MAY BECOME CONNECTED DEEP UNDERGROUND. THE EUROPEAN ELM BARK BEETLE ALSO SPREADS THE DISEASE: IF IT LAYS EGGS IN A DISEASED TREE, THE FUNGUS GROWS WITH THE EGGS AND THE BEETLE THEN GOES ON TO INFECT A NEW TREE. SPRAYING ELMS WITH INSECTICIDE TO STOP THE BEETLES LAYING THEIR EGGS HAS PROVED TO BE IMPRACTICAL OVER LARGE AREAS. HOWEVER, BIRDS DO HELP TO CONTROL THE DISEASE BY EATING THE BEETLES. THE ONLY LONG-TERM HOPE FOR THE ELM IS TO DEVELOP IMMUNITY. SOME TYPES HAVE ACHIEVED THIS— ALTHOUGH THE AMERICAN ELM IS SUSCEPTIBLE, THE CHINESE AND SIBERIAN ELMS ARE MUCH MORE RESISTANT.

JARGON

BACTERIA
SINGLE-CELLED ORGANISMS, USUALLY CLASSED AS PLANTS AND MAINLY PARASITIC, WHICH CAN CAUSE A WIDE RANGE OF DISEASES

EPIDEMIC
A PARTICULARLY WIDESPREAD DISEASE

GERM
POPULAR TERM FOR BACTERIA, VIRUSES AND FUNGI

PANDEMIC
A DISEASE WHICH SPREADS ACROSS A WHOLE COUNTRY OR THE WHOLE WORLD

CONTAGIOUS DISEASE
ONE WHICH CAN BE CAUGHT THROUGH CONTACT WITH A SUFFERER

PLAGUE
AS A MEDICAL TERM, ONE OF THREE SPECIFIC DISEASE TYPES, BUT USED GENERALLY TO DENOTE A WIDESPREAD AND INCURABLE CONDITION

VIRUS
THE MOST SIMPLE FORM OF LIFE, THE VIRUS IS A SUBMICROSCOPIC INFECTIOUS ORGANISM. IT IS INCAPABLE OF INDEPENDENT EXISTENCE AND CAN ONLY EXIST INSIDE ANOTHER LIVING CELL.

OF INFECTED VICTIMS

was most deadly in towns where cramped, unhygienic conditions caused the disease to spread rapidly, transmitted primarily by rat fleas. In England, 1,000 villages were completely wiped out by the Black Death, which struck rich and poor alike—some of the plague's most famous casualties were Queen Eleanor of Aragon and King Alfonso of Castile.

Cholera
A disease of the small intestine, cholera is caused by bacteria which spread to humans in water and food. Its symptoms include diarrhoea and vomiting so severe

that patients can lose 20 litres of water in 24 hours and die of dehydration. The disease usually takes 2–7 days to run its course. Poor hygiene in crowded living conditions is often the cause of a cholera epidemic. In India alone, cholera has killed 20 million people since 1900. In the 1980s and 1990s, the disease swept through refugee camps and slums in Ethiopia and Sudan. During 1991–92, over 500,000 cases of cholera were recorded in Peru, caused partly by the selling of contaminated food on the streets. Cholera is not always fatal and antibiotics can provide a cure.

Ebola
One of the most unpleasant diseases known to humans is the ebola virus. First discovered near the Ebola River in northern Zaire in 1976, its symptoms include high temperature, rashes, internal bleeding, loss of appetite, aches, vomiting and diarrhoea. Death can occur in as little as a week, during which blood can ooze from every orifice. There is no known treatment. The disease is spread by infected blood and other bodily fluids. In the year of its discovery, ebola killed hundreds of people. In 1996, an epidemic in Zaire infected 315 people; within eight months, 80% of them died.

Spanish 'flu
In 1918 an influenza pandemic swept the world, killing up to 40 million people—more than died in World War I. Despite its name, this unusual strain of influenza originated in China. Unlike most 'flus, which tend to kill the young and the elderly, this one hit people between the ages of 20 and 40, weakening the immune system and causing pneumonia. Major outbreaks occurred across the globe, but in India the mortality rate was particularly high: about 50 in every thousand people died.

Foot-and-mouth disease
In 1997 in Macedonia, thousands of animals had to be slaughtered due to an outbreak of foot-and-mouth disease. This incident was just one in the history of an animal disease which has been responsible for tremendous losses to livestock all over the world—mostly in Europe, Asia, Africa and South America. Foot-and-mouth disease causes fever and produces blisters on the tongue and lips and on the hooves—hence its name. Often the only way to stop it reaching epidemic proportions is mass slaughter because the virus which causes the disease is extremely hardy—it is able survive in the air for several weeks and on materials for months at a time.

Rabies
A lethal viral disease that attacks the central nervous system, rabies is one of the most feared of animal diseases. In theory, any fur-bearing mammal can carry the disease: in the USA, skunks and raccoon are common carriers, whereas in Africa and Asia dogs are especially vulnerable to infection and transmission. The virus, which is passed through saliva, causes foaming at the mouth accompanied by anxiety and uncharacteristic behaviour in animals. In humans, rabies can lead to hallucination, coma, paralysis and death.

DATA-BURST

HOW MANY PEOPLE CATCH THE PLAGUE TODAY?
THE WORLD HEALTH ORGANIZATION RECORDED 1,500 CASES A YEAR IN 1984–94. IN SOME COUNTRIES, THE DEATH RATE WAS UP TO 40%.

WHAT IS THE WORST OUTBREAK OF DISEASE TO DATE?
THE SPANISH 'FLU OF 1918 KILLED MORE PEOPLE IN ONE YEAR THAN THE BLACK DEATH OF THE 14TH CENTURY KILLED IN FOUR YEARS.

HOW DO BODIES DEAL WITH DISEASE?
ANIMAL AND HUMAN BODIES HAVE DEVELOPED EFFICIENT SYSTEMS TO HELP THEM SURVIVE THE THREAT THAT

DISEASE CAN BRING. THE MOST IMPORTANT OF THESE IS THE AUTO-IMMUNE SYSTEM WHICH CAN WAGE WAR ON INVADING FOREIGN BODIES.

IS THERE ANY PROTECTION AGAINST VIRUSES?
VACCINES PROTECT AGAINST INDIVIDUAL STRAINS OF A VIRUS, BUT AS SOON AS THE VIRUS MUTATES, RESISTANCE BREAKS DOWN.

WHICH ADVANCE HAS CONTRIBUTED MOST TO THE FIGHT AGAINST DISEASE?
THE DISCOVERY OF PENICILLIN BY SIR ALEXANDER FLEMING IN 1928 MARKED THE START OF ANTIBIOTIC TREATMENT, VITAL TO MODERN MEDICINE.

LEFT: CHOLERA BACTERIUM ENLARGED BY A FACTOR OF 16,300 SHOWING LONG FLAGELLUM

Death appears to be the final stage in the natural cycle of life. However, when an animal dies, its remains are broken down to form the vital organic matter which sustains all food chains. In this way, death is part of the natural recycling process. Sometimes animals die in order that their species as a whole will stand a better chance of survival. One animal's death can benefit another. A bee, for example, will sting attackers in defence of its hive, even though this act will result in its certain death.

Rot and decay
The body of an animal is broken down by a number of chemical and physical processes. Animal corpses are first attacked by scavengers such as hyenas, vultures, beetles and ants. Insect larvae will then feed on the nutritious meal that the flesh of a corpse offers them, reaching maturity within a matter of days. Two weeks after hatching, larvae crawl underground to pupate and the adult flies emerge a few days later. Only the hard, calcified parts of the animal, its skeletal bones, remain.

Elephant graveyards
The idea of elephant graveyards— places where old elephants withdraw when they sense they are about to die—has fascinated humans for generations. However, only finds of large quantities of buried elephant bones provide evidence that such places might exist. Some scientists explain these finds as mass drownings of elephants in quicksand or bogs.

Brief flight of the mayfly
Mayflies live as flying insects for only a very short time. These small, 4 cm-long flies live near streams

and ponds and pass the majority of their lives underwater. When they emerge from the nymphal stage they are genetically programmed to live for a day, sometimes only hours, even if conditions around them would allow them to survive for much longer. Mating is the only goal of the mayfly once it leaves the water, and death follows immediately afterwards. Male mayflies dance in swarms and the females fly into them. They mate in flight and copulation only lasts a

few seconds before they die and drop to the ground or river. Here they provide an important food source for other animals, such as fish. On the ground, huge piles of mayflies can sometimes be seen clogging gutters and making roads slippery. These mayfly graveyards can be several centimetres thick and often emit a rancid stench.

Beached whales
People have puzzled for years about why some whales swim too far inland and become trapped near the shore. It is possible that some whales accidentally swim too near land when their echo-sounding navigation system fails to work properly. But some scientists believe that there is more to beaching than just accident. Distressed whales have often been witnessed swimming towards a

shore where they become beached and die. In 1997 along the Pacific coast of North America, an unusually large number of beachings gave scientists further food for thought. These beachings were of young grey whales on their way from the coast of Alaska south to Mexico. Every year, an average of two young grey whales become beached during this migration, but in the first four months of 1997, five beached whales were found, four of which

were not only alive but also apparently healthy. It is possible that beaching may be a form of natural selection—the less robust whales become beached and die during their first migration. However, one of the young grey whales beached in 1997 was taken to San Diego's Sea World where it recovered sufficiently to be released into the wild again.

Bloodthirsty bluefish
The bluefish is a large fish which weighs up to 9 kg and is found in the Mediterranean, along the coast of Brazil, near Australia and around the southern tip of South Africa. Long known for its voracious feeding behaviour, as early as the 19th century this fish was dubbed the 'sea murderer' or 'assassin of the sea'. Its gruesome reputation comes from its habit of

attacking and killing any sea creatures smaller than itself. Up to 300 bluefish may group together to attack other fish, biting their victims in half with their powerful jaws. Squid and mullet are their favoured prey. Long after their hunger is satisfied, bluefish continue killing.

Self-sacrificing bees
Most of the 20,000 species of bee are solitary, living for only a few weeks after emerging from their

larval stage. Some species, however, such as bumblebees and honeybees, live in complex societies comprised of workers, drones and a queen. Part of the job of a worker bee is to protect the community from intruders. For this purpose, the workers are armed with a poisonous sting. However, each bee can sting only once: the act of stinging proves fatal. This is because the sting itself is armed with barbs which hold it in place in the skin of its victim. The poison sac is forced deeper into the victim's flesh. When the victim jerks to remove the bee, the sting holds fast and is ripped away from the bee's body, causing certain death for the bee. In this way, the act of stinging protects the community as a whole at the expense of the life of the individual bee.

DEATH

MAYFLIES MATE AND

RIGHT: SKELETAL REMAINS IN AN ARID LANDSCAPE

DIE WITHIN HOURS

DEATH PLAYS AN IMPORTANT ROLE IN THE CONTINUATION OF ANIMAL LIFE. INDIVIDUAL ANIMALS OFTEN DIE IN ORDER TO HELP THEIR SPECIES AS A WHOLE WHILE THE BIO-DEGRADATION OF CORPSES IS PART OF THE FOOD CHAIN

EXTINCTION

70 JAVAN RHINOS

Lack of food, cosmic events, global warming or cooling and changes in habitat and hunting by humans can cause extinction, a process which can take millions of years. The gradual development of new, specialized species, which become successful in their particular niche and supersede existing species, can also cause extinction. Although the process of extinction happens all the time, there have also been a number of mass extinctions in which a large number of species all died out simultaneously.

DEAD AS A DODO

THE DODO WAS BIGGER THAN THE TURKEY. THIS 23-KG FLIGHTLESS BIRD, WITH SMALL WINGS, A LARGE HEAD AND A HOOKED BILL, LIVED ON THE ISLAND OF MAURITIUS IN THE INDIAN OCEAN. THE BIRDS WERE FIRST SPOTTED BY SAILORS IN 1507. HUMANS AND THE ANIMALS THEY INTRODUCED TO THE ISLAND BOTH HUNTED AND ATE THE BIRD. ITS PLUMP BODY PROVIDED TASTY MEAT AND ITS TINY WINGS, USELESS FOR FLIGHT, MADE IT VULNERABLE TO ATTACK. IN 1681, THE LAST DODO DIED. TODAY, ONLY DODO SKELETONS REMAIN IN MUSEUMS.

THE GREATEST TESTAMENT TO THE ROLE OF HUMANS IN SPECIES EXTINCTION IS THE FATE OF THE DODO.

million years. It is one of the planet's most tenacious survivors. But the actions of poachers threaten to make the rhino extinct. Between 1970 and 1994, some 95% of Africa's black rhinos were wiped out. The forces which drive poaching—poverty, tradition, mismanagement and greed—are a powerful mix. Secret operations have exposed a flourishing trade in rhino horn: between 1988 and 1992, 100,000 items of rhino product were recorded, virtually all of which were exported from China. Rhino horn is considered a vital ingredient in oriental medicine and it has been used to produce dagger handles. Whereas hundreds of species of rhino once roamed the Earth, now only five survive.

EXIST WORLDWIDE

EXTINCTION HAPPENS WHEN DEATH OUTPACES BIRTH. IT IS AS OLD AS LIFE ITSELF: MOST SPECIES THAT HAVE LIVED ON EARTH ARE EXTINCT, REPLACED BY NEW LIFE-FORMS, BETTER ADAPTED TO SURVIVE IN THEIR HABITAT

Mass extinctions in history

At the end of the Permian period, 245 million years ago, 95% of all existing marine invertebrates died out. The reasons for this are thought to be related to changing climate and a very low sea level. The most famous mass extinction in Earth's history came at the end of the Cretaceous Period, 65 million years ago. For 150 million years, dinosaurs had dominated the Earth, but within the space of a million years they disappeared completely, along with much of the marine life of the time. A number of theories have been put forward to explain their sudden demise. One suggests that an asteroid struck the Earth causing a period of perpetual darkness, dust storms and freezing temperatures which

wiped out the habitat on which the dinosaurs depended. Other explanations are that widespread disease or the rise of egg-eating mammals could have contributed to their demise.

The giant panda

Only about 800 giant pandas remain on Earth—700 in the forests of China, where pandas are now confined to 13 reserves, and 100 in zoos around the world. Hunting is responsible for cutting down their numbers; even though China punishes those who trade in panda skins with the death penalty, poachers still sell to collectors. The other reason for the demise of the giant panda is the destruction of its natural habitat. The panda is a carnivore that has adapted to being

a vegetarian. It lives on bamboo which has very little nutritional value. As a result it spends up to 14 hours a day munching its way through 30 kg of the plant. Between 1974 and 1988, the panda's mountainous bamboo habitat shrunk to half its former size. Lost habitat leaves the panda starving. Difficulties also ensue from the fact that pandas are not able to reproduce easily: they cannot mate until they are seven-years-old and the female is on heat for a mere three days. Breeding in captivity has also proved difficult.

Poaching threat to rhinos

The prehistoric-looking rhinoceros, which wallows in Asian swamps or wanders the grasslands of Africa, has been evolving for some 60

Lonesome tortoise

The arrival of humans in an ecosystem that has evolved in their absence often disrupts animal species and starts them on a journey towards extinction. This fate has befallen the giant tortoises of the Galapagos Islands in the Pacific. When humans arrived, they killed the giant tortoises for food, and introduced new species which competed with them. A forest fire in 1994 destroyed 6,000 hectares of habitat. On neighbouring Abingdon Island, one aged male giant tortoise—dubbed 'lonesome George'—is the last remaining tortoise of its type.

Back from the dead

The fossil of the coelacanth, a large deep-sea fish, suggested to palaeontologists that the species had died out 60 million years ago. But to their astonishment, in 1938, a fisherman caught a live example in the Indian Ocean. Since then, several specimens of this 'living fossil', with its typical hollow fin spines, have been netted by fishermen off the Comoros Islands.

DATA-BURST

WHAT ARE THE WORLD'S RAREST MAMMALS?
IT IS ESTIMATED THAT THERE ARE ONLY 70 JAVAN RHINOS LEFT IN THE WORLD, 800 GIANT PANDAS, 2,000 BLACK RHINO AND 6,000 TIGERS.

WHAT ARE THE WORLD'S RAREST BIRDS?
ONLY TWO PAIRS OF THE KAUAI O-O, A HAWAIIAN SONGBIRD REMAIN IN THE WILD. WITH ONLY ABOUT 70 LEFT IN CAPTIVITY, THE CALIFORNIA VULTURE IS THE RAREST BIRD OF PREY.

WHAT IS THE WORLD'S RAREST FISH?
ONLY 200–500 OF THE DEVIL'S HOLD PUPFISH SURVIVE—AND ALL OF THEM LIVE IN ONE POOL IN NEVADA, USA.

WHAT IS THE WORLD'S RAREST REPTILE?
THE ROUND ISLAND BURROWING BOA WHICH LIVES ON AN ISLAND OFF MAURITIUS. IT IS POSSIBLE THAT THERE ARE NONE LEFT AT ALL.

WHAT IS THE WORLD'S RAREST AMPHIBIAN?
THE LATEST COUNT OF THE COSTA RICAN GOLDEN TOAD STANDS AT 11.

WHAT ARE ENDANGERED AND VULNERABLE SPECIES?
ENDANGERED SPECIES ARE IN GRAVE DANGER OF EXTINCTION. VULNERABLE SPECIES ARE THOSE THAT MAY BECOME ENDANGERED IF THEIR NUMBERS CONTINUE TO FALL.

LEFT: THE FACE OF THE GIANT PANDA · RIGHT: A RHINOCEROS, KILLED FOR ITS HORN BY POACHERS

DISCOVERIES

TEN NEW MAMMALS

New life—whether natural or manufactured by human hands— is forming around us all the time. In remote corners of the globe, entirely new species can be discovered, while existing species, once assumed to be extinct, can re-appear. Developments in modern science and medicine have led to the breeding of new animals solely for the purpose of experimentation to help us better understand the causes of diseases, such as cancer. In extreme cases, the scientific technique of cloning has been refined to enable genetic copies of species to be created. One product of such technology— Dolly the sheep—caused an international furore in 1997.

HELLO DOLLY

IN 1997 A SHEEP CALLED DOLLY WAS CLONED FROM GENETIC MATERIAL TAKEN FROM A SINGLE CELL OF AN ADULT SHEEP. A MAMMARY CELL FROM A SHEEP'S UDDER CONTAINING DNA WAS MERGED WITH EGG CELLS EXTRACTED FROM ANOTHER SHEEP, AND A PROTEIN WAS ADDED TO MAKE THE CELLS JOIN TOGETHER. THE RESULT WAS AN EGG CONTAINING NEW DNA. THE EGG WAS IMPLANTED IN ANOTHER SHEEP WHERE IT GREW NORMALLY. DOLLY HAS AROUSED A STORM OF CONTROVERSY INCLUDING CALLS TO PROHIBIT RESEARCH INTO HUMAN CLONING. THE FEAR IS THAT BECAUSE DOLLY WAS CLONED USING A SINGLE CELL, IN THEORY ANYONE COULD BE CLONED WITHOUT THEIR KNOWLEDGE IF THEY LIVED IN A COUNTRY WHERE HUMAN CLONING WAS NOT AGAINST THE LAW.

FOUND IN INDOCHINA

MANY SPECIES WHICH POPULATE THE REMOTE REGIONS OF THE WORLD ARE JUST BEING DISCOVERED. AT THE SAME TIME, SCIENTISTS ARE CREATING NEW LIFE USING NEW TECHNIQUES OF CLONING AND GENETIC ENGINEERING

Recent discoveries

The 1990s have produced a rich crop of new discoveries around the world. The largest new marsupial discovery is the bondegezou, or Mbaiso tree kangaroo, which was discovered by Dr Tim Flannery in Irian Jaya in 1994. A new monkey, the Satere marmoset, was discovered in Brazil as recently as 1996. Brazil was also the location for the discovery of the world's first vampire fish, described by Dr. Wilson Coasta in 1994. The most recently discovered whale is Bahamonde's beaked whale, which was described in 1996 when a skull was washed up on the beach at Robinson Crusoe Island, Chile. From the skull it is estimated that the whale must be as large as a fully grown elephant. The Nechisar nightjar, found in 1990, is known only by a single wing, all that was left of the bird after it was squashed by a truck on a road in Ethiopia's Nechisar National Park.

New finds in Indochina

During the 1990s an astonishing number of new species was discovered, or rediscovered, in Vietnam, Laos and Cambodia. In all, 10 new species of large land mammals were found. These included the Vu Quang ox, the holy goat, or kting voar, the giant muntjac and the Vietnamese warty pig. The largest of these, the Vu Quang ox, is the size of a small buffalo. So far, the holy goat is only known to scientists by its horns, which curl distinctively at the tips. The local people of southern Vietnam describe it as being brown and cow-like, but no official sighting has yet been made.

New bird in Brazil

In 1997, in marshlands 650 km from Rio de Janeiro, a bird was heard singing a song unlike any that had been heard before, even though Brazil supports a wide variety of birds. When the bird was captured it proved to be a new species, with no less than 11 unique features, including feather shape and bone structure. It was very small, and grey/black in colour. Known provisionally as the lowland tapaculo, it has yet to be given a scientific name.

New species in the Philippines

Dr Robert Kennedy has led 28 expeditions to the Philippines to document the wide variety of animals found in the rainforests. In 1993, in the eastern mountains of Mindanao, Dr Kennedy found a very beautiful and unusual-looking bird. Similar to a hummingbird, it had first been discovered by the Filipino ornithologist, Dioscoro Rabor in 1965, but Dr Kennedy established that it was actually a new species. The males are about 12 cm long, brilliantly coloured, with a curved bill. The bird has been named Lina's Sunbird after Rabor's wife, Lina. In 1996 Dr Kennedy found another new species, named the Panay cloudrunner, a mammalian tree-dwelling creature similar to a squirrel, with soft brown fur, small eyes and a long black tail.

Robo-roach

In 1997 Isao Shimoyama and his team at Tsukuba University, Tokyo, developed a cockroach which can be remote-controlled. Using a species of American cockroach known for its size and strength, a backpack has been surgically attached to its back to connect with the roach's nervous system. Its wings and antennae are removed and replaced with small electrodes. By using pulses of electricity, the roach can be made to turn left or right and go forwards or backwards. As cockroaches can lift 20 times their own weight, the backpacks, which only weigh twice as much as the roach, are easily carried. It is intended in the future to use electronically-controlled insects carrying tiny cameras or heat-sensing devices on their backs to crawl through earthquake rubble searching for victims.

Oncomouse

A mouse that has been genetically engineered to be highly likely to develop cancer, the oncomouse is intended to act as a tool in the fight against the disease. Designed specifically so that the animal will die from the disease, it has caused outrage among animal rights groups and religious activists. They believe that animals should not be subjected to such suffering, particularly as it has not yet been proved that the oncomouse's cancers will be comparable to human ones.

DATA-BURST

WHAT IS THE NEWEST BRITISH MAMMAL TO BE FOUND?
IN 1997 A NEW SPECIES OF PIPISTRELLE BAT WAS DISCOVERED.

HAVE ANY ENTIRELY NEW ECOSYSTEMS BEEN FOUND?
IN 1986 THE MOVILE CAVE MINI-ECOSYSTEM WAS DISCOVERED IN ROMANIA. THE CAVE HAS YIELDED AT LEAST 47 NEW SPECIES. SEALED OFF FROM THE SUNLIGHT, ALL OF THEM HAVE REDUCED EYES AND PIGMENTATION AND ENLARGED ANTENNAE TO COMPENSATE FOR THE LACK OF LIGHT.

HAS DOLLY'S CLONING LED TO OTHER DISCOVERIES?
YES, THE ABILITY OF DNA TO REVERT TO A PREVIOUS STATE OF BEING. IT HAD BEEN THOUGHT THAT A MAMMARY CELL COULD ONLY PRODUCE MAMMARY TISSUE, BUT IN THE CASE OF DOLLY, IT WAS ABLE TO REVERT TO FUNCTIONING LIKE AN EGG CELL.

COULD HUMAN CLONING BE MADE ILLEGAL?
IN BRITAIN IT IS ALREADY AGAINST THE LAW, AND OTHER COUNTRIES SEEM SET TO FOLLOW THE EXAMPLE.

WHAT IS TAXONOMIC CLASSIFICATION?
THE SYSTEM BY WHICH ANIMALS ARE GROUPED. IN DESCENDING ORDER— KINGDOM, PHYLUM, CLASS, ORDER, FAMILY, GENUS, SPECIES. THERE ARE MORE OF EACH GROUP AS THE LIST DESCENDS. FOR EXAMPLE, THERE ARE ONLY FIVE KINGDOMS, WHEREAS THERE ARE MILLIONS OF SPECIES, OF WHICH HUMANKIND IS JUST ONE.

WHAT IS DNA?
DEOXYRIBOSE NUCLEIC ACID IS THE GENETIC MATERIAL WHICH FORMS THE BASIC BUILDING BLOCK OF ALL LIFE ON EARTH. EACH STRAND OF DNA CONTAINS A SET OF GENETIC INSTRUCTIONS WHICH DETERMINES THE CHARACTERISITCS OF AN INDIVIDUAL.

LEFT: PROTOTYPE OF A ROBO ROACH SHOWING HI-TECH 'BACKPACK' CONTAINING MICROPROCESSOR AND ELECTRODE SET, TOKYO UNIVERSITY, 1997

UNEXPLAINED EVENTS ADD

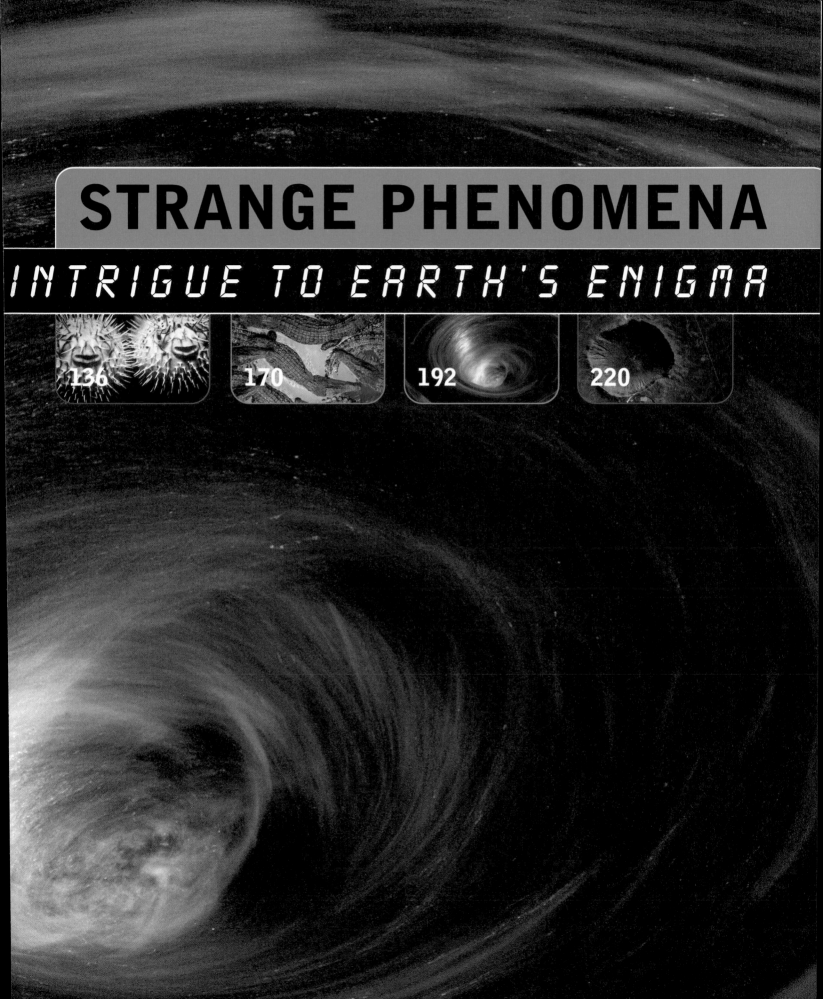

STRANGE PHENOMENA

INTRIGUE TO EARTH'S ENIGMA

Normally silent and invisible, the air around us is made of trillions of tiny particles that can glow, flash, pop or thunder when the conditions are right. For centuries, people have been mesmerized by mirages, auroras, streaks of lightning and other curiosities that light up the sky. Developing understanding of optics, electricity, magnetism and new technology have helped us to understand how nature creates these dramatic displays.

Bolt from the blue

Scientists flying over storms have photographed a form of lightning never seen from the ground. 'Blue jets' fire upwards, reaching distances of up to 50 km high. They have been caught on camera in storm clouds over Arkansas, USA. The cause of these streaks, which can travel at around 100 km/sec, are still unknown.

alarmed to see a silvery, cigar-shaped object hover over the ground then speed out of view, leaving a trail of purple clouds in its wake. Rather than an alien spacecraft, it is more likely that the couple had seen an unusual saucer-shaped cloud. These 'Lenticular' clouds often cause a spate of UFO sightings—they are formed when moist air crosses a mountain, and is met by air bobbing up and down, which generates the cloud formation.

streaks of light that glow in the sky. Auroras are usually generated when the solar wind, a stream of charged particles from the sun, collides with particles in the Earth's atmosphere. The *aurora borealis*, which is brightest at the North Pole, used to be visible over Japan but has drifted northwards over the last 40 years. Japanese newly-weds must now flock to Canada to see this phenomenon which is thought to bring good luck to their children.

section of the Earth's atmosphere. The atmosphere refracts (bends) and scatters the white light from the sun, creating a myriad of different colours in the sky—the colours of sunset. Normally, the green in the sun's scattered light is too faint to see. But if the conditions are right, for instance if the ground is very warm, it becomes much brighter. A green flash along the upper rim of the sun may be visible just before the sun disappears from view.

STRANGE SKIES
SCHOOLBOYS TURNED

Ball lightning

Balls of light have been observed in the sky for thousands of years. They vary from golfball to football-sized. Ball lightning has been observed floating through houses, aircraft and vehicles and is usually seen during or just after thunderstorms. On one Russian aircraft, two holes were pierced in the fuselage as a ball of lightning moved around the cockpit and passenger lounge. Despite this, no-one was hurt in the incident. There have been cases of electricity pylons collapsing in storms, sending huge balls of light cascading along the wire. Some physicists argue that ball lightning is comprised of electromagnetic fields of energy, with light at the centre. However, the most likely theory is that clouds, full of powerful electric charges, may leak electricity in the form of these glowing balls of light which, because of their magnetism, will be drawn towards confined spaces such as houses and aircraft.

Magnetic money

On 9 Sept 1989, unusual solar activity could have caused a crash on the Toronto Stock Exchange, Canada. Business in the Exchange was at that time regulated by a central computer and essential information was stored on a disk drive that was backed-up by two identical copies. Engineers were astonished when all three drives crashed at once, forcing trading to stop for three hours. They were later able to link the failures to a magnetic storm on Earth, caused by the arrival of a large number of charged particles from the sun. This storm was thought to be responsible for a wave of power cuts in Canada at the same time.

Clouded judgement

In November 1958, a doctor and his and his wife travelling through the deserts of Dakota were

Building sight

On a warm morning in 1879, viewers along the Firth of Forth, Scotland, saw a great city wall towering over May Island. This 300 m-high apparition was an example of a 'Fata Morgana'. Named after Morgan Le Fay, enchantress and sister of the legendary King Arthur, this mirage has been documented around the world since the 16th century. It can form whenever warm air rests above cooler air, usually over water. People have reported seeing ships, pillars, towers and even castles when a Fata Morgana appears on the horizon.

Bright hopes

Every year, thousands of Japanese newly-weds make a pilgrimage to the small town of Yellowknife, Canada. They fly there to chase the *aurora borealis* (northern lights),

Warning lights

On 17 Jan 1995, *Yomiri*, the daily newspaper in Kobe, Japan, reported that a fireman had seen a bluish-orange light hovering above the road. The fireman's story was stranger still as it coincided with one of the worst earthquakes ever experienced in the region. The Kobe earthquake, which left 2,500 people dead, created an array of aurora-like flashes over Kobe and nearby towns. These 'earthquake lights' may have been produced by the rocks as they squeezed together during the quake.

Green ray

A flash of green light around the rim of the setting sun was the subject of Jules Verne's classic book, *The Green Ray*, published in 1882. At sunset, the sun is low in the sky so the light emanating from it has to pass through a thick

Blue moon

In order to appear blue, there must be particles in the sky which disperse red light—this has the effect of leaving blue behind. On 20 Sept 1950, people from all over Europe saw a blue sun as well as a blue moon. This was caused by tiny particles sent up in to the atmosphere by fires in Alberta, Canada. In four days the oily particles, probably mixed with soot, reached Europe. The same blue tint of sun and moon resulted when Krakatau erupted in 1883.

LEFT: LENTICULAR CLOUD FORMED OVER MOUNTAIN · RIGHT: *AURORA BOREALIS* (NORTHERN LIGHTS) ILLUMINATE THE SKY OVER THE NORTHWEST TERRITORIES, CANADA

DATA-BURST

CAN BALL LIGHTNING HARM HUMANS?

THERE IS A SUGGESTED LINK BETWEEN BALL LIGHTNING AND SPONTANEOUS HUMAN COMBUSTION. A 27-YEAR-OLD VICTIM WHO DIED FROM SPONTANEOUS COMBUSTION NEAR BUDAPEST IN 1989 WAS SEEN TO BE ENGULFED BY BALL LIGHTNING JUST BEFORE HE DIED. SIGHTINGS OF GIANT BALL LIGHTNING HAVE BEEN REPORTED—WITNESSES IN WEST WALES, UK, IN 1977 SAW LIGHTNING ESTIMATED TO BE THE SIZE OF A BUS.

WHAT MAKES THE SOLAR WIND?

THE SURFACE OF THE SUN IS SO HOT THAT SOME ATOMS BECOME HIGHLY CHARGED AND BREAK FREE OF THE SUN'S GRAVITATIONAL PULL. THEY TRAVEL FREELY THROUGH SPACE UNTIL THEY ARE TRAPPED BY THE MAGNETISM OF EARTH.

WHY ARE AURORAS BRIGHTEST AT THE POLES?

AURORAS ARE USUALLY CREATED WHEN PARTICLES FROM THE SOLAR WIND COLLIDE WITH THOSE IN THE ATMOSPHERE. THIS CAN ONLY HAPPEN IF THE SOLAR WIND IS TRAPPED BY THE EARTH'S MAGNETIC FIELD (THE FIELD THAT MAKES THE NEEDLE OF A COMPASS TURN). THIS FIELD IS STRONGEST AT THE POLES.

CAN EXTREME PHENOMENA PRODUCE LIGHT SHOWS?

EARTHQUAKES ARE KNOWN TO GENERATE AURORAS. ELECTRICAL CHARGE CAN BE GENERATED BY PRESSURIZED ROCKS DURING A QUAKE. SIMILARLY, TORNADOES HAVE BEEN KNOWN TO PRODUCE LIGHTS, GLOWING FUNNELS AND BEAMS, PROBABLY AS A RESULT OF HIGH ELECTRICAL CHARGES.

GLOWING REPORTS

NAMED AFTER AN EARLY CHRISTIAN BISHOP, SAINT ELMO'S FIRE IS A BIZARRE WEATHER PHENOMENON WHICH TAKES THE FORM OF STRANGE LUMINOUS CORONA. DURING A THUNDERSTORM, GLOWING BALLS OF LIGHT HAVE BEEN OBSERVED IN THE MASTS OF SAILING SHIPS. THE PHENOMENON CAN ALSO AFFECT PEOPLE: ON 21 DEC 1976, THREE SCHOOLBOYS WATCHED IN HORROR AS THEIR FRIENDS' HAIR GLOWED AND STOOD ON END AFTER A SIMULTANEOUS CLAP OF THUNDER AND LIGHTNING. AMAZINGLY, THE SUDDEN ELECTRICAL DISCHARGE LEFT THEM UNHARMED. THE INCIDENT HAPPENED WHEN THE STORM WAS DIRECTLY OVER THEIR SCHOOL RUGBY FIELD. THE LUMINOUS BOYS ALL REPORTED THAT THEY HEARD A LOUD POPPING SOUND WHEN THEIR SPIKED HALOS FADED.

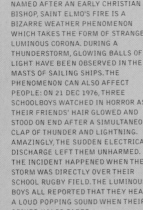

LUMINOUS BY ST ELMO'S FIRE

UNUSUAL ATMOSPHERIC CONDITIONS CAN GIVE RISE TO SPECTACULAR DISPLAYS OF LIGHT IN THE SKY AS PARTICLES IN THE AIR INTERACT IN COLOURFUL WAYS WITH THE FORCES OF SUNLIGHT AND ELECTRICAL ENERGY

The powerful forces of nature can combine to create some amazing, beautiful and often dangerous spectacles. Many of these, such as whirlpools or rainbows, are well understood by scientists, but occasionally these natural phenomena become manifest in unpredictable and inexplicable ways. An all-red rainbow, a huge spontaneous wave or a sonic boom out at sea are the kinds of weird distortions of natural phenomena that defy explanation by scientists.

Hindu pilgrimage

In August 1996, freak conditions led to disaster on a Himalayan trek to visit a holy site dedicated to the Hindu god, Shiva. Every year, upwards of 100,000 pilgrims visit the 3,880-m-high Amarnath cave in Kashmir, to worship an ice-stalagmite regarded as a phallic symbol of Shiva. In August 1996, the annual trek was disrupted—the 48-km-long pilgrimage route was battered by severe winds and heavy rain, and a freak snowstorm caused landslides en route. Many of the pilgrims were holy men; some of these 'sadhus' were naked, and so bore the full violence of the storms without protection. The death toll rose to 160 as blizzards, heavy fog and further snowstorms hindered the efforts of rescue workers. Almost 70,000 pilgrims, cut off from roads to safety, were stranded on the mountainside for three days as helpers sought to evacuate them. Ironically, Shiva is known as the god of destruction.

Whirlpools

A whirlpool is a mass of water which spins around with great force. It can occur when a water current strikes against a bank with a certain physical structure, where opposing currents meet, or when wind creates turbulence in a mass of water. Whirlpools have also been known to form when rocks and tides obstruct the course of an ocean current. There are several well known whirlpools around the world, including one in a gorge below the Niagara Falls. Here, 5 km below the actual falls, the Horseshoe whirlpool has swirling rapids so fierce that they cause

FREAK EVENTS

CINNAMON ODOUR RELEASED

8 cm of erosion to the river bank per year. Another famous whirlpool is the Maelstrom, in Norway. It sweeps and curls between two islands off the north-west coast of the country. A menace to sailors for centuries, it is most dangerous when the wind blows against it between high and low tide.

Rogue waves

Large waves are usually the result of earthquakes or high winds from hurricanes, but some seem to appear spontaneously. Known as rogue waves, they are caused when two waves combine to create a much larger one. They are short-lived, but can be disastrous, especially if aggravated by rocks

explanation. On 14 June 1903, a man living in Transvaal, South Africa, heard a massive explosion above his house, but there was no damage or visible signs of what could have caused the explosion. Similar noises have been heard by sailors at sea, some of whom have claimed to see a large burning fireball. The fireball could be ball lightning discharged during a thunderstorm. Alternatively, the explosion could be the sonic shockwave of a meteor as it streams through the atmosphere and converts its kinetic energy into sound and light energy. However, the lack of any impact zones does not help to confirm this theory. Other theories include rocks

Inexplicable subsidence

Subsidence is a common phenomenon, and can normally be explained by a host of geological or human reasons. However, every once in a while, holes appear in the Earth that are entirely inexplicable. One such incident occurred in 1984, in a field near Grand Coulee, Washington, USA. Two farmers who were herding cattle noticed a large depression 3 m by 2 m, extending to a depth of 3 m. Even more bizarrely, the earth that had once filled the gaping crater was found neatly placed some 22 m away. There was no plausible explanation as to how or why the earth had moved in such a way, and the phenomenon

Rainbows

Rainbows are caused when sunlight cuts through raindrops. The droplets of water act as prisms, and refract the light into the colours of the spectrum. While rainbows are familiar sights, some are more freakish. In 1945, Frederic Palmer observed a completely red rainbow. Others have seen rainbows that are entirely purple. Other anomalous rainbows include those which are not bow-shaped, but distorted into thin bands or large blocks in the sky. Some rainbows do not have any colour at all. These are known as fogbows, or Ulloa's Ring. These colourless rainbows are created on the edges of thick clouds or fog. Since the droplets are much smaller in fog, the light that has been refracted into its constitutive colours re-merges to form white light again.

Haloes and sun dogs

Another curious phenomenon is a halo around the sun, which is caused by high ice clouds. If the crystals of ice within these clouds are of a certain shape—a hexagonal prism—they can deflect light from the sun to form a halo around it. These cirrostratus clouds are also responsible for the halo that is occasionally visible around the moon. Sometimes, there can be more than one halo, or the halo may be only partial, which can produce a series of spectacular aerial sights. If conditions are right, these ice crystals bend the sun's rays into huge pillars of light stretching vertically above the sun. Sun dogs, sometimes known as mock suns, are a similar related phenomenon. False suns located to the side of the real sun, they become visible if the cirrostratus clouds that produce haloes do not form a blanket across the sky, but appear intermittently.

AFTER RAIN SHOWER

NOT EVERYTHING CAN BE EXPLAINED AWAY BY SCIENCE: PURPLE RAINBOWS, FREAK WAVES, BAFFLING NOISES AND ENIGMATIC HOLES IN THE GROUND ARE JUST SOME OF THE WAYS IN WHICH NATURE RETAINS ITS MYSTERY

and tides. A rogue wave struck a fishing boat off the San Diego coast, California, USA, on 5 Feb 1987. The wave, 6 m high, came without warning and overturned the boat. Ten sailors were killed. Rogue waves were also the cause of the demise of the yacht *Marques*, which sank in 1984 during a transatlantic race. Of the 27 crew, 18 were killed when the yacht sank in under 60 seconds.

Freak noises

There have been occasions when large, noisy sonic booms have sounded that have defied physical

cracking under pressure, pockets of trapped gas escaping from great depths following the settling of earth, or even an electrical discharge known as clear-sky thunder. One bizarre case of freak sonic booms happened in India in 1871. Near the town of Barisal, on the banks of the Ganges delta, a series of sonic booms were heard out to sea. They appeared to come from two directions. The booms, which were irregular, like cannon fire, became known as the Barisal Guns. Similar explosions have been heard in the Bay of Biscay and Seneca Lake, New York.

remains unexplained to this day. The only possible explanation was that a tornado had whipped up the earth and deposited it elsewhere, but this does not account for the neat construction of the earth pile. This was not an isolated incident. Other cases of inexplicable subsidence include a mysterious hole that appeared in a field near Poncey-sur-l'Ignon, France, in 1954, and, in Venice Center, New York, USA, a series of unexplained craters that were discovered in exactly the same place on the same date for three years in a row, from 1966 to 1968.

DATA-BURST

WHY DOES THE WORLD SMELL DIFFERENT AFTER A SHOWER OF RAIN? THE ATMOSPHERIC PRESSURE FALLS WHEN RAIN APPROACHES, TRIGGERING THE RELEASE OF FUNGAL SPORES, WHICH EMIT AN EARTHY CINNAMON ODOUR. CERTAIN SORTS OF SOIL EMIT A RICH 'RAIN SMELL' WHEN HUMIDITY RISES ABOVE 80%.

WHAT CAUSES A WHIRLPOOL? WHIRLPOOLS ARISE WHEN A CLASH OF TIDAL FLOWS OCCUR IN PLACES WHERE THE SEA FLOOR IS UNEVEN. CURRENTS RUSH TOWARDS EACH OTHER, AND, IF THEY HIT A ROCKY SHELF ON THE SEA FLOOR, WATER SURGES UPWARDS, TURNING THE SEA'S SURFACE INTO A WHIRLING MASS.

CAN MIST CREATE SPECIAL EFFECTS? YES. MIST DROPLETS CAN PRODUCE A STARTLING EFFECT KNOWN AS 'THE BROCKEN SPECTRE'. THE BROCKEN IS A MOUNTAIN IN GERMANY WHERE GIANT HUMAN SHADOWS HAVE BEEN OBSERVED. MIST DROPLETS BEHAVE LIKE TINY LENSES WHEN THE SUN'S RAYS HIT THEM AT A LOW ANGLE IN THE MORNING AND EVENING. THESE DROPLETS REFLECT HUGE SHADOWS ONTO THE SNOWY SLOPES WHICH ACT LIKE A LARGE CINEMA SCREEN.

CAN THE WEATHER BE MUSICAL? ALMOST. HILLS IN CHESHIRE, UK, HAVE BEEN HEARD TO MOAN—THEIR HOLLOWS ACT LIKE GIANT ORGAN PIPES WHEN EASTERLY WINDS BLOW.

THE RED TIDE

IN SPRING 1998 HONG KONG WAS PLAGUED BY A RED TIDE WHICH SWEPT ONTO BEACHES, KILLING MILLIONS OF FISH AND CAUSING THE DESTRUCTION OF MANY LOCAL FISH FARMS. THIS BIZARRE PHENOMENON, CAUSED BY AN INVASION OF ALGAE BLOOM MADE UP OF MICROSCOPIC ORGANISMS, IS SO- CALLED BECAUSE IT TURNS THE SEA A REDDISH-BROWN COLOUR. THE ALGAE MULTIPLY RAPIDLY WHEN THEY INVADE THE GILLS OF FISH, SUFFOCATING THEM. THE ROTTING CARCASSES OF THESE DEAD ANIMALS HAD TO BE REMOVED FROM THE SEA AS THEY WERE IN DANGER OF TRIGGERING A POLLUTION CRISIS. ALTHOUGH IT HAS ATTACKED BEFORE, THE 1998 STRIKE WAS ONE OF THE WORST IN HISTORY. THE ALGAE'S RAPID GROWTH MAY BE CONNECTED TO HONG KONG'S RISING POPULATION. THE ALGAE THRIVE ON CHEMICALS SUCH AS NITROGEN AND PHOSPHORUS—FOUND IN UNTREATED HUMAN WASTE, CHEMICAL FERTILIZERS AND DETERGENTS WASHED INTO THE SEA.

LEFT: A VIOLENT WHIRLPOOL ROTATES A MASS OF SWIRLING WATER AT GREAT SPEED

FLASH FLOODS
PROPERTY REPAIR

Flash floods are most common in areas where rain is infrequent but storms are fierce. Low-lying land is particularly prone to sudden flooding, especially in regions where rivers can be whipped up by hurricane-force winds. Arid regions are also vulnerable to flash flooding because the soil in these regions does not quickly or easily absorb or drain off surface water. The damage caused by flash floods is compounded by a lack of preparation and the absence of suitable flood protection schemes.

Storms over Leningrad
At least 208 people died in a flash flood that struck Leningrad (now St Petersburg), Russia, in Nov 1824. On the 6 and 7 of that month, a violent storm with heavy rains and hurricane-force winds caused the River Neva to overflow. By the morning of 7 Nov, the river had burst its banks; a few hours later, two-thirds of the city was submerged under water. The winds carried away bridges, wooden barges, roofs, trees, cattle and even people.

ART PAYS HIGHEST PRICE

THE FLOODS THAT HIT FLORENCE IN 1966 DESTROYED MANY PRICELESS WORKS OF ART AND DAMAGED MANY OF THE ITALIAN CITY'S MOST BEAUTIFUL BUILDINGS. ON 3 AND 4 NOV, ONE-THIRD OF THE CITY'S AVERAGE ANNUAL RAINFALL FELL IN JUST TWO DAYS. THE ARCHIVIO DI STATO AND THE BIBLIOTECA NAZIONALE, WHICH HOUSE MORE THAN 3 MILLION BOOKS, MANY DATING BACK TO THE RENAISSANCE ERA, SUFFERED SEVERE DAMAGE. MORE THAN A MILLION OF THE BIBLIOTECA'S BOOKS WERE DESTROYED. VOLUNTEERS EQUIPPED WITH GAS MASKS TO PROTECT THEMSELVES FROM THE STENCH OF SEWAGE AND ROTTING BINDINGS BRAVED THE MUD AND MANAGED TO RECOVER MUCH OF THE COLLECTION.

BILL $3 BILLION

SUDDEN UNEXPECTED SURGES OF FLOODWATER CAN RESULT WHEN TORRENTIAL RAIN FROM VIOLENT STORMS FALLS WITHOUT WARNING. THE RESULTING DAMAGE IS MADE WORSE BY LACK OF PREVENTATIVE ACTION

Britain's worst flood
In January 1607 gigantic waves struck the River Severn estuary in the Gloucestershire and Somerset area of south-western England. The resulting flood was so rapid that within five hours the entire low-lying coastal area was under water. The devastating floodwater spread 10 km inland, stretching from Bristol to Gloucester, wrecking everything in its path. North Devon was also hit; the town of Barnstaple was almost totally destroyed, with only the church tower rising above the floodwater in one part of town. At least 350 people died in the floods, largely because the whole area had been so unprepared for such a disaster.

Foul not fair
Arizona, USA, is known as the 'fair weather state' but it suffered terrible flash floods on 5 and 6 Sept 1970. They occurred when a tropical storm called Norma hit the region. This storm set new rainfall records, perhaps most spectacularly in the Sierra Ancha mountains, which received 28 cm of rain in a 24-hour period, double the previous record. This record-breaking rainfall caused 23 deaths, more than any other incident in Arizona's history. Eye witnesses claimed that river levels were rising by up to 3 m per hour. Many of the city's buildings, roads and bridges were damaged by the floodwater; trees were uprooted, huge boulders were carried along by fast-flowing streams and cars and buildings were swept away.

Australia's worst flood
The Great Australian Floods of January 1974 were probably the worst natural disaster to hit the continent since records began. They occurred when 48 cm of rain fell in just 17 hours in Western Australia. Floodwaters spread across the outback, where the dusty, dry river systems were more used to intense sunshine. In parts of north-west Queensland, the water rose above the level of the telegraph poles, and Broome and Darwin had to be evacuated. Many of those injured were trapped by the rising waters, and were forced to wait for help to arrive. Food supplies had to be dropped by air on isolated communities. Farmland in the north-west of the country was devastated, with drowned sheep left floating in the flooded grazing land. As the floodwaters advanced towards the Gulf of Carpentaria in the north, the rivers merged and water spread across 150 km of the gulf area. More than 1,200 houses were destroyed in the town of Ipswich; in Brisbane 20,000 people were left homeless.

Agnes strikes
Hurricane Agnes was probably the biggest natural disaster ever to hit the USA. The devastation that it caused in 1972 was so great that it brought flash floods from Georgia in the south up to New York State. Some 18 people were killed in the course of the flooding. As the hurricane developed it carried huge quantities of moisture from the deep tropics northwards. The resultant storm lasted for eight days, with short but very intense periods of rainfall; rivers and streams rose to unprecedented levels. From 18 to 25 June, up to 48 cm of rainfall fell in some parts of the country and an area of 93,000 km² received an average rainfall of 28 cm during the floods. In the capital, Washington DC, more than 28 cm of rain fell in less than 18 hours. Many of the most badly affected areas did have flood prevention schemes in place, but Hurricane Agnes simply proved too severe for them. The property repair bill reached around $3 billion dollars.

Freak storm in Black Hills
When a storm struck South Dakota, USA, on 9 and 10 June 1972, the average annual rainfall fell in just two days. An incredible 40 cm of rain fell in six hours on the evening of 9 June. The resulting flash flood was the worst natural disaster ever to hit the state. Among the most badly hit areas was Rapid City, where the normally pleasant mountain stream, Rapid Creek, swept through the area causing extensive damage. A total of 237 people died and 2,932 were injured. More than 750 homes were destroyed and around 2,000 cars were ruined. The repair bill was estimated to be $120 million.

Holiday disaster
Tragedy struck Las Nieves campsite in the Spanish Pyrenees in August 1996 when heavy rains caused devastating floods. In peak holiday season, the campsite, just outside Biseca, was engulfed by water within seconds. Trailers and cars were swept away and 84 bodies were later recovered from the site.

DATA-BURST

WHICH AREAS ARE MOST PRONE TO FLASH FLOODS?
ARID REGIONS, WITH DRY, DUSTY RIVER SYSTEMS WHERE HIGH LEVELS OF PRECIPITATION ARE NOT COMMON.

WHAT ARE THE MAIN FEATURES OF A FLASH FLOOD?
SUDDEN, HIGH LEVELS OF PRECIPITATION, TOGETHER WITH HURRICANES AND STORMS, WHICH WHIP UP RIVERS.

DOES NORMAL FLOOD PROTECTION WORK FOR FLASH FLOODS?
NOT NECESSARILY. WHEN A FLASH FLOOD HIT CALIFORNIA IN 1971, THE LEVEES WHICH WERE SUPPOSED TO PROTECT AGAINST WINTER FLOODING FAILED BECAUSE THE VOLUME OF WATER WAS SO HUGE, WITH WATER LEVELS RISING 6 M.

ARE FLASH FLOODS COMMON?
NO. EXPERTS PREDICTED THAT A FLOOD LIKE THE ONE THAT HIT SOUTH DAKOTA IN 1972 WOULD OCCUR ONLY ONCE EVERY THOUSAND YEARS.

WHAT IS THE CONNECTION BETWEEN HURRICANES AND FLASH FLOODS?
HURRICANES TEND TO CARRY A LOT OF WATER IN CLOUDS WHICH ACCOMPANY THEM; WHEN DRY AND COLDER AREAS ARE REACHED, THE DOWNPOURS CAN CAUSE FLASH FLOODS.

HOW MUCH WATER CAN FLASH FLOODS SPILL?
ONE OF NATURE'S MOST POWERFUL FORCES, THEY CAN SPILL MASSIVE AMOUNTS OF WATER—FOR EXAMPLE, A 1976 FLOOD IN COLORADO EMPTIED A MILLION LITRES OF WATER ONTO THE PLAIN EVERY SECOND.

LEFT: RAPID RUNNING FLASH FLOOD, TUCSON, ARIZONA · INSET: RESCUE TEAMS SEARCH FOR BODIES IN THE WAKE OF FLASH FLOODS AT LAS NIEVES CAMPSITE, SPAIN, AUGUST 1996

STORM SURGES

HURRICANE WAVES

At any given moment, there are approximately 2,000 thunderstorms in progress around the world. Storm surges are probably the most powerful consequence of such storms. A storm surge occurs when high winds combine with the low pressure in the eye of a storm to suck up the sea. This creates a wall of water up to 14 m high, which then crashes ashore, causing terrible damage particularly in low-lying, highly-populated coastal areas. The strength of such waves is incredible and they are all the more deadly because they are often so unpredictable, leaving little time for preventative action.

MONITORING STORM SURGES

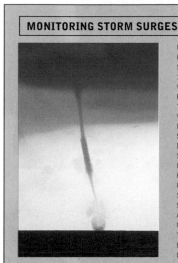

HUNDREDS OF SUNBATHERS ON A BEACH IN NEW ENGLAND, USA, WERE SWEPT AWAY BY STORM WAVES IN 1938 WHEN 4-M-HIGH WAVES STRUCK WITHOUT WARNING, FLOODING THE BEACH AND DROWNING MANY OF THOSE RELAXING THERE. THE DISASTER WAS A PERFECT EXAMPLE OF THE WAY IN WHICH UNPREDICTABLE VIOLENT SURGES CAN DO SO MUCH DAMAGE AND IT LED TO THE FORMATION OF BODIES SUCH AS THE SPECIAL PROGRAM TO LIST AMPLITUDES OF SURGE FROM HURRICANES, OR SPLASH. THIS RESEARCH GROUP MONITORS STORM SURGES WORLDWIDE, TO ASSESS THEIR SCALE AND TO PROVIDE FORECASTS AND ADVICE ABOUT PROTECTIVE MEASURES. THE GROUP ESTIMATES THAT A SURGE OF JUST OVER 1 M WILL BE ENOUGH TO DO CONSIDERABLE DAMAGE WHEN IT HITS THE SHORE.

in the storm waves of 1881, while waves were recorded reaching heights of 14 m around the Marshall Islands on 30 June 1905. The coast of China is also frequently bombarded. Low-lying areas, such as the land around the River Han, are particularly vulnerable. In August 1922, waves of more than 7 m were whipped up by winds of 150 km/h and water covered the entire delta, killing a staggering 60,000 people.

Gulf surges
The Gulf of Mexico is another part of the world which is frequently struck by storm surges. Between 1900 and 1919, waves killed 7,225 people in the region. The small town of Indianola, slightly north of the Mexican border, was hit particularly badly by a wall of waves and winds of more than 100 km/h in September 1875. Three-quarters of the town was destroyed and 176 people died. The town was nevertheless repaired, only to be struck again in August 1886, when every house in the town was damaged and some buildings were carried incredible distances by the waves. The town did not recover from this second disaster and was never rebuilt.

CAN REACH 14 M HIGH

STORM SURGES SWEEP IN FROM THE SEA TO STRIKE COASTAL DISTRICTS WITH A MASSIVE WALL OF WATER. VIOLENT AND UNPREDICTABLE, THE HIGH WINDS AND COLOSSAL WAVES CAN CAUSE CHAOS AND DESTRUCTION

Mass destruction
More people have lost their lives as a result of storm surges in the Bay of Bengal than anywhere else on Earth. The death toll on the fringes of the Indian Ocean is so high because the islands and coastal regions are densely populated and low-lying. Also, there is little to protect the population from the elements, particularly when hurricane waves can reach up to 12 m, the height of a four-storey building. Some 30,000 people died and thousands of ships and boats were destroyed during a storm around the delta of the River Ganges in October 1737. Worse

followed in October 1876, when the Bakhergunj hurricane swept ashore, covering the region south-west of Calcutta with several metres of water. Approximately 100,000 people were killed and many more died as famine and disease swept through the area afterwards. More recently, huge storm surges struck the Bay of Bengal in October 1960, and 15,000 people lost their lives. A wall of water 4 m high swept ashore near the city of Maji while winds of 160 km/h blew across the island of Ramgati, where the water rose to 6 m sweeping 2,764 people to their deaths. The island of

Hatiya was completely submerged in water, killing 3,450 inhabitants in the process. There was a further disaster in 1963, when three hurricanes whipped up violent storm surges in the bay, killing 10,000 people and leaving half a million homeless.

Hurricane fury
Camille was probably the most lethal storm to strike the US mainland. On 17 Aug 1969, it caused storm surges that killed 139 people in Mississippi and south-eastern Louisiana. This was despite the fact that the National Hurricane Centre had predicted the impending disaster and recommended the evacuation of the area. Many people recklessly ignored the advice; when 12 people in a third-floor apartment in Florida decided to hold a party to celebrate the coming of Hurricane Camille, they and 11 other people who remained in the complex were swept away as their building was flattened by the surges.

Pacific peril
Storm waves reach remarkable heights along the western shores of the Pacific Ocean. In the Haifong region, on the coast of north Vietnam, 300,000 people perished

Trouble in Europe
Storm surges are usually less severe in European waters, although waves of 4 m have been recorded. One particularly violent surge took place in the North Sea on 31 Jan 1953, when waves struck the coasts of Belgium, Holland and parts of eastern England. Residential areas were destroyed because the buildings were simply not designed to cope with such conditions. Holland suffered particularly badly on this occasion, with a surge up to 10 m high and water bursting through dams and dykes 65 km inland. Floods 9 m deep were recorded. The port of Rotterdam was extensively damaged and a total of 3,000 people were killed.

Shanty town tragedy
In June 1998, a tropical cyclone in western India caused terrible storm surges which completely wiped out a shanty town. Houses, some made only of corrugated iron and cardboard, were destroyed. Main roads were flooded as winds of 145 km/h, which gusted up to 185 km/h, tore across the ports of Vadinar and Kandla. Despite attempts by rescuers to evacuate the area, many victims were washed out to sea.

DATA-BURST

WHAT ARE STORM SURGES?
A COMBINATION OF HIGH WINDS AND LOW PRESSURE IN THE EYE OF A STORM AT SEA, WHICH COMBINE TO SUCK UP WATER INTO AN ENORMOUS, POWERFUL WAVE.

WHERE DO STORM SURGES STRIKE?
ACROSS MANY OF THE WORLD'S MAJOR OCEANS. THE AREA AROUND THE BAY OF BENGAL IN THE INDIAN OCEAN HAS BEEN PARTICULARLY BADLY HIT.

CAN STRUCTURES BE BUILT TO PROTECT AGAINST STORM SURGES?
IN SOME INSTANCES, WHEN FINANCES ARE AVAILABLE, ENORMOUS STEEL AND CONCRETE BARRIERS CAN BE

CONSTRUCTED. ONE AT NEELJE JANS, HOLLAND, FORMS PART OF A WATER PARK, DESIGNED TO SHOW THE POWER OF WATER.

WHAT IS THE DIFFERENCE BETWEEN A STORM SURGE AND A TIDAL WAVE?
A TIDAL WAVE CAN BE STARTED BY AN EARTHQUAKE A GREAT DISTANCE AWAY WHILE A STORM SURGE IS A FEATURE OF A LOCAL STORM OR HURRICANE.

WHY ARE THERE SO MANY CASUALTIES WHEN STORM SURGES OCCUR?
STORM SURGES OCCUR SUDDENLY AND PEOPLE ARE GENERALLY UNPREPARED. THEY ALSO TEND TO HIT DENSELY-POPULATED COASTAL AREAS

LEFT: THUNDERCLOUDS BREWING LOW OVER THE OCEAN CAN PRECIPITATE STORM SURGES · INSET: WATER CRASHES INTO A HOUSE DURING A VIOLENT STORM SURGE, FLORIDA, USA

STRANGE RAIN
YACHT RACE SPECTATORS

Weather-watchers are used to sudden squalls or heavy hail but strange rain can catch even the most seasoned meteorologists off guard. Since the days of the Old Testament, records have told of creatures tumbling from the sky. Over the centuries, people have witnessed falls of everything from frogs and birds to fish and insects. These bizarre accounts have precipitated much scientific enquiry. The reasons for such phenomena have been discovered to be not so much the stuff of simple superstition, but the result of explicable processes occurring in the natural world.

Cooking their goose
A bolt of lightning was a stroke of luck for the residents of Elgin, Canada. In April 1932, a large flock of geese were flying over the town while a thunderstorm was raging overhead. A lightning bolt hit the geese, killing and roasting them in an instant. Local legend reports that 52 of these 'pre-cooked' birds fell on the amazed and grateful townspeople below, many of whom scooped them up from the ground and took them home to eat for dinner.

Pennies from heaven
With winds that swirl at speeds of up to 120 km/h, tornadoes have the power to move the heaviest of objects. A tornado that whipped over a small village in Gorki, Russia, picked up 1,000 coins that had been buried in the ground since the 16th century. Sweeping over Merchery on 17 June 1940, it later deposited this treasure trove on delighted villagers.

Fisherman's friends
Spectators were showered with giant maggots while they were watching a yachting race on the coast of Acapulco, Mexico, in 1968. The creatures that fell, around a centimetre long, were still alive when they reached the ground. Upward air currents from a nearby thunderstorm had probably scooped the maggots high into the rain-clouds.

Catch a falling star
The Welsh dubbed it *pwdre ser*, meaning 'star rot', but no-one really knows the origin of the foul-smelling jellied ball that was spotted in a garden in the British Isles in June 1978. A day after Mrs Ephgrave had prodded the

ON HEARING THE SOUND OF FALLING LUMPS OF MUD, THE MANAGER OF A SWIMMING POOL IN TROWBRIDGE, UK,

HOPPING MAD

WAS SURPRISED TO SEE HUNDREDS OF TINY FROGS TUMBLING FROM THE SKY. MR E. ETTLES FOUND THE FROGS SCATTERED ON A CONCRETE PATH AND NEARBY GRASS, EVEN IN AN OLD BATH TUB THAT HAD BEEN LEFT OUTSIDE THE POOL. HE WAS EVEN MORE SURPRISED TO SEE A FEW OF THEM LEAP AWAY, ALIVE AND WELL AFTER THIS UNLIKELY DOWNPOUR ON 16 JUNE 1939. A SHOWER OF FROGS WAS ALSO REPORTED ON 27 JULY 1979 WHEN MRS MCWILLIAM OF BEDFORD, UK, FOUND A HUGE NUMBER OF SMALL FROGS COVERING HER GARDEN AFTER A HEAVY SHOWER OF RAIN, LEAVING THE BRANCHES OF TREES DRAPED WITH WHAT APPEARED TO BE FROGSPAWN. ON 24 OCT 1987, NEWSPAPERS COVERED THE STORY OF AN OLD LADY WHO HAD REPORTED A FALL OF PINK-COLOURED FROGS ON HER HOME IN STROUD, UK, DURING A TORRENTIAL SHOWER OF RAIN A WEEK EARLIER.

football-sized mass that had settled behind her Cambridge home, she was astonished to see it had disappeared. Although star rot undoubtedly falls from the sky, it is unlikely this material is of cosmic origin. A slightly more plausible explanation is that the star rot is frogs' innards vomited by overhead birds or blue-green algae carried by the wind.

Drops of blood
When red sand from the Sahara Desert is picked up by high winds, it can fall over Europe or northern Africa like drops of blood. After the rain dries, the red dust remains, looking like a thin layer of rust. Around 300,000 kg of 'blood rain' from the Sahara fell on the French city of Lyon on 17 Oct 1846.

SHOWERED WITH MAGGOTS

DEFYING RATIONAL EXPLANATION AND PREVAILING WEATHER SCIENCE, OUTLANDISH OBJECTS, UNIDENTIFIED MATERIALS AND SOMETIMES EVEN LIVING ANIMALS HAVE ALL FALLEN FROM THE SKY IN STRANGE RAIN SHOWERS

DATA-BURST

HAS STRANGE RAIN BEEN SCIENTIFICALLY STUDIED?
YES. THE FAMOUS PHYSICIST ROBERT BOYLE, FOR INSTANCE, REPORTED EXAMINING 'A GOODLY QUANTITY' OF STAR ROT. NATURALIST CHARLES DARWIN ESTIMATED THE SPREAD OF A BLOOD RAIN SHOWER OVER CAPE VERDE, AND OTHERS HAVE ANALYZED SAMPLES OF FALLEN MATERIAL.

DO SCIENTISTS KNOW WHAT CAUSES STRANGE RAIN?
NOT FULLY. THEY THINK POWERFUL WINDS CAN PICK UP CREATURES AND OBJECTS BUT THERE ARE STILL MANY UNANSWERED QUESTIONS: FOR INSTANCE, WHY DOES STRANGE RAIN ONLY EVER PICK UP ONE SPECIES OF ANIMAL AT A TIME? HOW CAN WIND EXPLAIN STRANGE RAIN THAT CONTAINS DEEP SEA FISH?

WHAT IS THE MOST GHASTLY RAIN?
ACCORDING TO URBAN MYTH, SOME PEOPLE HAVE BEEN SHOWERED WITH BLUE ICE, FROZEN WATER AND OTHER MATERIAL FROM THE TOILETS OF OVERHEAD AIRCRAFT.

IS STRANGE RAIN EVER SALTY?
NO. ALTHOUGH MARINE ANIMALS HAVE FALLEN AS STRANGE RAIN, THE RAIN THAT DROPS WITH THEM IS FRESH WATER, NOT SEA WATER.

HOW MUCH DEBRIS FALLS WITH STRANGE RAIN?
NONE. ANOTHER MYSTERY IS HOW OBJECTS AND CREATURES CAN BE SCOOPED UP AND DROPPED BY THE WIND BUT THE SOIL SURROUNDING THEM IS LEFT BEHIND.

HOW FAR CAN STRANGE RAIN TRAVEL?
IT CAN TRAVEL FOR THOUSANDS OF MILES. A SCIENTIST ANALYZING THE BLOOD RAIN THAT COVERED LYON IN 1846 WAS ASTOUNDED TO FIND IT CONTAINED TINY ORGANISMS ALL THE WAY FROM SOUTH AMERICA.

ARE ALL STRANGE RAINS GENUINE?
ALMOST CERTAINLY NOT, FOR INSTANCE FLESH THAT WAS THOUGHT TO HAVE RAINED ONTO A FIELD IN TENNESSEE, USA, IN 1841 WAS LATER FOUND TO HAVE BEEN SPREAD THERE BY DISGRUNTLED WORKERS.

With added fibre
When Captain J.N. Gowrie looked at the decks of his ship on 12 March 1993, he was amazed to find them littered with wool and cotton. Somehow, the wind and rain had carried strands of these fibres onto his vessel. The material must have travelled a long way before it hit the deck; Gowrie and his ship were in the middle of the South Pacific Ocean.

Going haywire
Heavy showers of falling hay have been known to darken skies. On 14 July 1875, the Reverend T. Power raised the alarm when he saw a cloud of hay raining on Monkstown, Ireland. Wet and heavy with dew, the hay seemed to drop in individual stems. This peculiar downpour, which lasted for about five minutes,.left hay scattered over an area of 0.5 km².

Singularly odd
The strangest rain comes in a single drop. On a summer's evening in 1990, one P.W. Becker was sitting in his car when something fell on its roof with an enormous thud. When he went out to see what it was, he was surprised to find a frozen chunk of pizza which had presumably fallen from the sky. Other objects that have fallen from the sky include an ice sheet the size of a grand piano which fell in Connecticut, USA in June 1985, crushing a garden fence.

Animal, mineral, vegetable
A wide variety of bizarre matter has rained down on the unsuspecting public, including: fish in East Ham in London in 1984; hazelnuts in Dublin in 1987; crayfish in Florida in 1954; and coal in Bournemouth in 1983. On 12 Feb 1979, a shower of mustard seeds struck a house in Southampton, followed by broad bean and haricot bean seeds the next day. Among the multifarious items to have rained down during the last 100 years are apples, peas, nails, crabs and pieces of crockery as well as less identifiable slimes, goos and jellies.

LEFT: ICE-COATED COAL AND GRIT THAT FELL DURING A HAILSTORM OVER POOLE, UK, 5 JUNE 1983 · RIGHT: SPECIMENS OF THE FISH FALL AT EAST HAM, LONDON, MAY 1984

As meteorologists have begun to understand the mechanisms of the atmosphere, some have wondered if they can control it like any other machine. Just 100 years ago, any scientist wishing to manipulate the weather would have been regarded as arrogant. But dustbowls, wars and the famines of the 20th century have encouraged a more receptive attitude to the rainmakers. Ironically, while they have discovered what makes complex systems like the atmosphere tick, scientists have realized that it may be more dangerous than they imagined to meddle with the world's weather.

Rainbow warriors

An exploded nuclear bomb releases millions of charged particles that can interact with the air, making it glow. In this way, the particles can create aurora or northern lights—brilliant colours illuminating the sky. Synthetic aurora seen around the planet in July 1962 caused worldwide fury. The result of a nuclear test codenamed Operation Dominic, the light displays were generated by a series of 'rainbow bombs' detonated in the air around Christmas Island in the South Pacific by US government scientists. Hailed as a research experiment to increase our understanding of the stratosphere, Operation Dominic helped to fuel Cold War paranoia.

Stealing thunder

Experimenters in the USA and Japan have been zapping thunderclouds with high-powered laser beams in an attempt to strike back at lightning. A beam of laser light can charge a channel of air between a thundercloud and the ground, acting as a short circuit for a lightning bolt. Every year, lightning causes around $100 million worth of damage to crops and property in the USA alone. It is therefore not surprising that companies are willing to invest millions in a bid to control storms.

First fall

A group of scientists felt a flurry of excitement when snow fell on 13 Nov 1946. The flakes, which sprinkled over Pittfield, USA, were the first ever to be artificially coaxed out of the clouds. Minutes beforehand, meteorologists had thrown just over a kilogram of dry ice into a cloud. As they pulled away in their aircraft, they were amazed by what happened to the cloud. As team member Vincent Schaefer explained, "it seemed as though it had almost exploded, the effect was so widespread and rapid". Snow burst from the cloud in seconds, showing them they could change the weather on tap.

HUMAN WEATHER
70% OF WATER CAN BE

Cloud crackers

A self-styled rainmaker in the 1890s blamed birds for the lack of rain. Michael Cahill wrote to the governor of Kansas, USA, to explain how high-flying birds 'open vents for the vapour' where clouds could form. He urged the governor to train birds to fly on command, making rain when needed. In the 1930s, at the height of the US drought, rainmaking still attracted a fair number of eccentrics. James Boze, an enthusiastic experimenter, died while detonating 'moisture bombs' in the air. Frank Clark, a spare-time mechanic, made a fruitless rainmaking machine that could also pick up radio signals.

Rain factory

After studying the clouds that formed over a paper mill, meteorologist Graeme Mather found a new way to coax rain from the sky. He noticed how clouds above the mill produced far more rain than others. Later he discovered that the mill's chimneys were belching fine particles into the air that were inadvertently 'seeding' the cloud, making rain fall. Experimenting with flares that blew dust into clouds, he found a way to coax up to 70% of the water out of cloud. Earlier attempts to seed the clouds had only managed to make 20% of rainwater fall.

Silver lining

The Taiwanese government regularly sprinkles clouds with a fine dust of silver iodide. This helps the clouds to produce rain that can be captured in huge dams to fuel the country's hydroelectric power stations. Tiny drops of silver iodide in a cloud eventually freeze, forming large lumps that fall from the sky.

City heat

Visitors to Columbia, South Carolina, USA, are guaranteed a warmer welcome than ever because the city acts as an 'urban heat island'. Between 1968 and 1975, the population of Columbia grew from 200 to 20,000. Now a mini-metropolis, Columbia is packed with houses, offices and cars that burn fossil fuels, all of which feed heat into the city's air. Rural Columbia was thick with soil and vegetation that could cool the air by evaporating water. But much of the modern city is covered with tarmac and paving, materials that trap heat. As a result, Columbia is now around 8°C warmer than it was in the 1960s.

STRANGE TRAIL

THERE IS NOTHING UNUSUAL ABOUT A PLANE'S VAPOUR TRAIL, THE STREAM OF WHITE CLOUDS THAT STRETCH OUT BEHIND IT. BUT IN 1994, T. SURENDONK SAW ONE THAT WAS SO CURIOUS, HE DECIDED TO DESCRIBE IT IN A LETTER TO THE 'NEW SCIENTIST'. A 'THIN TUBE OF MISTY AIR' PASSED HIM AT HIGH SPEED JUST 25 SECONDS AFTER A PLANE LANDED. MOVING AT A VERY LOW ALTITUDE, IT WAS 'ACCOMPANIED BY A RATHER LARGE FLAPPING SOUND'. IT IS QUITE LIKELY THAT THE BODY OF AN AIRCRAFT, NOT ITS ENGINES, CAUSED THIS PECULIAR STREAM OF MOISTURE. IN VERY HUMID WEATHER, AIR CRUSHED AROUND A LOW-FLYING AIRCRAFT CAN CONDENSE TO FORM THIN LINES OF CLOUD IN A SIMILAR WAY, AND FORMULA 1 CARS CAN CREATE SWIRLS OF VAPOUR AS THEY CUT THROUGH THE AIR.

RIGHT: DARK STORM CLOUDS · INSET: EXPERIMENT SHOWING AN ARTIFICIAL CLOUD 'SEEDED' WITH SILVER IODIDE CAUSING RAIN AND SNOWFALL, WILTSHIRE, UK, 1955

COAXED FROM CLOUDS

NOT CONTENT WITH SIMPLY OBSERVING THE ELEMENTS,
SCIENTISTS ARE NOW FINDING WAYS TO MANIPULATE
THE WORLD'S WEATHER—THE HUMAN IMPACT ON THE
ATMOSPHERE COULD CHANGE THE CLIMATE FOR GOOD

About 65 million years ago, dinosaurs roamed the Earth. Then a giant asteroid struck, wiping out the dominant lifeforms and radically reshaping evolution. A repeat could theoretically occur at any time and, if the world's entire nuclear arsenal were to explode at once, the consequence would be nothing compared with such a natural disaster.

The biggest bang
Around half of the species living on Earth were wiped out by the giant asteroid 10 km in diameter that struck the Earth in the Yucatan region of Mexico 65 million years ago. Known as the KT Event, the asteroid hit Earth travelling at a phenomenal rate of 20 km per second, forming a crater nearly 200 km wide. The surrounding 20,000 km³ were instantly vapourized, and more than 1 trillion tonnes of carbon dioxide and sulphur were

cataclysm, which saw mass extinction of many life forms. Dust from the collisions was propelled into the atmosphere, blocked out the heat of the Sun, destroying many life-forms. The cooling may also explain the formation of the first Antarctic ice sheets, which developed at around this time.

The Devil's Canyon
The Meteor Crater, in the Canyon Diablo region of the Arizona desert, USA, was formed about 50,000

This would have caused climatic upset, as large quantities of dust and debris were hurled into the atmosphere, bringing significantly cooler temperatures worldwide.

Cosmic near miss
On 30 June 1908, a huge explosion rocked the scarcely-populated basin of the Podkamennaya Tunguska River in Russia. The cause was almost certainly an asteroid or comet exploding 7–10 km above the Earth's surface. Eyewitnesses

miss. Travelling at 40 km per second, if it were to hit the Earth, the effects would be catastrophic. A direct collision would wipe out most life forms. Its next predicted near-miss will be on 29 Sept 2004, when it should pass within 1.55 million km of the Earth.

Calculated gamble
Media interest in cosmic impacts reached fever pitch in March 1998 when it was announced that an asteroid was on a direct collision

COSMIC IMPACT
800-KM FIREBALL

described a great flash in the sky, followed by intense heat and a giant fireball 800 km long and as bright as the Sun. The explosion could be heard 800 km away, and the fireball was visible in Kirensk, 400 km away. No deaths were reported, although people were blown off their feet, sheep were incinerated and an area of forest 3,900 km² was devastated. Despite a long and extensive search, no fragments of the cosmic body have ever been recovered.

Lessons from space
In 1994, a fragmented comet called Shoemaker-Levy 9 crashed into the planet Jupiter, teaching us a great deal about the possible effects of a similar cosmic impact on the Earth. Fragments up to 3 km in diameter struck Jupiter with a force equivalent to the explosion of 11 million atomic bombs of the size that were dropped on Hiroshima. A fireball rose 3,000 km into the air, forming craters the size of our planet.

Erratic behaviour
An asteroid known as 4179 Toutasis orbits the Earth and has come very close to collision on several occasions. Measuring 4.8 km in diameter, the asteroid has an unusual dumbbell shape and a complex rotation. Despite attempts to plot its path, its erratic route makes it impossible to say with certainty whether it will ever collide with our planet. On 29 Nov 1996, Toutasis passed 5.3 million km from the Earth which, in astronomical terms, is a very near

course with Earth. Astronomers had first identified the potential for a serious cosmic impact in late 1997 and having charted its course since then, they predicted that the space rock called 1997 XF11 would pass within 50,000 km of the Earth on 26 October 2028. If these calculations were only slightly out, the asteroid could have hit the Earth head on with awesome force. However, subsequent calculations have suggested that the asteroid will actually pass about 500,000 km from our planet, substantially reducing the risk of impact.

released into the atmosphere, later bringing global warming and acid rain. The species that survived the fires and floods had to endure thousands of years in which conditions were unstable and food was scarce, thus the hierarchies of life were radically transformed. This precipitated the evolution of mammals, and therefore humans, at the expense of the dinosaurs and other large reptiles.

Double impact
The KT impact of 65 million years ago was followed 35,200,000 years ago by another large mass extinction. The massive Popigai crater in central Siberia and another in Chesapeake Bay, off the eastern coast of the USA, are evidence of two cosmic impacts that occurred in relatively quick succession. This double impact may have been the cause the Eocene

years ago by a nickel-iron meteorite 60 m in diameter. The meteorite was virtually intact when it hit the ground, at which point it was vapourized, dispersing thousands of tonnes of material over a 260 km² region, to form a crater 1,219 m across. The energy of the impact has been estimated at about 60,000,000,000,000,000 joules, or 750 times the explosive power of the atomic bomb dropped on Hiroshima, Japan, in 1945.

Ancient destruction
For centuries, historians have puzzled over the reasons why flourishing ancient civilizations in China, Egypt, Greece, India and Israel all collapsed in rapid succession. The answer could be that a shower of 100 metre-wide meteorites, perhaps fragments from a single larger body, pounded the Earth around 4,300 years ago.

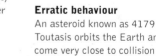

JARGON

ASTEROID WINTER
A COLD AND LIFELESS PERIOD OF TIME CAUSED BY ASTEROID DEBRIS BLOCKING THE HEAT OF THE SUN

CHICXULUB IMPACT
AN IMPACT 65 MILLION YEARS AGO OFF THE YUCATAN PENINSULA, MEXICO, WHICH IS BELIEVED TO BE RESPONSIBLE FOR THE KT EVENT

EARTH-CROSSING ASTEROID [ECA]
AN ASTRAL BODY WHICH CROSSES THE PATH THAT THE EARTH MAKES IN ITS ORBIT AROUND THE SUN

KT-BOUNDARY
THE PLACE AT WHICH THE KT EVENT TOOK PLACE

KT EVENT
GEOLOGICAL SHIFT 65 MILLION YEARS AGO THOUGHT TO HAVE WIPED OUT THE DINOSAURS. SO-CALLED BECAUSE IT MARKED THE TRANSITION FROM CRETACEOUS (K) TO TERTIARY (T) PERIODS

NEAR-EARTH-OBJECTS [NEOs]
ASTEROIDS AND COMETS THAT ARE IN CLOSE ENOUGH PROXIMITY TO EARTH TO POSE A SERIOUS THREAT

LEFT: ARTIST'S IMPRESSION OF A SUPER IMPACT OF AN ASTEROID 800 KM IN DIAMETER · RIGHT: AERIAL VIEW OF THE METEOR CRATER, CANYON DIABLO, ARIZONA, FORMED 50,000 YEARS AGO

DATA-BURST

HOW MANY NEOs ARE THERE?
MILLIONS OF COSMIC BODIES CROSS THE EARTH'S ORBIT. ABOUT 2000 OF THESE ARE GREATER THAN 1 KM IN DIAMETER.

HOW OFTEN DO POTENTIALLY CATASTROPHIC NEOs STRIKE EARTH?
THE ODDS OF AN OBJECT STRIKING THE EARTH WITH GLOBALLY CATASTROPHIC CONSEQUENCES IS 1 IN 2 MILLION.

HOW FAST DO IMPACTORS HIT?
IMPACTORS CAN HIT EARTH AT SPEEDS FROM 10–70 KM PER SECOND, EQUIVALENT TO 36,000–252,000 KM/H.

HOW MUCH DO NEOs WEIGH?
ESTIMATES SUGGEST THAT OBJECTS IN THE 1-KM CLASS COULD WEIGH A BILLION TONNES. HALE BOPP HAD A MASS OF AROUND 10 MILLION TONNES.

HOW MANY IMPACT CRATERS EXIST?
THERE ARE 120 TERRESTRIAL IMPACT CRATERS ON EARTH AT THE MOMENT. DYNAMIC PROCESSES, SUCH AS VOLCANOES, HAVE DESTROYED MANY.

WHAT COULD BE DONE TO PREVENT A DISASTER?
THE EARTH'S NUCLEAR ARSENAL COULD BE RE-DIRECTED TOWARD ANY ONCOMING HEAVENLY BODIES, OR SEEK AND DESTROY MISSIONS COULD BE CARRIED OUT, USING STAR WARS DEFENCE MECHANISMS, LASERS OR KINETIC ENERGY WEAPONS.

HOW MANY PEOPLE HAVE BEEN KILLED BY IMPACTS?
ALTHOUGH ANCIENT CHINESE RECORDS DESCRIBE DEATH BY METEORITES, NO HUMAN DEATHS HAVE BEEN REPORTED IN THE LAST MILLENNIUM.

THE END IS NIGH?

USING ADVANCED COMPUTER SIMULATIONS ON SUPERCOMPUTERS, GEOPHYSICAL DATA OF PAST IMPACTS AND OBSERVATIONS FROM OTHER CELESTIAL BODIES, SCIENTISTS ARE ABLE TO CONSTRUCT A SCENARIO OF FUTURE IMPACT. THE SCALE OF THE COSMIC IMPACT AND ITS ENSUING EFFECTS WOULD OBVIOUSLY DEPEND ON THE SIZE OF THE ASTEROID. ANY OBJECT MORE THAN 2 KM IN DIAMETER WOULD CERTAINLY HAVE GLOBAL IMPLICATIONS. A CRATER 10–15 TIMES THE SIZE OF THE OBJECT WOULD BE CREATED, TSUNAMI 100 M HIGH WOULD BE GENERATED AND THERE COULD WELL BE A SERIES OF SERIOUS EARTHQUAKES. A FIREBALL WOULD COMBINE WITH THE NITROGEN IN THE AIR TO PRODUCE NITRIC ACID, WHICH WOULD RESULT IN GLOBAL ACID RAIN OF CATACLYSMIC PROPORTIONS. A JET OF DUST WOULD BE PROPELLED INTO THE STRATOSPHERE, WHICH WOULD BLOCK OUT THE HEAT AND LIGHT OF THE SUN, AS WELL AS GENERATING ENOUGH NITROUS OXIDE TO DEPLETE THE OZONE LAYER AND PERHAPS EVEN DESTROY IT. AS TEMPERATURES BEGAN TO DROP BY TENS OF DEGREES CENTIGRADE, A 'NUCLEAR WINTER' WOULD SET IN, WIPING OUT BILLIONS OF LIVES. THE BITTER COOLING OF THE EARTH WOULD EVENTUALLY END IN A GREENHOUSE EFFECT AS ADDITIONAL CARBON DIOXIDE RELEASED IN THE EXPLOSION WARMED UP THE EARTH. LIFE AND CIVILIZATION WOULD BE ALTERED BEYOND ALL RECOGNITION. IT IS ESTIMATED THAT A SERIOUS COSMIC IMPACT OCCURS ABOUT ONCE EVERY 500,000 YEARS, GIVING ABOUT A ONE IN 10,000 CHANCE THAT IT WOULD OCCUR IN OUR LIFETIME.

BURNS BRIGHT AS THE SUN

SPACE IS A COSMIC JUNKYARD. AT ANY TIME, ONE OF THE COUNTLESS ASTEROIDS THAT LURK IN SPACE AND CIRCLE OUR PLANET COULD COME CRASHING TO EARTH WITH POTENTIALLY CATASTROPHIC CONSEQUENCES

Fossils preserved in rocks are the remains of creatures, often extinct, from the distant past. They provide the evidence from which it is possible to chart the history of life on Earth. The earliest fossils are found in rocks 3.5 billion years old: tiny organisms, such as bacteria and blue-green algae, are thought to have been the Earth's first life forms. The oldest animal fossils are of soft-bodied worm-like creatures that date back 700 million years. Fossils of animals and plants that are still alive today can only be found in rocks formed 570 million years ago. Animals with backbones, or vertebrates, only appear in rocks aged around 400 million years.

The first fossils

Palaeontologists used to believe that fossils preceding the beginning of the Cambrian period, 550

any organized fossil record were found in 1818 in Connecticut, USA. At the time, they were thought to be of human origin, but were later identified as Anchisaurus. In the 1820s, fossils of Megalosaurus and Iguanodon, including a jawbone with teeth intact, were found in the UK, and in 1834 the partial skeleton of another Iguanodon was found near Brighton, UK, and gave scientists the first insight into what dinosaurs looked like. Over 150

animals, like modern reptiles. Palaeontologists at Oregon State University, USA, discovered that dinosaurs lacked a particular bone in their nasal passages that was present in the warm-blooded mammals of the time. In 1996, palaeontologists at the University of Chicago made a further dinosaur breakthrough when they added two new dinosaurs to the fossil record. They found the new remains in Morocco and dated them to about 90 million years

palaeontologists regard Homo habilis as the first true hominid. But a species much more closely recognizable as an ancestor of modern humans had already been found. This was Homo erectus, a hominid that lived in Africa, Asia and Europe during the Pleistocene epoch, surviving until 200,000 years ago. The first specimen was found in Java in 1890 and was followed by finds in China, Tanzania, Morocco, Algeria, Germany and finally Hungary in

FOSSILS
10,000 YEARS OF

million years ago, were very simple life forms. However, studies of the Ediacaran rock formation in Australia have revealed the existence of complex organisms living before this time. The rock has preserved the soft bodies of plants and animals living in the area between 600 and 700 million years ago. These include jellyfish and other free-floating animals, some of which have body parts for movement and digestion.

Big bones

The word 'dinosaur' was coined in 1841 by Richard Owen, an English palaeontologist. It comes from the Greek meaning deinos (terrible) sauros (lizard). The extensive picture of dinosaurs we have today is built entirely from fossil records. Palaeontologists estimate that the dinosaur remains which have been discovered so far represent less than 0.0001% of all the dinosaurs that ever lived on Earth. The earliest bones to be catalogued in

years later, we know much more about the variety and habits of dinosaurs and their connections with modern animals. They appear to be most closely related to crocodiles, but may well be linked to many of today's species. Some of them clearly walked upright, such as Tyrannosaurus rex, while others, such as Diplodocus, walked on four legs. Fossils found in groups tell us that dinosaurs may have travelled or lived in herds, and bones found close to crocodile and turtle remains suggest that some species lived in or near water. But there is much that fossils cannot tell us—such as what dinosaur skin was like, how developed their senses were and how they communicated with each other.

Cold-blooded

Recent breakthroughs in the field of dinosaur palaeontology include the discovery in 1995 of evidence which seems to confirm that dinosaurs were cold-blooded

ago. Both were large, carnivorous dinosaurs. Carcharodontosaurus saharicus, had a 1.6 m long skull; the other, Deltadromeus agilis, had long legs for speed and agility.

Swamp life

Plants which lived and died in swamps millions of years ago were transformed at first into peat, and then, due to heat and pressure from overlying layers of mud and silt, into fossil fuels such as coal, oil and gas. A 30-cm deep section of coal represents 10,000 years of peat accumulation. Most fossil fuel used today was formed 65 million years ago.

Human remains

Fossilized bones and teeth provide the only evidence we have about members of the family Hominidae from which modern humans, or Homo sapiens, are thought to have descended. In 1924, in a cave at Tuang, South Africa, the first remains of the species Australopithecus were discovered. The find consisted of a child's skull, dating from the earlier Pliocene epoch, 5.3–1.6 million years ago. The discovery of this hominid was followed 35 years later by the discovery of some remains of a hominid species from the Pleistocene epoch, 1.6 million to 10,000 years ago. Later called Homo habilis, this species was first discovered in the Olduvai Gorge in northern Tanzania in 1959. Tools were also found in the Gorge and the brain of Homo habilis was much larger than that of its predecessor. For this reason, many

1965. The earliest known Homo sapiens remains were unearthed by workmen in the Neander Valley in Germany in 1856. Later called Neanderthals, or cold-adapted humans, these hominids lived in Europe about 200,000–100,000 years ago. Remains of another form of Homo sapiens—Cro-Magnons—were found in a rock shelter in the Dordogne, France, in 1868. Debate still rages among palaeontologists about the exact places in the fossil record of all these hominids, their various routes of migration and their connection to modern humans.

JARGON

EXOBIOLOGY
THE STUDY OF LIFE ON OTHER PLANETS

EXTANT
STILL LIVING ON EARTH

EXTINCT
NO LONGER LIVING ON EARTH

FOSSIL RECORD
ALL THE FOSSILS AND DATA CONNECTED WITH THEM GATHERED FROM AROUND THE WORLD

INDEX FOSSIL
A FOSSIL USED TO ESTIMATE GEOLOGICAL TIME

PALAEOBOTANISTS
SCIENTISTS SPECIALIZING IN THE STUDY OF FOSSILIZED PLANTS

PALAEONTOLOGISTS
SCIENTISTS SPECIALIZING IN THE STUDY OF FOSSILS

PETRIFICATION
THE CONVERSION OVER TIME OF SKELETAL PARTS OF ANIMALS INTO A STONE-LIKE SUBSTANCE

LEFT: THIS CARBONIFEROUS FOSSILIZED FERN MAY HAVE BEEN PRESERVED IN ROCK FOR HUNDREDS OF MILLIONS OF YEARS · RIGHT: THE BONES OF A FOSSILIZED FISH

DATA-BURST

CAN ALL ANIMALS SURVIVE AS FOSSILS?
NO. MOST FOSSILS ARE OF ORGANISMS WITH A PROMINENT BACKBONE. IN SOME CASES, ENTIRE SHELLS ARE FOUND IN LAYERS OF ROCK, SUCH AS THOSE OF CLAMS, BUT MOST FOSSILS ARE PETRIFIED BONES.

WHY ARE FOSSILS NOT FOUND IN COAL?
COAL ITSELF IS A MASS OF COMPRESSED FOSSILIZED PLANT MATERIAL. PLANT FOSSILS ARE FOUND ONLY BETWEEN LAYERS OF COAL.

HOW ARE FOSSILS PRESERVED AT THE BOTTOM OF THE OCEAN?
THE LEVELS OF OXYGEN AND BACTERIA ON OCEAN FLOORS ARE LOW, SO DEAD ORGANISMS EITHER DECOMPOSE VERY SLOWLY OR NOT AT ALL, PARTICULARLY

IF THEY ARE QUICKLY BURIED BY LAYERS OF SEDIMENT. THIS CREATES VERY WELL PRESERVED FOSSILS.

CAN FOSSILS REVEAL USEFUL INFORMATION ABOUT THE ENVIRONMENT OF THE DISTANT PAST?
YES. BY ANALYZING FOSSILIZED PLANT POLLENS AND SPORES, FOR EXAMPLE, PALAEOBOTANISTS WORKING IN PANAMA IN 1994 WERE ABLE TO ESTABLISH THAT LEVELS OF CARBON DIOXIDE IN THE ATMOSPHERE HAVE FLUCTUATED DURING THE EARTH'S HISTORY.

WHAT ARE ZONE FOSSILS?
ZONE FOSSILS, OR MARKER FOSSILS, ARE THOSE WHICH APPEAR IN ALMOST ALL SEDIMENTARY ROCKS OF THE SAME AGE. EACH GEOLOGICAL PERIOD HAS A ZONE FOSSIL.

FOSSILS FROM OTHER WORLDS

IN 1996, THE US SPACE AGENCY, NASA, DISCOVERED THAT A METEORITE KNOWN AS ALH84001, FOUND IN THE ALLAN HILLS ICE FIELD OF ANTARCTICA, CONTAINED FOSSILIZED ORGANIC MATERIAL AND BACTERIA THAT WAS AN ESTIMATED 3.6 BILLION YEARS OLD. BY COMPARING THE METEORITE TO MATERIAL COLLECTED BY THE VIKING SPACECRAFT WHICH LANDED ON MARS IN 1976, SCIENTISTS WERE ABLE TO DEDUCE THAT THE 1.9-KG LUMP OF ROCK FOUND IN ANTARCTICA WAS FORMED 4.5 BILLION YEARS AGO WHEN MARS ITSELF APPEARED. IT PROBABLY LEFT MARS AROUND 16 MILLION YEARS AGO AND REACHED EARTH AS A METEORITE 13,000 YEARS AGO. THE FOSSILS ON AND IN THE METEORITE RESEMBLE BACTERIA ALSO FOUND ON EARTH 3.6 BILLION YEARS AGO.

PEAT EQUALS 30 CM OF COAL

FOSSILS ARE ANIMALS AND PLANTS WHICH HAVE BEEN PRESERVED IN THE LAYERS OF THE EARTH'S CRUST. THEIR DISCOVERY HAS PROVIDED US WITH TANTALISING CLUES ABOUT LIFE ON THE PLANET MANY MILLIONS OF YEARS AGO

FROZEN IN TIME
5,000-YEAR-OLD MAN

Phenomena which defy the processes of decay brought on by the passage of time fascinate humans. Ancient cultures, such as the Egyptians, often developed unique ways of preserving the bodies of their dead. When animals or humans are frozen in time, scientists are provided with an ideal resource for studying prehistoric DNA and gaining insights into ancient customs.

Semi-precious time capsules

When prehistoric insects became trapped in sticky tree resin, they were suspended in time, to be discovered intact 40–60 million years later. Prehistoric plants onto which the resin dripped were also

JOURNEYS BEYOND DEATH

THE INCAS OF SOUTH AMERICA AND THE ANCIENT EGYPTIANS BOTH PRACTISED ELABORATE DEATH RITES, PERFECTING THE TECHNIQUE OF EMBALMING. THEY WRAPPED CORPSES AS A MARK OF RESPECT AND ALSO TO ENSURE THEIR SAFE PASSAGE INTO THE NEXT WORLD. IN ANCIENT EGYPT, WHERE A NUMBER OF MUMMIES STILL REST WITHIN THE PYRAMIDS AT GIZA, THE BODY WAS PRESERVED TO HELP THE SOUL IN THIS JOURNEY. IN THE OLD TESTAMENT, JOSEPH AND JACOB ARE MUMMIFIED WHILE THE TIBETAN BOOK OF THE DEAD RECORDS THAT THE DALAI AND TASHI LAMAS WERE BOTH MUMMIFIED. IN PEKING, CHINA, THE 2,000-YEAR-OLD MUMMIFIED BODY OF A WOMAN WAS FOUND IN A PYRAMID. SCIENTISTS WHO EXAMINED HER SKIN AND HAIR WERE AMAZED BY HOW WELL THEY HAD BEEN PRESERVED.

FROZEN IN ALPINE ICE

BRIEF MOMENTS OF LIFE CAPTURED IN FREEZE-FRAME, SUCH AS AN EGG-LAYING MOTH PRESERVED BY STICKY TREE RESIN OR A FULLY-CLOTHED HUMAN BODY FROZEN IN ICE, HELP US TO RECONSTRUCT THE JIGSAW OF OUR PAST

preserved as the thick liquid hardened to form translucent golden-yellow amber. Most amber finds have been made on the shores of the Baltic Sea, but in the hills of the Dominican Republic in the Caribbean, a local miner found some 25 million-year-old amber in which several insects were trapped. They included a praying mantis, a queen ant, a stingless bee and a large termite. Other remarkable amber legacies include a weevil trapped in Lebanese amber which contains DNA 125 million years old—the oldest known to science. Some animals caught in the resin have been freeze-framed in the middle of their daily lives. These preserved action scenes include two gall midges mating and a moth laying eggs. Even desperate struggles to escape the sticky resin have been recorded: one piece of amber contains the body of a gecko with a broken back, which probably snapped as it tried to escape the glue-like liquid.

Ice mammoths

For thousands of years, the frozen landscape of Siberia has preserved the bodies of huge elephant-like mammoths, which wandered the Earth during the Pleistocene epoch 1.6 million–10,000 years ago.

The hairy prehistoric giants reached 4 m high at the shoulder and had dense coats and a layer of fat 8 cm thick to protect them in their cold environment. Scientists believe that the frozen mammoths may have accidentally stumbled into crevices and, unable to get out, they became literally frozen in time. Their deep-frozen bodies are often remarkably well preserved. There have even been cases of Siberian dogs feeding on the meat of frozen mammoths 30,000 years old. Some of the earliest mammoth discoveries, found in the 1770s, were still covered in hair.

Bog men

Over the past 50 years, some 2,000 well preserved human bodies have been discovered in peat bogs all over Europe. Peat bogs have similar preservative qualities to ice. In 1938, a 3,000-year-old man was discovered in a bog in Emmer-Erfscheidenveen in Holland. His clothes were in a good state of repair and included a sheepskin cap, deerskin shoes, a coarsely-woven undergarment with an embroidered hem which hung to his knees, and an animal-skin cape. This discovery gave historians a remarkable insight into Bronze Age culture. Perhaps the most

famous peat body is Tollund Man, found in 1950 in Jutland, Denmark. He had a leather cord around his neck, indicating that he may have been hanged or committed suicide. Moreover he was naked apart from a belt and a hat, suggesting the possibility of a ritual killing or human sacrifice.

Pete Marsh

In 1984, a peat worker in Cheshire, UK, discovered human skin and bone hidden in a bog. The fragments were soon found to be part of the well-preserved body of a man estimated to have died shortly after the birth of Christ. The body, named Lindow man, or Pete Marsh, was in a good enough condition for scientists to learn much about him. His stomach revealed he had eaten a last meal of bread while his general health was found to be good—except for slight arthritis and a problem with worms. His teeth and nails were also in good condition. The man had a hole in the top of his skull and on his skin were traces of chemicals which suggested that he had been painted green or blue. A cord of animal sinew hung around his neck. A forensic expert helped to establish several possible causes of death: a blow to the head; a blow to the back which broke a rib; or strangulation, which would have caused a broken neck and blocked windpipe.

The Ice Man

The oldest complete human body ever found is the Ice Man, or Ötzi, discovered by a German tourist on the border of Italy and Austria in 1991. This man, dated to 3,300 BC, is thought to have died of exposure as he tried to cross the Alps. He lay in a small hollow in the ice of the Similaun Glacier where he was lost for over 5,000 years until the ice started to melt. He is estimated to have been about 30 years old when he undertook his journey and was small by modern standards—standing only 1.5 m tall and weighing 50 kg. His leather shoes were stuffed with grass and the hairs remaining on his head showed that he used to have it cut—the earliest evidence yet found of haircutting. He carried equipment for his expedition, including a small copper-bladed axe and a flint dagger, both with wooden handles, as well as a bow made of yew and arrows carried in a fur quiver. Even some of his food supplies were preserved: a sloe, some mushrooms and a few chewed animal bones.

DATA-BURST

HOW DOES AMBER PRESERVE THE BODIES OF ANIMALS?
CELLS NORMALLY DECOMPOSE IF WATER IS PRESENT. RESIN VAPOURS REPLACE WATER IN THE BODY CELLS OF ANIMALS TRAPPED IN AMBER, SO CELLS DO NOT DECOMPOSE BUT STAY AS THEY WERE WHEN THE ANIMAL DIED.

HOW DOES ICE PRESERVE BODIES?
ICE ACTS AS A PRESERVATIVE BY INHIBITING THE DESTRUCTIVE ACTION OF BACTERIA, YEAST AND MOULD.

HOW DOES PEAT PRESERVE BODIES?
BODIES IN PEAT ARE SANDWICHED BETWEEN LAYERS OF VEGETATION. MUCH OF THIS, SUCH AS SPHAGNUM

PLANTS, DECOMPOSES SLOWLY BECAUSE OF A CHEMICAL MAKE-UP THAT NEUTRALIZES THE CORROSIVE EFFECTS OF ACIDITY. THIS PROCESS PRESERVES PLANTS AND HUMANS.

CAN FROZEN ANIMALS TEACH US ABOUT ANCIENT LIFE ON EARTH?
PLANTS HAVE BEEN PRESERVED IN STOMACHS OF FROZEN MAMMOTHS, LEAVING THEM WELL PRESERVED FOR SCIENTIFIC ANALYSIS.

WHERE DOES THE WORD MUMMY COME FROM?
FROM THE ARABIC 'MUMIYAH' WHICH MEANS BITUMEN—A TAR-LIKE SUBSTANCE USED FOR PRESERVATION.

LEFT: EXPLORER HOLDS A 500-YEAR-OLD PERUVIAN MUMMY. FOUND IN AN ICY PIT WEARING THE FINEST CLOTHES, SHE HAD PROBABLY BEEN SACRIFICED · INSET: INSECT TRAPPED IN AMBER

For millennia, humans have been curious to explore anything that is not immediately comprehensible. This pursuit of knowledge has uncovered many of the world's secrets and mysteries, but there are still many natural phenomena that cannot, as yet, be explained by modern scientific techniques.

The Bermuda Triangle

Located in the North Atlantic Ocean, between Bermuda, the American coast and the Greater Antilles, the Bermuda Triangle has become infamous for the 50 ships and 20 aircraft that have been lost within its boundaries. Reports of disappearances date back to the 19th century, although there are legends that state that Columbus' 1492 voyage of discovery met with difficulties in the region. Craft have been discovered completely abandoned, while others have vanished without trace. Perhaps the most famous case was the disappearance of Flight 19, a squadron of US Navy Avenger torpedo-bomber planes. On the night of 5 Dec 1945, the entire squadron vanished after setting off in good weather from Fort Lauderdale. A search plane also went missing as it sought to locate the squadron. While the US Navy's official report stated that the squadron compass had failed and the aircraft had run out of fuel, a host of more outlandish theories have grown up to account for the mystery of the Bermuda Triangle. These include attacks by sea monsters, alien attack, tsunami, and methane gas release.

Nazca Lines

The Nazca lines are found on the flats of the Nazca plain, Peru, and are possibly the world's largest works of art. They comprise a series of zig-zagging lines and curves, some of which appear to depict animals. These drawings, etched on the landscape, are of massive proportion. They can only be seen from aircraft and the tops of hills. Because no-one knew they were there, the PanAmerican Highway was built straight through the desert, across the lines. The ancient land scars are thought to date from 300 BC to AD 540, and cover an area of 1,300 km². The straight lines are remarkable: they can be up to 8 km long, and run so true that they do not deviate by more than 3 m in every 1.5 km. The animals depicted include a

STRANGE PLANET

50 SHIPS LOST IN

180-m-long lizard and a 45-m-long spider. Nobody knows the exact purpose of the lines, but they may have been ritualistic religious markings depicting symbolic kinship systems or astrological charts. The most outlandish theory is that the lines and trapezoids are runways for extra-terrestrial craft.

MYSTERIOUS GIANT BALLS

LAS BOLAS GRANDES, THE GIANT BALLS, LITTER THE DIQUIS DELTA OF COSTA RICA. THESE GRANITE ORBS, OF WHICH THERE ARE MORE THAN 1,000, ARE PERFECTLY SPHERICAL. THEY VARY IN SIZE FROM A FEW CENTIMETRES TO 2.5 M IN DIAMETER. THE FORMATION OF THESE ROCK BALLS IS A MATTER OF GREAT MYSTERY, ALTHOUGH MOST RESEARCHERS

BELIEVE THAT THE BALLS ARE MAN-MADE. THEY ARE ASSOCIATED WITH THE PRE-COLUMBIAN ERA, BUT THE PRECISE SOURCE OF THE GRANITE USED TO CONSTRUCT THEM REMAINS UNKNOWN. AS WELL AS BEING STUNNING EXAMPLES OF PRECISION SCULPTING, THESE STONES ARE ALSO EXTREMELY HEAVY. THE BIGGEST WEIGHS AS MUCH AS 16 TONNES.

Signs in the corn

Over the last two decades, there have been hundreds of cases of perhaps the most visually dramatic of all strange phenomena—crop circles. Appearing on farmland, they consist, in their most basic form, of a single circle in the middle of a field in which the crop is bent to the ground. The crop, which is often corn, is flattened but not broken. The circle sometimes has attendant smaller circles surrounding it. The patterns have become increasingly complex, with one discovered near Royston in southern England in 1991 with the shape of a mathematically intricate fractal set. Until 1980, crop circles were only known in the south of England—since then they have begun appearing on farms throughout the UK and in other parts of the world. Explanations for these stunning phenomena include UFO activity, the effects of bird flocks, fungal infections, over-fertilization of crops and military experiments. However, there are two more plausible theories. Dr Terence Meaden, a Canadian academic, suggests that wind hitting a hill will create a vortex on the other side, which sucks in atmospheric electricity and more wind.

This phenomenon has been dubbed the plasma vortex. This theory is backed up by evidence from Gary and Vivienne Tomlinson who, in 1991, were caught up in spiralling winds in Surrey, England. When the vortex disappeared, they found themselves in the midst of a corn circle. However, the most plausible theory to explain crop circles is that they are all hoaxes. Many fraudsters have recently admitted to fabricating these complex and elaborate designs.

Moving stones

In Death Valley, California, one phenomenon that remains to be explained is the rocks that move when nobody is looking. They are found on the Racetrack Playa, a 5-km-long and very flat dry lake surrounded by mountains. The rocks, which range in size from pebbles to boulders and can be anything up to 315 kg in mass, create long shallow furrows in the dried mud. They have been known to move up to 200 m in one run, while the bigger rocks can still manage 70 m. Suggestions as to the cause of these moving stones include wind, or a thin layer of ice on the land surface which facilitates wind movement. No-one has ever seen the rocks move.

RIGHT: AERIAL VIEW OF THE NAZCA LINES, PERU, SHOWING A SYMBOLIC BIRD ETCHED IN THE LANDSCAPE · INSET: CROP CIRCLES, WILTSHIRE, UK, 1990

BERMUDA TRIANGLE

WHILE MOST OF NATURE'S AMAZING PHENOMENA CAN NOW BE UNDERSTOOD AND EXPLAINED AWAY, CERTAIN WEIRD EVENTS AND BIZARRE OBJECTS ARE BEYOND THE REALM OF SCIENTIFIC REASONING OR UNDERSTANDING

OBJECTS IGNITED BY

There are some naturally occurring phenomena which, although well-documented, still present us with bizarre and unexplained mysteries. Strange isolated incidents appear to fall outside the framework of natural laws. Some humans suffer death from spontaneous combustion while others claim to be capable of starting fires using only the power of their minds. Freak children are discovered living in the wild while grotesque animal mutilations remain unexplained.

room. SHC has several plausible explanations. The most obvious is that the burning is not truly spontaneous in that a source of fire nearby, such as a fire or a candle, sets the body ablaze. The body is fuelled by its fat, which explains why spontaneous combustion tends to affect overweight people more. However, this theory does not explain why furniture and fittings remain untouched, when they should also have been burnt to ashes in the searing heat required to burn a human body.

A LIKELY TAIL

RATS HAVE BEEN FOUND LINKED TOGETHER BY THEIR TAILS: SUCH PHENOMENA ARE CALLED RAT KINGS. IN DECEMBER, 1822, TWO RAT KINGS WERE FOUND IN AN ATTIC IN DÖLLSTEDT, GERMANY. ONE HAD 28 RATS, THE OTHER 14. ABOUT 38 RAT KINGS ARE DOCUMENTED, WHILE MICE AND SQUIRREL KINGS HAVE ALSO BEEN DISCOVERED. ONE EXPLANATION FOR THE PHENOMENON IS THAT FRIGHTENED RATS HUDDLE TOGETHER AND ENTWINE THEIR TAILS. THESE BECOME ENTANGLED, FORMING THE BIZARRE LINKAGE WITNESSED.

POWER OF THE MIND

SOME PHENOMENA ARE SO BIZARRE THAT THEY DEFY OUR CURRENT UNDERSTANDING OF THE PHYSICAL WORLD. INEXPLICABLE FIRES, UNACCOUNTABLE RADIATION AND QUIRKS OF BIOLOGY CONTINUE TO BAFFLE AND BEMUSE

Human fireballs

Spontaneous human combustion (SHC) is one of the most bizarre of all reported phenomena. SHC is the ignition and burning of a human without contact with a source of fire. Human bodies, which do not burn very well, have been known to burst into flames. Mrs Mary Reeser of St Petersburg, Florida, USA, was one of the first notorious victims of this bizarre phenomenon. She was last seen alive on 1 July 1951. The next morning, her landlady, smelling smoke and noticing heat from Mrs Reeser's room, broke in to find the widow burnt to ashes. Strangely, her left foot remained unburnt, as did the rest of the items in the

Flame-throwers

Some people have claimed to be able to set objects alight using only the power of their minds. In 1982, a 10-year-old Italian boy named Benedetto Sepino claimed he could set objects alight by gazing at them and concentrating hard: he first set alight a comic in a dentist's waiting room. Fires would spontaneously occur around the boy and he later escaped death when his bedclothes ignited while he was asleep. The boy was brought to the attention of Italy's top scientists who suggested that the source of his power could be static electricity. Later that same year, a 19-year-old nanny working in Italy named Carole Compton, found

herself charged with the attempted murder of children in her charge after one of the infants' cots was discovered engulfed in flames. Compton was labelled a witch by local people but held as an arsonist by the Italian police. Curiously, no trace of inflammable substances could be found by forensic experts at the scene of the crime and the fire itself was discovered to be of a particularly intense heat, not capable of being started by a naked flame. Although found guilty at her trial, few believed Compton was capable of starting such fires and she was eventually set free.

Floating on air

According to the rules of Western physics it is impossible to defy gravity. However, Hindu fakirs have on occasion demonstrated their seeming ability to levitate. One famous case was of Subbayah Pullavar in India in 1936. Outdoors, in front of 150 people, including photographers, he hovered in the air, resting his hand lightly on a cloth stick. No hidden wires were discovered.

Feral children

There have been many documented cases of children being raised by animals. They are known as feral children because they are brought up in the wild. One famous example came from Midnapore, India, in 1920. Following a claim of human phantoms sighted near the village,

two girls were discovered living with a group of two wolves and several cubs. One girl was 18-months-old, the other was about seven. They were taken to an orphanage, where the younger girl died. The older girl, named Kamala, lived on for a further nine years. Other documented cases of feral children include humans raised by other animals. These include the bear child of Lithuania (1694), a leopard child of India (1920), the gazelle child of Syria (1946) and an ape child of Tehran (1961). Perhaps the most famous feral child was Genie, a 13-year-old-girl found in the USA in 1970.

Cattle mutilations

There have been tens of thousands of reported cases of cattle that have been horrifically mutilated. The cows are found dead, with their blood drained and, often, their reproductive organs removed. To confuse matters further, high levels of radiation have been found near the carcasses, and scavenging animals ignore the meat. The mutilations are often characterized by a lack of footprints to and from the animal. The phenomenon was first reported in the autumn of 1973 in Minnesota and Kansas, USA. Horses have also been found mutilated—one reported incident occurred at Saskatoon, USA, in October 1989. The two most widely heard explanations for the gruesome killings are satanic cults and UFO activity.

Winged cats

One very eerie sight in nature is a cat with wings. A rare skin disorder, feline cutaneous asthenia, causes increased elasticity of the cat's skin, so wing-like projections protrude from the side of the cat. One famous example was discovered in a builder's yard in Manchester, UK, in 1975. The wings do not cause the cat any discomfort, and they can be peeled off without causing bleeding.

LEFT: THE FOOT OF DR JOHN IRVING BENTLEY WAS ALL THAT REMAINED FOLLOWING HIS DEATH BY SPONTANEOUS HUMAN COMBUSTION, PENNSYLVANIA, USA, 1966

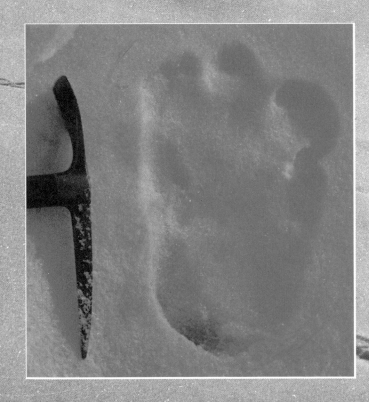

CRYPTOZOOLOGY
BIG FOOT REPUTED

When zoologists study a new creature, they seek evidence—some footprints, the remains of a meal or better still, a living specimen. But unusual creatures, like the Yeti of the Himalayan Mountains and the Beast of Bodmin, rarely offer such useful material. Surprise is in the very nature of these beasts and scientific observers are rarely on hand to glimpse them in action. Armed with nothing more than a shaky camera, it is not surprising that observers infrequently produce the hard evidence that is required. The rarity of these beasts is what makes them so daunting to study, and also what makes them so compelling.

MAD DOGS

AN INFAMOUS IMPORT, THE CHUPACABRA IS SAID TO BE A BLOOD-SUCKING BEAST ORIGINALLY FROM PUERTO RICO. AS MIGRANTS FROM PUERTO RICO SETTLED IN NEW HOMES AROUND THE GLOBE, SIGHTINGS OF THIS CREATURE HAVE SETTLED WITH THEM. THIS RED-FANGED, GREY-SKINNED, DOG-LIKE CREATURE HAS BEEN SPOTTED IN PLACES AS FAR APART AS NEW YORK, MIAMI AND MOSCOW. A FAVOURITE OF TELEVISION TALK-SHOWS AND RADIO PHONE-INS AROUND THE WORLD, THE CHUPACABRA HAS BEEN DISMISSED AS A MYTH BY MOST LAW ENFORCEMENT AGENCIES. AFTER AN AUTOPSY ON ONE OF ITS SUPPOSED ANIMAL VICTIMS, AMERICAN POLICE DECLARED THAT THE ANIMAL HAD BEEN THE VICTIM OF NOTHING MORE THAN A PACK OF HUNGRY STRAY DOGS.

before, were all that was washed up in Kuwait in July 1997. Remains the size of a whale caused a similar riddle when they were first discovered by two boys on the shore of Saint Augustine, USA. Found in November 1896, the tangled mess of body parts included several long limbs. They probably belonged to a giant squid.

Monster flesh
Much excitement was generated in April 1997, when a Japanese fishing vessel dredged up what appeared to be the rotting carcass of a giant sea monster measuring 9.7 m, and weighing 1.8 tonnes. However, on closer inspection, it was found to be the body of a decaying basking shark, a massive creature whose remains have often been confused with sea serpents. One specimen washed up in Egypt in 1950 was found to be nearly 17 m long.

Marine mystery
Every year, there is at least one authenticated sighting of a Cadborosaurus off the coastline of British Columbia, Canada. Known affectionately as 'Caddy', this giant, long-necked creature may be a descendant of the prehistoric plesiosaur. Marine biologists hope to confirm the existence of this possible Jurassic survivor.

TO BE 2.5 M TALL

ALTHOUGH STILL THE STUFF OF LEGEND, CREATURES LIKE BIG FOOT AND THE LOCH NESS MONSTER ATTRACT SERIOUS SCIENTIFIC RESEARCH. ZOOLOGISTS HOPE THAT THESE BEASTS WILL HELP SHED NEW LIGHT ON EVOLUTION

Meet the ancestors
Maybe they are just mountain bears or men in shaggy suits, but it is hard to explain away all the sightings of the creature known as Big Foot—sightings are from the earliest history of the Native Americans. As recently as August 1995, this ape-man was caught on camera by a film crew who were working near Crescent City, California. Standing 2.5 m tall

with a heavy, boned brow, Big Foot could provide the missing link between hominids and apes.

A small step
Taken from the Tibetan words meaning 'that thing', the Yeti is the name given to Big Foot's Himalayan counterpart. In a memorable set of pictures shot in 1951, Eric Shipton and Michael Ward photographed the footprints

of this creature, after stalking it for several minutes. Compared to Big Foot, the Yeti they found had surprisingly dainty feet, only 18 cm in length and 10 cm in width.

The beast of Bodmin
A teenage boy who found a fanged skull in Cornwall, UK, thought he had stumbled on the remains of the beast of Bodmin. Since 1983, locals had reported that a giant black cat had been stalking livestock on the desolate moor. Found in a river in 1996, the skull was taken to the Natural History Museum, London, for further investigation. Curators there confirmed it was from a leopard but also spotted telltale signs that it had been imported into the area after death. This specimen had been dumped in the river by hoaxers, but the real Beast of Bodmin, if there is one, continues to stalk the moors.

All washed up
Zoologists identifying cryptic creatures sometimes have nothing more than a few body parts to work with. The Al-Fintas Monster of the Persian Gulf defies identification to this day. An upper head, jaw and spinal cord, unlike those of any living creature seen

Loch Ness enigma
On 8 Aug 1972, Dr Robert Rhine and his Acadamy of Applied Science team detected a very large object, 6–9 m long, pursuing a shoal of fish in Loch Ness, Scotland. After underwater photos were developed, they showed a flipper-like structure attached to a much larger body. The Loch Ness Monster has evaded searches by sonar but many argue it is not surprising in the 250-m deep lake. If there is any substance to Nessie's numerous sightings, she could be one of Caddy's prehistoric plesiosaur cousins.

Jurassic bark
Countless dinosaur movies have undoubtedly inspired some amateur spotters of animal throwbacks. A huge striped dog tracked down in Tasmania may well be a surviving member of the Tasmanian wolf family. But zoologists are less confident about the lineage of a creature that has been buzzing the backyards of Texas, USA. While many residents believe it is a flying dinosaur called a Quetzalocanthus, zoologists think it is more likely to be a giant bird.

DATA-BURST

HAVE PEOPLE ALWAYS SPOTTED CRYPTIC CREATURES?
ACCOUNTS OF APE-MEN, DRAGONS, GIANT WATER-HORSES AND MERMAIDS CAN BE FOUND IN ANCIENT HISTORY AROUND THE WORLD. NESSIE, FOR INSTANCE, WAS SPOTTED BY THE VIKINGS AND BIG FOOT FEATURES IN NATIVE AMERICAN MYTHOLOGY.

HAS ANYONE EVER CAUGHT A BIG FOOT OR YETI?
NO-ONE ON RECORD, ALTHOUGH PEOPLE CLAIM TO HAVE SEIZED YETI SCALPS AND HANDS (NOW PROVEN TO BE FAKE).

HOW COULD A SPECIES LIKE NESSIE HAVE SURVIVED?
SOME PEOPLE HAVE SUGGESTED THAT AN UNDERWATER DINOSAUR LIKE NESSIE COULD HAVE SETTLED IN A LOCH WHILE IT WAS STILL A FJORD, A LAKE WITH AN OUTLET TO THE SEA. AS THE CONNECTION TO THE SEA CLOSED OVER, CREATURES WOULD HAVE BEEN TRAPPED IN THE LAKE,

BIOLOGICALLY ISOLATED FROM OTHER UNDERWATER SPECIES.

ARE THERE ANY COMMON FAKES?
SAILORS IN THE 18TH CENTURY SOMETIMES BROUGHT HOME FAKE MERMAIDS, SPECIMENS THAT WERE ASSEMBLED BY PIECING TOGETHER THE BODIES OF MONKEYS AND FISH.

DO SCIENTISTS THINK CRYPTIC CREATURES ARE NONSENSE?
FAR FROM IT, SOME ARE ACTIVELY SEEKING CREATURES LIKE NESSIE AND THE TASMANIAN WOLF IN THE HOPE THEY CAN SHED SOME LIGHT ON THE EVOLUTION OF LIFE ON EARTH.

HOW CAN SCIENCE HELP US TO FIND CRYPTIC CREATURES?
SONAR ON SHIPS CAN HELP US LOCATE CREATURES LURKING IN DEEP WATER, ULTRAVIOLET AND INFRARED CAMERAS ENABLE US TO SEE THEM IN THE DARK. DNA FINGERPRINTING ENABLES IDENTIFICATION OF DESCENDANTS.

LEFT: A TRAIL OF YETI FOOTPRINTS IN THE SNOW · INSET: CLOSE-UP OF A YETI FOOTPRINT

On a cosmic scale, the Earth is fairly young. Formed 4.65 billion years ago, it arrived in the last quarter of the universe's history. In these terms, the existence of the human species seems almost inconsequential—we have only been here for around 5 million years. The fossilized remains of extinct creatures illustrate how short-lived any stay on Earth can be. And as we search deeper into the universe, we can see that the Earth itself also has an age limit.

Cold facts

While scientists argue about global warming, the long-term forecast is for a much cooler planet. That is because the Earth will eventually plunge into another ice age. Every 150 million years or thereabouts, global temperatures plummet by 20°C, making the ice caps extend over huge tracts of land. These developments could be triggered by

temperature profile, due to global warming for instance, could destroy the winds that push these currents. This could leave vast areas of the northern hemisphere far too cold for human habitation.

The only way is up?

Compasses made today may point south in the future. That is because the Earth's magnetism is likely to swing upside down. Scientists studying rocks that formed millions of years ago have noticed that the

Toughing it out

According to the theory of Gaia, other species on Earth will outlive us. Scientist James Lovelock first proposed Gaia in the 1980s. He suggested that all living things on Earth act together as one giant organism, securing life's overall survival. Although human activity may change Earth's climate, other organisms on the planet could work to stabilize it again. If the planet was heated by global warming, for example, more algae

Smash hit

The dinosaurs may have been wiped out by a cosmic collision—and there is no reason why humans will not suffer a similar fate. Traces of unusual metals like iridium in the Earth's crust can only have come from outer space. Many scientists think they were deposited here by a huge comet that hit the Earth around 65 million years ago. Vaporizing water and rock, this comet would have sent enough debris into the air to block out the

FUTURE WORLD
SUN WILL CONSUME

minute changes in ocean currents or irregularities in Earth's orbit around the sun. Fortunately, the last ice age ended only 2 million years ago so the next big chill is still a distant prospect.

Winter warmer

Northern Europe and the USA would be left out in the cold if the Gulf Stream and North Atlantic Drift stop flowing. These two currents of tropical ocean water bring about 40% of the heat to the land on their shores. Without them, countries like Greenland and Denmark would be as chilly in the winter as Iceland. The gulf stream transports water from the equator with a surface temperature around 25°C, which makes the average winter in Bergen, Norway, about 0.5°C warmer than the average winter in Philadelphia, USA. Subtle changes in the world's

Earth's magnetism switches periodically. The last magnetic reversal was 780,000 years ago but no-one is sure when it will happen again. With the aid of supercomputers, scientists are beginning to model the complex motions of the Earth's molten core that create magnetism.

Mind children

Will future evolution on Earth be in machine form? Artificial intelligence guru Hans Moravec expects it will. He is convinced that we will eventually be able to build machines which are truly intelligent. Predicting that they will go on to evolve intellectual capabilities way beyond our own, Moravec has called these machines our 'mind children'. He expects they will ultimately leave us behind and find their own destiny somewhere else in the universe.

could thrive, reflecting more heat away from Earth's oceans. There is no reason why evolving life could not create a stable climate that is far too warm for humans. In this way, Earth could reject us like unwelcome guests.

Earth calling

Our understanding of life on Earth could change for good if we find out we are not alone. A document written in 1989 shows how scientists and governments are ready to deal with such a discovery. Grandly titled the *Declaration of Principles Concerning Activities Following the Detection of Extraterrestrial Intelligence*, it outlines what governments and scientists must do in response to an alien message. There is every reason to be cautious before sending a reply—we have no way of knowing whether or not our new neighbours will be friendly.

Death star

Whatever the fate of the Earth, the sun itself has to end one day. Like every other star in the universe, the sun consumes itself as it burns, turning its mass into energy. In another 4.5 billion years, the sun will be all used up. Its remaining mass will be unable to stay together so it will swell to form a red giant, a large ageing star. In this state, the sun will swallow the remains of the solar system, including Earth. But life on Earth will probably have faded long before this, unable to survive in the heat of the dying sun.

sun from the surface of the planet. This may have led to the dinosaurs' extinction. Another comet could wipe out life on Earth again—but the chances of it happening in our lifetime are remote.

Bubble trouble

A huge, interstellar gas cloud is heading our way—it will be here in 50,000 years. That is the warning given by Gary Zank, a US cosmologist with an eye for a disaster. Zank thinks we should be more worried about cosmic clouds than giant comets. When a large gas cloud reaches the solar system, it could burst the 'heliosphere'—a band of charged particles from the sun that surround the solar system acting as a shield. Without the heliosphere, Earth will be bombarded with particles from outer space. These could trap heat in the atmosphere, causing runaway global warming. They could also mutate the genes of any surviving life forms—and even destroy life itself.

A bang or a whimper?

All scientists agree that the universe will end one day—but they cannot agree if it will go with a bang or a whimper. Ever since the Big Bang, the event that created all time, space, energy and matter, the universe has been expanding. Some scientists think it will carry on growing forever—eventually dying in a slow, cold 'heat death'. Others have estimated there is enough matter in the universe to pull it together again, ending it in a giant Big Crunch.

LEFT: ILLUSTRATION DEPICTING THE EARTH'S SURFACE BEING MELTED BY AN EVER-GROWING SUN · RIGHT: X-RAY SATELLITE IMAGE OF THE SUN SHOWING ACTIVITY OF ITS OUTER LAYER

DATA-BURST

CAN WE SEE ANY RED GIANTS FROM EARTH?
YES – ANTARES AND BETELGEUSE ARE TWO WELL-KNOWN EXAMPLES OF RED GIANTS VISIBLE FROM EARTH. IN FACT, ANTARES, MEANING 'NOT MARS', WAS SPECIALLY NAMED TO PREVENT EARLY ASTRONOMERS CONFUSING IT WITH MARS, THE RED PLANET.

WHAT IS A COMET?
IT IS A MASS OF ICE-COVERED ROCK THAT TRAVELS THROUGH SPACE. AS A COMET APPROACHES THE SUN, ITS ICY COVER MELTS SO IT EJECTS SOME OF ITS ROCKY INTERIOR, FORMING FIERY TAILS OF DUST AND GAS.

DO COMETS HIT THE EARTH?
YES – THOUSANDS OF TINY COMETS MAY ENTER EARTH'S ATMOSPHERE EVERY DAY, PROVIDING THE PLANET WITH WATER FOR ITS OCEANS. METEORS ARE DEBRIS FROM THE TAIL OF COMETS THAT HAVE PASSED CLOSE TO EARTH. THE COMET THAT MAY HAVE BEEN RESPONSIBLE FOR WIPING OUT THE DINOSAURS WAS ABOUT 5 KM IN DIAMETER—IMPACTS LIKE THIS ARE EXTREMELY RARE.

HOW LONG WILL HOMO SAPIENS LAST?
IT IS USUAL FOR SOME SPECIES TO BE REPLACED BY OTHERS AND HUMANS MIGHT NOT PROVE AN EXCEPTION TO THIS RULE. FEW SPECIES LAST LONG ON OUR PLANET, AROUND 5 MILLION YEARS ON AVERAGE.

HOW COULD THE UNIVERSE END IN A HEAT DEATH?
THE UNIVERSE COULD DIE IF ALL THE HYDROGEN THAT IS USED IN STELLAR REACTIONS IS EXPENDED.

SPREAD OF THE SUPERBUG?

SUPERBUGS CAPABLE OF RESISTING THE STRONGEST ANTIBIOTICS COULD POSE A SERIOUS THREAT TO HUMAN LIFE ON THE PLANET. IN DECEMBER 1997, MEDICAL EXPERTS IN LONDON CALLED FOR SPECIAL PRECAUTIONS AFTER JAPANESE DOCTORS IDENTIFIED A NEW STRAIN OF SUPERBUG. DR KEIICHI HIRAMATSU, AT JUTENDO UNIVERSITY IN TOKYO, FOUND A STRAIN OF THE COMMON INFECTION CALLED STAPHYLOCOCCUS AUREUS WHICH DID NOT RESPOND TO VANCOMYCIN, THE LAST LINE OF DEFENCE AGAINST INFECTION. SINCE THE LATE 1970S, STRAINS OF RESISTANT BACTERIA HAVE BEEN FOUND AROUND THE WORLD, BUT ALL RESPONDED TO VANCOMYCIN. WERE THIS LATEST STRAIN TO BECOME AIRBORNE, DOCTORS WOULD BE HELPLESS TO DEFEND AGAINST ITS EFFECTS.

ITSELF IN 4.5 BILLION YEARS

PLANET EARTH IS CONSTANTLY CHANGING AND ADAPTING TO DIFFERENT CLIMATES AND CONTINUES TO DEVELOP NEW LIFE FORMS. IT HAS EXISTED FOR 4.65 BILLION YEARS, BUT NOBODY REALLY KNOWS WHAT THE FUTURE HOLDS...

FROM DISASTERS TO PHENOMENA

8   38   72   106

EARTH EXTREMES

THIS IS A SUPERLATIVE PLANET

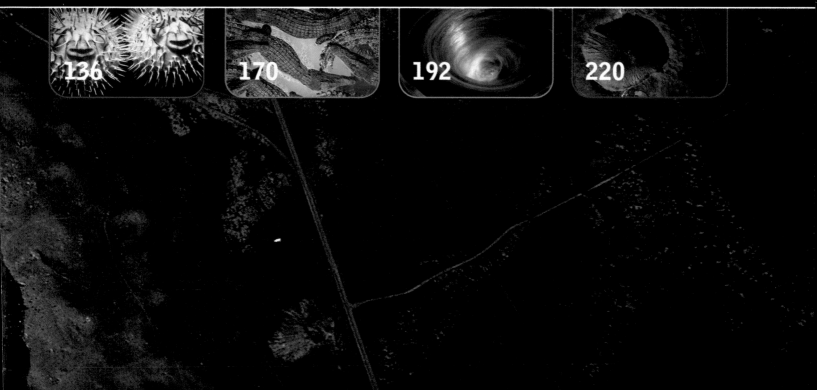

136

170

192

220

MOST DEADLY TROPICAL STORMS

NO.	AREAS OF LARGEST LOSS	YEAR	TYPE OF STORM	APPROXIMATE DEATH TOLL
1	EAST PAKISTAN (NOW BANGLADESH)	1970	CYCLONE	300,000-500,000
2	BANGLADESH	1991	CYCLONE	131,000
3	SOUTH-EASTERN INDIA	1977	CYCLONE	100,000
4	EAST PAKISTAN (NOW BANGLADESH)	1964	CYCLONE	35,000
5	INDIA & EAST PAKISTAN (NOW BANGLADESH)	1965	CYCLONE	30,000
6	WEST INDIES (LESSER ANTILLES)	1780	HURRICANE	22,000
7	EAST PAKISTAN (NOW BANGLADESH)	1963	CYCLONE	15,000
8	EAST PAKISTAN (NOW BANGLADESH)	1964	CYCLONE	15,000
9	TEXAS, USA	1900	HURRICANE	12,000
10	BANGLADESH	1985	CYCLONE	11,000
11	HONG KONG	1906	TYPHOON	10,000
12	HONDURAS	1974	HURRICANE	8,000
13	CUBA & HAITI	1963	HURRICANE	7,000
14	EAST PAKISTAN (NOW BANGLADESH)	1960	CYCLONE	6,000
15	PHILIPPINES	1991	TYPHOON	6,000
16	GUADELOUPE	1776	HURRICANE	6,000
17	JAPAN	1959	TYPHOON	5,000
18	NEWFOUNDLAND	1775	HURRICANE	4,000
19	FLORIDA, USA	1928	HURRICANE	4,000
20	LOUISIANA, USA	1893	HURRICANE	2,000

EARTH EXTREMES 1

DEADLY STORMS, VOLCANOES,

MOST DEADLY VOLCANOES

NO.	NAME	LOCATION	YEAR	DEATH TOLL
1	TAMBORA	JUMBAWA, INDONESIA	1815	92,000
2	KRAKATOA	KRAKATOA, INDONESIA	1883	36,000
3	MONT PELEE	MARTINIQUE, WEST INDIES	1902	29,000
4	NEVADO DEL RUIZ	ARMERO, COLUMBIA	1985	25,000
5	MT ETNA	SICILY, ITALY	1669	20,000
6	LAKI	ICELAND	1783	20,000
7	MT VESUVIUS	BAY OF NAPLES, ITALY	79	20,000
8	KELUD	JAVA, INDONESIA	1586	10,000
9	KELUD	JAVA, INDONESIA	1919	5,500
10	MT LAMINGTON	PAPUA NEW GUINEA	1951	5,000

MOST DEADLY TSUNAMIS

NO.	LOCATION	YEAR	DEATH TOLL
1	LISBON, PORTUGAL	1755	60,000
2	EAST INDIES	1883	36,000
3	JAPAN	1707	30,000
4	ITALY	1783	30,000
5	JAPAN	1896	27,122
6	CHILE	1868	25,000
7	RYUKYU ISLANDS	1771	11,941
8	JAPAN	1792	9,745
9	PHILIPPINES	1976	8,000
10	JAPAN	1498	5,000

MOST DEADLY EARTHQUAKES

NO.	LOCATION	YEAR	DEATHS	RICHTER SCALE
1	SHANSI, CHINA	23 JAN 1556	830,000	8.3 (EST.)
2	CALCUTTA, INDIA	11 OCT 1737	300,000	UNKNOWN
3	TANGSHAN, CHINA	27 JULY 1976	242,000	7.9
4	ALEPPO, SYRIA	9 AUG 1138	230,000	UNKNOWN
5	DAMGHAN, IRAN	22 DEC 856	200,000	UNKNOWN
6	GANSU, CHINA	16 DEC 1920	200,000	8.2
7	NAN-SHAN, CHINA	22 MAY 1927	200,000	8.3
8	ARDABIL, IRAN	23 MARCH 893	150,000	UNKNOWN
9	KANTO PLAIN, JAPAN	1 SEPT 1923	142,807	8.3
10	CHIHLI, CHINA	SEPT 1290	100,000	UNKNOWN
11	SHEMAKHA, AZERBAIJAN	NOV 1667	80,000	UNKNOWN
12	MESSINA, SICILY, ITALY	28 DEC 1908	80,000	7.5
13	TABRIZ, IRAN	18 NOV 1727	77,000	UNKNOWN
14	LISBON, PORTUGAL	1 NOV 1755	70,000	8.7
15	GANSU PROVINCE, CHINA	26 DEC 1932	70,000	7.6
16	[NORTHERN] PERU	31 MAY 1970	66,800	7.7
17	SICILIA, TURKEY	1268	60,000	UNKNOWN
18	SICILY, ITALY	11 JAN 1693	60,000	UNKNOWN
19	CALABRIA, ITALY	4 FEB 1783	50,000	UNKNOWN
20	WESTERN IRAN	21 JUNE 1990	40,000	7.3

Volcanic time-bombs

Some of Earth's most dramatic and unpredictable features, active volcanoes perpetually steam and bubble beneath the surface, sporadically erupting in a massive explosion of red hot molten lava, ash and debris which is propelled high into the air and is capable of burying entire cities.

TSUNAMIS AND EARTHQUAKES

EARTH EXTREMES 2

MOUNTAINS, AVALANCHES,

HIGHEST MOUNTAINS

NO.	NAME	HEIGHT (M)	RANGE
1	MT EVEREST	8,848	HIMALAYA
2	K2 (CHOGORI)	8,610	KARAKORAM
3	KANGCHENJUNGA	8,598	HIMALAYA
4	LHOTSE	8,511	HIMALAYA
5	MAKALU I	8,481	HIMALAYA
6	DHAULAGIRI I	8,167	HIMALAYA
7	MANASLU I (KUTANG I)	8,156	HIMALAYA
8	CHO OYU	8,153	HIMALAYA
9	NANGA PARBAT (DIAMIR)	8,124	HIMALAYA
10	ANNAPURNA I	8,091	HIMALAYA

WORST AVALANCHES/LANDSLIDES

NO.	LOCATION	INCIDENT	YEAR	DEATH TOLL
1	HSIAN, SHENSI, CHINA	LANDSLIDE	1556	1,000,000
2	KANSU, CHINA	LANDSLIDE	1920	200,000
3	DOLOMITES, ITALY	AVALANCHES	1916-18	80,000
4	MT HUASCARAN, PERU	AVALANCHE	1970	25,000
5	HUARAZ, PERU	AVALANCHE	1941	7,000
6	MT HUASCARAN, PERU	AVALANCHE	1962	4,000
7	VAJONT DAM, ITALY	LANDSLIDE	1963	1,925
8	MEDELLIN, COLOMBIA	LANDSLIDE	1987	683
9	BIASCA, ALPS	LANDSLIDE	1512	UP TO 600
10	CHUNGAR, PERU	AVALANCHE	1971	600

LARGEST METEOR CRATER

NO.	NAME	AGE (MILLIONS OF YEARS)	DIAMETER (KM)
1	SUDBURY, ONTARIO, CANADA	C. 1,850	200
2	CHICXULUD, MEXICO	C. 65	170
3	ACRAMAN, AUSTRALIA	C. 570	160
4	VREDEFORT, SOUTH AFRICA	C. 1,970	140
5	MANICOUAGAN, CANADA	C. 212	100
6	POPIGAI, RUSSIA	C. 35	100
7	CHESAPEAKE BAY, USA	C. 36	85
8	PUCHEZH-KATUNKI, RUSSIA	C. 220	80
9	KARA, RUSSIA	C. 73	65
10	BEAVERHEAD, MONTANA, USA	C. 600	60
11	SILJAN, SWEDEN	C. 368	55
12	TOOKOONOOKA, AUSTRALIA	C. 128	55
13	CHARLEVOIX, CANADA	C. 357	54
14	KARA-KUL, TAJIKISTAN	C. 25	52
15	MONTAGNAIS, CANADA	C. 51	45
16	ARAGUAINHA DOME, BRAZIL	C. 249	40
17	SAINT MARTIN, CANADA	C. 220	40
18	CARSWELL, CANADA	C. 115	39
19	CLEARWATER WEST, CANADA	C. 290	32
20	TEAGUE, W. AUSTRALIA	C. 1,685	30

Nature shapes the Earth
Mountains, which make up some of the world's most stunning landscapes, are formed over millions of years—steep slopes and precipitous ravines are carved into the Earth by the force of retreating ice sheets and battering winds, while river erosion produces broad sweeping hills and valleys.

LANDSLIDES, METEOR CRATERS

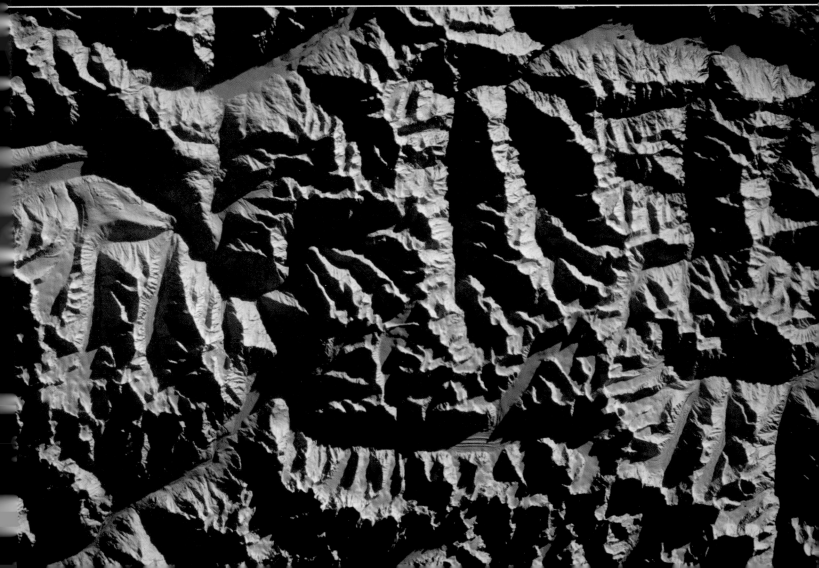

LONGEST RIVERS

	NAME	LENGTH (KM)	SOURCE	COMMENTS
1	AMAZON	6,750	PERU	15,000 TRIBUTARIES. DELTA EXTENDS 400 KM INLAND. NAVIGABLE 3,700 KM UPSTREAM
2	NILE	6,670	BURUNDI	NAVIGABLE TO ASWAN DAM—1,545 KM
3	YANGTZE (CHANG JIANG)	6,300	WESTERN CHINA	ESTUARY IS 190 KM LONG
4	MISSISSIPPI-MISSOURI	6,020	SOUTHERN MONTANA, USA	MISSISSIPPI ACCOUNTS FOR 3,778 KM OF TOTAL LENGTH
5	YENISEY ANGARA-SELENGE	5,540	MONGOLIA	ESTUARY IS 386 KM LONG. YENISEY ITSELF IS 3,540 KM LONG
6	HUANG HO (YELLOW RIVER)	5,464	QINGHAI PROVINCE, CHINA	CHANGED MOUTHS BY 400 KM IN 1852. ONLY LAST 40 KM IS NAVIGABLE
7	OB'-IRTYSH	5,409	MONGOLIA	ESTUARY IS 725 KM LONG
8	PARANA	4,880	BRAZIL	EMERGES INTO CONFLUENCE WITH R. URUGUAY TO FORM RIO DE LA PLATA
9	CONGO	4,700	ZAMBIA-CONGO BORDER	NAVIGABLE FOR 1,730 KM FROM KISANGANI TO KINSHASA
10	LENA	4,400	LAKE BAIKAL, RUSSIA	ESTUARY IS FROZEN BETWEEN OCTOBER AND JULY
11	MEKONG	4,350	CENTRAL TIBET	SOURCE DISCOVERED 1995
12	AMUR-ARGUN	4,345	NORTHERN CHINA	AMUR IS 2,824 KM LONG
13	MACKENZIE-PEACE-SLAVE	4,241	BRITISH COLUMBIA, CANADA	PEACE RIVER IS 1,923 KM LONG; MACKENZIE IS 1,733 KM LONG
14	NIGER	4,181	GUINEA	DELTA'S COASTAL LENGTH IS 200 KM
15	MURRAY-DARLING-CONDAMINE	3,750	QUEENSLAND, AUSTRALIA	DARLING IS *c*.2,740 KM LONG; PERMANENT STREAMS OF MURRAY ARE 2,590 KM
16	ZAMBEZI	3,540	ZAMBIA	NAVIGABLE 610 KM UP TO QUEBRABASA RAPIDS
17	VOLGA	3,530	WESTERN RUSSIA	EUROPE'S LONGEST RIVER
18	MADEIRA	3,380	BOLIVIA	WORLD'S LONGEST TRIBUTARY
19	JURUA	3,283	PERU	MOST PRONOUNCED MEANDERS IN AMAZON BASIN
20	PURUS	3,211	PERU	NAVIGABLE FOR 2,575 KM. PURUS WAS FORMERLY CALLED COXIUARA

EARTH EXTREMES 3

RIVER SYSTEMS, WATERFALLS

WORST FLOODS

NO.	YEAR	LOCATION	DEATH TOLL
1	1931	HUANG HO, CHINA	4,000,000
2	1887	HONAN, CHINA	UP TO 900,000
3	1642	CHINA	300,000
4	1911	YANGTZE RIVER, CHINA	100,000
5	1786	JAPAN	UP TO 30,000
6	1828	JAPAN	UP TO 10,000
7	1951	MANCHURIA	UP TO 5,000
8	1991	JOWZJAN PROVINCE, AFGHANISTAN	UP TO 5,000
9	1992	GULBAHAR, AFGHANISTAN	3,000
10	1996	HUANG HO, CHINA	2,300

WATERFALLS

NO.	NAME	HEIGHT (M)	LOCATION
1	ANGEL	979	VENEZUELA
2	TUGELA	947	KWAZULU NATAL, S. AFRICA
3	UTIGARD	800	NESDALE, NORWAY
4	YOSEMITE	800	YOSEMITE VALLEY, USA
5	MONGEFOSSEN	774	MONGEBEKK, NORWAY
6	OSTRE MARDOLA FOSS	656	EIKESDAL, WEST NORWAY
7	TYSSESTRENGANE	646	HARDANGER, NORWAY
8	KUKENAAM (OR CUQUENAN)	610	VENEZUELA
9	SUTHERLAND	580	OTAGO, NEW ZEALAND
10	KILE (OR KJELLFOSSEN)	561	NR. GUDVANGEN, NORWAY

OCEANS/ SEAS

NO.	NAME	AREA (KM²)	AVERAGE DEPTH (M)
1	PACIFIC	166,240,000	4,188
2	ATLANTIC	86,560,000	3,736
3	INDIAN	73,430,000	3,872
4	ARCTIC	13,230,000	1,205
5	SOUTH CHINA SEA	2,974,600	1,200
6	CARIBBEAN SEA	2,753,000	2,400
7	MEDITERRANEAN SEA	2,503,000	1,485
8	BERING SEA	2,268,180	1,400
9	GULF OF MEXICO	1,542,985	1,500
10	SEA OF OKHOTSK	1,527,570	840
11	EAST CHINA SEA	1,249,150	180
12	HUDSON BAY	1,232,300	120
13	SEA OF JAPAN	1,007,500	1,370
14	ANDAMAN SEA	797,700	865
15	NORTH SEA	575,300	90
16	BLACK SEA	461,980	1,100
17	RED SEA	437,700	490
18	BALTIC SEA	422,160	55
19	PERSIAN GULF	238,790	24
20	GULF OF ST. LAWRENCE	237,760	120

The source of life

Although they account for a relatively small proportion of the world's water—just 1% compared to the 97.2% contained in the oceans—rivers are the main force in shaping the landscape. They provide essential routes for navigation and trade and play a pivotal role in settlement location.

FLOODS, OCEANS AND SEAS

LARGEST CAVE SYSTEMS

NO.	NAME	LOCATION	LENGTH (M)	DEPTH (M)
1	MAMMOTH CAVE SYSTEM	KENTUCKY, USA	379,000	116
2	OPTIMISTICESKAJA	UKRAINE	183,000	20
3	JEWEL CAVE	SOUTH DAKOTA, USA	166,000	212
4	HOLLOCH	SCHWYZ, SWITZERLAND	156,000	87
5	SIEBENHENGSTEN-HOHLENSYSTEM	BERN, SWITZERLAND	126,000	1,110
6	WIND CAVE	SOUTH DAKOTA, USA	119,000	172
7	LECHUGUILLA	NEW MEXICO, USA	113,000	486
8	OZERNAJA	UKRAINE	111,000	20
9	FISHER RIDGE SYSTEM	KENTUCKY, USA	104,000	88
10	GUA AIR JERNIH - LUBANG BATAU	SARAWAK, MALAYSIA	101,000	355
11	SYSTEME DE OJO GUARENA	BURGOS, SPAIN	97,400	UNKNOWN
12	RESEAU DE LA CUOMO D'HYOUERNEDO	HAUTE-GARONNE, FRANCE	90,500	1,004
13	ZOLUSHKA	MOLDARSKAJA, MOLDAVIA	85,500	30
14	SISTEMA PURIFICACION	TAMAULIPAS, MEXICO	78,600	904
15	RAUCHERKARHOHLE	OBEROSTERREICH, AUSTRIA	70,000	725
16	HIRLATZHOHLE	OBEROSTERREICH, AUSTRIA	70,000	612
17	FRIARS HOLE SYSTEM	WEST VIRGINIA, USA	68,800	188
18	EASEGILL SYSTEM	YORKSHIRE, UK	66,000	211
19	ORGAN (GREENBRIER) CAVE SYSTEM	WEST VIRGINIA, USA	63,600	148
20	RED DEL RIO SILENCIO	CANTABRIA, SPAIN	58,600	492

EARTH EXTREMES 4

CAVE SYSTEMS, DESERTS,

LARGEST DESERTS

NO.	NAME	AREA (KM²)	LOCATION
1	SAHARA DESERT	8,600,000	NORTH AFRICA
2	ARABIAN DESERT	2,330,000	ARABIAN PENINSULA
3	AUSTRALIAN DESERT	1,550,000	AUSTRALIA
4	GOBI DESERT	1,040,000	MONGOLIA, CHINA
5	KALAHARI DESERT	520,000	BOTSWANA, S. AFRICA, NAMIBIA
6	TAKLA MAKAN	320,000	XINJIANG, CHINA
7	NAMIB DESERT	310,000	NAMIBIA
8	SONORAN DESERT	310,000	USA, MEXICO
9	KARA KUM	270,000	TURKMENISTAN
10	SOMALI DESERT	260,000	SOMALIA

LARGEST ISLANDS

NO.	NAME	AREA (KM²)	LOCATION
1	GREENLAND	2,175,600	ARCTIC OCEAN
2	NEW GUINEA	808,510	WESTERN PACIFIC
3	BORNEO	757,050	INDIAN OCEAN
4	MADAGASCAR	594,180	INDIAN OCEAN
5	SUMATRA (SUMATERA)	524,100	INDIAN OCEAN
6	BAFFIN ISLAND	476,070	ARCTIC OCEAN
7	HONSHU	230,460	N.W. PACIFIC
8	GREAT BRITAIN	229,870	N. ATLANTIC
9	ELLESMERE ISLAND	212,690	ARCTIC OCEAN
10	VICTORIA ISLAND	212,200	ARCTIC OCEAN

LARGEST RAINFORESTS

NO.	COUNTRY	AREA OF TROPICAL FOREST/ WOODLAND (THOUSAND KM²)
1	BRAZIL	5,611
2	CONGO (EX-ZAIRE)	2,268
3	INDONESIA	1,812
4	CHINA	1,555
5	PERU	679
6	COLOMBIA	541
7	INDIA	517
8	BOLIVIA	493
9	MEXICO	486
10	VENEZUELA	457
11	SUDAN	430
12	PAPUA NEW GUINEA	360
13	TANZANIA	336
14	CENTRAL AFRICAN REPUBLIC	306
15	MYANMAR (BURMA)	289
16	ANGOLA	231
17	CAMEROON	204
18	CONGO (-BRAZZAVILLE)	199
19	GUYANA	184
20	GABON	182

Magical underground world
Carved from rock by the power of underground streams and rivers over thousands of years, caves can be as mighty as cathedrals with intricate features such as stalactites and stalagmites, while complex labyrynthine passageways may zigzag underground for several thousand metres.

ISLANDS AND RAINFORESTS

THREATENED MAMMALS		
NO.	COUNTRY	MAMMAL SPECIES AT RISK
1	INDONESIA	128
2	CHINA	75
3	INDIA	75
4	BRAZIL	71
5	MEXICO	64
6	AUSTRALIA	58
7	PAPUA NEW GUINEA	57
8	PHILIPPINES	49
9	MADAGASCAR	46
10	PERU	46
11	KENYA	43
12	MALAYSIA	42
13	CONGO (EX-ZAIRE)	38
14	VIETNAM	38
15	ETHIOPIA	35
16	USA	35
17	COLOMBIA	35
18	THAILAND	34
19	SOUTH AFRICA	33
20	TANZANIA	33

THREATENED BIRDS		
NO.	COUNTRY	BIRD SPECIES AT RISK
1	INDONESIA	104
2	BRAZIL	103
3	CHINA	90
4	PHILIPPINES	86
5	INDIA	73
6	COLOMBIA	64
7	PERU	64
8	ECUADOR	53
9	USA	50
10	VIETNAM	47
11	THAILAND	45
12	AUSTRALIA	45
13	MYANMAR (BURMA)	44
14	NEW ZEALAND	44
15	ARGENTINA	41
16	RUSSIA	38
17	MEXICO	36
18	MALAYSIA	34
19	JAPAN	33
20	PAPUA NEW GUINEA	31

EARTH EXTREMES 5

PROTECTED AREAS, MAMMALS

THREATENED SPECIES

NO.	COUNTRY	NUMBER OF THREATENED SPECIES
1	USA	854
2	AUSTRALIA	483
3	INDONESIA	340
4	MEXICO	247
5	BRAZIL	240
6	CHINA	213
7	SOUTH AFRICA	205
8	INDIA	193
9	PHILIPPINES	188
10	TANZANIA	132
11	JAPAN	132
12	PAPUA NEW GUINEA	122
13	PERU	122
14	MADAGASCAR	120
15	COLOMBIA	119
16	ECUADOR	117
17	CONGO (EX-ZAIRE)	113
18	RUSSIA	113
19	THAILAND	110
20	KENYA	107

NB: THE USA HAS THE HIGHEST TOTAL NUMBER OF ENDANGERED SPECIES
BECAUSE ITS RECORDS ARE MORE COMPLETE

PROTECTED AREAS

NO.	COUNTRY	NO. OF PROTECTED AREAS	AREA PROTECTED (HA)
1	USA	1,494	104,238,016
2	GREENLAND	2	98,250,000
3	AUSTRALIA	892	93,545,457
4	CANADA	640	82,545,492
5	RUSSIA	199	65,536,759
6	CHINA	463	58,066,563
7	BRAZIL	273	32,189,837
8	VENEZUELA	100	26,322,306
9	INDONESIA	175	18,565,292
10	INDIA	374	14,350,738
11	TANZANIA	30	13,889,975
12	CHILE	66	13,725,125
13	ALGERIA	19	11,919,288
14	CHAD	9	11,494,000
15	ECUADOR	15	11,113,893
16	BOTSWANA	9	10,663,280
17	NAMIBIA	12	10,217,777
18	ZAIRE	8	9,916,625
19	MEXICO	65	9,728,732
20	SUDAN	16	9,382,500

Threatened mammals
Both the panda and the gorilla face uncertain futures and possible extinction if their natural habitat continues to be encroached upon by humans. These environmental issues, compounded by poaching, mean that only around 800 pandas and 600 mountain gorillas remain on Earth.

AND BIRDS UNDER THREAT

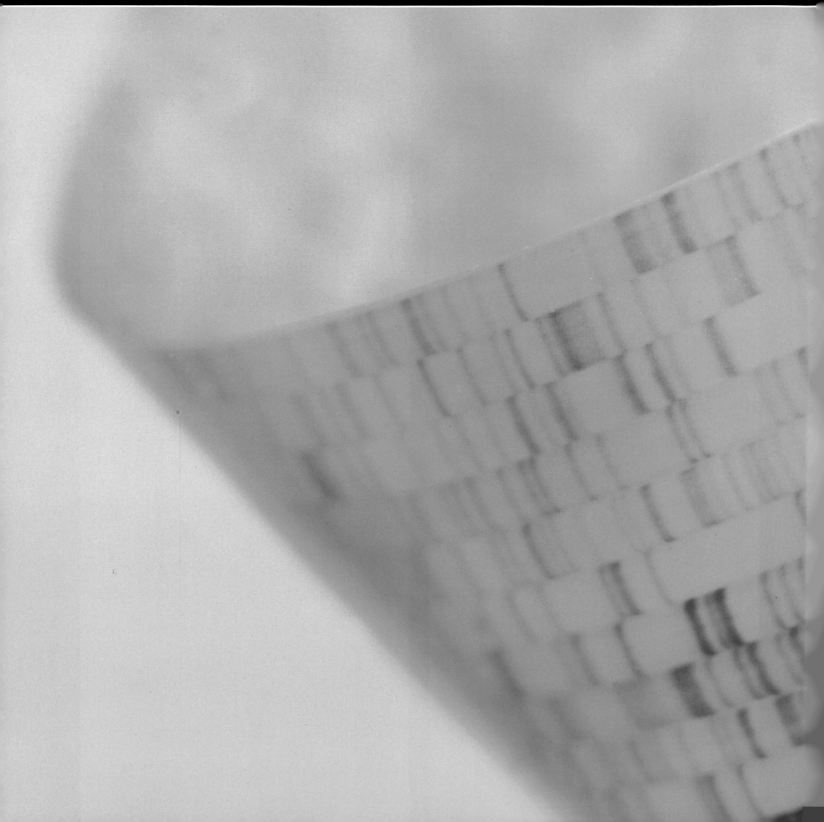

3,000 ALPHABETICAL ENTRIES

INDEX

ABERFAN TO ZONE FOSSILS

t=top;b=bottom
Page 8: Roger Ressmeyer/Corbis
Page10: Reuters/Popperfoto
Page 10 inset: Michael Yamashita/Corbis UK Limited
Page 12: Topham Picturepoint
Page 13t: Stef Lamberti/Tony Stone Images
Page 13b: David Parker/Science Photo Library
Page 14: James Balog/Tony Stone Images
Page 15t: Hulton Getty
Page 15b: Roger Ressmeyer/Corbis
Page 16: Image Makers/The Image Bank
Page 16 inset: Sigurgeir Jonasson/Frank Lane Agency/Corbis
Page 17: NASA/Corbis
Page 18: Roger Ressmeyer/Corbis
Page 18-19: Roger Ressmeyer/Corbis
Page 20: Jonathan Blair/Corbis
Page 21: Popperfoto
Page 22: Reuters/Popperfoto
Page 23t: Popperfoto
Page 23b: Galen Rowell/Corbis
Page 24: Yann Arthus-Bertrand/Corbis
Page 25: John Hestletine/Corbis
Page 25 inset: Richard Hamilton/Corbis
Page 26: Reuters/Popperfoto
Page 27: Galen Rowell/Corbis
Page 28: W Perry Conway/Corbis
Page 29t: Ross Parry/Rex Features
Page29b: Yan Arthus-Bertrand/Corbis
Page 30: Franz Camenzind/Planet Earth Pictures
Page 30inset: G.S.O Images/The Image Bank
Page 31: Wolfgang Kaehler/Corbis
Page 32: Darrell Gulin/Tony Stone Images
Page 33t: Hilarie Kavanagh/Tony Stone Images
Page 33b: Will & Deni McIntyre/Tony Stone Images
Page 34: World Perspectives/Tony Stone Images
Page 35: Nigel Press/Tony Stone Images
Page 36: Mike Vines/Tony Stone Images
Page 37t: Bettmann/Corbis
Page 37b: Ken Fisher/Tony Stone Images
Page 38-39: Annie Griffiths/Corbis
Page 40: Cameron Davidson/Tony Stone Images
Page 41: Gianni Dagli Orti/Corbis
Page 42t: Reuters/Popperfoto
Page 42b: NASA/Science Photo Library
Page 43: Annie Griffiths/Corbis
Page 44T: William J Hebert/Tony Stone Images
Page 44b: UPI/Bettmann/Corbis
Page 45: Danny Lehman/Corbis
Page 46: UPI/Bettmann/Corbis
Page 47t: Tony Arruza/Corbis
Page 47b: Hulton Deutsch Collection/Corbis
Page 48: Barrie Rokeach/The Image Bank
Page 49t: Nationalmuseum,Stockholm/The Bridgeman Art Library
Page 49b: Tom Dietrich/Tony Stone Images
Page 50: Popperfoto
Page 50 inset: Warren Faidley/Oxford Scientific Films
Page 51: Reuters/Popperfoto
Page 52: Kent Wood/Science Photo Library
Page 53: Reuters/Popperfoto
Page 54t: Reuters/Popperfoto
Page 54b-55: Warren Faidley/Oxford Scientific Films
Page 56: Kevin Morris/Corbis
Page 57: Associated Press/Topham Picture point
Page 58: USGS-Hawai Volcano Observatory/Corbis
Page 59: Hulton Getty
Page 60: Agencia Estado/Associated Press
Page 62t: Morton Beebe-S.F./Corbis
Page 62b: Jim Sugar Photography/Corbis
Page 63: Vinc Streano/Corbis
Page 64: World Perspectives/Tony Stone Images
Page 65t: Popperfoto
Page 65b: Image Makers/The Image Bank
Page 66: Martin Puddy/Tony Stone Images
Page 66t: Joel Rogers/Corbis
Page 66b: Earl Kowell/Corbis
Page 68: Popperfoto
Page 69: Annie Griffiths Corbis
Page 70: Historical Picture Archive/Corbis
Page 71: CP/Associated Press
Page 72-73: Digital Image/Original Image Court/Corbis
Page 74: NASA/Corbis
Page 75: Robert Holmes/Corbis
Page 76: Gianni Dagli/Corbis
Page 77: Digital Image/Original Image Court/Corbis
Page 78: Alison Wright/Corbis
Page 79: Frans Lanting/Tony Stone Images
Page 79 inset: Wolfgang Kaehler/Corbis
Page 80: Pat OiHara/Corbis
Page 81: Tom Bean/Corbis

Page 82: Phil Schermeister/Corbis
Page 82 inset: Philip Gould/Corbis
Page 83: Nik Wheeler Corbis
Page 84t: Paul McCormick/The Image Bank
Page 84b: Lowell Georgia/Corbis
Page 85: Scott Smith/Corbis
Page 86: Bryn Campbell/Tony Stone Images
Page 87: Moreton Beebe s.f./Corbis
Page 88: Digital Image/Original Image Court/Corbis
Page 89: Japanese National Tourist Office
Page 90: Tom Till/Tony Stone Images
Page 90 inset: David Hiser/Tony Stone Images
Page 91: The Bridgeman Art Library
Page 92-93: Joseph Sohm;Chromo Sohm Inc./Corbis
Page 93t: Robert Frerck/Tony Stone Images
Page 94: Ric Ergenbright Corbis
Page 95t: Gary Cralle/The Image Bank
Page 95b: Chris Noble/Tony Stone Images
Page 96: Steve Kaufman/Corbis
Page 97t: George Lepp/Tony Stone Images
Page 97b: Richard Nowitz/Corbis
Page 98: Robert Hessler/Planet Earth Pictures
Page 99t: Jonathan Blair/Corbis
Page 99b: Verena Tunnicliffe/Planet Earth Pictures
Page 100: Stephen Frink/Corbis
Page 101t: Stephen Frink/Corbis
Page 101b: Paul Chesley/Tony Stone Images
Page 102: Ralph White/Corbis
Page 103: Stuart Westmorland/Tony Stone Images
Page 103 inset: Pal Hermansen/Tony Stone Images
Page 104: Robert Van Der Hilst/Tony Stone Images
Page 105: Space telescope science institute/Corbis
Page 106-107: Robert Van Der Hilst/Tony Stone Images
Page 108: Horst Baender/Tony Stone Images
Page 109: Jacques Jangoux/Tony Stone Images
Page 110: Peter Johnson/Corbis
Page 112: The Image Bank
Page 113: Vittoriano Rastelli/Corbis
Page 114: Associated Press
Page 115: Hulton Getty
Page 116: Reuters/Popperfoto
Page 117t: Dave Bartruff/Corbis
Page 117b: Otto Lang/Corbis
Page 118: Kyodo Press
Page 119: Poppetfoto
Page 120: David Simonson/Oxford Scientific Films
Page 121t: Rex Features
Page 121b: Stephen Studd/Tony Stone Images
Page 122: Robert Van Der Hilst/Tony Stone Images
Page 123: Reuters/Popperfoto
Page 124: A.B.Dowsett/Science Photo Library
Page 125: Bettmann/Corbis
Page 126: Associated Press
Page 127: David Woodfall/Tony Stone Images
Page 128: Sylvain Coffie/Tony Stone Images
Page 129t: Peter Poulides/Tony Stone Images
Page 129b: Rex Features
Page 130: Kevin Morris/Corbis
Page 131: Judyth Platt/Corbis
Page 132: Nik Wheeler/Corbis
Page 133t: UPI/Bettmann/Corbis
Page 133b: Nik Wheeler Corbis
Page 134: European Space Agency/Science Photo Library
Page 135t: UPI/Bettman/Corbis
Page 135b: NOAA/Science Photo Library
Page 136-37: Marc Chamberlain/Tony Stone Images
Page 138: Joseph Van Os/The Image Bank
Page 139: Illustrated London News/Corbis
Page 140: Kim Taylor/Bruce Coleman Limited
Page 141t: Malcolm Kitto/Pappillo/Corbis
Page 141b: Hal Horwitz Corbis
Page 142: Hans Christoph Kappel/BBC Natural History Unit
Page 143t: Wolfgang Kaehler/Corbis
Page 143b: Rex Features
Page 144: Michael and Patricia Fogden/Corbis
Page 145: Kevin Horan/Tony Stone Images
Page 146: Art Wolfe/Tony Stone Images
Page 146 inset: Marc Chamberlain/Tony Stone Images
Page 147: Tim Flach/Tony Stone Images
Page 148: Karen Tweedy-Holmes/Corbis
Page 149: Steve Taylor/Tony Stone Images
Page 150: Jose Luis Gonzalez Grand/Bruce Coleman Limited
Page 151: Bruno Dittrich/Tony Stone Images
Page 152: Tim Flach/Tony Stone Images
Page 153: Wayne Bilenduke/Tony Stone Images
Page 154: John Holmes/Frank Lane Picture Agency/Corbis
Page 155: Pat OiHara/Tony Stone Images
Page 156: James Solliday/BPS/Tony Stone Images
Page 157: Lester Bergman/Stephen Frink/Corbis

Page 158: Clem Haagner/Corbis
Page 159t: Jonathan Blair/Corbis
Page 159b: Guido Rossi/The Image Bank
Page 160: George Lepp/Corbis
Page 161t: Robert Yinn/Corbis
Page 162t: Alastair Shay/Papillo/Corbis
Page 162b-163: Gerard Rollando/The Image Bank
Page 164: Peter Johnson/Corbis
Page 165: John Beatty/Tony Stone Images
Page 165 inset: Roger Garwood/Planet Earth Pictures
Page 166: Chris Harvey/Tony Stone Images
Page 166 inset: Renee Lynn/Tony Stone Images
Page 167: Daniel J Cox/Tony Stone Images
Page 168: Wayne Lawler/Corbis
Page 169t: Michael Freeman/Corbis
Page 169b: Darrell Gulin/Corbis
Page 170-71: Art Wolfe/Tony Stone Images
Page 172: Peter Dazeley/Tony Stone Images
Page 173: Art Wolfe/Tony Stone Images
Page 174: Michael Yamashita/Corbis
Page 175: Ben Osbourne/Tony Stone Images
Page 176: Jonathan Blair/Corbis
Page 177t: John Banagan/The Image Bank
Page 177b: Tony Malmquist/The Image Bank
Page 178t: Darryl Torckler/Tony Stone Images
Page 178b-179: Hans Christoph Kappel/BBC Natural
   History Unit
Page 180: John Beatty/Tony Stone Images
Page 181: Gerben Oppermans/Tony Stone Images
Page 181 inset: Chris Thomaidis/Tony Stone Images
Page 182: John Beatty/Tony Stone Images
Page 183: Wolfgang Kaehler/Corbis
Page 184: Hans Gelderblom/Tony Stone Images
Page 185: Roger Tidman/Corbis
Page 186: The Acadamy of Natural Sciences
   Philadelphia/Corbis
Page 187: Associated Press
Page 188: Keren Su/Corbis
Page 189t: Hulton Getty
Page 189b: Sharna Balfour/ABPL/Corbis
Page 190: Popperfoto
Page 191: Reuters/Popperfoto
Page 192-3: Jim Sugar Photography/Corbis
Page 194: Galon Rowell/Corbis
Page 195t: Fortean Picture Library
Page 195b: George Lepp/Tony Stone Images
Page 196: Jim Sugar Photography/Corbis
Page 197: Associated Press
Page 198: A Willett/The Image Bank
Page 198 inset: Popperfoto
Page 199: Poppefoto
Page 200: Ed Simpson/Tony Stone Images
Page 200 inset: Rex Features
Page 201: Ken Graham/Tony Stone Images
Page 202t: Dr Meaden/Fortean Picture Library
Page 202b: Llewellyn Publications/Fortean Picture Library
Page 203: Dr Meaden/Fortean Picture Library
Page 204: Terje Rakke/The Image Bank
Page 205: Grant Taylor/Tony Stone Images
Page 205 inset: Popperfoto
Page 206: NASA/Science Photo Library
Page 207: Jonathan Blair/Corbis
Page 208: Kevin Schafer/Corbis
Page 209: Associated Press
Page 209b: Antonio Rosario/The Image Bank
Page 210: National Geographic Society/Associated Press
Page 211: Charles and Joset Leners/Corbis
Page 212: Buddy Mays/Corbis
Page 213: Alejandro Balaguer/Tony Stone Images
Page 213 inset: Frederick Taylor/Fortean Picture Library
Page 214: Larry E.Arnold/Fortean Picture Library
Page 215: Peter Samuels/Tony Stone Images
Page 216: Hulton Deutsch Collection/Corbis
Page 217: John Sibbick and Fortean Times/Fortean Picture
   Library
Page 218: David Hardy/Science Photo Library
Page 219t: Mark Douet/Tony Stone Images
Page 219b: Jisas/Lockheed/Science Photo Library
Page 220-21: NASA/Corbis
Page 223: Gary Braasch/Corbis
Page 227: Digital Image/Original Image Court/Corbis
Page 229: Robert Dowling/Corbis
Page 230: Wayne Lawler/Corbis
Page 231: Karen Su/Corbis
Maps, pages 222-28: Mountain High Maps® Copyright© 1993
Digital Wisdom, Inc.
Cover t: George Lepp/Tony Stone Images
Cover b: Roger Ressmayer/Corbis
End papers: Digital Image/Original Image Court/Corbis